COMPUTER CONTROL & AUDIT

AUDIT

by
William C. Mair, CDP, CPA
Detroit, Michigan

Donald R. Wood, CPA
Chicago, Illinois

Keagle W. Davis, CPA
Minneapolis, Minnesota

Partners
TOUCHE ROSS & CO.

Published and distributed by The Institute of
Internal Auditors, Inc., 249 Maitland Ave., P.O.
Box 1119, Altamonte Springs, Florida 32701,
with the permission of the copyright owner,
Touche Ross & Co.

ISBN 0-89413-063-3

Foreword

The computer has been described as a dominant advance of the 20th Century. Certainly it is a primary reason for the accelerating evolution of business methods. Applications are no longer computerized simply to gain the benefit of the speed and reliability of automated equipment but to use a new approach in performing applications.

The advent of electronic funds transfer systems, on-line data bases, and networks of interconnected computers provides management with new challenges which have created new problems. For one thing, the traditional methods used to control organizations in a manual environment are not effective in a computerized business environment. New control techniques are needed to be responsive to and complement the characteristics of the computer.

These changes are reflected in the problems auditors have in evaluating the reliability of computerized applications. Without established internal control mechanisms, auditors are turning to external measures to control computerized applications. This is because data processing personnel have not spent enough time evaluating computer-generated exposures and risks to their organizations or developing adequate internal control systems for monitoring computer functions. Weaknesses are particularly evident where manual and computerized portions of an application interface.

Computer Control & Audit by Mair, Wood, and Davis of Touche Ross & Co. addresses these problems. The prerequisite to effective auditing is effective control. This book discusses controls from a preventive, detective, and corrective viewpoint. The objective of controls, to reduce exposures, is discussed in detail together with practical methods of improving controls in data processing applications.

Written by practitioners who worked in conjunction with many large corporations to present practical data processing control concepts from the viewpoint of control-oriented personnel, the book is a valuable addition to the personal library of data processing systems analysts and managers as well as auditors. For the first time, control is adequately explained from an accountant's and auditor's viewpoint. The book answers the key question: Why is the total system of control over data processing applications a major concern of data processors? In answering this question, the authors take a practical and logical approach to the analysis of all varieties of controls used in computerized and manual information systems.

Ruth Davis
Deputy Director (Research and Advanced Technology)
Office of the U.S. Director of Defense, Research, and Engineering

Preface

Recognizing the need to provide auditors with information on the audit and control of computer systems, The Institute of Internal Auditors issued a manual entitled *Internal Auditing of EDP Systems* in 1968. This book helped innumerable audit groups to establish the EDP audit function and to become involved in the audit and control of computer applications.

IIA's International Research Committee recognized in the early 1970's that *Internal Auditing of EDP Systems* was becoming outdated and that it would have to be replaced. The committee's recommendation was to amplify an existing book published in 1972 by Touche Ross & Co. with the same title as this volume. The International Research Committee formed a task force under the direction of Robert Logue of the 3M Company to work with Touche Ross' authors of the original book. The objective of the task force was to supplement the book with the viewpoints of internal auditors, top management, and data processing personnel and, at the same time, to update the book to reflect current technology. The result was the publication of this book.

This comprehensive manual on computer audit and control outlines a methodology for evaluating the process of internal controls in computer systems. To date, most auditing literature has alluded to the process of evaluating controls without defining this process. It is not intuitively obvious to many auditors what is meant by adequate control in data processing. A prime objective of this manual is to help answer that question. The manual is developed from actual field experience by practicing internal auditors and certified public accountants.

The Institute is deeply indebted to the authors of this book: William Mair, CPA; Don Wood, CPA; and Keagle Davis, CPA. We are also very grateful to Touche Ross & Co. for having donated this book to The Institute.

This book represents the diligent efforts of numerous individuals, and The Institute of Internal Auditors expresses its appreciation to all those who made this manual possible.

John D. Bradt, CIA
International President
1975-1976

Acknowledgments

We are deeply indebted to a large number of individuals whose advice and assistance were essential in writing this book.

The following members of Touche Ross & Co. directly contributed their ideas and enthusiasm to the contents:

Paul Hamman, CPA	James Loebbecke, CPA
Hugh Hardie, CA	Carl Pabst, CPA
John Lehman, CPA	Richard Webb, CPA

Advice, review, and editing were provided by an IIA committee of reviewers that included:

Willard E. Hick, III
Massachusetts Mutual Life Insurance Company
Robert P. Logue, CIA, CPA
3M Company
Frederick B. Palmer, CIA
Chairman, International EDP Audit Committee,
Institute of Internal Auditors
Raymond S. Perry
Xerox Corporation
William E. Perry, CIA, CPA
The Institute of Internal Auditors

In addition to these individuals, who are easy to identify, we must offer our thanks also to a multitude of associates whose efforts and experience developed the accumulation of knowledge related herein. A list of these individuals would be so vast that space does not permit it here.

Finally, we would like to thank Brenda Walton for her extensive labors in preparing the manuscript.

William C. Mair
Donald R. Wood
Keagle W. Davis

Contents

Contents

LIST OF FIGURES AND ILLUSTRATIONS

LIST OF FIGURES AND ILLUSTRATIONS

Prologue

**Why should computer controls be of concern to businessmen?
Should auditors give them special attention?**

The Equity Funding fraud, for all of the millions of dollars that it cost investors, is somewhat facetiously credited for providing the greatest contribution in recent years to the goal of strong computer controls. The authors' accounting firm was engaged by the bankruptcy court to produce more realistic financial statements after the discovery of the fraud. Although the press credited the success of the fraud to the sophisticated use of computers, we found, rather, that only 19% of the fictitious assets claimed by Equity Funding had any relation to the use of computers. In fact, most of the assets were wholly without any type of support by computer or anything else. The only role that a computer actually played was to create some rather weak support for certain fictitious insurance policies that Equity Funding was selling to legitimate insurance companies.[1] If Equity Funding were all we had to worry about regarding computer fraud, we wouldn't really have much to worry about.

The opportunity for computer fraud that should cause greater concern is the programmer's ability to manipulate the computer as though it were a puppet. He does not need to have direct access to the actual computer equipment. By submitting programs with subtly imbedded routines to perpetrate a fraud or evade existing controls, he may gain control of huge quantities of assets.

A case of programmed computer fraud occurred in a revolving-credit-card system. A programmer provided a little "extra" maintenance along with some routine program changes. Thereafter, on the tenth day of each month, the first $100 payment processed was credited to the programmer's own account. The second $100 payment was credited to the account of the first payment, and so on. A complaint resulting from the eventual shortage in the last account could never be traced to the programmer. The programmer never came near the computer room.

In spite of these examples, relatively few cases of computer fraud or embezzlement are uncovered — particularly when one considers the number of opportunities that exist. Based upon our obser-

---

[1]*Report of the Trustee of Equity Funding Corporation of America Pursuant to Section 167(3) of The Bankruptcy Act [11 U.S.C. §567(3)]* by Robert M. Loeffler. Trustee United States District Court Central District of California, February 22, 1974, p. 38 and October 31, 1974, pp. 137-139.

vations, relatively few companies have sufficient internal controls to reliably prevent or detect acts of computer fraud and embezzlement. Apparently, the only reason computer fraud and embezzlement are not more common is that data processing personnel are generally honest. In comparison to the other problems that exist, the exposures to computer fraud and embezzlement seem to be relatively minor. This is not to say that they are negligible but, rather, that other and more substantial problems should command the greater concern and attention.

The business records maintained today on a computer may constitute virtual "information assets" of the organization. Although not negotiable, these assets may even be more critical to the successful operation of the business. If they are damaged or destroyed, they may threaten the very existence of the business enterprise.

Probably the greatest threat to these assets, like their more tangible cousins, is fire. The computer equipment and machine-readable records can be damaged by temperatures as low as 120° F. While fire seldom occurs within computer equipment, fire in an adjacent area may easily spread.

A computer manufacturer experienced a serious fire in a computer center used to distribute software products. The fire started in the basement used to store packing materials for the shipment of the software products. The intensity of the heat structurally damaged the computer room floor on the level above and entered the computer room via conduits provided for electrical cables. Water used to extinguish the fire added to the destruction. Millions of dollars of computer hardware and information assets were destroyed.

What makes the risk from catastrophes greater with computers is the totally new level of concentration of information assets that they promote. The comparison of information assets between a paper environment and a computerized one is like comparing a cash register to a bank vault. The consequent effects on risk management may be compared to an insurance company having all of its policies on buildings within a single block. Although the probability of destruction is not increased, the potential consequences certainly are.

The risks provided by this concentration of assets do not involve only the catastrophic destruction. Daily operating errors may also have massive consequences.

The computer operator in a medical institution forgot to remove the "protect ring" on a magnetic tape that constituted the sole record of approximately $.5 million in cash receipts. He accidentally mounted the tape on the wrong tape drive, and it was erased. As a result, past-due receivables could not be identified and pursued. To assist in the reconstruction, additional labor had to be hired. About the time that the reconstruction was finally complete, the same accident happened again.

Computer records often play an essential role in the business information systems. A serious deficiency in the quality of these records or their complete loss can cause "organizational amnesia." This occurs when the business information system fails to provide accurate and timely information regarding the activities of the organization. As businesses grow and must deal with an increasingly complex society, the effects of organizational amnesia become of greater concern. Businessmen must take positive steps to assure that their survival is not threatened.

A small aerospace manufacturing company developed a high-technology consumer product having great appeal. Within two years it grew from a business that serviced only 20 customers to a household name selling directly to more than 15,000 retail establishments. However, its information system for the collection of receivables was completely inadequate to control the growth. Three years after its successful product introduction, the company declared bankruptcy — a victim of organizational amnesia.

While serious threats, catastrophe and organizational amnesia are still not the primary reason for concern with modern computer systems. Fires do not occur every day; and many businesses can continue to exist, even though their internal information is limited or inaccurate.

Based on our experience, *the greatest sources of computer losses are innocent errors and omissions.* Users may be excluded from development and operation of computer applications and, therefore, never really understand the meaning of the information they receive nor the role they play in controlling it.

A receivables application included excellent controls: starting when the data entered the computer room and ending when the reports left it. Since a computer produced the reports, they were regarded as infallible. Auditors soon discovered, rather, that customer payments were so hopelessly misapplied that they could only request that the customers inform the company of the amounts owed per their records. The company eventually went out of business.

Although computers are highly reliable at what they do, they only do that which is programmed and, then, only with information that is provided from humans. Errors and inaccuracies in these inputs may be the source of millions of dollars of losses.

A medical institution developed a sophisticated computer system to gain better control over patient billings and collections. One major feature of this system was an error suspense file that controlled follow-up on items submitted with apparently erroneous information. The system provided capacity to control 100,000 error items in suspense at any time. Within three months after inauguration of the system, this file contained 120,000 items and was completely out of control. No one had ever dreamt that the volume of erroneous information being submitted could be so massive. Auditors had to be called in to institute computer-assisted auditing techniques to resolve most of the exception items.

Even one error in certain types of inputs can have a persistent, recurring effect.

A large wholesaler was forced to raise prices in order to recover inflationary increases in costs. However, the "new" price list that was fed into the invoicing system was actually the list of six months previous. Incorrect billings were issued for two months for a loss of $80,000. Recovery efforts cost another $20,000 for a total of $100,000.

Computers lack the tolerance for erroneous inputs that manual systems previously could handle. Clerks who operated manual information systems would often recognize ridiculous situations and correct them without hesitation.

A manufacturing company converted its inventory control system from a manual system to a computerized one. They were pleasantly surprised but somewhat perplexed when the reported inventory increased by approximately $1 million. Subsequent investigation eventually disclosed that the instruction manuals for their product were classified under the same part number as the machine they described. The 50 manuals in stock were treated by the computer as also being worth $20,000 apiece.

Even when proper inputs are provided to computers, they can still produce absurd results.

Depreciation calculations of an aerospace company contained assets with a negative net book value. Although the programming staff was instructed regarding the various acceptable depreciation methods, none of the finance people had ever informed them that depreciation calculations stop when the net book value reaches zero.

Logic problems in computer processing do not simply evolve from any natural process. They are caused! The vast majority of the cases are caused by poor or nonexistent communications between the data processing personnel and the other members of the business organization. However, even perfect communications will not eliminate all problems.

In a financial institution, the interest calculation on savings accounts was erroneously programmed as if there were 31 days in every month. In the five months before it was discovered, over $100,000 in excess interest was paid out.

The error rate in programmed functions is intolerably high. Even "tried-and-true" applications may contain subtle defects that exist for years.

A large retail establishment computed its aging of receivables incorrectly for three years before it was detected. It was impossible to determine what effect this had on its collections of receivables.

Experienced EDP auditors may expect to encounter programmed errors in 30% of the applications they test. This percentage is lower among financial institutions and higher in manufacturing and service organizations. Rates of as high as 60% have been observed. Fortunately, the majority of the errors that are detected do not have material financial consequences. On the other hand, some of them amount to millions of dollars.

Another financial institution was making discounted installment loans. Upon receiving the information of the amount of discount, the computer would calculate the effective yield on the loan and store that yield for use in subsequent interest-earned calculations. Unfortunately, the programmers did not allow the system to accept any discount values of $1,000 or more so that, when such amounts were occasionally submitted, they would be truncated and produce a lower apparent yield than the actual loan. By the time this was discovered by the auditors, misstatements in earnings had already accumulated to $1.5 million; and more than $.5 million had already been allowed in excess rebates to individuals who repaid loans early.

Approximately five percent of the items carried by a company in the distribution industry were so-called "catalog items" whose unit cost was based upon the volume purchased in a year. The company's rule was that inventory items would be valued at the lowest amount of such sliding-scale prices representing the highest possible purchase volume. Prices paid in excess of the minimum would be expensed as variances from standard. A minor error in the logic of valuing inventory reversed this rule, however, and valued these items at the maximum price or minimum quantity. The effect was to increase the reported value of inventory by approximately $10 million.

Not only do the applications being developed contain numerous subtle and not-so-subtle errors, but they also cost far more to develop than ever intended. One popular seminar on EDP controls presents materials stating that cost overruns in the development of computer applications of 250% are "typical."

There is a tremendous need for better controls designed more economically and reliably. Systems design personnel may be trained in "systems analysis" but rarely are trained in the design of controls. Many controls that they institute are not even recognized as controls. They are just the way things are done . . . sometimes. Auditors, who are supposed to be the control experts, will list off numerous controls that they think should be provided but rarely provide any explanation as to *how* they reach their conclusions. As a result, the systems designers repeat the same errors and omissions with the next system.

The data processing personnel of a large mail-order house designed a "perfect system." It would only operate if everything else worked perfectly. After implementation, the auditors discovered that errors were occurring at the rate of almost 50 percent. The system swiftly collapsed and had to be abandoned after investment of approximately a quarter of a million dollars.

In spite of the absurd results they occasionally produce, computers have come to be considered an essential part of the business environment. At the end of 1973, 133,000 computers valued at almost $30 billion were in use. The number of installed computers will grow to 500,000 by 1978 with a projected value of over $50 billion. The reason for the increase in value being less than proportionate to the number of units is because the heaviest growth is taking place in the very small units, although a heavier rate of growth is also noted in the very large machines.[2] Given this phenomenal growth, we must ask what need are these machines satisfying?

A medium-sized company in a service industry installed a medium-sized computer for which the rent was approximately $100,000 per year. When their utilization was evaluated, it was found that the machine was being used only 22 hours per month. The equipment had obviously been installed based upon the management's desire to appear progressive and modern rather than any economic evaluation of the actual needs.

In spite of the horror stories on things that go wrong with computers, some systems are designed and function properly.

A service organization designed a "cradle-to-grave" automated accounting system. Their design methodology followed a textbook approach precisely and was performed by trained and expert systems personnel. After careful design for more than seven man-years, the system was implemented and has now been operating for five years with an almost perfect record for reliability and accuracy.

Strong, well-directed management is what makes the difference. Data processing management is a very new profession. Business applications of computers only reached a wide scale in the early 1960's. Current standards for effective EDP management may be quite unfamiliar to individuals who entered the electronic data processing profession only a few years ago. Such persons must not allow themselves to become obsolete.

The great waste is that so many organizations seem to have to learn the hard way rather than by the experience of others. So often professional data processors complain that integrity controls "cost too much." They are sadly unaware that many techniques to improve record integrity pay for themselves by also improving productivity.

A perpetual inventory system contained inaccuracies in 70% of its on-hand balances. By expanding cycle-count efforts, the rate was reduced to 30%. This then permitted a reduction of 15% in the

---

[2]*EDP Industry Report*, James Peacock, editor, International Data Corp., quoted in *Computerworld*, August 7, 1974, p. 29.

levels of inventory carried to protect against stock-outs. The reduced carrying costs saved from four times the cost of the additional controls.

Fortunately, some organizations eventually reach a state where they start to use computers creatively rather than merely extending payrolls . . . and even doing that wrong. Just as the maturation of humans is accompanied by an increasing concern for distant future events, this same phenomenon is noted in business organizations that achieve a mature level of comprehension of this invaluable tool.

A distribution company now projects anticipated future sales of each product by dividing its inventory into hundreds of demand classifications and comparing recent sales with historical sales trends for products of each type. Using this approach, they have managed to reduce inventory levels by 25% while improving the level of service.

We absolutely *must* learn to control and audit computers in a more reliable and efficient manner. Even the sophisticated applications of today barely hint at the potential of what computers will be used to do tomorrow.

One of the fundamental concepts of computers is the "stored-program" concept. This recognizes that stored programs are identical in form to stored data; therefore, programs may be modified by programs just as data can. From this recognition, we already have computer programs that appear to "learn" to play chess or to perform other advanced logic. While these applications appear to constitute "artificial intelligence," they are still merely sets of computer instructions designed by men. However, the program can modify its own instructions according to its "experience." The actual instructions that are being performed may change dynamically and be unrecognizable when compared to the original set. If we can't even design a receivables-aging program that operates correctly by using the same logic rules for years, how are we ever going to control or audit a program that changes itself each second?

What we are really witnessing is a "computer revolution" that has potentially greater consequences than the Industrial Revolution. While the Industrial Revolution harnessed machines to multiply the power of man's muscles, computers can be harnessed to multiply the power of his mind. The successful and effective use of this power demands control. The people who can provide this control will be able to guide the future.

This book was written expressly for those who are concerned about the future of their organizations and the impact computers and computer control will have upon them. For a capsule summary of what this book is and what it is not, read chapter 1.

Section I
GENERAL TOPICS

1
Introduction

WHAT THIS BOOK IS ABOUT

This book is about the effective development, control, and audit of business information-processing systems using computers. The text may be considered a basic introduction to computer control and audit for the reader who is already versed in elementary business and computer terminology and auditing in general. It will describe the problems and relative merits of alternative solutions to controlling and auditing computerized information systems. Its structure should ease the reader into progressively more challenging areas of interest rather than immediately plunging him into the deep waters of technical jargon and exotic machinery.

WHAT THIS BOOK IS NOT

This book will not present a "cookbook" solution to any and all problems. To our best knowledge, universal, standard solutions simply do not exist in today's complex computerized business environment. Neither is this book a reference manual. Full comprehension of materials in many of the latter chapters is dependent upon reading certain earlier chapters.

However, once the reader reads the book, subsequent reference will be facilitated by an index. While extremely technical activities will not be discussed in detail, more detailed, as well as general, discussions of specific subjects are listed in the recommended-readings section.

CONTROLS IN AN EDP ENVIRONMENT

The form of information controls is changed with the utilization of computers. However, fundamental concepts remain the same. To put these concepts into perspective, we have dedicated chapter 4 to describe certain basic concepts of control whether manual or computer implemented.

Before we can effectively consider the appropriate use of controls, however, we must first thoroughly comprehend the environment in which they exist. In a business, there are certain common, universal consequences that may arise from the many things that can go wrong. Controls act upon these things that can go wrong which, in turn, leads to the reduction of exposures (the consequences times the probability).

While the utilization of a computer in an information system does change the specific controls that are employed, it will rarely eliminate the need for numerous controls implemented by humans. Therefore, many of the comments presented in this book will be seen to be mutually applicable whether or not a computer is involved.

In practice, different types of controls with different objectives will be provided at all levels of management, creating a hierarchy of controls. We will deal with all levels in this book, integrating line-operation controls with quality-assurance functions and the controls implemented by middle and top management as well as the stockholders and directors.

We can diagram the relationship between electronic data processing, computer controls, and the overall organization as in Figure 1-1. In brief, it is composed of the various business applications, the development and maintenance of those applications, and the information processing facility where the actual computer operations are performed. This trimodal distribution of controls provides the organization of the book.

IMPACT OF EDP ON AUDITING

This book should not be considered a basic text on the subject of auditing. Rather, it will presume the reader of the chapters on auditing already has a general knowledge of auditing. It will then emphasize the many factors in auditing that change with the introduction of a computer.

Even more specifically, the book will concentrate on those aspects of auditing that are of mutual concern to all types of auditors: compliance with appropriate internal controls. Substantive auditing of results, which is primarily a concern of external auditors, will not be included. Rather, the book will emphasize the auditor's need to predict the reliability of information systems based upon internal control.

The book will provide a rational and workable structure to the activities of an auditor of computerized systems. This has been seriously lacking in the past. One colorful comparison of the auditor's problem has been likened to dropping him blindfolded at midnight during the rain into the center of a well-used cow pasture and then

Relationship Between Electronic Data Processing, Computer Controls, and the Overall Organization

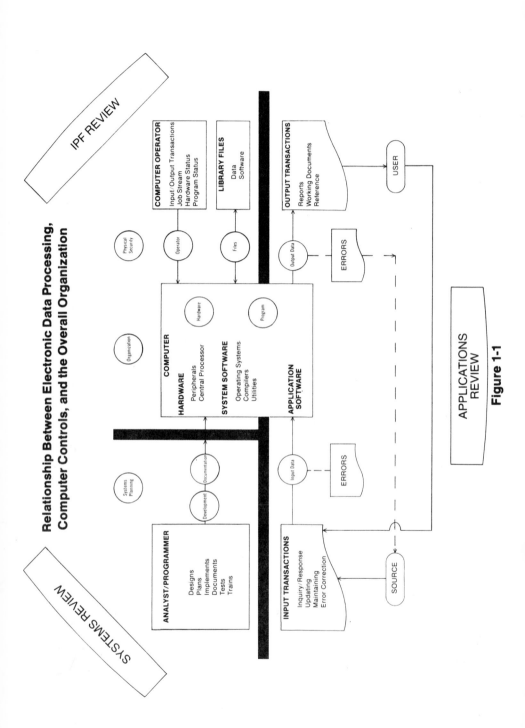

IPF REVIEW

SYSTEMS REVIEW

APPLICATIONS REVIEW

ANALYST/PROGRAMMER

Designs
Plans
Implements
Documents
Tests
Trains

COMPUTER

HARDWARE

Peripherals
Central Processor

SYSTEM SOFTWARE

Operating Systems
Compilers
Utilities

APPLICATION SOFTWARE

COMPUTER OPERATOR

Input/Output Transactions
Job Stream
Hardware Status
Program Status

LIBRARY FILES

Data
Software

OUTPUT TRANSACTIONS

Reports
Working Documents
Reference

INPUT TRANSACTIONS

Inquiry/Response
Updating
Maintaining
Error Correction

Systems Planning

Organization

Physical Security

Development

Documentation

Hardware

Operator

Files

Program

Input Data

Output Data

ERRORS

ERRORS

SOURCE

USER

Figure 1-1

4

telling him to jump over the fence without getting his shoes dirty. Since he has no idea where he is, where he should be going, or where danger lies, it is not hard to imagine that he is very unlikely to leave that field with clean shoes or clean anything else for that matter.

Applying this analogy to the EDP auditor, we may understand why so many have emerged rather disheveled from the field of computer auditing.

Since computers are a significant element in the environment in which the auditor of today must operate, he has no choice but to recognize their existence. The effective auditor of computer systems must become "bilingual." An auditor who remains ignorant of the techniques for computer control and audit will soon become obsolete and capable of functioning only as a "manual audit specialist."[1]

In addition to responsibilities for financial examinations, the auditor, particularly the internal auditor, is held increasingly responsible for providing assurance that operational information is controlled and used effectively. The auditor is responsible for modifying his methods to assure effective, efficient examinations in a changing environment. Operating in this new dimension, the auditor must use the power of the computer to meet his expanding obligations.

Accordingly, we will deal with the issue of auditing "around or through" the computer. Using a slightly different viewpoint, we will answer the question more by dealing "with or without" the computer. This deals with the decision of using the computer as a tool in the examination as an alternative to strictly manual procedures. If there is a choice, we will recommend that the auditor evaluate the alternatives in terms of costs and effectiveness and decide on the basis of comparison. If this comparison results in a tie, the auditor will be advised to decide in favor of the computer. The next situation he encounters may not be a tie, and each experience builds his EDP auditing capability for the future.

Computer service bureaus will not be dealt with as a separate topic. Rather, they will be viewed as a distinct, major element in a complete business information processing system.

ORGANIZATION OF THE BOOK

The remaining chapters of Section I will continue with discussions of several general and important fundamental topics. These topics include many basic, but possibly unfamiliar, concepts that are essential to the understanding of the subsequent sections. Even if some of the concepts discussed are already familiar to the reader, all of Section I should be read so as to provide the reader with an appreciation of certain viewpoints on relationships that are unique to this text.

[1]F. Andrew Best, "Obsolescence: A Do-It-Yourself Game," *The Internal Auditor,* The Institute of Internal Auditors, March/April 1975, pp. 43-49.

Some readers may view Section I as a refresher course in the "basics" of EDP control and audit. Such a refresher is often of value even to the most experienced.

In the remainder of Section I, we will present:

- The relationship between controls, causes, and consequences
- Typical organization and EDP functions
- Approaches to classifying and analyzing controls
- A universal structure for compliance auditing

The subsequent three sections of the book discuss the three major aspects of electronic data processing: applications, systems development, and the information processing facility. These three dimensions of EDP activity relate to each other logically in the typical education and experience pattern of the businessman and the auditor. Computerized business applications closely resemble the procedures familiar in manual business information activities and, thus, is the preferable starting point for the businessman or the auditor to whom EDP is new.

The control of applications, however, must include in a single sweep the control of both manual and computerized phases. This is due to the interdependence between the two activities. The manual entry of a single transaction may automatically impact a chain-related series of computer activities without further manual involvement.

The studies of implemented applications lead naturally to review and participation in development of new systems. This involves studying and assisting in the planning of new systems to assure inclusion of adequate operating controls.

Finally, the EDP familiarity gained in the study of existing and new applications leads to an evaluation of control of the more technical activities within the information processing facility.

Within each one of the sections above, a particular structure is followed:

- Presentation of the activities constituting the specific function
- Discussion of the controls peculiar to that function
- The tools, techniques, and effective approach to auditing the controls within the function

Section V of the book deals with various advanced topics that contain significant elements of more than one of the basic functions covered in sections II, III, and IV. We do not intend to belabor the reader with intricate and esoteric controls lying in the domain of the computer scientist. We do not believe that this level of knowledge is necessary for effective utilization, even of so-called "advanced systems." Instead, we will continue to emphasize the organization used in the preceding three sections of the book: activities, causes of exposures, controls, and effective techniques for auditing. The level of detail will be that which is generally common rather than unique to specific manufacturers.

Specifically, the topics covered in Section V include:
- Advanced application systems (real-time, data bases, etc.)
- Minicomputers
- Computer abuse
- Operational auditing

In conclusion, Section VI addresses audit management. This will be of interest not only to the audit manager but to anyone who is concerned about efficient audit decisions and the relative goals of internal and external auditors.

A schematic diagram of the organization of the book is presented in Figure 1-2. Each reader should start with the general topics and move outward to the areas of his personal, specific interest.

ORGANIZATION OF THE BOOK

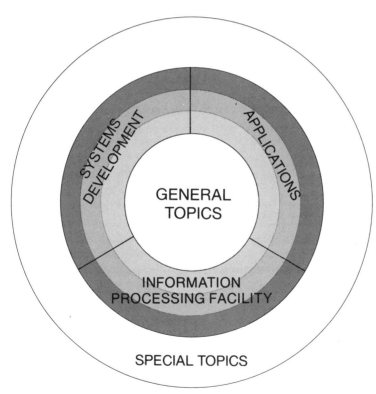

Figure 1-2

ACTIVITIES
CONTROLS
AUDITING

WHO SHOULD READ WHAT?

The authors anticipate that a significant variety of backgrounds and interests will be represented among the readers.

Specifically, the following major interest groups are addressed within this text:

- EDP systems designers
- EDP operations personnel
- Internal auditors
- Certified public accountants and chartered accountants
- All business managers using computer applications

EDP systems designers will be particularly interested in the methods described to analyze and to evaluate controls. Systems analysts must be capable of not only designing computer systems but really designing entire business information systems with proper controls. "Control analysis" is not yet really a standard part of the curriculum for a systems analyst. In addition to the controls that they must build into application systems, systems analysts will also be interested in the extensive presentation of the controls that they may establish over their own development process.

EDP professionals in computer operations will have a special interest in computer operating controls, security and recovery, computer abuse, and operational auditing. The operational auditing chapter will deal with several efficiency-related controls.

Internal auditors, certified public accountants, and chartered accountants will have a broad interest in this book. Of special interest, however, will be the methods for evaluating controls in all areas of activity and then selecting those specific controls, tools, and techniques to audit with maximum efficiency. Emphasis will be placed on auditing "with" the computer in order to harness its power and to replace manually performed audit tests with better, more efficient methods.

Business managers using computer applications will have a broad interest in all of the materials in this book. Some of the topics that will be least familiar will be the descriptions of systems development, information processing facility activities, application and systems development controls, advanced application systems, mini-computers, and computer abuse.

Figure 1-3 illustrates many of the specific topics that may fall within the particular interests of various types of readers.

Throughout the book, we will emphasize not only what controls should exist but also the relative roles and responsibilities of various members of the business team.

PHILOSOPHY OF THE AUTHORS

The one guiding philosophy that ties all of these diverse interests together is that business information systems must *serve* the busi-

INTERESTS OF VARIOUS TYPES OF READERS

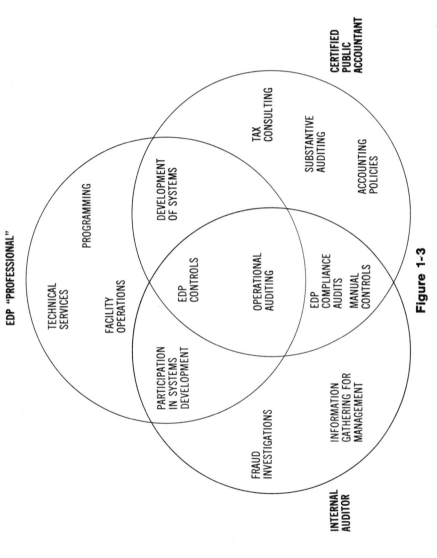

EDP "PROFESSIONAL"

TECHNICAL SERVICES

PROGRAMMING

FACILITY OPERATIONS

DEVELOPMENT OF SYSTEMS

EDP CONTROLS

PARTICIPATION IN SYSTEMS DEVELOPMENT

OPERATIONAL AUDITING

EDP COMPLIANCE AUDITS

MANUAL CONTROLS

TAX CONSULTING

SUBSTANTIVE AUDITING

ACCOUNTING POLICIES

CERTIFIED PUBLIC ACCOUNTANT

FRAUD INVESTIGATIONS

INFORMATION GATHERING FOR MANAGEMENT

INTERNAL AUDITOR

Figure 1-3

ness. This is equally applicable when the organization is not actually a business enterprise but, rather, a government or charity.

Our intent may best be summarized by quoting from a famous book that is highly relevant to the field of computers — *Future Shock* by Alvin Toffler.

"It is no longer sufficient for Johnny *(businessmen* or *auditors)* to understand the past. It is not even enough to understand the present, for the here-and-now environment will soon vanish. Johnny must learn to anticipate the direction and rate of change. He must, to put it technically, learn how to make repeated, probabilistic, and increasingly long-range assumptions about the future.

"The individual must know how to classify and reclassify information, how to evaluate its veracity, how to change categories when necessary, how to move from the concrete to the abstract and back, how to look at problems from a new direction — how to teach himself."

We hope that this book will provide some direction and assistance to the reader's efforts to teach himself to deal with the future.

2
Exposures, Causes, and Controls

EXPOSURES

Controls are needed for a purpose. This purpose is the reduction of exposures. Therefore, before we can begin to evaluate controls in any context, we must identify the *exposures* which controls should prevent, detect, or correct. The following list of exposures includes most of the adverse effects that a business organization might encounter:

- Erroneous record keeping
- Unacceptable accounting
- Business interruption
- Erroneous management decisions
- Fraud and embezzlement
- Statutory sanctions
- Excessive costs/deficient revenues
- Loss or destruction of assets
- Competitive disadvantage

Erroneous record keeping is the recording of financial transactions contrary to established accounting policies. The errors may involve the time of recognition, value, or classification.

Unacceptable accounting is the establishment or implementation of accounting policies which are not generally accepted or are inappropriate to the circumstances. This could also lead to further exposures such as statutory sanctions.

Business interruption may include anything from a temporary suspension of operations to a permanent termination of the enterprise. At the extreme, this also affects the accounting principal regarding a "going concern."

Erroneous management decisions are objectionable in themselves but may also lead to other exposures. Such decisions may arise due to misleading information, lack of information, or errors in judgment.

Fraud and embezzlement may be perpetrated at different levels — *against* management or *by* management. Direct misappropriation of funds is only one ramification of fraud. Deliberately misinforming management or investors is also fraudulent, even if only to keep one's job.

Statutory sanctions refer to any of the penalties which may be brought by judicial or regulatory authorities having jurisdiction over an organization's operations.

Excessive costs include any expense of the business which could be readily avoided. A related exposure is also a loss of revenues to which the organization is fairly entitled.

Loss or destruction of assets refers to the unintentional loss of physical assets, monies, claims to monies, or information assets.

Competitive disadvantage relates to any inability of an organization to effectively remain abreast of the demands of the marketplace or to respond effectively to competitive challenges.

Obviously, these exposures are not all mutually exclusive. However, they do include most of the adverse effects that a business may encounter. We introduce these here because we will refer to them repeatedly throughout the remainder of this book. *Their purpose is to communicate in basic business terms,* not to be philosophically elegant. To the extent that other terms may express a commonly recognized adverse business situation, such terms are also appropriate to describe exposures.

CAUSES OF EXPOSURES

Exposures do not arise simply due to lack of controls. Exposures are caused. Controls act to reduce or to eliminate these causes; but even without controls, *the causes must exist before exposures result.*

A cause may generate more than one type of exposure. No simple one-to-one relationship exists. Furthermore, the various exposures that may arise from a particular cause would not normally arise with equal probability.

Example — In a bank, the loss of a check after it had been partially processed would certainly cause erroneous record keeping because credit would have been given for the deposit; but it could not be charged against the proper account. Excessive costs would also result because an extensive error-correction activity would be necessary. If very many items were lost, the bank might have to interrupt normal operations in an attempt to recover. The granting of credit for the deposit, without being able to deduct from the appropriate account, would constitute the loss of assets. Finally, the depositor's awareness that the bank was losing such transactions could cause him to place his business with a competitor.

These relationships can be illustrated in tabular form. On a table, the causes of exposure could be listed across the top and the potential resulting exposures along the side. We could then place numerical values opposite each exposure under the cause to indicate the probability that the cause would lead to the exposure.

Using this approach, the table that would result from our cause of exposure, "losing a check," would be as illustrated in Figure 2-1.

POSSIBLE EXPOSURES CAUSED BY LOSING A CHECK

Magnitude of Exposure	Types of Exposures
3	ERRONEOUS RECORD KEEPING
—	UNACCEPTABLE ACCOUNTING
1	BUSINESS INTERRUPTION
—	ERRONEOUS MANAGEMENT DECISIONS
—	FRAUD AND EMBEZZLEMENT
—	STATUTORY SANCTIONS
2	EXCESSIVE COSTS
3	LOSS OR DESTRUCTION OF ASSETS
2	COMPETITIVE DISADVANTAGE

KEY TO MAGNITUDE OF EXPOSURE
3 — Virtually certain
2 — Probable
1 — Possible but unlikely
Blank — Very unlikely

Figure 2-1

CONTROLS

An exposure is the effect of a cause (stated in dollars) times the probable frequency of its occurrence. The term "exposure" is often misused. Fire itself is not an exposure. An exposure is the *destruction* that fire may cause. A control acts to reduce a cause of exposure rather than directly impacting the exposure. Therefore, while controls are intended to limit exposures, they really act upon a cause.

Once again, there is no simple one-to-one relationship between controls and causes. Various control techniques may effect a particular cause, and a particular cause may be controlled by various techniques.

All of the controls that could be exercised over a particular cause need not be utilized — only those which are sufficient to effectively limit the exposure. When auditors find that a particular control is not used, they are usually tempted to consider this a *weakness*. However, no net exposure will result if another control exists to limit the same cause to the desired degree.

Auditors are sometimes tempted to request that all the potential controls that are conceivable be implemented simultaneously over a particular process. This is not necessary (and is, in fact, wasteful) if the implemented controls are sufficient by themselves. This effect of one control serving in lieu of another is generally referred to as "a compensating control."

We can also depict this relationship between controls and causes in a table. Again, we can list the causes of exposures across the top but with the *controls* along the side. Furthermore, we can also use numbers in the intersecting squares to signify the order of magnitude with which the particular control will effect the particular cause. An illustration of such a table is provided in Figure 2-2.

RELATIONSHIP OF CONTROLS TO CAUSES OF EXPOSURE

	CAUSE OF EXPOSURE
CONTROLS	LOSING A CHECK
Training	1
Secure custody	2
Prenumbered form	3
Endorsement	1
Transmittal document	2
Amount control total	3
Document control count	3
Reconciliation	3
Discrepancy reports	2

KEY TO STRENGTH OF CONTROLS
3 — Very reliable
2 — Moderately reliable
1 — Useful but not reliable
Blank — No significant use

Figure 2-2

14

These relationships may be combined into one "control evaluation table" by simply placing one over the other so that the causes of exposure are aligned. We can then trace the three-element relationship of control, cause, and exposure to analyze the control quality. This is illustrated in Figure 2-3.

CONTROL EVALUATION TABLE

CONTROLS	CAUSES OF EXPOSURE	
	Lose a Check	KEY TO STRENGTH OF CONTROLS
Training	1	
Secure custody	2	3 — Very reliable
Prenumbered form	3	2 — Moderately reliable
Endorsement	1	1 — Useful but not reliable
Transmittal document	2	Blank — No significant use
Amount control total	3	
Document control count	3	
Reconciliation	3	
Discrepancy reports	2	
		EXPOSURES
	3	Erroneous record keeping
KEY TO MAGNITUDE OF EXPOSURE		Unacceptable accounting
3 — Virtually certain	1	Business interruption
2 — Probable		Erroneous management decisions
1 — Possible but unlikely		Fraud and embezzlement
Blank — Very unlikely		Statutory sanctions
	2	Excessive costs
	3	Loss or destruction of assets
	2	Competitive disadvantage

Figure 2-3

ANALYSIS OF CONTROLS

Once we have developed a control evaluation table, we can evaluate the quality of control. We first assume that all of the causes do exist. No "perfect system" has ever been devised. By "perfect system," we do not mean one which is perfectly controlled but, rather, a system where no causes of exposure exist. The system is then called "perfect" because, since everything always functions perfectly, there is no reason to have controls. Unfortunately, many computer systems have been designed on this fallacious premise.

Given the recognition that causes of exposure always exist, we can analyze the various controls that would have an effect on those causes and determine whether they are effectively implemented in a particular situation.

Controls that are found to be ineffective or nonexistent are deleted from the evaluation table with deletion of the associated effect on causes of exposures. Each cause of exposure is then reviewed for the controls over it. This review includes consideration of exactly how reliable each control could be expected to be in the specific situation.

Following this review, a judgment may be made regarding the likelihood that each cause of exposure could occur, remain undetected, or fail to be corrected. Then another judgment may be made regarding the probable exposures.

Given this analysis of controls, we may then conclude whether the particular cause is likely to occur and, if so, the resulting exposures.

EFFECT OF EDP ON MAJOR CONCERNS

Three general areas of business operations generally provide concern: financial data, business assets, and efficiency of operations. Accordingly, control and audit emphasis may be directed to any of these major concerns. The introduction of computerized data processing does not change these concerns, but it does change the things that may happen within these areas of concern.

First, the use of a computer usually involves the storage of large amounts of information in one place. This information is in itself an asset. The record of a customer's account balance may be one of the most important assets that the organization has.

Second, the introduction of a computer has an impact on the basic organization of most businesses. Whereas the processing of a particular business function is usually centralized within one department under precomputer organizations, the introduction of a computer normally adds two more departments to this processing: a systems development and programming department and the information processing facility.

16

As a result, where there formerly was only one department under one department head who was responsible for the processing of a particular business information application, the addition of a computer to perform this processing centrally will actually decentralize the processing of the various business applications. Where a single department head could formerly control all aspects of processing, he must now share his supervisory control with two more department heads.

This may lead to a situation where the only executive having common authority over all phases of the application processing is as high as the president of the organization. This authority over all phases of processing may be termed *"lowest level of common supervision."* The phenomenon that we often observe with the introduction of a computer is an upward shift in this lowest level of common supervision.

The control implications of this are obvious. *Where a single manager could formerly exercise overall supervision, now no one does*. Certainly, no business president has the time available to exercise the same level of supervision over all the various business information-processing applications as did the many individual managers when they had supervisory control over all phases of processing.

This upward shift in the lowest level of common supervision is the source of increased needs for effective internal audit. The internal auditor becomes the reconnaissance force for top management. Because no one below top management has authority over a complete process and because top management has limited time, the internal auditor is called upon to act as the eyes and ears of top management. To effectively perform this role, the auditor must not only have the skills to evaluate the activities of the many functional departments but also the technical skills needed to review the activities of the computer departments.

Therefore, the manual auditor of old must grow and become the EDP auditor of today — with all of the skills of before — plus!

EDP AUDITING

We may define EDP auditing as the verification of controls in three areas of the organization:

- *Applications*
- *Systems Development*
- *Information Processing Facility*

Applications include all of the business information functions where a computer plays any role in the processing. Applications systems involve one or more departments of the organization as well as computer operations and systems development.

Systems development covers the activities of the systems analysts and programmers who develop and modify application files, computer programs, and other procedures.

The information processing facility includes all of the activities actually involving the computer equipment and files. This includes the computer operations, the library of computer files, data-entry equipment, and data distribution.

Concerns with computer operations are not eliminated simply because they are performed by a third party — a service bureau. The utilization of an independent service bureau may allow numerous economies as well as relieve the user of many concerns about operational efficiency, but it does nothing to relieve him of his concerns for the safeguarding of assets and accuracy of information.

INTERNAL AUDIT CONCERNS

The modern internal auditor is equally concerned with all of the potential exposures to the business. The degree of concern is not influenced by the nature of the particular exposure but rather by the potential financial consequences — no matter from what source. Therefore, if the exposure to competitive disadvantage could be measured for a particular situation as affecting operations by $100,000, this causes no less concern than if an exposure to fraud were measured in the same magnitude. Some methods to measure such exposures will be discussed in subsequent chapters. The point at this stage of the discussion is that the *internal auditor must be concerned with good management* so that everyone concerned with the business will prosper in the long run.

EXTERNAL AUDIT CONCERNS

The certified public accountant may be engaged by the Board of Directors and stockholders for the specific and limited objective of rendering an opinion over the fairness of the presentation of financial statements for the benefit of investors, creditors, and other third parties.

Although we will use the title "certified public accountant" consistently throughout this book, we intend to include "chartered accountants" and all other international equivalents when we designate "CPA."

Accordingly, the CPA's primary concern has been limited to the exposures to unacceptable accounting practices and erroneous record keeping. He also has significant secondary concerns with exposures to interruption of the business and loss or destruction of assets where they threaten the presentation of the business operations as a "going concern." Lower on his scale of priorities are excessive costs, statutory sanctions, and fraud. Finally, he will seldom be involved with specific marketing or competitive decisions or the quality of management decisions. Increasingly, however, the external auditor is being asked to assist management in evaluating and recommending improvements to all areas of exposures and controls. These additional objectives may be met by utilizing the consulting staff that is common to most major CPA firms.

USER CONCERNS

Auditors are certainly not the only ones concerned with controls. The various managers who utilize information and products of computers, as well as top management, are concerned with all of the potential exposures to an equal or greater degree than any auditor. Their advancement or continued employment often depend directly upon the success of computer processing and the decisions that are based upon computer-produced information. The prudent user will not accept a cheap (but uncontrolled) operation or operating results that are favorable (but inaccurate). These situations *may* benefit him in the short run but will be disastrous in the long run.

WHO IS RESPONSIBLE?

With the managers of systems development, the information processing facility, and user departments involved and with top management, external auditors, and internal auditors also concerned, who is responsible for the controls of a particular operation? This question has frequently been debated, but it is usually resolved that *the users must be primarily responsible.* Their performance is being affected by the computerized system; they have the most immediate knowledge of a computerized application; and they have the most to lose. However, where the user manager cannot reasonably be expected to have adequate technical comprehension to exercise total control responsibility, higher levels of management should provide necessary support to assure proper technical controls. This is often provided by a separate quality-assurance function.

EFFECTS OF COMPUTER ON CAUSES

The introduction of a computer for business information processing does not directly affect the exposures that may occur to a business. Rather, it changes the types of causes of exposure as well as their relative frequency.

Example — Human errors in multiplication would be expected several times a day, whereas actual errors in such calculations by a computer may only occur a few times a year.

EDP AUDIT OBJECTIVES

The objective of an audit of compliance with controls is to predict the reliability and related exposures which should be expected from the system in operation in the future. The auditor is not supposed to be a "cop." *Enforcement of daily operating controls is a function of line management.* Of course, where such enforcement is lacking and would improve the reliability of the system, the auditor must call for implementation and enforcement of proper controls. But this is a secondary function. *The internal auditor's primary function is to evaluate controls, verify their implementation, and provide his conclusions to management.* To the extent that he is qualified, the auditor will also submit constructive recommendations with his conclusions.

In meeting the objectives of a financial audit, the certified public accountant seeks evaluations of reliability of controls so that he may limit the extent of substantive audit work required to render an opinion on financial statements. A certified public accountant refers to this evaluation and verification of controls as "compliance auditing." While not his primary function, it is usually essential to his obtaining a conclusive and economical opinion on the fairness of financial statements. The relationship between "substantive" and "compliance" auditing is discussed in chapter 24 under the topic of "scope."

Controls, causes, and exposures are the elements for evaluating the reliability of a particular function. *Exposure* is the financial effect of a cause times the probable frequency of its occurrence. *Causes* are the activities or circumstances that adversely affect a business. *Controls* are anything that acts upon causes so as to tend to reduce exposures.

The same general exposures exist for every business. The introduction of computerized information processing does not change the nature of the exposures but, rather, changes the nature and frequency of the causes. Accordingly, different controls must be adopted.

While the internal auditor should be concerned with all types of exposures, the external auditor is primarily concerned with those exposures affecting the fairness of the financial statements.

Effective EDP auditing may be performed by splitting the efforts according to application systems, system development, and the information processing facility.

3
The EDP Organization

DIVERSE EDP ORGANIZATION FUNCTIONS

The EDP activity in most organizations is unique in its breadth of functions, responsibilities, skills, and characteristics. The data processing manager needs effective skills in three distinct management areas:

- Production and operations experience to manage line functions such as computer operations, data conversion, input-output controls, and output distribution.
- Project orientation to manage an almost-equivalent level of effort in development areas. These will include feasibility studies, systems analysis, system design, and programming.
- Research background to keep abreast of enhancements in hardware, software, and systems technology.

These basic responsibilities and functions of an EDP Department lend themselves to natural organizational groupings. Recognizing these natural groupings and providing the appropriate organizational structure and personnel are critically important. They mark a first step toward effectiveness and internal accounting control within an EDP Department. The major functional groupings are:

- Operations and production (includes data conversion, computer operations, input-output controls, and output distribution).
- Project-type functions (includes feasibility studies, systems analysis, systems design, programming, testing, and conversions).
- Technical services functions (includes analysis of hardware, software, systems technology, communications, and quality control).

The characteristics and responsibilities of these three major functional areas are discussed below and are summarized in Figure 3-1

CHARACTERISTICS AND RESPONSIBILITIES OF EDP FUNCTIONS

FUNCTIONAL GROUPINGS	FUNCTIONS INCLUDED	GROUP CHARACTERISTICS	RESPONSIBILITIES
INFORMATION PROCESSING FUNCTIONS	Operation of computer and related equipment Data conversion Library Control group	Highly repetitive work loads predictable and subject to scheduling Operations routine require supervision Instructions necessary Operations subject to performance measurement Visible results for users Quality of controls, readily determinable	Achieve efficiency for group as a whole Maintain committed schedules High level of accuracy for data processed Maintain quality consciousness for group as a whole
PROJECT FUNCTIONS	Systems development Procedures and forms Quantitative analysis Programming	Only nominally repetitive Long duration Projects with structured activities for visible interim results High level of interpersonal skills Numeric orientation (quantitative analysis) Systems analysis skills necessary	Understand objectives, responsibilities and functioning of user organization Improve effectiveness of user through application of EDP processing
TECHNICAL SERVICES FUNCTIONS	Equipment selection Software and operating system selection Program maintenance Quality assurance	Highly technical Results may have low user visibility	Technical support to operating and project functions Improve efficiency and effectiveness of operating and project functions Development and maintenance of standards for computer operations Monitor compliance with standards

Figure 3-1

EDP OPERATIONS FUNCTIONS

A computer information processing facility (IPF) functions as any other production-oriented segment of a company. From a management standpoint, operation of an IPF has a number of functions and characteristics in common with a manufacturing operation including:

- Highly repetitive, day to day and hour to hour.
- Predictable work loads subject to long- and short-range scheduling.
- Routine operations subject to close supervision.
- Utilization of equipment for processing with attendant investment, maintenance, etc.
- Rapid personnel turnover.
- Explicit, detailed instructional standards required to cover all operations.
- Operations subject to performance measurement and performance standards.
- Unlike many manufacturing operations, the results of IPF operations are clearly visible to users; therefore, the quality of control may be quickly determinable.

Overall Performance Emphasis

The nature of the work done by the EDP operations group emphasizes four objectives:

- Operational efficiency in production of varied but tangible products.
- Maintenance of committed schedules for delivery of outputs.
- A high level of accuracy for data processed.
- Responsibility to maintain a quality consciousness within the group as a whole.

Usually, 50 percent or more of the budget of the total EDP activity will be devoted to the IPF; thus, failures to meet operations commitments may be extremely costly in both money and level of service.

Functions of the IPF

The functions of an IPF may be divided into four general areas:

- **Data conversion operations** which take in written source documents from originating departments and record those data in machine-readable form. The most used data conversion technique is keypunching. However, this function may also be performed on devices which operate from keyboards and record on magnetic tape or disc. Data may also be entered directly into a computer file for on-line editing and immediate or subsequent processing.

- **Operation of the computer and related equipment.** This includes the console, peripheral devices, and auxiliary equipment necessary for further processing and distribution of outputs.
- **A library** responsible for storage of and accountability *for data files and programs.*
- **A "control" function** which initiates all production and follows the status of the jobs as they move through the facility. Input is accepted from users or sources and forwarded to data conversion and operations. Logs are maintained to record and balance input and computer processing control totals. All outputs are also logged and balanced. Adherence to established schedules is also noted. In many cases, the group is also responsible for delivering reports or documents to users.

PROJECT FUNCTIONS

Project function responsibilities within the total EDP activity fall into three broad areas:

- **Systems development,** the most significant of the three in terms of budgetary commitment and management attention, incorporates the study of existing systems, user needs, and design of new or improved methods to meet identified requirements.
- **Procedures and forms,** covering responsibility for creating and maintaining procedures manuals and forms for new and ongoing systems.
- **Quantitative analysis,** which applies mathematical logic and modeling techniques to appropriate areas of company operations and planning (including operations research).

Common Characteristics

Activities associated with system projects are only slightly repetitive. Each project has the same overall activity structure; but the velocity and degree of repetition would be measured in months or weeks, as compared with days or hours. Primarily since they are accomplished over a much longer period, results are often less visible than in operations.

The long duration of projects illustrates one of the chief advantages for the setting up of structured activities for the development of EDP systems. With a structured sequence of activities, visible interim results are more likely; end items may be planned and predicted through periodic review of activity status.

The emphasis of project functions is largely in the area of providing a bridge between business problems and technical solutions. Project personnel, therefore, must demonstrate a high level of multidiscipline skills. Systems analysts and other project personnel within the EDP Department must be at home in dealing with both technicians and users on their own terms.

Analysts working on computer and clerical systems must interact closely with personnel in departments outside the EDP area. By contrast, operations and technical services personnel deal largely with computers, software, and technical information. The potential for personnel problems is greater in project work.

Quantitative analysis skills are also crucial in the project area and are becoming more so continually. Project personnel within the EDP Department must have technical and practical skills in dealing with numbers. These skills must transcend accounting considerations and extend to simulation, modeling, and other requirements likely to be encountered in the analysis and development of advanced EDP systems.

TECHNICAL SERVICES FUNCTIONS

Technical services include a grouping of functions which are both technical and supportive in nature. In other words, technical services activities are performed primarily through other functions of EDP departments.

Common Characteristics

Technical services skills and responsibilities revolve around a highly technical orientation. The results of technical services activities are frequently unseen outside EDP departments.

This function is enjoying a growing stature, particularly as departments and budgets expand (largely because dependence on technical services people increases as hardware and software become more sophisticated). Furthermore, there has been an increased understanding of the potential and real impact of technical services in the improvement of operating effectiveness and reduction of costs. One area for application of technical services skills lies in optimization of file design and software. Through these, EDP activities are continually reducing system development and operating costs while providing better user services.

Functional Responsibilities

The range of functions, responsibilities, and skills which fall under technical services personnel includes:

- IPF software selection and maintenance.
- Analysis of equipment, including comparisons of capabilities of continually announced new equipment with units presently installed.
- Development and maintenance of EDP standards. This generally takes in standards for system projects as well as for IPF hardware, software, and operations.

- Quality control responsibility for the technical services group plus monitoring all operations and project activities for compliance with standards.
- Application programming is a technical services function closely related to project activities, calling for the preparation of detailed coding instructions for the processing of applications on computers. One of the major investments of any EDP activity — both in people and dollars — goes into its programming group.

The most valuable skills within the technical services function will generally be among senior and supervisory personnel in the programming area and among technical specialists responsible for evaluating and specifying hardware and software.

Program Maintenance

Program maintenance generally falls outside the scope of the system development function largely because of the limited size and scope of most maintenance projects and the faster response times required.

Where maintenance responsibility is positioned in the organization will vary with conditions and policies. Depending on the organization, such as when a company uses a sophisticated data base, responsibility may be assigned to the application programming area of the technical services function. However, if the organization has a comparatively large number of implemented applications in use and running smoothly, this responsibility might be assigned to the operations function.

EDP STAFF FUNCTIONS

The size and scope of the EDP Department's staff functions vary with its size and scope and that of the company as a whole.

Staff functions necessary to the conduct of the business of an EDP Department will include at minimum:
- Administration of the department
- Personnel administration
- Departmental planning
- Membership on or leadership of task forces or steering committees operating at an interdepartmental level. These may be either committees specializing in EDP projects or in other areas affecting the company as a whole.

EDP ORGANIZATIONAL STRUCTURE

The organizational structure of an EDP activity will vary. Within a large corporation, the functions in the EDP activity may be grouped as shown in Figure 3-2. This illustration assumes that the EDP activity is headed by a person at the director level who reports to a top execu-

STRUCTURE OF A LARGE EDP ORGANIZATION

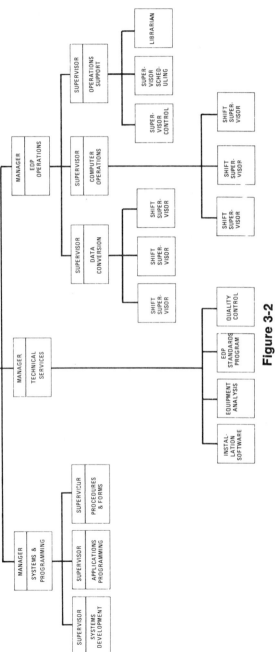

Figure 3-2

tive of the company. Manager and supervisor-level positions are designated for the separate functions. Even before we have the opportunity to address the subject of controls, a study of organizational structures inevitably leads us to note the control known as "segregation of duties." A careful analysis of this organizational structure will show the segregation of responsibilities for:

- Accounting for and custody of data
- Processing of data
- System development and programming

In contrast, Figure 3-3 represents implementation of a satisfactory segregation of responsibilities for a small EDP organization. The head of this department is at a manager level. Heads of the functional areas are supervisors. A definite separation has been maintained between programming, computer operations, and data control. In such an organization, the computer operations supervisor may be involved in console operation. Similarly, the supervisor of systems and programming may be a project leader or senior systems analyst. Also, in a small organization, functions in the project area may be combined by assigning personnel as programmer/analysts. A data conversion supervisor may be the librarian and the head of the control operation.

Even in a small organization, these two organization charts indicate that substantial control measures may be applied through separation of responsibilities.

CONTROL RESPONSIBILITIES

All the various departments and individuals involved in EDP must understand their appropriate role with regard to control. Many of the "computer" problems in businesses today stem from confusion as to who should do what.

Responsibility of Users

As an information system becomes increasingly centralized, the user gives up control; and the information processing facility acquires a greater degree of information file custody. In considering control responsibilities, it is important to recognize that there are marked differences between physical custody of media and hardware and control over accuracy and reliability of the data.

But it is still up to the EDP user to conduct himself as a prudent businessman. The user must understand and specify what controls are necessary in the handling of transactions, the processing of data, and the availability of information output. The user must still understand the information processing system at a logical level. This is the level of detail that the user can compare with generally reasonable business practices. While he should not be expected to become an

STRUCTURE OF A SMALL EDP ORGANIZATION

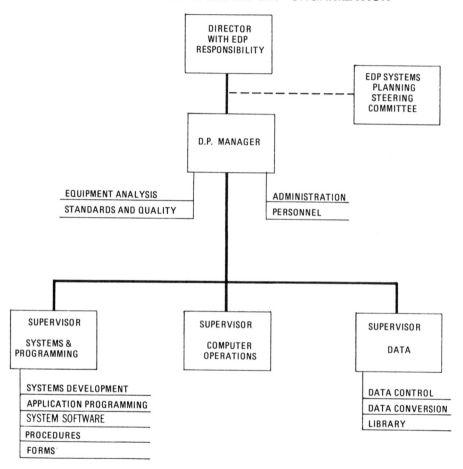

Figure 3-3

expert in computer technology, he must retain the responsibility to operate and to test controls.

Data Processing Responsibilities

Data processing management, in turn, is responsible for all custodial processes associated with handling, processing, storing, and output of data between receipt of input data and delivery of results to users. In meeting custodial responsibilities, data processing people should apply the same types and degrees of care expected of the treasurer in the handling of cash and negotiable securities.

Additionally, the EDP activity has central responsibilities in the area of technical design of systems. Data processors must determine that levels of service and control acceptable to users are specified and designed into systems. Trade-offs are made between manual and computerized systems on the basis of economies, compensating controls to offset abridged manual procedures, and company policy.

Quality assurance is an important responsibility assumed by data processing management with centralization of processing and file custody. Data processing is in a position to assure that control procedures meet defined requirements and is the primary entity which can assure quality in information processing.

MANAGEMENT PARTICIPATION

One of the lessons of the early failures in the development of EDP systems was that *management involvement is essential.* The reasoning is that EDP efforts and expenditures have grown to sufficient size to warrant full use of capital budgeting techniques used in other areas within well-managed companies.

The typical mechanism which has emerged for dealing with system development in many companies is a management committee, generally known as an EDP steering committee. Gradually, a rationale has evolved for the purposes, functions, roles, and responsibilities of EDP steering committees. As a management activity, a steering committee changes its purpose for being and its role to fit the situation of the company. As an EDP Department develops its own management capabilities, a steering committee may become less necessary.

In time, a rationale has emerged in many companies for the formation of management committees with EDP responsibility at two different levels:

- An EDP steering committee is a top-level group with responsibilities and functions akin to the capital budgeting process.
- EDP task-force committees are made up of directors or managers at the departmental level. These committees tend to have project responsibilities.

There will, of course, be variations in the way companies appoint and use EDP management committees. The discussion which follows is not intended as a specific set of directions; rather, committee functions will be discussed at two clearly separate levels for management emphasis.

EDP Steering Committees

An EDP steering committee is the top-management mechanism in the EDP area and is composed of persons who can commit the capital and other resources of the company to EDP purposes and projects. This comparison of an EDP committee with the capital budgeting function is particularly appropriate. If a company has strong, functioning capital-budgeting capability, the EDP steering function might well fall under the Capital Budgeting Committee. Such a committee would typically be well situated for evaluations of EDP and other investment programs. However, at least with regard to its EDP function, the steering committee should include the organization's general auditor, even if he is not normally involved in capital decisions. It would also have the reporting and follow-up mechanisms to trace EDP investments and evaluate results.

Like a capital budgeting committee, an EDP steering group should be small. It should also apply its attentions and efforts at the highest decision levels. A top-level steering committee, for example, might have five to seven members — nine at most. During its first few months of existence, it might meet every two weeks. Sessions could run from two to four hours, certainly no more. After a few months of meetings to establish policy and scope, sessions could be spread out to a monthly and eventually to a bimonthly basis.

Responsibilities and deliberations of such a group would fall into two broad categories: topics of a capital budgeting nature and those related to management of the EDP function. In the capital budgeting area, interests and activities of the committee would deal with resource allocation, progress reporting and analysis, and postimplementation reviews.

In the resource allocation area, interests and activities would deal with both projects and the EDP function itself. Projects would be dealt with at an overview level only. A management committee at this level should not be burdened with reports and decisions involving individual activities within projects. This responsibility should fall to the next level of management, the project task-force committee.

Decisions relating to the EDP function itself would include selecting and dealing with the EDP director, levels of staffing, major equipment decisions, facilities decisions, and so on. Reviews and analyses of reports on progress would also be at the capital budgeting level. Essentially, the committee at this level has the responsibility for follow-up on progress and utilization of resources.

Postimplementation reviews would be aimed at monitoring values received from allocations of resources. In addition, these after-the-fact studies would be aimed at sharpening EDP management's capabilities for future decisions.

Resources available to the committee should be variable, depending on the deliberations at hand and the status of the EDP function. At the very minimum, one person who should be present at all sessions should be the EDP director. He may be a member of the committee or an outside resource. He can provide an information resource, answering questions raised by committee members; and he will understand management positions better if he is a witness or a party to them.

In many companies, a top-level steering committee will be a temporary management mechanism only. If this committee is assigned to the EDP function only, its role may be to get a data processing capability established and running smoothly. Once this happens, the need for the committee may diminish or disappear. This would be particularly true if a company has a capital budgeting mechanism in place to assume responsibility for allocating resources.

EDP Task-Force Committees

An EDP task-force committee assumes responsibilities at an operational level. Its primary role is coordination, serving to establish the cooperation and collaboration necessary for the implementation of projects involving multiple departments.

Membership of a task-force committee will generally be larger than a steering committee. At a minimum, membership in such a group will include directors or managers of all departments which are major EDP users. In addition, members will include the EDP director, managers of any projects being monitored, and senior auditors assigned to participate in development projects. On larger projects, key user departments may appoint supervisors to committee-coordination roles on a full-time basis for the duration of the project. Obviously, such persons should be active participants in committee activities.

The value of a task-force committee includes providing a sounding board for evaluation of EDP projects, coordination of projects, active direction and support of projects, and assuming responsibility for results. Since membership will include managers of key user departments, the committee is in an excellent position to recommend priorities for EDP projects. Once agreement has been reached on the ordering of projects, task-force committee members are also in the logical position to establish coordination and to provide direction.

The ability to monitor results is possibly a special value for a committee at this level. Departmental managers hold ultimate responsibility for identifying values and benefits of new applications during the system planning and specifications activities of a project. The task-force committee, if it functions effectively, becomes the logical group to monitor accountability of such commitments.

Demands and commitments for time and participation upon members of a task-force committee will obviously be greater than for a steering committee. Individual department heads might have to devote from 10 to 40 hours per month to committee activities. And, as indicated, these commitments may have to be supplemented with assignment of knowledgeable supervisors to committee work full time.

In summary, it might be said that responsibilities of management committees in the EDP area divide logically along lines of planning and doing. A steering committee, as described here, would be a planning group. A task-force committee would be charged with doing the job.

4
Control Concepts and EDP

CONTROL OBJECTIVES

"Control objectives" means the same within any information processing system whether or not it employs computers. However, with computers, special emphasis is necessary to deal with the mechanical nature of processing and the centralization of files and operations.

WHAT ARE CONTROLS?

Control is anything that tends *to cause the reduction of exposures.* Control can accomplish this by reducing harmful effects or by reducing the frequency of occurrence.

The utilization of computers does not change any of the basic concepts of controls. The effects that computers have on controls are to change the effectiveness of different types of controls and change the medium in which they are implemented. Therefore, while nothing fundamental has changed in the nature of controls themselves, something very radical does occur in the surface appearance of the controls that are implemented in computerized systems:

- The extent of manual controls is abbreviated.
- Sources of data have shifted and are often independent of data users.
- Transaction trails are subject to discontinuity because there may no longer be a one-for-one correspondence between data entry and output.
- There may be a shift in the points at which controls are implemented: from clerks and supervisors to computer and systems analysts.

- Controls must be more explicit because many of the processing points which formerly presented opportunities for human judgment have been abridged or eliminated.
- The quality of documentation is more critical because records which might have existed previously in hard-copy form are frequently imbedded in computer files.
- Information file custody has shifted. Responsibilities for custody of information assets are being assigned to central data processing facilities.

For all these reasons, the structure and application of controls must be clear to all parties concerned. In this respect, two levels of controls exist within a computerized system: *logical* and *technical*. The distinction between these two levels is chiefly in their respective degrees of complexity.

Before we go into these specific surface appearances of the various controls that are implemented over computer-related activities, let us delve into the *fundamental nature of* these *controls* so as to build a common foundation to relate them with the controls that we were familiar with under manual systems.

We can classify controls in several different ways. Each of the different classifications tells us something different about the ways controls change — and change the auditor's viewpoint — in computerized information processing situations.

LOGICAL versus TECHNICAL CONTROLS

Business-trained managers and auditors find that many controls in computerized systems include simple and obvious incorporations of business logic. Such logical controls are functional in nature. They may be implemented either by people or by computers without any significant change to their surface appearances.

> *Example — Supervisory approval of the work performed by a computer operator appears little different from supervisory approval being provided over bookkeeping clerks.*

There are also a significant number of controls which are new and peculiar to the technology of electronic digital computers.

> *Example — Parity controls are incorporated by the manufacturers of computer equipment to detect electronic failures in the transmittal or recording of binary-coded data. No parallel situation can be found in purely manual processing.*

Particular controls would not normally be considered purely business logic or technical. Rather, controls over computer functions lie in a *spectrum* of relative technical complexity. While the examples above are probably extremes, many other controls might be considered in grey areas between these extremes. This is not to say that there is anything *illogical* about technical controls . . . given an appreciation of the technical environment that brings rise to their use. Rather, this classification relates controls to the relative degree of technical education that is found among business managers and auditors.

VERTICAL versus HORIZONTAL CONTROLS

Another way of classifying controls is to segregate them between controls that follow the vertical lines of authority of an organization chart and those which follow processing flows that cut across such lines.

Example — Supervisory controls are exercised upward along the vertical lines of the organization chart, whereas transmittals between departments might be diagrammed as horizontal between equal levels of the organization.

As indicated previously, the implementation of computers in many situations brings about an *upward shift in the lowest level of common supervisory or line management control.* This upward shift affects the nature of vertical controls because individuals having overall line authority over the processes are higher in the organization and have less time to provide detailed supervision. Also, as additional departments (computer operations and systems development) become involved in a process where only one department existed before, the need for more horizontal controls emerges. Accordingly, an organizational structure that provided adequate controls for a manual system will generally not provide an equal level of control for a system after the introduction of computers and integrated application systems.

This is not to say that the vertical controls, such as supervision and segregation of duties, are no longer important to a computer system. However, their effectiveness and the related emphasis upon them is reduced. This emphasis must be shifted more toward the horizontal types of control such as transmittals, control totals, and edits.

PREVENTIVE, DETECTIVE, AND CORRECTIVE CONTROLS

The final technique for classification of controls that we will discuss in this chapter relates to whether a particular control technique will *prevent* a cause of exposure from happening, *detect* the fact that it has already happened, or *correct* the effects of it after it has been detected.

Preventive controls are those which reduce the frequency with which causes of exposure occur. Detective controls do not keep causes of exposure from happening but, rather, detect them after the fact. The mere detection of a cause of exposure is not sufficient. When such situations are detected, a decision must be made as to what is appropriate corrective action and then that action must be taken.

A *preventive* control acts as a guide to help things happen as they should. Often they are passive with no physical activity directly involved. Also, such controls often allow a significant percentage of violations. In Figure 4-1, we depict this as a funnel. One may liken it to a cattle chute that passively directs most of the herd into the pen but may be evaded by some of the mavericks. Preventive controls are often so subtly imbedded within a process that persons involved in the operation may not even be conscious of their existence.

A *detective* control does not prevent a cause of exposure from happening but instead triggers an alarm after it has happened. The detective control may terminate further processing or merely register the occurrence. This "monitoring" function is often quite reliable. However, the detection that a cause has actually occurred is just that and no more. Detective controls will alert persons involved in the process so that they will be conscious of the existence of a problem. This consciousness is mandatory if they are to take action to correct the effects of the cause.

The final type of control is *corrective.* This assists in the investigation and correction of causes of exposures that have been detected. Corrective action is always needed to resolve the causes of exposures that are detected. A decision might be made that corrective action is not worth the effort, but this decision must be made consciously and consistently — not by default. The alarm provided by a detective control is useless if no one is listening. Since preventive controls are often passive (like the instructions on a form), a detective control is needed to determine whether the preventive control is functioning. Even if it were certain that the preventive control was functioning, such controls would still be needed to detect exposures that evade the preventive control.

Furthermore, items that cause errors are often more difficult to handle than more normal ones; otherwise, the error would not have been made in the first place. Proper correction may also be difficult. Therefore, all items that are corrected must be subsequently processed through the same or even more stringent detective controls. Even when the correction is easy, it is likewise very easy to process it in the wrong direction so that something that should be added is really subtracted. Detective controls over corrective controls are quite essential because *error correction itself is a highly error-prone activity.*

FUNCTIONS OF CONTROLS

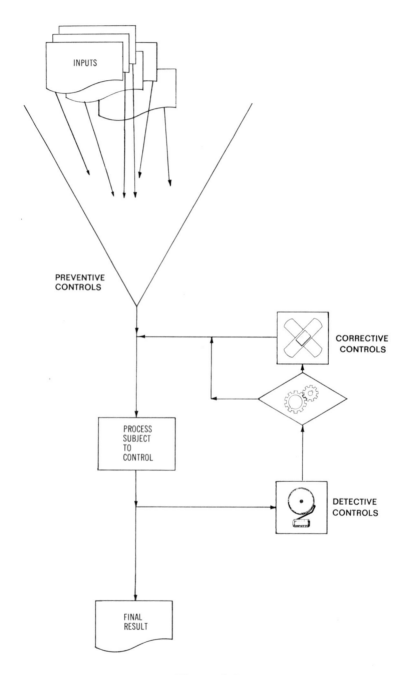

Figure 4-1

COST versus BENEFIT OF CONTROLS

In information systems, as elsewhere, each control has a cost factor. No control should cost more than the potential errors it is established to detect, to prevent, or to correct. The cost of understanding and correcting errors should not be overlooked in this cost-risk concern. To the extent that controls are poorly designed or excessive, they become burdensome and are under threat of being ignored. A review should be made to see if the errors may be caught earlier in the processing cycle, minimizing:

- The control points required.
- The damage which may be done to the file.
- The necessary correction effort.

The needs of management and the significance of any given error — as well as the evaluation of costs and risks — are effective balances. They help determine where and to what extent controls should be applied.

Preventive controls are generally the lowest in cost. Detective controls usually require some moderate operating expense. On the other hand, corrective controls are almost always quite expensive. It takes three to ten times more effort to correct something that occurs improperly than it takes to do it right the first time.

The design of optimum controls, therefore, requires a set of trade-offs. Preventive controls are the cheapest to operate but are seldom adequate alone. Therefore, some error-correction activity is virtually always necessary. The cost-benefit balance must be struck between the cost of implementing further preventive controls and that of operating the correction activities. Elimination of detection controls is seldom an appropriate means of cost reduction. Without them, neither the effectiveness of preventive controls nor the resulting exposure can be measured.

USE OF CLASSIFICATIONS IN CONTROL ANALYSIS

The significance of these various control classifications in a computerized environment should now be apparent. Just as a businessman without technical expertise in computer controls cannot design, implement, or evaluate a complete set of effective controls, neither can a data processing technician who is lacking in business skills. Successful controls require a combination of business and computer technical expertise. Businessmen and data processing technicians must effectively merge their skills for the success of the resulting operations.

The *specifications* of controls for reliable processing of business *applications* depend primarily upon knowledge which is already familiar to businessmen. Some factors change; but once the businessman acquires a moderate knowledge of this new technology, he will find that the data processing environment is really not so mysterious after all.

The development and implementation of new business applications on the computer require a greater degree of technical expertise. A business-trained individual can substantially increase his effectiveness by acquiring a limited knowledge of the activities which comprise the systems development process. Knowledge of file concepts, programming languages, hardware, and other technical elements are rarely essential for the businessman who has adequate technical support.

Finally, the *evaluation* of the information processing facility (IPF) is the most heavily oriented toward computer technology, since it handles the functions of actually operating the computer and the machine-readable files. An individual with limited technical expertise may encounter difficulties in evaluating his findings and persuading technical management to follow his recommendations. At the same time, however, many activities of IPF operations are still essentially business judgment; e.g., physical security. Effective evaluation of these activities lies well within the capabilities of an individual having only moderate technical background. The more tangible nature of IPF operations, as compared to application processing, further reduces the evaluation difficulties that could be encountered by a nontechnician.

The incorporation of various levels of technical expertise in controls over computer systems does not prohibit a manager or auditor who has a sound business background but limited technical knowledge from effectively designing, implementing, or evaluating the controls over computerized application processing or computer operations. However, a greater level of technical expertise will be required when concerned with the controls over the systems development process or the technical aspects of computer operations.

The second classification of controls, *vertical* versus *horizontal*, indicates that *greater emphasis* and concern must be placed upon the *horizontal* type than was the case in manual systems. As a result, application controls can no longer be evaluated on a department-by-department basis. Effective control of computerized activities depends upon the adequacy of controls during development, computer operations, and within all user departments. An evaluation of any single department will omit highly relevant supplementary controls existing in other departments. Only in this way can the entire picture be seen and properly evaluated.

Example — The reliable processing of a mortgage payment to a bank is dependent upon controls exercised by the branch tellers, the mortgage department's staff, programs developed by the Systems Development Department, and handling and security

40

of files maintained by computer operations. This chain is only as strong as its weakest link.

Third, an analysis of controls according to their preventive, detective, or corrective characteristics clearly indicates that, for purposes of auditing, *detective controls are the most important.* They measure the effectiveness of both preventive and corrective controls. This, then, will provide the primary approach that we use in the succeeding materials to guide the evaluation and audit of controls.

AREAS OF CONTROL

Areas of control within computer systems include:
- Application controls, which are unique to individual user systems.
- Systems development controls, which assure that the planning and development of systems are performed in a systematic manner.
- Information-processing facility (IPF) controls, which apply to the physical processing location and to how most or all applications are processed within that facility.

Application Controls

Application controls are probably the *most* important in the entire EDP area in a review of overall control reliability. This is true because:
- Controls over system development and IPF activities ultimately affect applications and meet their final test.
- Applications lend themselves best to audits by persons familiar with logical controls, providing them an opportunity to develop experience with the technical aspects of auditing computer systems.

Systems Development Controls

Systems development consists of those functions which plan, develop, and modify application and IPF procedures. Evaluation of systems development should be done by persons who are highly experienced in systems development.

In evaluating systems management as a system control factor, good performance results from:
- Using a consistent set of activities which is comfortable and acceptable to both users and systems analysts. These should be carried forward as standards from one project to another.
- Providing project direction. This is accomplished by establishing appropriate project objectives and scope, setting up realistic schedules which consist primarily of standard activities, and assigning responsibilities.

- Making sure that the results from each activity are documented and understood and agreed to by those involved.
- Reviewing project progress at predetermined intervals for specified purposes.

The documentation referred to is one of the primary results of an adequate, strong systems management program. The presence or lack of adequate documentation in reviewing applications and IPF controls is, in itself, an evaluation of the effectiveness of systems development.

IPF Controls

In addition to controls for individual user applications, separate controls are applied to the information processing facility as a whole. This segregation of application and IPF controls is aimed at making best use of available resources. Application controls can be reviewed effectively by persons with minimum EDP exposure. IPF controls, however, require a higher degree of familiarity with EDP operations. This additional level of skill may be acquired gradually through computer application audits under appropriate supervision.

These areas and classification of control will be used as the framework for describing and evaluating controls throughout the remainder of this book.

5
Compliance Audit Methodology

OBJECTIVE

The purpose of evaluating controls is to predict the reliability of the process under control. Sound audit methodology dictates that, before testing controls for compliance, a determination must first be made (1) that control standards exist and (2) that these standards are adequate to provide the desired level of reliability.

THE NEED FOR STANDARDS

The major prerequisite to consistent utilization of controls is that standards exist that call for them. If the controls that are examined and evaluated are not also to be used in the future, no prediction based upon an examination of them is valid. Without some standards for operations, the auditor has no foundation upon which to base a prediction.

PURPOSE OF STANDARDS

Information system standards describe operations and requirements for all activities and results of information systems. Standards are developed and applied to both manual and machine functions. In effect, *a standard is a formal written statement of "the way we do things around here."*

Today, the majority of EDP IPF's have or are developing some type of formal documentation of standards. This trend is noteworthy, even though the quality of controls expressed in standards varies widely and tends to be less than adequate in many cases.

Growth and acceptance of system standards result from a number of factors:

- Management has demanded that data processing resources be used more effectively. Standards have become a formal representation of the way management wants things done.
- Centralization of processing and file custody in a data processing department eliminate much of the face-to-face communication contact which formerly played an important part in making information processing systems work. With integration and centralization of processing and files in an information processing facility, standards become communication vehicles, bridging the gaps in processing distance.
- An EDP system requires a high degree of uniformity. In most cases, formal standards are a necessity for achieving this required uniformity.
- Standards provide a basis for measuring performance and costs. For instance, if invoices are prepared in several branch offices, standards establish uniform procedures which facilitate comparing productivity among locations.

System standards cover the full scope of information system activities. They are applied at both the logical and the technical level. Technical standards are necessary for the programming and actual operation of computers. However, logic-level standards provide the key to the control and audit of EDP applications. This introductory overview, therefore, will deal primarily with logical standards.

OBJECTIVES OF SYSTEM STANDARDS

System standards are designed to meet varying objectives. In general, system standards provide three things:
- Direction
- Documentation
- Measurement

Direction Objectives

Direction standards tell personnel operating or using a system what they are to do and, often, how they are to do it. Their objective is to provide a required level of consistency in the performance of people associated with information systems. Direction standards are prepared at three different levels, depending on the functions being performed and the degree of judgment to be exercised by the personnel involved:
- Policies
- Guidelines
- Instructions

Policies are direction standards calling for the highest level of judgment and discretion.

Guidelines are used as standards in situations where room for judgment must be provided in the execution of defined responsibilities.

The nature of guidelines may be illustrated with the analogy of maximum and minimum speed limits posted on expressways. These posted limits are, at best, guidelines. Obviously, drivers are not expected to move at maximum speed limits during rush hour. However, under ideal conditions, highway authorities expect these limits to be followed.

Another characteristic of guidelines is that they may be violated at the expense of a calculated risk. A driver moving at 70 miles per hour in a 55-mile-limit area realizes that he is running a risk to achieve an objective of earlier arrival. He is aware of both the probabilities and the consequences of the risks he is taking.

Instructions are generally issued for clerical operations to be performed according to set patterns. Specific instructions are designed to achieve a high degree of uniformity in job performance. Activities are typically repetitive clerical functions which involve preparation of documents or data for use within an EDP system. Volumes of work involved are also material in determining whether instructions or lower levels of control should be incorporated in standards. In general, the higher the volume of work involved, the more specific the instructions should be.

A typical instruction-level standard is illustrated in Figure 5-1. This shows a written procedure.

Documentation Objectives

The documentation inherent in systems standards serves to provide communications and to record accomplishments.

Although effective policies, guidelines, or instructions may be communicated orally, this medium is rather unreliable. Spoken words can be changed too easily, forgotten, or never even heard. This lack of reliability may be quite serious when an effort is made to evaluate the reliability of the activities implemented as a result of such policies.

Measurement Objectives

EDP standards also provide a basis for measuring performance and progress. The most obvious value of standards in performance measurement is with operational systems. If systems development documentation standards describe the activities to be performed, the schedules to be met, and the results to be achieved, they become a vital tool for comparing accomplishments with what was expected. Similarly, to understand and to control costs, it is valuable to:
- Establish standard activities
- Measure the costs of these activities over time, among locations and projects

JOB INSTRUCTIONS

ACTIVITY NAME: Sales Order X27A

TASK NAME: "Manual Inventory" Sales Order

PERSONNEL: Customer Service Representative

FORMS: Sales Order (101A/101B/101C)
Customer Purchase Order

REPORTS: None

INTRODUCTION: "Manual Inventory" includes custom made and personalized items stocked in the regional warehouse but not recorded on the computer Merchandise Master File. The Customer Service Representative prepares a Sales Order Requesting the charge-off and shipment of manual inventory.

STEPS PERFORMED:

1. Receives or prepares Sales Order (Refer to Procedure Number A431-1, Full Code Customer), including the following information:

   a. Enters billing only "RR" suffix in the Sales Order Number suffix box..

   b. Enters complete "Ship To" information on Sales Order.

   c. Enters "Ship from Manual Inventory" on Sales Order in the "Remarks" section.

2. Sends Sales Order and Customer P.O. to Purchasing Supervisor.

Figure 5-1

Management considerations would seem to dictate that system development efforts be similarly scheduled and budgeted. This may be done by establishing standards for a system development methodology. Within this structure, standard activities are repeated on multiple projects; and realistic estimates are developed.

System development costs and schedules may then be estimated with increasing ease. Reasonableness and progress may be checkpointed frequently, measuring actual progress against the working plan. Without standards for measurement of system development, these efforts are highly subject to cost overruns and schedule delays.

APPLICATION AND IPF STANDARDS

Within the discussion, it is important to establish an understanding of *where* detailed standards fit within the EDP requirements *and why.*

In the application and information processing facility (IPF) areas, detailed standards are particularly important to the auditor. They establish the framework for determining reliability of an organization's operational systems and financial statements. This is true because application and IPF standards cover every phase of clerical activity, processing, and reporting, providing the actual basis for evaluations of system reliability and tests of compliance performed during an audit.

Application standards are primarily logical in the sense of a general description of a *business* process. They must cover every activity involving clerical or computer processing of data through the entire cycle of an operational system. Even in activities involving use of the computer, processing steps and controls should be described at a level where the reasonableness of the activity will be apparent to an informed businessman. This enables the user and the auditor to test and evaluate the system, using techniques which are already familiar. Where computer processing is to be tested, a familiarity with general purpose audit software, acquired in a few weeks of training *and use,* should provide the special knowledge necessary for most audits of application programs.

> *Examples — Such logical standards include specifications that the operator is to process jobs in the sequence scheduled, that he makes no adjustments to application data, that he logs all use of files, that he follows set procedures in mounting tapes or discs, that he does not have application code listings available, and so on.*

IPF standards should be expected to cover those functions which apply to most or all applications processed in an EDP facility. IPF standards include elements that are both technical and nontechnical in nature. In evaluating technical IPF standards, however, the auditor may require assistance from EDP specialists. Areas covered by technical IPF standards include:

- Hardware-software control trade-offs
- Equipment configuration
- Operating system features and versions

Detail-level standards should be expected in the application and IPF areas chiefly because of high volumes and the repetitive nature of the work involved. Operating instructions should be explicit. Only limited judgment or application of operator decisions should be expected or allowed. Thus, the degree to which application and IPF standards are explicit in directing, documenting, and measuring the manual and computer activities is an important measure of the reliability of these standards.

The value of a comparatively high level of detail in application and IPF standards is enhanced because repetitive functions tend to have a relatively great exposure to loss. In most clerical-oriented situations, heavy volumes of work make for major exposure to potential for financial loss. Thus, the more explicit the standards, the lower the risk and the greater the capability for supervision and/or detection of nonstandard practices or errors as well as for monitoring the activities of new people.

DEVELOPMENT AND PLANNING STANDARDS

Guideline and policy standards apply mainly to the systems development areas of EDP activity. These will be discussed in greater depth in Section III.

The primary characteristics of development work which lend themselves to control by standards are:

- The moderate degree of repetition in the work performed
- The importance of efficient and predictable results from these activities

The repetitive characteristic is offset by evaluation and decision criteria which are too extensive to make specific, instructional standards feasible. Thus, in these areas, guidelines and policy statements are designed to set general boundaries for the work to be done, the schedules to be followed, and the resources to be utilized without impairing the application of judgment.

Guideline standards and policy statements also supply the degree of consistency necessary for effective system planning and development. This consistency should be sufficient so that development activities follow established patterns and produce predictable results.

If these standards are really to exist, it is critically important that they be documented, formal, and clear. Informal or assumed guidelines or policies are not standards because they do not allow reliable prediction of results.

48

Guideline and policy levels of directional and documentation types of standards establish a base of communication. Using these standards, the project team can look back and benefit from experience in building and working a plan. This approach is of particular value to users who might never have been associated with system projects before. Even for the experienced systems analyst, directional guidelines provide an activity structure which makes for consistency in his work.

Specific communication *content of documentation standards* includes:

- **Detailed standard documentation** of application processing logic and data flow understandable to all parties associated with system development users, analysts, programmers, EDP operations personnel, managers, and auditors.
- **Directional guidelines** establishing definitions and responsibilities for standard activities of system development projects. The specification of responsibilities builds a measure of error prevention into the system development cycle, because an understanding of these activities and responsibilities provides an indication of where errors may occur.
- **Performance guideline standards** provide for the specification of resources — in equipment, money, and personnel — to be used in the development of a new EDP system. Everyone connected with a system project must understand what resources will be available, in what amounts and under what schedules.

Another important consideration is that documentation created during a system development project becomes the basis for the preparation of instruction standards to be applied when the new application becomes operational. Thus, the quality of instruction standards developed for applications relates directly to the quality of the guideline and policy standards used in system planning and development. Logically, then, documented guideline and policy standards are also important in determining the auditability of a newly developed information processing application.

There is a general tendency to downgrade the importance of documenting guidelines and policies for systems development. One line of reasoning holds that thorough documentation increases the costs of a system project unnecessarily. There is a tendency to rush or compromise the documentation of system project activities and to regard this documentation as an unnecessary frill.

This is not the case! Documentation of development projects is essential for quality assurance and for reliable application controls. Training and maintenance also require documentation. Although short-run cost reductions might be realized by shortcutting documentation, the long-range cost implications may be very substantial. Increasingly, documentation of guidelines, policies, and system project activities is being recognized as essential for effective control rather than as an option or a frill.

STANDARDS AS AN AID TO AUDITING

The availability of formal written system standards eases and improves the process of understanding, evaluating, and testing system reliability. By observing the operation and results of system processing, the auditor can determine whether the actions and controls specified in system standards actually exist in the implemented procedures. The documentation required for communication between users and EDP specialists is also suitable for the auditor.

Furthermore, the value of the audit activity is enhanced because the auditor's level of knowledge of system functions and performance goes further than is possible without system standards. With documentation available, the auditor can plan his work to review the reliability of systems and controls adherence to both application and installation standards simultaneously.

In the past, documented standards were a rarity. However, increasing numbers of data processing and general managers are recognizing that precise descriptions of systems pay for themselves by:

- Improving controls
- Reducing costs
- Facilitating the conduct of audit examinations
- Minimizing the interruptions caused by audit activities

In many cases, this requirement for documentation during an audit should stimulate the preparation of standards.

Any audit engagement involving the examination of EDP systems on which the auditor intends to rely should include an assumption that, before an application review takes place, the auditor will familiarize himself with application standards. Their absence or inadequacy is cause for comment by the auditor and revision of the planned scope of substantive audit procedures. This initial review should relate directly to the level of work being done in the examination. *The ability to review system documentation at the logic level is probably the most critical requirement in the audit of EDP applications.*

This area of activity presents a whole new dimension of opportunity for auditors. With appropriate application documentation, the auditor will understand the alternatives and the reasoning behind the decision rules used in applications and evaluate their effectiveness. Findings in the review of operational computer systems can also be evaluated against project development. In effect, a new dimension of operational auditing will be added to the conventional attest function performed by the auditor. Thus, where adequate standards exist, the presence of a computer will enhance rather than diminish auditability.

System standards are the appropriate basis for auditing control over EDP systems. The presence, absence, or degree of control relates directly to the extent, the completeness, and the comprehensibility of documentation. Documentation is the key element of a standards program. Without documentation, standards cannot reliably exist. With documented standards, the work of the auditor is facilitated and his role is made more meaningful.

A more meaningful audit of compliance with controls will only occur after adequate standards have been established.

COMPLIANCE AUDITING

Audits to verify compliance with controls are performed by both internal auditors and certified public accountants. In the case of internal auditors, this is generally their primary function. In the case of certified public accountants, compliance audits are performed so as to predict the degree of reliability of the financial statements prepared by the organization and thereby limit the extent of substantive testing performed over the actual year-end financial statement balances. Compliance auditing is a major concern to certified public accountants because it is extremely important to them in rendering an opinion on financial statements within reasonable cost and time limitations. Few organizations are so small or simple that their financial statements may be readily verified through substantive audit procedures only. In practically every case, particularly with larger organizations, reliance upon controls by the certified public accountant is absolutely essential to the completion of an audit.

The goal of a compliance audit is to identify and to verify the existence and effective operation of controls over a specific information processing function. In order to do this, the auditor must first have specific objectives: to verify financial or management controls and to evaluate efficiency or the safeguarding of assets.

The objectives of the certified public accountant are fairly clear: to evaluate the quality of accounting and other controls that could affect the quality of financial reporting.

The objectives of an internal auditor are not always so clear. Although we have previously stated that the internal auditor *should* be attentive to all types of exposures and their causes, the actual fact is that few internal audit organizations maintain a balance to their efforts. This is not necessarily wrong.

Internal auditors must be responsive to the desires of top management and to the special needs of their own company. Furthermore, the skills required to evaluate various types of exposures may call for a division of the internal audit staff into various specialties.

Example — Auditors of exposures to erroneous bookkeeping or unacceptable accounting should possess a sound background in accounting. Auditors for excess computer processing costs should be experts in computer hardware and system software.

COMPLIANCE AUDIT STEPS

Seven specific steps should be found in every compliance audit examination:

- Define objectives
- Gather basic information
- Gather detailed information
- Evaluate control
- Design audit tests
- Perform tests
- Evaluate findings

Each of these steps should be directed toward the preparation of a particular set of audit documentation. Such documentation provides a definable beginning and ending for each step of the audit, allows effective supervision, and facilitates staffing changes and subsequent reference. *The primary control over the conduct of an audit is documentation and review.* This process is illustrated in Figure 5-2.

Define Objectives

The first step is always to clearly state the specific objectives of the compliance audit. This does not mean that the objectives need to be limited or narrow. It means that explicit, tangible *goals* be stated so that the auditor, as well as his superiors, will be able to determine later whether the objectives were met.

Basic Information Gathering

With his objectives and goals firmly in mind, the second step for the auditor is to obtain a general understanding of the system standards and flow of transactions: its general purpose, magnitude, functions, and controls. This general understanding need have little direct bearing on the specific objectives. It is simply an effort to acquire a general comprehension of the system in question so that subsequent steps may narrow in on the specific objectives effectively. The information gathered should be the policies and possibly some of the more significant guidelines.

The documentation for basic information gathering is rather simple: interview notes, completed general questionnaires, organization charts, and similar information about the general structure of the system.

Detailed Information Gathering

Once he understands the general characteristics of the overall system, the auditor goes about obtaining a more detailed understanding. This differs from a general understanding in that it involves

STANDARD METHODOLOGY FOR EXAMINATION
OF INTERNAL CONTROLS

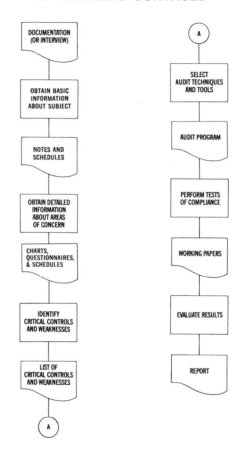

Figure 5-2

a greater level of detail and limits that detail to the aspects of the system that relate solely to his particular objectives.

Example — An auditor concerned only with predicting the reliability of financial information in an inventory system could exclude perpetual inventory records from his detailed information gathering if such records were used for production control purposes only and did not relate to the financial books.

Here he should gather remaining relevant guidelines as well as relevant instruction-level standards. This detailed information is also carefully documented in the form of completed detailed questionnaires, additional notes, examples of documents, flowcharts, and detailed charts of other types.

Evaluation of Control

Once the auditor understands the system thoroughly, he must identify and evaluate the controls. First, this involves differentiating between the activities in the system which are *subject to control* and those which *provide control*. Once this differentiation is made, the auditor (1) identifies those controls whose absence would allow significant exposures and (2) searches for exposures which exist under the system but which could be eliminated by the addition of further controls. The exposures will be limited to those covered by his objectives.

This evaluation process is often done informally and intuitively. Some evidence exists that even experienced auditors, given identical circumstances, will provide varied evaluations of the controls and exposures. This evaluation will be substantially improved if this step is made into a formal process.

The documentation resulting from this evaluation should be a listing of significant control features and weaknesses with an estimate of the resulting business exposures on an overall basis.

The one major assumption that must be made by the auditor in evaluating exposures is known as Murphy's Law: "Anything that can go wrong, will!" At the same time, however, he must realize that the probability of certain things going wrong is greater than the probability of others. Even though precise probabilities are not known in most situations, general orders of magnitude may be assigned. Even the fact that nothing has ever gone wrong in the past is no proof that this situation will continue. Some serious causes of exposure, such as fire, would not be expected to occur frequently, even when no controls exist. However, managements which refuse to institute controls because they have never been harmed in the past are merely gamblers — and the dice don't remember.

54

CONTROL REVIEW

The three steps that we have just presented above — basic information gathering, detailed information gathering, and evaluation of control — are often called a "control review." Nothing has yet been done to obtain conclusive evidence that the controls that have been reviewed *actually* exist or function effectively. Neither has anything actually measured the magnitude of the exposures allowed by the apparent weaknesses. A control review is not a compliance audit; it is merely the first phase.

Design Audit Procedures

To verify the controls and to measure the weaknesses, the auditor must next design his auditing procedures, using the most appropriate tools and techniques. A specific testing procedure must be applied to verify each control which he considers important and to measure the effect of each weakness which he considers significant. Many of these procedures may be delegated to audit assistants.

The documentation of this phase is generally called an "audit program." It typically describes the system under examination, discusses the evaluation of control, and lists the auditing procedures to be performed. Often columns are placed adjacent to the list of auditing procedures. These are to be dated and initialed by the auditor upon completing the procedure. Another column referencing the working papers produced is often used.

Testing

The next step is the performance of the audit tests. While this phase is what most people would just call "auditing," actually five distinct steps have had to be performed before this point is reached.

The performance of the various audit tests involves an auditor using various techniques, which may include the utilization of various tools. The distinction between techniques and tools is important. *A technique is an action that the auditor may perform, whereas a tool is something tangible that he can use.*

Techniques may include interview, observation, examination of documentation, confirmation, etc., whereas *tools* may range anywhere from a simple pencil to a complex computer program. Some techniques, such as interviewing, do not necessarily require any tools; but the utilization of any tool naturally involves the application of some technique.

The results of the audit compliance tests include working papers and memoranda which indicate to what items the tests were applied and exactly what was found. Working papers are essential for quality control of the audit. To a large extent, they are another phase of information gathering that may be provided to audit management personnel for their review to assure that the tests were properly performed and that meaningful findings were recognized and reported.

Evaluation of Findings

The final step is to produce conclusions from the detailed findings documented in the working papers. These findings should provide evidence that the various controls do or do not exist, that they function effectively, or have measured the historical effects of a particular weakness.

The predictions drawn from these findings should generally assume that the events of the past will continue at a similar rate in the future. However, this assumption should not be followed blindly because some events that have rarely occurred would not be expected to be found in any relatively small test sample. At the same time, events that occur rarely will seldom concern the auditor unless the consequences of a single occurrence would be significant. Given this information, the auditor should produce a prediction or forecast of the reliability of the system under examination as it relates to his objectives. If at all possible, this evaluation should be stated in terms of the financial exposure. Commonly, the exposures would be quantified on an annual basis.

Example — The resulting exposure to excessive costs is estimated at approximately $500,000 per year.

This prediction should also be accompanied by constructive suggestions as to what actions may correct any problems that have already occurred and what controls might be added to minimize future recurrences.

INTERIM DECISIONS

After each step, the auditor must review his own documentation and decide whether he is ready to commence the next step. He may detect something that was omitted from a previous step and go back and get it. He may also realize that, for some reason, his initial objectives cannot be met. He could then either redefine his objectives or abort the entire examination. Finally, he may determine that controls are so weak that no meaningful prediction of reliability will be possible. If this is the case, it must be reported and a "weakness examination" instituted to attempt to evaluate and to correct the consequences.

SUMMARY

A diagram of the general compliance audit methodology is shown in Figure 5-2. You will note that the completion of each of the seven steps is marked by a particular set of documentation. In subsequent chapters, we will describe how this general methodology is applied toward major areas of EDP auditing.

Section II
APPLICATIONS

6
Application Activities

INTRODUCTION

This section of the book will deal with the nature and controls of computerized business information application systems and the methods for auditing their reliability.

In this section we will describe:

Chapter 6 — Application Activities
- Inputs
- Processes
- Outputs
- Causes of application exposure

Chapter 7 — Application Controls
- Prevention
- Detection
- Correction

Chapter 8 — Application Audit Tools
- Information gathering
- Evaluate controls
- Verify controls

Chapter 9 — Application Audit Techniques
- Information gathering
- Evaluate controls
- Verify controls

Chapter 10 — Auditing EDP Applications
- Steps

Applications are the broad area of business information systems. Common examples are:
- Payroll
- Receivables
- Inventory
- Deposits, etc.

Computer usage in application systems may be comprehensive or merely as a printing device. Some applications are primarily accounting oriented, whereas others provide nonaccounting management information.

The application function is the objective of the EDP activities. For evaluation of controls, these activities will be examined in detail.

ACTIVITIES SUBJECT TO CONTROL

The following are activities which take place within operational computer applications and require explicit consideration in designing, evaluating, and testing system controls.

Initiation

Initiation is creating a transaction which will cause a demand for processing. Transaction initiation may be performed either manually or by processing within a computer program. The content and format of transaction initiation results from agreement by users and systems analysts on explicit logical specifications.

Transactions are records which are in a transitory state within the application. This classification excludes historical files of transactions that are typically retained for reference or analysis after the original purpose of the transactions has been served.

Transaction type provides a useful classification both for inputs and for processing. Distinct characteristics may be found that have a definite relationship to the frequency and magnitude of exposures.

Increasingly, systems are being developed in which initiation of an extended series of processes occurs without human involvement. The initiation may be triggered by the passage of time, accumulation of other transactions, or a particular set of circumstances conveyed by some input. *Internally initiated transactions* will be quite reliable in the sense of consistency but can readily be misapplied in circumstances that were not anticipated.

Recording

Recording refers to the entering of data on any media: paper, punched cards, magnetic tape discs, etc., in the initial capturing of data on a source document such as a customer order. Recording often occurs simultaneously with initiation, whereas a transaction may be initiated but not recorded.

The probability of introducing errors varies widely with different approaches to the recording of data. The main problems are with the accuracy and completeness of all relevant data.

Coding

Codes serve a variety of functions, including specification of records and files to be affected by an input, data elements of a record to be changed, and how they are changed.

Codes may utilize any type of symbol: numeric or alphanumeric. Their distinguishing feature is that their meaning may only be interpreted by a "key." Their outward appearance will not provide any interpretation. Codes are widely employed in computer files to conserve storage space.

Example — In a billing system, elements of a customer's account code might automatically approve or disapprove credit purchases.

Transcription

The subsequent transcription of data from one medium to another is similar to recording.

Transmission

The interaction implicit in information systems requires transmission of data between departments and processing points. At its inception, data must be moved from source to data processing. Within an information processing facility, movement takes place between the control group and other sections, including data conversion, computer operations center, library, output handling, and so on.

There is always an exposure to loss of data or insertion of improper data during physical or electronic transmission.

Processing Logic

The term "processing logic" is used to describe all functions applied to data and files within computers. Processing logic includes:

- Comparison
- Calculations
- Updating
- File maintenance
- Summarization
- Sorting

These processes may be combined into extremely complex sequences and alternatives. The speed with which they can be performed is generally the primary reason for utilizing a computer to process information.

Data Storage

Storage is the retention of data files for subsequent processing, reference, or backup for any period of time.

Output Preparation

Ultimately, the purpose of every information processing system is to provide some useful output, which must then be transmitted to its users.

While these are the activities that make up any application system, they may be either the activities subject to control or those used to implement control. Therefore, while their identification at a detailed level will be quite important, they must also be classified and analyzed according to whether they act as controls. This will be discussed further in the next chapter.

IMPORTANCE OF INPUTS

Input, the entry of data for processing within an application, is traditionally the most significant area for application of controls to computer systems. This is a recognition of the fact that there is no way to operate a reliable computer system without adequate measures to assure the quality of input. This recognition is aptly summarized in the expression "garbage in, garbage out."

This traditional concentration on input can be expected to expand in the future. Continued emphasis on input becomes particularly necessary where data processing facilities are centralized and where input transactions are often initiated remotely from multiple sources. As transaction points become more and more scattered from the central data processing facilities, both geographically and organizationally, the input activities must become more structured in order to achieve compatibility with the requirements of a central data processing system.

TYPES OF INPUT

Although there are many variables of environment, procedures, and controls, inputs may be divided into four general types:

- Update
- File maintenance
- Inquiry
- Error correction

Each of these types of input has a separate set of characteristics and associated concerns.

Update

Update transactions generally involve large volumes of data. Processing of updating transactions is usually routine and highly repetitive. Also, each individual update transaction will tend to have a limited impact on data files.

Updating transactions are frequently chain related to each other. Manual authorizations are frequently applied to the first transaction in a chain with authorizations for succeeding transactions handled automatically or assumed. Typically, linked transactions are carried forward routinely by the computer. Relatively heavy use of integrated

ACTIVITIES SUBJECT TO CONTROL

Activities Subject to Control	Explanation of Activity
INITIATE	Any financial or other event which should be recorded
RECORD	
Recording	The creation of a record of a transaction on some medium
Coding	The recording of values or characters having meanings which are not readily apparent
Transcription	The copying of recorded information from one medium to another
TRANSMIT	The movement of data from one location to another
PROCESSING	
Comparison	The examination of data using logical or conditional tests to determine or identify similarities or differences
Calculation	The performance of various mathematical operations yielding a numeric result
Updating	Changing information in a file through the addition or subtraction from a value in a field
File maintenance	Changing information in a file through addition, deletion, or replacement usually to information that will have a sustained impact on future processing
Summarization	To combine detail items having the same "key" into a single item with the same "key" and accumulated value
Sorting	To place items or records into sequence
DATA STORAGE	
File	Storage of transactions or records so that they may be retrieved upon request
OUTPUT PREPARATION	
Reporting	Summary or exception information printed and used for management decisions or accounting entries
Working documents	Functional documents used to transfer assets or information
Reference documents	Documents that serve to store information for reference
INQUIRY	A request to obtain information without altering it

Figure 6-1

files, reasonableness checks, and application program logic make chain authorization feasible.

Example — A record for a new customer was approved and inserted into a computer file. The system may be preauthorized at this point for the processing of updating transactions for pricing, billing, shipping, and applying cash. This may be done on the basis of only a test of correct account number, current balance, and credit limit.

The order-entry application represents only one of many different types of processing chains which have become commonplace in EDP systems. Other chains of transactions are triggered in purchasing, payroll, or production work orders.

File Maintenance

File maintenance transactions are characterized by limited volume, particularly in comparison with update transactions. File maintenance transactions are generally received from fewer, more restricted, and more secured sources. They have a semipermanent or permanent impact upon the data files. Their effect is residual until they are changed or revoked.

Example — Considering the transaction chain described previously, file maintenance transactions would include the initial establishment of a customer's record or those transactions which might change some continuing content of the file such as customer's address, credit limits, standard discount allowances, and so on.

Inquiry Transactions

The primary characteristic of an inquiry transaction is that there is no addition or change to the significant content of data files. Some systems maintain logs of inquiry activity, but these do not affect the information content of the file. Inquiry transactions frequently lead to decisions regarding initiation or other processing of subsequent updating or file maintenance transactions.

Example — Before initiating a credit sale, the salesman will inquire whether the customer's credit limit will permit it.

Error Correction Transactions

Of the four categories of inputs, error corrections are probably the most difficult to process and require the highest degree of thought and effort for effective control. Error correction inputs are data entries correcting either previously rejected transactions or data elements contained on the files of the system. By definition, a problem already exists before an error correction transaction is initiated.

Therefore, the handling of an error correction will be more complex than any other type of input.

Example — An update transaction had already affected an application file before an error condition was discovered. The error was detected; the transaction was recorded in a suspense file and reported on an error listing. The correction procedure, therefore, includes a determination of which files have to be returned to the status that existed before the erroneous transaction was processed. Correction procedures also have to determine the processing necessary for file updating on a current basis as well as steps required to remove the error item from the suspense file.

Many error corrections are initiated in response to reports of errors identified during input or processing. These error-output reports provide controls which assure that identified errors are corrected with new input transactions. Where errors are concerned, it is important that the role of output reports be identified and understood as a potentially critical element of input transaction processing.

It is paradoxical, but true, that error correction transactions run a high risk of engendering errors. Even an error which is relatively simple in its initial commission becomes more complex to handle through formal correction procedures. Correction procedures generally involve:

- Analysis of the error report data
- A decision as to whether any corrective action is necessary
- New input documents
- File updating for error control records
- Entry of the data into its proper processing files
- Reestablishing balances which might have been harmed by the initial error

This complexity is often compounded because errors are more likely to occur with more difficult or complex input entries. Because of concerns for the complexity and error probability of the correction process, the handling of inputs for corrections is usually assigned to more experienced people than those who handle normal input functions. Controls for error correction input should be at least as stringent as those where the original errors were encountered — and more so, if possible.

A final concern in this area is establishing controls to make sure that the causes of errors are corrected where feasible. This requires that documentation on the commission of errors be reviewed with an eye toward future prevention measures which can be implemented through either changes in procedures or through further training of personnel.

CHARACTERISTICS AND CONCERNS FOR INPUTS

TYPES OF INPUTS	CHARACTERISTICS	CONCERNS
UPDATE	Large volumes Chain related and processed from initial authorization Transaction value limited to one-time impact on files Routine and repetitive processing	Increasing concentration of processing Verifying initial authorization in transaction chains Completing the processing chain Authorization of adjustments and deviations Controls must be efficient
FILE MAINTENANCE	Limited volumes Restricted sources Permanent or semipermanent impact on data files	Authorization is critical Timing of transactions affects content of processing cycle
INQUIRY	File reference only; no impact on file content May trigger subsequent decisions or inputs	Security of data in custody Accuracy of data displayed must be in keeping with the decisions to be made and actions to be taken
ERROR CORRECTION	Records were entered and rejected previously Processing is more complex than for routine input transactions	Reentry controls must be as stringent or more stringent than for original input Correction is more complex than original entry; error probability is higher with corrections Errors should be reviewed to determine causes for potential system improvement or user training

Figure 6-2

ROLE OF OUTPUTS

Outputs are the specific end products delivered by a computer system to meet user specifications incorporated within application programs.

TYPES OF OUTPUT

There are four basic types of output:

- Reports
- Working documents
- Reference documents
- Error reports

Reports are summary-level documents that provide a wide variety of information for general information, management decisions, or accounting entries.

Working documents are items that have some functional use: to transfer assets or to play some role in future transactions. Examples would be checks, savings bonds, invoices, etc.

Reference documents provide storage outside of the computer for detailed information that may be subject to future inquiry. Typical examples are trial balance, transaction lists, etc.

Error reports list exceptions noted in processing.

Each has its specific characteristics and its associated concerns for control.

Reports

Reports tend to be periodic in nature. They also have more limited volumes than are normally associated with working documents. The very existence of a report presupposes consolidation, integration, or summarization of data.

Reports are primary conveyors of management and accounting information; thus, two important characteristics of reports are that they are specified in advance and that their format and content are anticipated. Another important characteristic is that wide variances may be expected in the uses to which reports are put and in the impact of the data they contain.

Some reports may be produced only when prespecified conditions occur. These are called "exception reports." Nevertheless, the user must be aware of these programmed decisions and also understand what is not being reported.

Since many reports have a special purpose and are confidential in nature, security of distribution is a subject for concern. Intensifying this concern is the fact that some reports have great potential value to outsiders — particularly competitors. Therefore, the degree of concern should have a direct relation to the content of the report and the potential impact of the information on company operations.

Concern should be applied to evaluating whether the content is timely and the format of each report is consistent with its use. Persons associated with the development and use of EDP systems should satisfy themselves continuously that reports issued by computer systems are of constructive use.

Working Documents

Working documents are usually related to or derived from specific inputs. Most working documents provide direct support for transactions associated with internal operations of a business, with the need for communicating with or paying its employees, or for dealing with outside individuals and companies. Such sensitive documents (checks, savings bonds, etc.) are major security concerns.

Concerns over working documents center chiefly on the trade-offs between the effectiveness and efficiency of control alternatives. One of the trade-off considerations is large volumes involved. Because of volumes, detailed clerical controls of individual transactions will be time-consuming and costly. More desirable control solutions utilize the power of the computer. These controls apply concepts of chain transaction authorization and approval discussed earlier.

Reference Documents

Outputs of this type serve as references. They are also prime elements in a recovery system if computer services are interrupted. Compared with other outputs, reference documentation is used comparatively infrequently.

An increasingly important characteristic of this type of output is that it can be recorded and retrieved through the use of micro-image techniques.

Error Reports

Error reports are characterized, hopefully, by limited volumes. What error outputs lack in volume, they more than make up in critical importance, in complexity of logic associated with their handling, and in demands for attention in their processing.

A high degree of control and judgment must be applied in seeing that output error reports are distributed to the proper parties for corrective action. Further, stringent controls are necessary for follow-up to be such that correcting entries are initiated and processed. Therefore, throughout the processing of error corrections, it is important that documentation and procedures provide for ease in identifying and categorizing types of errors and fixing responsibility for their correction and their future elimination.

ROLE OF PROCESSING

Application processing may be the implementation of transactions initiated internally or from inputs. Accordingly, the first set of processing functions is the same as for inputs (excluding error correction):

- Updating
- File maintenance
- Inquiry

CHARACTERISTICS AND CONCERNS FOR OUTPUTS

TYPES OF OUTPUTS	CHARACTERISTICS	CONCERNS
WORKING DOCUMENTS	Wide range of forms and uses; orders, invoices, shipping papers, checks, statements, etc. Large volumes Usually generated by or related to specific inputs Routine and repetitive in nature	Trade-offs between effectiveness of control and efficiency of operations with large volumes
REPORTS	Limited volumes Primarily preplanned and repetitive Wide variation in uses of information and impact of company operations	Are content and timing of reports consistent with use of information and decisions to be made? Greater concern and control efforts should be applied to one-time or intermittent reports than to those issued regularly and frequently
REFERENCE DOCUMENTS	Periodically produced Voluminous, especially when whole files are "dumped" Increasingly being stored in micro-image format	Conscientiousness of production; reports should not be put off because they get little use Safe custody for reports in event they are needed for recovery Application of stipulated cutoff dates for report production
ERROR REPORTS	Limited volumes Complex transactions requiring greater application of logic and judgment than other input transactions	Distributed to proper parties for corrective action Establish control to assure entry of corrections Experienced people should process because of complexities Learn reasons for errors and avoid recurrence where feasible through training or system modification

Figure 6-3

Similarly, processing may be the implementation of output requirements (excluding error reports):

- Reports
- Working documents
- Reference documents

In short, processing is directed by either the nature of the transactions or the outputs. Processing for its own sake would serve no useful function.

Therefore, classifications of processing are meaningless outside of their transaction or output relationships. Their control concerns are dependent upon their functions listed above.

CAUSES OF APPLICATION EXPOSURES

The concept of causes of exposures was discussed in a previous chapter. Exposures arise from active causes, not directly from an absence of controls. The causes of exposures which are attributable to computer applications may be categorized within four major classifications:

- Input
- Processing
- Output
- Other

INPUT CAUSES OF EXPOSURE

The input causes of exposure exist whenever a transaction or file is subjected to a new process. This process may be either manual or computerized and may involve a transmittal over a considerable distance or merely to the next desk. The principal input causes of exposure are:

- Inputs lost
- Inputs duplicated
- Inaccurate contents on input
- Data missing on inputs
- Transaction never recorded
- Transactions authorized on a blanket basis
- Transactions initiated internally by the computer

Inputs Lost

The loss of inputs is very common. It may occur any time an item is transmitted from one location to another, including those times when the transmittal is to implement a control.

Inputs Duplicated

Inputs may also be duplicated erroneously. This may arise through the mistaken understanding that they had been lost when in fact they had not.

Inaccurate Contents on Input

The data conveyed on inputs may be recorded inaccurately at the time of initiation or during some subsequent transcription operation. Numbers may be recorded incorrectly or inverted. Names may be misspelled, or the recording may be sloppy and be misread.

Data Missing on Inputs

The correct processing of transactions may require different information in different circumstances. Absence of the information needed under certain circumstances may cause processing to be erroneous or impossible.

Transactions Never Recorded

One of the most difficult problems in recording financial transactions is knowing whether all of the transactions which actually occurred were ever recorded in the first place. This applies particularly in situations where the individuals have reason *not* to record them such as in the case of accident, theft, embezzlement, etc.

Transactions Authorized on a Blanket Basis

Computerized systems are often implemented where transactions are authorized on a "blanket" basis. This is usually due to having a massive volume of inputs that exceeds management's capability to authorize each input on an individual basis. While this situation may be justified by the circumstances, it may also lead to various problems that would not otherwise exist.

Transactions Initiated Internally by the Computer

Computer programs are often designed to automatically perform the logical processes that cause the initiation of various types of financial transactions. Common examples of such programs include recognition of interest, automatic stock reorders, and payment of accounts payable. In effect, a blanket authorization for such transactions is made when the computer program is designed and implemented. As long as the program operates in a manner appropriate to the circumstances of each situation, the programming could be considered a control over the consistency of such transactions. However, situations which the program designers have not anticipated often arise and cause exposures.

PROCESSING CAUSES OF EXPOSURE

While the causes of exposure related to the inputs were noted as the source of the expression "garbage in, garbage out," *garbage may result from defective processing,* even though the inputs are complete, accurate, and appropriate to the situation. These processing causes of exposure include:

- Processing with the wrong file
- Processing transactions against the wrong record
- Incomplete processing
- Incorrect processing
- Untimely recognition
- Processing inappropriate to the circumstances
- Loss of files
- Loss of programs
- Loss of knowledgeable people

Processing with the Wrong File

Although a file might be considered the input to a specific computer program, whichever way you prefer to classify files, there is no doubt that the wrong ones may be used. The most common form of this error is the use of an obsolete file (retained for backup and recovery purposes) against current transactions. The resulting file then lacks the effects of the previous cycle of transactions.

Processing Transactions Against the Wrong Record

Even though the proper file is used, the transactions may be processed against the wrong record. This is most likely to happen in the logic of updating.

Incomplete Processing

Due to a variety of subtle problems in the application's logic, problems may exist even in spite of reports showing proper record counts as well as in situations involving rare combinations of transactions.

Incorrect Processing

Despite good intentions, persons or programs may perform processing activities in an incorrect manner. Errors by people (clerical errors) usually occur intermittently (about 5% of the time). Programmed errors will occur every time the same conditions occur. Such errors originate in the system design.

Untimely Recognition

Not only must processing be correct, but it must frequently also occur within a limited span of time after the event being recorded has occurred. Untimely recognition of transactions may lead to recognition in the incorrect accounting period, inaccurate outputs, or unnecessary error correction.

Processing Inappropriate to the Circumstances

The only processes that transactions and records should be subjected to are those which were anticipated by the designers. If unusual circumstances arise, the processing designed for the general situation may be wholly inappropriate. Computers exercise no judgment on their own.

Loss of Files

While the actual loss of files may also arise within the computer operations environment, situations may occur which are unique to specific applications. Such situations would include files retained by the users outside of the information processing facility or programmed processes which cause the destruction of record contents, either quickly or slowly.

Loss of Programs

Here, again, loss of programs may also be considered within the computer operations environment. We include this as an application cause of exposure because many controls are available that are applied to individual applications.

Loss of Knowledgeable People

The key ingredient in many application processes is the people, not the computer. These people may be lost either temporarily or permanently through vacations, terminations, illness, or death.

OUTPUT CAUSES OF EXPOSURE

The production by the computer of information that is complete, accurate, and meaningful is not the end of the application. Such information exists for the use of people somewhere. In order to fulfill their objectives, such information must reach its proper users and convey the results of input and processing in a legible and plausible manner in hard copy, microimage, optical, audio, or some other media. The major output causes of exposure include information:

- Improperly distributed
- Late or lost
- Obviously erroneous
- Erroneous but plausible
- Excessive error resolution
- Unsupportable results

Improperly Distributed

Output information may be transmitted to the wrong persons or delivered in an incomplete or damaged condition.

Late or Lost

Even when they are properly distributed, such outputs may be so late as to have lost their function. They may also go undelivered.

Obviously Erroneous

Even when input and processing are inaccurate, only limited damage may result if the users recognize the results as being obviously erroneous. This will normally, however, cause the users to lose confidence in the existing system.

Erroneous but Plausible

This is a general cause of exposure which relates to many of the previous causes discussed above. Trust in plausible but erroneous results may have widespread, harmful consequences.

Excessive Error Resolution

Even when controls exist to detect erroneous results due to any of the causes noted, large volumes of such detected errors may exceed the capacity of an organization to correct them on a timely basis. This may have the same effect as if the inputs were never processed or the processing were never performed.

Furthermore, most of the other causes of exposure may also arise in the process of error correction.

Unsupportable Results

The persons in charge of processing are usually held accountable for the results they produce. This is particularly important where the processing involves a fiduciary responsibility. Statutory and regulatory authorities such as the Internal Revenue Service often require support of costs, deductions, etc. Also, customers may demand support for charges.

OTHER CAUSES OF EXPOSURE

Three additional causes of exposure exist that do not fall into the previous three major categories:

- Shadow systems
- Unlimited access
- Management override

Shadow Systems

A "shadow system" is an application system that accepts inputs, performs processing, and produces outputs that are also being produced by the formal system authorized by management. Shadow systems are not all bad. They frequently compensate for deficiencies in the formally authorized system. However, since they are outside of the authorized application system, they may also be the source of many problems relating to their underground nature and absence of management participation.

Unlimited Access

Unlimited access to inputs, processing, or outputs provides the opportunity for persons to introduce exposures due either to their ignorance or their desire to perform some act contrary to law or company policies. The availability of unlimited access widens the opportunities for computer abuse. Submission of inputs, performance of processing, or receipt of outputs by unauthorized personnel may also cause harm simply because those persons are not qualified for the tasks they are performing.

Management Override

Operating or higher-level management may override any routine controls. Their reason for this should be to deal with unusual circumstances not foreseen by the system designers. However, their reason may be self-serving.

The things that can go wrong (causes of exposure) are related to the individual activities subject to control in Figure 6-4.

RESULTING EXPOSURES

The general exposures to which a business is subjected were discussed in a previous chapter. These exposures do not change according to computer involvement. They are:
- Erroneous record keeping
- Unacceptable accounting
- Business interruption
- Erroneous management decisions
- Fraud
- Statutory sanctions
- Excessive costs
- Loss or destruction of assets
- Competitive disadvantage

The precise exposures which result from the causes listed previously will depend on the particular application. Obviously, unacceptable accounting cannot result from a computer application that produces no accounting entries. A table showing the relationships between causes of exposures and exposures which are fairly typical of many computerized business applications is shown in Figure 6-5. *Generally, this figure should not be used for evaluation of specific applications;* rather, the specific exposures and the probable results from the causes should be individually tailored for each major application area.

74

RELATIONSHIPS OF ACTIVITIES SUBJECT TO CONTROL TO CAUSES OF EXPOSURE

CAUSES OF EXPOSURE

ACTIVITIES SUBJECT TO CONTROL	INPUT							PROCESS									OUTPUT						OTHER		
	LOST	DUPLICATED	INACCURATE	MISSING DATA	NEVER RECORDED	BLANKET AUTHORIZATION	INITIATE INTERNALLY	WRONG FILE	WRONG RECORD	INCOMPLETE	INCORRECT	UNTIMELY	INAPPROPRIATE	FILE LOST	PROGRAM LOST	PEOPLE LOST	IMPROPER DISTRIBUTION	LATE OR LOST	OBVIOUSLY ERRONEOUS	ERRONEOUS BUT PLAUSIBLE	EXCESSIVE ERRORS	UNSUPPORTABLE RESULTS	SHADOW SYSTEMS	UNLIMITED ACCESS	MANAGEMENT OVERRIDE
Initiate	×	×	×	×	×	×	×									×						×	×	×	×
Record	×	×	×	×			×							×		×					×		×	×	×
Transcribe	×	×	×	×			×							×		×					×		×	×	
Code			×				×							×		×					×		×	×	
Transmit	×	×	×	×			×	×						×		×					×		×	×	×
Compare								×	×	×	×	×	×	×	×	×					×		×	×	×
Calculate								×	×	×	×	×	×	×	×	×					×		×	×	
Update								×	×	×	×	×	×	×	×	×					×				×
File Maintenance								×	×	×	×	×	×	×	×	×							×	×	×
Summarize								×	×	×	×	×	×	×	×	×					×		×	×	
Sort								×	×		×			×	×	×					×		×	×	
File								×		×	×		×	×	×	×	×	×			×		×	×	
Report								×	×		×	×	×	×	×	×	×	×	×	×	×		×	×	×
Working Document								×	×	×	×	×	×	×	×	×	×	×	×	×	×		×	×	
Reference Document								×	×	×	×		×	×	×	×	×	×	×	×	×		×	×	
Inquiry									×					×	×	×					×		×	×	×

Figure 6-4

APPLICATION RELATIONSHIPS OF CAUSES AND EXPOSURES

	INPUT							PROCESSING									OUTPUT						OTHER			EXPOSURES
	LOST	DUPLICATED	INACCURATE	MISSING DATA	NEVER RECORDED	BLANKET AUTHORIZE	INITIATED INTERNALLY	WRONG FILE	WRONG RECORD	INCOMPLETE	INCORRECT	UNTIMELY	INAPPROPRIATE	FILE LOST	PROGRAM LOST	PEOPLE LOST	IMPROPERLY DISTRIBUTED	LATE OR LOST	ERRONEOUS BUT PLAUSIBLE	OBVIOUSLY ERRONEOUS	EXCESSIVE ERROR CORRECTION	UNSUPPORTABLE	SHADOW SYSTEM	UNLIMITED ACCESS	MANAGEMENT OVERRIDE	
	3	3	3	3	3	2	2	3	3	3	3	3	3	3		2	2	2	3	2	2	1	1	1	1	Erroneous record keeping
	1	1	1	1		2	2		1	1	2	2	3	2	2	2	2	2	2	1		2		2	1	Unacceptable accounting
	2	2	2	2	2	1	1	2	1	2	1	1	1	2	2	2	2	2	2	1	2	1		2	1	Business interruption
		1	1	1		1	1		2	1	2	2	2	1		1	2	1	3	1	2	2	1	1	1	Erroneous management decisions
	2	2	1	1	1	1		2	2	2	1	1	1	2	3	1	2	2	1	1	1	3	1	2	1	Fraud
	2	2	2	2		1	1	2	2	1	2		2	2		1	1	1	2	2	3		3	1	1	Statutory sanctions
									1		2	1	2	2	1	3	1	1			1			2	1	Excessive costs/deficient revenues
	1	1	1	1	1	1	1	1	1	1	1	1	1		1	1				1					1	Loss or destruction of assets
																			1		1					Competitive disadvantage

CAUSES OF EXPOSURES

IMPACT OF CAUSES

3 — Very likely to occur

2 — Likely to occur

1 — May occur

Blank — Generally little effect

Figure 6-5

CLASSES OF APPLICATIONS

Applications come in many sizes and shapes. We will describe a few broad classes that provide useful relationships to the technical expertise required to evaluate them. These classes are:

- Small
- Common
- Sophisticated
- Unique

Classification Criteria

The criteria we use to establish these four classifications of applications include the following:

- Number of computers processing application functions
- Capacity of the computers utilized (memory size and processing speeds)
- The processing mode, batch or on-line
- Number of user departments
- The decisions included in application functions, according to their level, from clerical to management
- The extent to which transactions are initiated externally or internally
- The degree of reliance on exception and summary reports rather than detail-printed hard copy
- The availability of visible transaction trails
- The extent to which the system relies upon programmed versus user controls
- The maintenance of files on off-line media or on-line data bases

Naturally, with these many criteria, many applications will not fall neatly into one category or another. The appropriate classification for an application will depend upon where the preponderance of these criteria fall under the four general definitions. Since the purpose of these classifications is to gauge the relative technical expertise required of management and auditors who are attempting to evaluate controls, any decisions as to questionable classifications should be made with this purpose in mind. A summary table of the major classifications and their criteria is shown in Figure 6-6.

Small Applications

These are the systems generally implemented on a single computer having limited capacity (32,000 characters of main memory or less) and processed by batches. Alternatively, larger equipment may be off site at a service bureau or other facility. Each individual application will have one primary user. The processing functions will be limited to general clerical processes with extremely limited decision levels. Almost all of the transactions will be initiated externally. The outputs will be highly detailed and may require significant amounts

CHARACTERISTICS OF APPLICATION CLASSES

APPLICATION CLASS	MEMORY (000)	NUMBER OF USERS	BATCH OR REAL TIME	DATA BASE	PROGRAMMED DECISIONS	INTERNALLY INITIATED TRANSACTIONS	VISIBLE TRANSACTION TRAIL	EMPHASIS ON PROGRAMMED OR USER CONTROLS	NUMBER OF CPU'S	LEVEL OF EXCEPTION REPORTS
SMALL	Up to 32	1	Batch	No	Negligible	No	Abundant	User	1	Negligible
COMMON	32-196	1	Batch	No	Some	Some	Adequate	User	1	Some
SOPHISTICATED	124-556	2 or 3	Some Real Time	Some	Many	Many	Limited	Programmed	Several	Many
UNIQUE	335-1,500+	3 +	Extensive Real Time	Yes	Massive	Massive	Negligible	Programmed	Many	Massive

Figure 6-6

of subsequent manual processing. However, as a by-product, the transaction trail will be readily available. The users will exercise the principal control over the application inputs and processes. The files will be small and stored off-line when not in use.

Example — An IBM System/3 with 16,000 bytes of capacity may be utilized to post invoices and cash receipts on accounts receivable. Batch processing of the application may require two hours each afternoon on a file of 10,000 customers. It would produce frequent trial balances, statements, and transaction listings which are monitored by a collections clerk for accuracy and collection.

Common Applications
The majority of computer users fall into this broad category. Processing would be in house on a single machine of moderate capacity in the batch mode. Besides the volume, it is different from a small system in that the programmed functions involve more business decisions. Some transactions may be initiated internally. The outputs would still include detail trial balances and transaction listings, but they would be supplemented by more analytic reports. Clerks would still be capable of resolving inquiries and discrepancies, using reports produced regularly. While user controls are still the most important, the computer programs would provide agings and listings of edit exceptions. Most files are likely to be stored off-line, but the magnitude would be fairly significant.

Example — A common application system for accounts receivable might include, in addition to those functions performed by a small system, pricing and automatic calculation of interest on past-due balances. This might be performed on an IBM 370/125 operating under DOS. Accounts in excess of their credit limit would be reported for manual resolution. Agings would be produced monthly, and extensive edit routines would be employed on inputs. The files would be on magnetic tape and amount to 100,000 records or more.

Sophisticated Applications
These applications involve higher levels of programmed management decisions as well as larger equipment. More than one user department in related functions may be primary users. Extensive use may be made of internally initiated transactions. Relatively few detailed reference documents are printed on a regular basis because the volume would be prohibitive. A transaction trail is available on request through on-line terminals or from microfilm (COM) files. The users are significantly dependent upon programmed controls, since they are seldom involved with day-to-day processing and volumes

exceeding manual control capabilities. Although the primary update processing is still in a batch format, on-line terminals are available for inquiries and transmission of input data from remote locations for editing and subsequent batch processing. Although the files still relate to individual applications, most of the time they are kept in storage directly accessible to the main computer to accommodate the on-line capabilities.

Example — To continue our accounts receivable example, a sophisticated-level application may require an IBM 370/155 supplemented by CRT terminals at remote locations. The credit and marketing departments are primary users of the system as well as accounts receivable. The application is programmed to automatically dun past-due accounts and to write them off eventually. The only detailed documents produced are invoices, dunning notices, and monthly customers' statements. Copies of the customers' statements are maintained on microfilm to provide a transaction trail. All other reports are produced on a summary or exception basis. The only user controls exercised are the run-to-run controls inherent in posting the general ledger for accounts receivable. Customers' inquiries may be answered immediately by operators assisted by cathode-ray terminals. The customer master files amount to several hundred thousand records stored on high-speed access disc drives.

Unique Applications

The state of the art is represented by this level of application. Multiple information processing facilities are integrated into massive systems that serve a multitude of users. Extensive use may be made of on-line updating. The files may be massive integrated data bases. The level of decisions may be no higher than with sophisticated systems, but they may utilize information in files not normally related to the application. Although working documents must still be produced, virtually no detailed reports are produced. Extensive programmed controls attempt to hold down the number of exceptions since transaction history information must be obtained by request, making error resolution difficult.

Example — In a unique-level application, our accounts receivable system may be integrated with production scheduling, purchasing, and inventory. A customer's request may be accepted at a remote location and, via on-line terminals, stock availability checked against inventory records. If the item on order is readily available, the transmissions would be sent to the most appropriate warehouse, generating shipping documents at that location. If the item were not readily available, the demand would be recorded and included in production schedules. Whenever the item was shipped, receivables follow-up would proceed as in a separate, sophisticated system.

Reports produced by this system would be simply summaries of status and agings of problem accounts or orders. Because of the interrelationship of the functions, the many users would be substantially dependent upon programmed controls built into the system and often implemented by different users. All of the related files would be permanently kept on-line to the computer, occupying a large number of large-capacity disc packs.

We will refer to these four classifications of applications at several subsequent points in our discussions of controls and audit considerations.

7
Application Controls

A great variety of controls and techniques for their employment are available for application systems. In this chapter we will describe these controls and discuss some of the more significant aspects of their effective use.

APPLICATION CONTROL OBJECTIVES

Contrary to established custom, we will not organize controls according to the location of their implementation: input, process, output. The location of controls is not important to their *evaluation*. What is important is the objective they serve, no matter where they accomplish this service.

The objectives of application controls are to prevent, detect, or correct the various application causes of exposure discussed in the prior chapter. Since the *potential* for these causes is always *assumed* to exist, we will summarize the objectives of application controls in five positive statements:

- Assure that all authorized transactions are completely processed once and only once
- Assure that transaction data are complete and accurate
- Assure that transaction processing is correct and appropriate to the circumstances
- Assure that processing results are utilized for the intended benefits
- Assure that the application can continue to function

Individual controls often affect more than one of the causes of exposure and, therefore, serve multiple control objectives.

Example — An edit of a paycheck for a value greater than $600 might serve each of the first three objectives above.

82

As noted previously, a single cause (or objective) will also relate to one or more exposures.

Since no simple one-to-one relationship exists among controls, causes (objectives), and exposures, we cannot readily organize our presentation of controls according to these relationships without burdensome redundancies. Instead, we will present the various controls according to whether they prevent, detect, or correct causes of exposure and then describe which causes or objectives they affect through use of a table.

CONTROL DESCRIPTIONS

Since most of the controls over computer applications are already well known to experienced EDP professionals, business managers, and auditors, we will not define or describe all application controls in detail. A comprehensive list of application controls and a description with examples is provided in Figure 7-3 at the end of this chapter. In this portion of the chapter, we will discuss those controls which are *unique* to EDP systems or which *commonly cause questions* as to their nature and utilization. We will also discuss the manner in which these controls should be utilized to provide adequate control over complete application systems.

Reliability of People Versus Machines

Even the best qualified people lack total consistency. Even though they know what to do and are capable and willing to do it, every human is subject to some lapses. A typical rate for clerical errors is generally around five percent.

Mechanization can eliminate this inconsistency and is, indeed one of the greatest strengths of computerizaton. Computerized application processing may not be correct, but it will be consistent.

Exception Inputs and Default Options

One common approach to the elimination of input errors is to eliminate the inputs themselves in other than *exception* conditions.

Example — A salary payroll application may be designed to produce a check for a standard 40-hour week unless an input indicating more or less time is submitted.

The activity performed, given no input, is called a "default option." The use of these two alternatives will avoid a large variety of input errors, but there is also a risk that the loss of an input will not be recognized and that the resulting process will not be appropriate to the true conditions.

Hash Totals

A type of control total that is found only in computerized systems is a *hash total*. Since all data being processed by computers are represented by some type of binary code, a control total can be developed for not only numeric account numbers or quantities but also for alphabetic and character symbols. While the results of a hash total are, by definition, meaningless, they are not useless. They will allow a strong control over loss or alteration of data.

Editing and Reviewing

Both of these terms actually include a large number of specific controls, including format checks, limit checks, reasonableness tests, etc. The primary difference is that *edits* are performed by machines, whereas *reviews* are performed by people. Neither of these terms are particularly useful in evaluating controls. More specific terms must be used to define what types of edit or review activities are being accomplished.

Sequence Checking

The *sequence check* is an extremely important control in the customary logic of updating and file maintenance as well as in other situations. The update and file maintenance logic of batch processing systems usually requires two files to be in sequence and advances each file so as to match transactions with the appropriate master record. Even though such files may supposedly be sorted prior to the update or file maintenance processing, sequence checks should still be mandatory. If, somehow, those files should not be in proper sequence, the processing of certain transactions or records may be completely omitted.

Overflows

Any mechanized arithmetic computation can produce a result having more digits than the device is designed to accept. This happens on modern electronic digital computers just as we are accustomed to having it occur on mechanical adding machines and calculators. When overflow conditions occur, most computer hardware generates an internal signal or "flag." This can be recognized by the program so that corrective action may be taken. The key to implementing this control lies in standard systems software or application program routines which interrogate such hardware flags and specify actions to be taken based upon the conditions discovered. If an application has no explicit provision to interrogate overflow flags, such conditions may exist undetected.

Format Checks

Data in computers are stored in various formats: character, packed decimal, binary, etc. All of these representation systems except that of character (also known as binary coded decimal or extended binary coded decimal) will accept only numeric data. An attempt to process unacceptable values with these systems may result in an equipment halt called by the operating system (a "dump"). However, this depends upon the specific operating system used.

Character or "alphanumeric" fields may contain both numeric and nonnumeric data. The control called *format checking* is an examination of actual input data to see whether it is acceptable for the data format that is defined in the application program.

Check Digits

Another control that is feasible only with computerized processing is the "check digit." This detective control is designed to establish the validity and appropriateness of numeric-indicative data elements such as account numbers. In creating a check-digit account number, one digit within the number is a mathematical function of the other digits. It is appended to the basic account or record number for the specific purpose of establishing the validity of the other digits by using those other digits with some mathematical routine that should generate a digit equal to the check digit.

Check-digit verification may be applied through inexpensive attachments to keypunch machines and other key-entry devices. This allows performance of the check-digit testing at the point of entry or data conversion. A variety of algorithms may be applied with this technique, which, generally, will catch 90 percent or more of all key-entry errors in account or record numbers.

The disadvantage of using check digits is the associated cost. If check digits are to be appended to already-existing sets of numbers, major maintenance changes in catalogues and other documents may be necessary. The detected error date will also increase due to errors in recording or transcribing the check digit itself.

Keystroke Verification

The completeness and accuracy of inputs which are keypunched are customarily tested using a machine called a "verifier." This is a redundant keystroke operation wherein the source documents are rekeyed and compared to the original transcription. Cards having no differences will receive a notch in the side. If a difference is noted, the machine will halt; a red light will come on; and a notch will be cut in the position of the difference.

The machine may be operated so that only certain fields of the record are verified. Furthermore, the key-verifying operation is just as error prone as was the original keypunch operation. Accordingly, key verification will eliminate only 75 to 90 percent of keypunching errors.

Key verification may also be implemented on key-to-tape and key-to-disc equipment. The operation is quite similar to the use of punched cards except that the media are different.

Authorization Versus Approval

These two terms should not be confused. *Authorization* is the *advance* permission to initiate a transaction or perform a process. It is not the same as *approval,* which occurs *after the fact.* Approval also carries the assumption that some edit or review was performed. Authorization is a preventive control, whereas approval is detective.

Reconciliation Versus Balancing

Balancing is the test of control totals for equality. If any differences exist, some exception condition is generally indicated. *Reconciliation* implies that differences will normally occur and is essentially an analytic operation. The detection of errors depends upon detailed analysis of the nature of the reconciling items. Of course, reconciling items should bring one total into balance with the other.

File Labels

Header and *trailer records* provide strong controls over the identification of transactions, files, outputs, and some aspects of processing. Header labels customarily include an identification of the records as well as a variety of other information. A standard header record format is shown in Figure 7-1. Trailer records customarily carry control totals of blocks, records, or control amounts.

Periodic Audit

Auditing may be performed by many people other than internal or external auditors. Individuals, departments, and group offices can audit the results of their own processing as an internal control. The most common example of this is the annual confirmation of customers' accounts.

Quality-assurance groups are often established where auditing must be performed over a particular application on a regular basis. A common example is found in the insurance industry where claims auditing is exercised by a separate staff within the Claims Department.

Auditing is a strong control over virtually every cause of exposure. However, it is relatively expensive and will still not be effective if other controls are extremely deficient.

86

FORMAT OF TAPE HEADER RECORD ANSI (American National Standards Institute, Inc.) STANDARD

TAPE HEADER RECORD

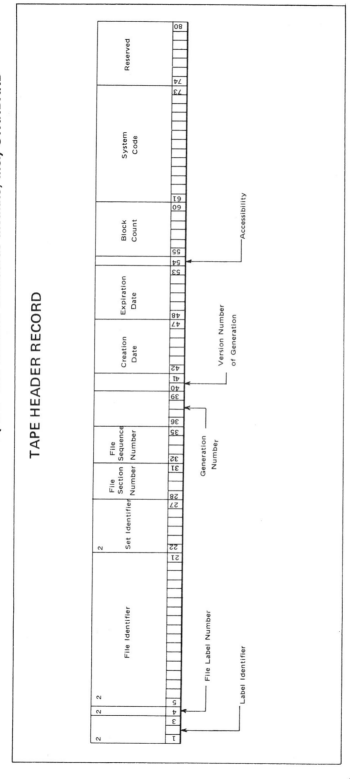

Figure 7-1

87

Transaction Trails

Contrary to popular belief, transaction trails do not exist for the convenience of auditors. For this reason, we avoid the use of the term "audit trail" throughout this book. Neither do transaction trails exist primarily for the enlightenment of management. Rather, they are primarily a tool for follow-up and correction of exceptions. They are mostly utilized by clerical personnel assigned to various types of error correction or quality control functions.

Transaction trails are rarely an effective medium for detective controls in a computerized application system. The volume of transactions customarily found exceeds the capacity of any individual to effectively review them. Manual review of numerous transactions should always be replaced by computerized edits.

Since no application is "perfect" (error free), a transaction trail in some medium is always essential. Transaction trails may also be essential to the support of tax deductions, for external audits, and to support the proper discharge of fiduciary responsibilities. Where volumes are large, machine-readable transaction trails may not only be adequate but preferable. Their high-speed characteristics may assist in retrieval and analysis. The Internal Revenue Service of the United States recognized the desirability of such transaction trails in their Revenue Ruling 71-20.

Upstream Resubmission

After an error is corrected, it should be resubmitted into the application subject to the same, or more stringent, controls to which it was subjected before. Error correction is a highly error-prone activity. Error correction inputs should not be allowed to be processed without further scrutiny once the transaction has been initiated.

Documentation

The nature and content of documentation for various purposes is discussed throughout this book. It has not only preventive characteristics but also important application control features for detection and correction. Its preventive characteristics arise from the self-checking opportunities that are inherent in the preparation of application documents. Its detective characteristics are found in its communication capabilities that provide a medium for subsequent inspection. Its corrective capabilities are found through the availability of documentation for subsequent reference. The availability of adequate application documentation will usually allow the reconstruction of practically any application process — given enough time and resources.

The reader should scan Figure 7-3 for any other controls which are unfamiliar or which differ from his previous understanding.

CONTROLS ASSOCIATED WITH INPUT AND OUTPUT FUNCTIONS

Updating

Control over updating transactions must consider the establishment of checkpoints, methods, and techniques for authorization which are suitable for the volumes being handled and the extent of the subsequent transactions that are preauthorized.

Example — In an order processing system based upon preauthorization, one of the conditions for initiating the processing chain is that customer authorization be recorded on the appropriate master file and that a credit limit be established. The status or condition of customer organizations is subject to change. Therefore, active customer status in system files should be subject to experience. Thus, if a customer did not place an order within a specified time, the account record should be formally reviewed or automatically removed from the file.

Dollar controls should be maintained all the way through the processing chain. However, where the value of any one transaction is not significant and where the dollar value of the transaction is determined within the computer, a particular problem arises. The cost of establishing dollar-control totals prior to computerized dollar extension may be infeasible or prohibitive. An alternative approach may be available.

Input transaction controls may be set up only by number of units or line items. Dollar controls may be established when the computerized evaluation is performed. Subsequently, controls will be carried in dollars only.

These dollar controls should be carried from pass to pass within a particular cycle of the application and for combining the old master files with subsequent transactions from run to run (cycle to cycle).

Many times updating occurs in what are essentially "suspense files." This is particularly true for orders awaiting shipment, accounts receivable awaiting payment, inventories awaiting sales, etc. All open items in such suspense files should be subjected to automatic aging. Items which remain open beyond the time span customary to the industry should be reviewed.

Where chain processing of update transactions takes place, concerns develop in three major areas:

- Authorization for the first transaction in the chain is critical. In addition, there should be continued assurance that the authorization remains valid.
- Completion of the processing chain should be tracked and controlled through the system.
- All adjustments to or deviations from the established processing cycle must receive full and complete approval. This approach

provides a balance of efficiency between the use of the computer for repetitive processing of routine, high-volume items and application of human attention for exception items or for low-volume processing.

File Maintenance

Initiation and authorization for file maintenance inputs frequently takes place at a higher level within the organization than for updating. This reflects a greater concern over the potentially greater impact of erroneous transactions that have a lasting effect on the files.

Where *limited* volumes permit, file maintenance transactions, for which processing has been completed, should be printed out in full detail, permitting visual review by someone at the same level as or higher level in the company than the individual initiating the transaction. This action should verify the original transaction and that processing has modified the files as specified. This review of detailed transaction printouts is intended to control both the validity and accuracy of the process. This should also guard against improper entries from authorized sources and from unauthorized entries.

The level at which authorization takes place may vary widely according to the significance of the transaction chain which might result. Authorization for setting up a master record in a system with many customers, each with a small minimum credit limit, might be comparatively perfunctory with authorization at a relatively low level within the organization. However, in a system dealing with large individual items, authorization procedures for opening a new record would be far more extensive, possibly even requiring approval of an officer. Another aspect for concern over file maintenance transaction controls lies in the time of processing. Frequently, file maintenance transactions will carry specific dates on which the values or conditions to which they apply become effective. This is obviously important. For example, a price change may occur which will change the value of other updating transactions.

A sequence of transactions where both file maintenance and updating inputs are processed in a single computer run presents a critical control situation. The consequences of whether the file maintenance transactions are processed before or after the updating transactions could be substantial, since processing sequence determines whether file content changes apply to the updating transactions currently being processed.

Inquiries

An important concern in the control of inquiry transactions is file security. Information should be provided only in response to a qualified inquiry from an authorized source.

A concurrent concern is the accuracy of the data that are reported. The degree of control applied over this aspect should be commensurate with the purposes of the inquiries being accepted. Accuracy standards for data reporting should be in line with the potential actions or decisions which would be based upon use of that Information.

Error-Correction Inputs

The error-correction situation is often complicated because errors are more likely to occur when the input transactions are unusually difficult or complex. Due to this greater complexity and the probability of errors in the correction process, the handling of error-correction inputs is usually assigned to more experienced personnel than those who handle normal input functions. Controls for error correction should be *at least as stringent,* and more so if possible, as those where the original errors were encountered.

A final concern in this area is the establishment of controls to assure that the causes of error are corrected where feasible. This requires that documentation be maintained concerning the commission of errors so that future preventive measures may be implemented through either changes in normal procedures or through further training of personnel.

CONTROL RESPONSIBILITIES

One of the obvious requisites for application control is the fixing of responsibilities for all persons and departments initiating, processing, or using the data or media involved. Five separate areas of responsibility are found:
- Input-source departments
- Systems designers
- The information processing facility
- The IPF or user control group
- The users

Input-Source Departments

The source of input transactions has a major responsibility for control over and reliability of input transactions, including error correction. Carefully planned input procedures will provide both data processing control and valuable operating statistics such as:
- Dollar control totals
- Document counts
- Line-item counts

These control totals are also important productivity and backlog indicators. Source department managers are responsible for assuring that the procedures built into an application are followed in areas under their responsibility. Once an application is implemented, the quality of controls applied to input transactions becomes substantially dependent upon the caliber of work performed by source department personnel.

Systems Designers

The designers of application systems have a range of responsibilities which, cumulatively, provide assurance that:

- Control alternatives are considered
- The controls used are effective and economical for the specific application
- The processes and controls are thoroughly documented for review and reference

Systems designers must also assure that instructional procedures are prepared which explain the various manual phases of processing. These procedures should include the handling of both normal transactions and error conditions. This responsibility is exercised in a coordinating role. Departments or persons who act as sources of inputs or users of outputs frequently should, in so far as possible, prepare their own instructional standards manuals. In addition, involvement with source and user departments is more likely to promote a sense of involvement in the system design and the control measures.

The Information Processing Facility

The operations personnel within the information processing facility (IPF) are responsible for determining that, at fixed points in the processing cycle, input transactions are either in balance or that corrections are required. Operating procedures should indicate that processing is to continue only if balances are established. If balances are not established, alternate procedures should be specified. In most cases, this should indicate that the processing cannot proceed until input transactions and files are in a condition of acceptable balance.

The personnel in the computer operations area are responsible for applying the specific procedures established for processing control data and for detecting and correcting errors caused within their jurisdiction. Computer operators should not be asked, nor even be permitted, to initiate transactions or to reenter data so as to establish balances which have not been carried forward in processing. Responsibilities in the operations center extend only to formally documented limits.

IPF or User Control Group

Responsibility for balancing output data to input and processing controls — a primary set of controls over an application — falls frequently upon an organization known as a "control group." This group is most frequently a part of the information processing facility but independent of computer operations. Alternatively, it may be within a user department. No matter where it is located, the control group must follow adequate procedures for verifying balances and documenting actions taken.

Where the control group is within the information processing facility (IPF), it frequently serves as a chief contact and service point to the users. It is also responsible for receiving input items from source departments and recording or establishing control totals.

A control group within the IPF will frequently be responsible for applying anticipation controls and in setting up jobs for computer operations.

The IPF control group should also scan each set of output reports. However, the members of the control group may have only limited backgrounds upon which to judge these documents. Their responsibility will fall chiefly in the area of looking for data or pages which are garbled or unreadable. They should make sure that all reports were processed to their conclusion, including the printing and recording of any necessary summaries. They should also scan the report to make sure that all pages and sections are included in the distributions. Other operational responsibilities of the IPF control group are included in the chapter on the EDP organization.

Finally, a critically important responsibility of the control group, often associated with user controls, is monitoring and reporting input errors and file control totals. Furthermore, this group is responsible for establishing controls to assure reentry of corrections for outstanding errors submitted to source or user departments.

Users

The user's role is essential in the application of controls to the results of applications.

Example — In a Sales Department, the person who is working with a customer's account continuously will be in a good position to scan the order and the shipping information so as to spot unusual situations. He will know if there is anything out of the ordinary in the product specified, shipping routes indicated, etc.

Another critical responsibility of users lies in the handling of error conditions. Prime responsibility for corrections lies solidly with the users. Furthermore, the user must perform the primary analysis of errors and evaluate how they may be reduced or eliminated.

SELECTION OF APPROPRIATE CONTROLS

The combinations and arrangements of application controls over a particular application function are almost infinite. Adequate control may be achieved in many ways.

Furthermore, the question of whether existing controls provide an adequate level of reliability is highly subjective. The question involves a balance between costs of control versus speculation as to the probabilities of the causes of exposures. Because the occurrence rate is speculative, no "optimum" level of control may be precisely determined in advance.

The question that must be answered by designers, users, and auditors of information processing applications is whether, *in their subjective opinion,* the controls which they design, operate, or examine are reasonable and adequate in the circumstances. While subsequent sections of this book will provide aids in preparing relevant information for analysis, nothing can replace the judgment of the responsible persons.

A summary chart of the relationships between controls and causes of exposure is provided in Figure 7-2. This figure provides an example of the strengths of controls in a "normal" situation. These relationships will require revision before they can be applied to any particular application.

Development and evaluation of optimum application controls remains much more of an art than a science. The primary considerations of sound control were summarized in an earlier chapter on control concepts. All alternatives, their effectiveness, and cost must be considered.

RELATIONSHIPS OF APPLICATION CONTROLS TO CAUSES OF EXPOSURES

APPLICATION CAUSES OF EXPOSURES

PREVENTION CONTROLS	INPUT							PROCESSING											OUTPUT				OTHER		
	LOST	DUPLICATED	INACCURATE	MISSING DATA	TRANSACTIONS NEVER RECORDED	BLANKET AUTHORIZE	INITIATED INTERNALLY	WRONG FILE	WRONG RECORD	INCOMPLETE	INCORRECT	UNTIMELY	INAPPROPRIATE	FILE LOST	PROGRAM LOST	PEOPLE LOST	IMPROPERLY DISTRIBUTED	LATE OR LOST	ERRONEOUS BUT PLAUSIBLE	OBVIOUSLY ERRONEOUS	EXCESSIVE ERROR CORRECTION	UNSUPPORTABLE	SHADOW SYSTEM	UNLIMITED ACCESS	MANAGEMENT OVERRIDE
Definition of responsibilities	1	2	2	2	2	2	2	1	1	2	2	2	1	1	1	2	1	2	1	1	1	2	2	2	1
Reliability of personnel	1	1	1	1	1	2		1	1	2	2	2	2	2	1	2	2	1	2	2	2	2	2	2	1
Training	1	1	1	2	2			1	1	2	2	2	2	1	1	1	2	1		2	2	2	2	1	
Competence	2	2	1	2	1			2	2	1	2	2	2	1	1		2	1	2	2	2	2	1	1	2
Mechanization	2	2					3	1	1	2	2	3	2		1				1	1	1	1		1	2
Segregation of duties																									
Rotation of duties																									
Standardization	1	2	1	2	2			1	1	2	2	1	1	1	1		2	2	1	1	1	1	2	2	1
Authorization	1	2	1	1	1	2		1	1		2	1	2	1	2	2	2	1	1	2	1	1	1	3	
Secure custody	2			2				2							2								2	3	
Dual custody	1							2																	
Forms design	2	2	2	2	1				2	2	2	2	2		1			1		1	1	1	2		
Prenumbered	2	2		1						2	2		2		1							1		2	
Preprinted													2									1			
Simultaneous preparation	2	2	2		3					2	2	2	2							1		1			
Turnaround document			1							2	2												1		
Drum card												2													
Endorsement	2		2	2				2																	
Cancellation		2															1		1					1	2
Documentation	2	2	2	2	2		2			2	2	1	2	2	2		2	2	2	2	2	3			
Exception input										2															
Default option								1	1	2		1	2												
Passwords								1	1				2											3	2

RELIANCE ON CONTROLS

3 — Reliably controls applicable cause

2 — Controls cause but should be accompanied by additional controls

1 — Useful but not especially effective

Blank — No significant contribution

Figure 7-2 (page 1 of 3)

95

APPLICATION CAUSES OF EXPOSURES

DETECTION CONTROLS	INPUT — LOST	DUPLICATED	INACCURATE	MISSING DATA	NEVER RECORDED	BLANKET AUTHORIZE	INITIATED INTERNALLY	PROCESSING — WRONG FILE	WRONG RECORD	INCOMPLETE	INCORRECT	UNTIMELY	INAPPROPRIATE	FILE LOST	PROGRAM LOST	PEOPLE LOST	OUTPUT — IMPROPERLY DISTRIBUTED	LATE OR LOST	ERRONEOUS BUT PLAUSIBLE	OBVIOUSLY ERRONEOUS	EXCESSIVE ERROR CORRECTION	UNSUPPORTABLE	OTHER — SHADOW SYSTEM	UNLIMITED ACCESS	MANAGEMENT OVERRIDE
Anticipation	3				3					3		1		2	2	2	3	3							
Transmittal document	2	2	2						2								2								
Batch serial numbers	3	3						2		2	2														
Control register	3	2	2					2		2	1			3											
Amount control totals	3	3	2					3		3				2											
Document control count	3	3						2																	
Line control count	3	3						2	1	2	1														
Hash totals	3	3	2					3	2	2	1														
Batch totals	3	3	2						2	2	2														
Batch balancing	3	3	1		2			3	2	2	1						2								
Visual verification	2	1	1					3		1	1									3					
Sequence check	2		2	2				2		2	2		1	1											
Overflow check			2		2						2		2												
Format check			2	2				2	2	2															
Completeness check			2	2				2	2	2	2	1													
Check digit		2	3	2			2	2	2		2								1	2		1			
Reasonableness	1	2	2	2			2	1	2		2	1	2							2					
Limit check			2					2			2		2							2					
Validity check			3			2																			
Readback	2		3	2																2					1
Dating		1			2			2				2	2	2						3		3	2	3	
Expiration		2			2								2	1						3					
Keystroke verification		1	2	2				3		1	2	1	2												
Approval			2							2	2		2												
Run-to-run totals										2				3											1

RELIANCE ON CONTROLS
3 — Reliably controls applicable cause
2 — Controls cause but should be accompanied by additional controls
1 — Useful but not especially effective
Blank — No significant contribution

Figure 7-2 (page 2 of 3)

RELATIONSHIPS OF APPLICATION CONTROLS TO CAUSES OF EXPOSURES

APPLICATION CAUSES OF EXPOSURES

RELIANCE ON CONTROLS
3 — Reliably controls applicable cause
2 — Controls cause but should be accompanied by additional controls
1 — Useful but not especially effective
Blank — No significant contribution

DETECTION CONTROLS (continued)	INPUT							PROCESSING											OUTPUT				OTHER		
	LOST	DUPLICATED	INACCURATE	MISSING DATA	NEVER RECORDED	BLANKET AUTHORIZE	INITIATED INTERNALLY	WRONG FILE	WRONG RECORD	INCOMPLETE	INCORRECT	UNTIMELY	INAPPROPRIATE	FILE LOST	PROGRAM LOST	PEOPLE LOST	IMPROPERLY DISTRIBUTED	LATE OR LOST	ERRONEOUS BUT PLAUSIBLE	OBVIOUSLY ERRONEOUS	EXCESSIVE ERROR CORRECTION	UNSUPPORTABLE	SHADOW SYSTEM	UNLIMITED ACCESS	MANGEMENT OVERRIDE
Balancing	2	2	2	1				3	3	3	2								2	3	2	2			
Reconciliation	2	2	2	2	2			3	3	2	3		1							3	2	1	2	3	1
Aging	2	2	1	1	2				2	2	2	2	1									1		1	
Suspense file	2	2		2	2				2	2	1	2	1								2	1			
Suspense account	2	2	3	2	2			3	3	2		2	1								2	2			
Matching	3	3	3	2			3	3	3	2	1	2	1						2	3					
Clearing account	2	2	2	2	2				2	2	2	2	1												
Tickler file	2				1							2													
Periodic audit	2	2	3	2	2		3	3	2	2	2	2	2	2	2	2	2	2	2	3	2	3	2	3	1
Redundant process			2	2		2				3	1				2		2							1	
Summary process			2	2				2		3				2	2		2								
Label	1	1			1			2						2				2							
Trailer record	2	2	1	1				3		3				2				3							

CORRECTION CONTROLS	LOST	DUPLICATED	INACCURATE	MISSING DATA	NEVER RECORDED	BLANKET AUTHORIZE	INITIATED INTERNALLY	WRONG FILE	WRONG RECORD	INCOMPLETE	INCORRECT	UNTIMELY	INAPPROPRIATE	FILE LOST	PROGRAM LOST	PEOPLE LOST	IMPROPERLY DISTRIBUTED	LATE OR LOST	ERRONEOUS BUT PLAUSIBLE	OBVIOUSLY ERRONEOUS	EXCESSIVE ERROR CORRECTION	UNSUPPORTABLE	SHADOW SYSTEM	UNLIMITED ACCESS	MANGEMENT OVERRIDE
Discrepancy reports	2	2	2	2	2			3	3	3	3	2	2					2							1
Transaction trail		3	3	2	2			3	3	2	3		2												1
Error source statistics	2	2	3	2				2	2	2	2	2	2												1
Automated error correction			2	2					2	2	2		2							3	3				
Upstream resubmission			2	2					2	2	2		2	3	3	3	2	3		3	3				
Backup and recovery	3													3	3	3	2	3					2		2

Figure 7-2 (page 3 of 3)

DEFINITIONS OF APPLICATION CONTROLS

PREVENTIVE CONTROLS:	EXPLANATION:	EXAMPLE:
Definition of Responsibilities	Descriptions of tasks for each job function within an information processing system. These indicate clear beginning and termination points for each job function. They also cover the relationship of job functions to each other.	The cashier disburses petty cash and prepares deposits but does not sign checks or maintain accounting records.
Reliability of Personnel	Personnel performing the processing can be relied upon to treat data in a consistent manner.	The cashier has a record for regular attendance, few errors, and keeping sober.
Training	Personnel are provided explicit instructions and tested for their understanding before being assigned new duties.	All tellers attend a one-week school before starting work.
Competence of Personnel	Persons assigned to processing or supervisory roles within information systems have the technical knowledge necessary to perform their functions.	The controller is a CPA.
Mechanization	Consistency is provided by mechanical or electronic processing.	Calculation of gross and net pay is performed by computer.
Segregation of Duties	Responsibility for custody and accountability for handling and processing of data are separated.	The cashier does not maintain the cash accounting records.
Rotation of Duties	Jobs assigned to people are rotated periodically at irregularly scheduled times, if possible, for key processing functions.	Payroll clerks are always rotated within two years.
Standardization	Uniform, structured, and consistent procedures are developed for all processing.	A controller's manual describes the processing of all financial applications.
Authorization	Limits the initiation of a transaction or performance of a process to the selected individuals.	Only the timekeeper may submit payroll-hours data.

Figure 7-3 (1 of 8)

DEFINITIONS OF APPLICATION CONTROLS (Continued)

PREVENTIVE CONTROLS:	EXPLANATION:	EXAMPLE:
Secure Custody	Information assets are provided security similar to tangible assets such as cash, negotiable securities, etc.	The general ledger is locked in a safe every night.
Dual Access/Dual Control	Two independent, simultaneous actions or conditions are required before processing is permitted.	A safe deposit box requires two keys to open it.
Forms Design	Forms are self-explanatory, understandable, concise, and gather all necessary information with a minimum of effort.	The form to establish a new account has instructions for each space and spacing indicated to assist in keypunching.
Prenumbered Forms	Sequential numbers on individual forms printed in advance so as to allow subsequent detection of loss or misplacement.	Checks are provided with preprinted numbers.
Preprinted Forms	Fixed elements of information are entered on forms in advance and sometimes in a format which permits direct machine processing so as to prevent errors in entry of repetitive data.	The MICR encoding of bank and account number on checks.
Simultaneous Preparation	The one-time recording of a transaction for all further processing, using multiple-copies, as appropriate, to prevent transcription errors.	A payment form having check, check copy, and voucher.
Turnaround Document	A computer-produced document which is intended for resubmission into the system.	A utility bill.
Drum Card	Automatic spacing and format shifting of data fields on a keypunch machine.	The tab key on a typewriter is replaced by a drum card on a keypunch.
Endorsement	The marking of a form or document so as to direct or restrict its further use in processing.	Endorsing a check "for deposit only."
Cancellation	Identifies transaction documents to prevent further or repeated use after they have performed their function.	Punching "PAID" into invoices.

Figure 7-3 (2 of 8)

DEFINITIONS OF APPLICATION CONTROLS (Continued)

PREVENTIVE CONTROLS:	EXPLANATION:	EXAMPLE:
Documentation	Written records for the purpose of providing communication.	Standard forms for journal entries.
Exception Input	Internally initiated processing in a predefined manner unless specific input transactions are received that specify processing with different values or in a different manner.	A salaried employee must submit a separate request for payment of overtime.
Default Option	The automatic utilization of a predefined value in situations where input transactions have certain values left blank.	Salaried employees receive pay for a 40-hour week automatically.
Passwords	The authorization to allow access to data or processed by providing a signal or "password" known only to authorized individuals.	Computer access by a time-sharing terminal requires a user identification and a secret code word.
DETECTIVE CONTROLS:		
Anticipation	The expectation of a given transaction or event at a particular time.	Every employee expects his paycheck at 3:00 PM, Friday.
Transmittal Document (Batch Control Ticket)	The medium for communicating control totals over movement of data, particularly from source to processing point or between processing points.	Receipts for deposit are accompanied by a deposit slip indicating the account, listing the currency and checks, and total.
Batch Serial Numbers (Batch Sequence)	Batches of transaction documents are numbered consecutively and accounted for.	Daily receipts are batched together and numbered, using the Julian date.
Control Register (Batch Control Log)	A log or register indicating the disposition and control values of batches or transactions.	A logbook records the time and batch number of receipts picked up by the armored-car service.
Amount Control Total	Totals of homogeneous amounts for a group of transactions or records, usually dollars or quantities.	The receivables file totals $1,237,629.53.
Document Control Total	A count of the number of individual documents.	The receivables file contains 3,721 accounts.

Figure 7-3 (3 of 8)

DEFINITIONS OF APPLICATION CONTROLS (Continued)

DETECTIVE CONTROLS:	EXPLANATION:	EXAMPLE:
Line Control Count	A count of the individual line items on one or more documents.	The December invoices had 4,261 line items.
Hash Total	A meaningless, but useful, total developed from the accumulated numerical amounts of nonmonetary information.	The hash total of account numbers is 47,632,177.
Batch Totals (Batch Control)	Any type of control total or count applied to a specific number of transaction documents or to the transaction documents that arrive within a specific period of time.	The December 17 invoices total $44,755.68.
Batch Balancing	A comparison of the items or documents actually processed against a predetermined control total.	A teller will compare currency and checks with the list and total on the deposit slip.
Visual Verification	The visual scanning of documents for general reasonableness and propriety.	A quick scan revealed that the printer's ink roll was dry.
Sequence Checking	A verification of the alphanumeric sequence of the "key" field in items to be processed.	Account number A16352 precedes account number A16567.
Overflow Checks	A limit check based upon the capacity of a memory or file area to accept data.	The product of 10,736 x 37,667 = (404,392,912) cannot be displayed on an 8-digit calculator.
Format Check (Form)	Determination that data are entered in the proper mode – numeric or alphanumeric – within designated fields of information.	The characters 4 H 6 1 are not an acceptable invoice amount.
Completeness Check	A test that data entries are made in fields which cannot be processed in a blank state.	The computer will not print the check if the payee is all blanks.
Check Digit	One digit, usually the last, of an identifying field is a mathematical function of all of the other digits in the field. This value can be calculated from the other digits in the field and compared with the check digit to verify validity of the whole field.	$$\begin{array}{cccccc} 1 & 2 & 3 & 4 & 5 & 6 \\ \underline{\times 2} & \underline{1} & \underline{2} & \underline{1} & \underline{2} \\ 2+2 & +6+4+10 & = 24 \\ & & -30 \\ \hline & & 6 \end{array}$$

Figure 7-3 (4 of 8)

DEFINITIONS OF APPLICATION CONTROLS (Continued)

DETECTIVE CONTROLS:	EXPLANATION:	EXAMPLE:
Reasonableness	Tests applied to various fields of data through comparison with other information available within the transaction or master records.	A male patient should not receive charges from the obstetrics ward.
Limit Check (Range Check)	Tests of specified amount fields against stipulated high or low limits of acceptability. When both high and low values are used, the test may be called a "range check."	A paycheck should be between zero and $900.
Validity Check	The characters in a coded field are either matched to an acceptable set of values in a table or examined for a defined pattern of format, legitimate subcodes, or character values, using logic and arithmetic rather than tables.	375-44-006 is not a proper social security number. They all have nine digits.
Read Back	Immediate return of input information to the sender for comparison and approval.	Information transmitted over the phone is repeated back to the sender.
Dating	The recording of calendar dates for purposes of later comparison or expiration testing.	A date is placed on all paychecks.
Expiration	A limit check based on a comparison of current date with the date recorded on a transaction, record, or file.	The paycheck is marked "void after 90 days."
Keystroke Verification	The redundant entry of data into keyboards so as to verify the accuracy of a prior entry. Differences between the data previously recorded and the data entered in verification will cause a mechanical signal.	A punch card verifier closely resembles a keypunch.

Figure 7-3 (5 of 8)

DEFINITIONS OF APPLICATION CONTROLS (Continued)

DETECTIVE CONTROLS:	EXPLANATION:	EXAMPLE:
Approval	The acceptance of a transaction for processing after it has been initiated.	The controller approves the journal entry prepared by the payroll clerk.
Run-to-Run Totals	The utilization of output control totals resulting from one process as input control totals over subsequent processing. The control totals are used as links in a chain to tie the one process to another in a sequence of processes or one cycle to another over a period of time.	Beginning receivables plus invoices and minus receipts and adjustments should equal the ending receivables balance.
Balancing	A test for equality between the values of two equivalent sets of items or one set of items and a control total. Any difference indicates an error.	The detail of accounts receivable differs from the general ledger by $326.11.
Reconciliation	An identification and analysis of differences between the values contained in two substantially identical files or between a detail file and a control total. Errors are identified according to the nature of the reconciling items rather than the existence of a difference between the balances.	The bank reconciliation indicates an unrecorded service charge as well as outstanding checks and deposits in transit.
Aging	Identification of unprocessed or retained items in files according to their date, usually transaction date. The aging classifies items according to various ranges of dates.	Receivables are aged "current, 30, 60, 90, over 90."
Suspense File	A file containing unprocessed or partially processed items awaiting further action.	The receivables file contains invoices on which neither payment nor partial payment were received.
Suspense Account	A control total for items awaiting further processing.	The total value of the receivables file should agree with the general ledger balance for receivables.

Figure 7-3 (6 of 8)

103

DEFINITIONS OF APPLICATION CONTROLS (Continued)

DETECTIVE CONTROLS:	EXPLANATION:	EXAMPLE:
Matching	Matching of items from the processing stream of an application with others developed independently so as to identify items unprocessed through either of the parallel systems.	The payables clerk matches purchase orders to receiving reports and invoices.
Clearing Account	An amount which results from the processing of independent items of equivalent value. Net control value should equal zero.	Intercompany accounts should eliminate upon consolidation.
Tickler File	A control file consisting of items sequenced by age for follow-up purposes. Such files are usually manual.	Copies of invoices filed in invoice-date sequence.
Periodic Audit	A verification of a file or a phase of processing intended to check for problems and encourage future compliance with control procedures.	The Accounts Receivable Department confirms all of its accounts every June 30.
Redundant Processing	A repetition of processing and an accompanying comparison of individual results for equality.	A second payroll clerk recalculates each gross pay multiplication.
Summary Processing	A redundant process using a summarized amount. This is compared for equality with a control total from the processing of the detailed items.	Total straight-line depreciation can be calculated for each asset class (where everything in an individual class has the same useful life). This balance is compared to total net book value of the property file.
Labeling	The external or internal identification of transaction batches or files according to source, application, date, or other identifying characteristics.	See Figure 7-1.
Trailer Record	A record providing a control total for comparison with accumulated counts or values of records processed.	The trailer record indicates 373 blocks, which agrees with the actual count.

Figure 7-3 (7 of 8)

DEFINITIONS OF APPLICATION CONTROLS (Continued)

CORRECTIVE CONTROLS:	EXPLANATION:	EXAMPLE:
Discrepancy Reports	A listing of items which have violated some detective control and require further investigation.	Each month, a list of delinquent accounts is sent to the Credit Department.
Transaction Trail (Audit Trail)	The availability of a manual or machine-readable means for tracing the status and contents of an individual transaction record backward or forward, between output, processing, and source.	A list of property additions and retirements supports changes to the property file.
Error-Source Statistics	Accumulation of information on type of error and origin. This is used to determine the nature of remedial training needed to reduce the number of errors.	The Keypunch Department keeps track of the number of errors made by each operator and detected by key verification.
Automated Error Correction	Automatic error correction of transactions or records which violate a detective control.	A debit memo is automatically produced and sent to vendors whose invoices exceed purchase order terms.
Upstream Resubmission	The resubmission of corrected error transactions so that they pass through all or more of the detective controls than are exercised over normal transactions (e.g., before input editing).	All rejected inputs are resubmitted the next day after correction as if they were new inputs.
Backup and Recovery	The ability to recreate current master files using appropriate prior master records and transactions.	Prior day's master files and transactions are retained in case the current master file is destroyed.

Figure 7-3 (8 of 8)

105

8
Application Audit Tools

Before we can realistically evaluate the various available techniques for auditing application processes and controls, we must first be aware of the various tools that exist to ease the task. As noted previously, an "audit tool" is any tangible aid that assists an auditor in the implementation of an audit technique. In this chapter, we will cover:

- Tools to obtain information
  - Questionnaires
  - Analytic audit flowcharts
  - Flowcharting software
- Tools to evaluate controls
  - Application controls matrix
- Tools to verify controls
  - Test data generators
  - Tailored computer programs
  - General purpose audit software

TOOLS TO OBTAIN INFORMATION
Questionnaires

Standardized audit questionnaires are an audit tool that has been traditionally employed in gathering information with regard to internal controls. An example is shown in Figure 8-1.

To be particularly effective, questionnaires for application controls need to be oriented toward the general type of application; e.g., payroll, inventory, purchasing, etc. Any broader scope will generally allow nothing more explicit than a set of general guidelines.

Application questionnaires need not be specifically designed for applications using computers. As noted previously, most application functions are built on general business logic rather than any par-

106

EXAMPLE OF AUDIT QUESTIONNAIRE

	Yes	No	N/A

21. Does this application use internal labels (both header and trailer) on all files to identify the proper file? ✓ __ __

   a) If yes, are the labels used according to normal installation standards?   a. ✓ __ __

   b) If no, briefly describe exceptions.

           N/A
_____

_____

_____

   c) Do the programs contain procedures to ensure the proper file is being processed?   c. ✓ __ __

22. When processing transactions against a master file for this application:

   a) Does the program prevent duplicate master records from being established?   a. ✓ __ __

   b) Are listings printed for all master file changes, showing:
     1) the master record before change?   b.1. __ ✓ __
     2) the master record after change?   2. ✓ __ __
     3) the nature of the change?   3. __ ✓ __

   c) Does the program check for illogical conditions prior to changing the master record (e.g., record to be deleted still has a balance; inventory quantity would become negative, etc.)?   c. __ ✓ __

   d) Is a transaction that changes a key field(s) in a master record checked for proper authorization when appropriate?   d. ✓ __ __

   e) Are all transactions not processed:
     1) reported, with reason(s)?   e.1. ✓ __ __
     2) Placed in a suspense file?   2. __ ✓ __

23. Where corresponding records exist on more than one file, are there routines that assure accuracy, completeness, and consistency of those records?   __ ✓ __

24. If master files used by this application are "shared" with other applications (generally in an on-line environment), is there a priority for updating the file in the event of simultaneous update?   ✓ __ __

25. Are master files periodically reviewed by a special program that reads the entire file and:

   a) Counts all records (possibly by type)?   a. ✓ __ __
   b) Totals all hash and other amount fields used to control the file?   b. ✓ __ __
   c) Samples records and lists them for review by user or owner?   c. ✓ __ __
   d) Crossfoots records where applicable?   d. ✓ __ __
   e) Checks key fields for reasonableness or validity?   e. ✓ __ __

   If so, how often, and when was the program last used? *monthly*

26. Are files periodically purged of obsolete records?   ✓ __ __

TR CP-42Q(II)
  1975

Figure 8-1

ticular approach to implementation. Nevertheless, the causes of exposure differ between manual and computerized applications; and any evaluation must recognize this.

No matter how well designed an internal control questionnaire may be, it is not designed with provisions for all the unique circumstances that actually exist in any single application system. As such, questionnaires may only be used as guides and reminders. Under no conditions should they be allowed to replace thorough audit analysis.

Analytic Audit Flowchart

A useful audit analysis tool is an analytic flowchart, which identifies all manual and computer processing in an application. It shows all files and transactions subject to processing, who does the processing, and what is done. The complexity of the application will determine how extensive the flowchart must be.

An example of an analytic flowchart of an application is presented in Figure 8-2. This illustration was drawn with standard flowchart symbols. The special characteristic of an analytic flowchart is that separate columns are drawn to designate each significant organizational entity performing processing. Normally, columns will be assigned at the department level on the basis of processing, handling, decisions, or control responsibilities. However, where there are several processing points within one department, columnar breakdowns can represent responsible sections or individuals.

The flowchart identifies and traces each transaction document and file through the application, emphasizing processing tasks which apply control.

Typically, a separate column of the analytic flowchart would show the various application processes that take place within the information processing facility. As indicated in Figure 8-2, each significant processing step should be appropriately labeled or accompanied by a brief descriptive narrative.

In many cases, transaction controls will involve flows of documents or batches of documents which move in parallel through the principal processing sequence. For the auditor's purposes, it is important to identify and trace these parallel flows. For instance, a batch transmittal form would be identified and followed separately from the documents themselves. This is a particularly important feature of an analytic flowchart. The points at which control totals incorporated in documents and batches are compared should be stressed. The course of processing in the event that the totals do not match should also be shown.

For the auditor, there are two good reasons for the columnar arrangement of analytic flowcharts:

EXAMPLE OF A PORTION OF AN ANALYTIC FLOWCHART

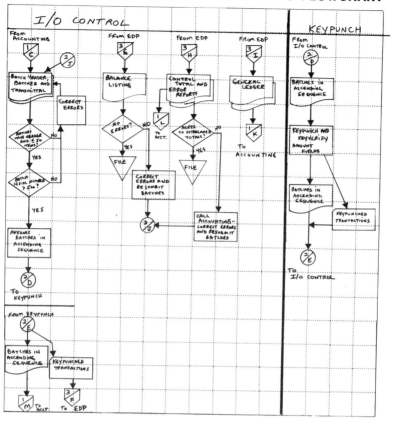

Figure 8-2

- The representation of processing by responsibility provides a good mechanism for evaluating segregation of duties within each application.
- This flowcharting format highlights one of the most error-prone types of situations which may arise in the evaluation of systems — the interface or interaction between departments or other organizational entities.

While a system flowchart is a basic item of documentation during the development of application systems, many times such flowcharts cover only the computer processing phases of the system. While this indicates a serious weakness in the systems development process, it doesn't provide much help to the auditor. Accordingly, the auditor must often prepare his own comprehensive, analytic flow-chart.

Generally, it is necessary to interview several persons; and analytic flowcharts must sometimes be prepared two or three times before they represent the application understandably and fairly. One typical revision requirement between flowchart drafts is the rearrangement of columns. If the flow lines cross a minimum number of unaffected columns, they depict the system more clearly.

It is generally possible for a trained person to complete the preparation of an analytic flowchart in a few hours. Experienced auditors can readily draft rough versions of the flowcharts during their interviews, right at the desks of the personnel involved. However, the total analysis may take much longer.

When completed, the analytic flowchart presents a comprehensive picture which assists in the further analysis of the application in several ways. They depict:

- What is happening during the normal processing of transactions, files, and outputs
- Many of the controls incorporated in the processing sequence of the application
- The relative status of the various files which will exist and be used within the application

As the auditor completes the flowchart, he should note specifically whether detailed transaction listings covering errors are prepared early enough within the processing cycle for effective use in error correction. The importance and value of this control feature usually relate directly to the order and accessibility associated with files of transaction documents.

As the analytic flowchart is being completed, it should be studied in the course of each draft to evaluate the adequacy of controls and identify those which are essential to the successful completion of the application. If the application is extremely complex, the auditor may find it convenient to select only those processing steps and control points which concern him and redraft the flowchart in a condensed format. The new flowchart may then represent only those control and processing points within the application which will require testing.

Flowcharting Software

The program source-language listing is a useful, but technically demanding, reference for detailed information regarding programmed application functions and controls. While logic-level program flowcharts are normally also prepared during application development, they are frequently *not* updated for subsequent program modifications.

Such flowcharts may be generated directly from the source code by "flowcharting software." Although generally intended as a program maintenance and debugging aid, such software may also be employed by auditors or others who require a detailed understanding of program logic. An example of a logic flowchart generated by STRATA[1] is in Figure 8-3.

TOOLS TO EVALUATE CONTROLS
Application Controls Matrix
In determining which controls must be verified, the auditor must first identify and distinguish between the *characteristics that constitute controls* and the *activities subject to control*. The analytical flowchart discloses all major activities but does not segregate those which are controls and those upon which controls act. To accomplish this identification, the auditor may use a control matrix like the one shown in Figure 8-4.

CHARACTERISTICS THAT CONSTITUTE CONTROLS
Along the left-hand side of the matrix, the auditor lists the potential controls that may be used. For convenience in analysis, the controls may be segregated into these categories:
- Preventive
- Detective
- Corrective

ACTIVITIES SUBJECT TO CONTROL
Across the top of the matrix are listed all the activities or transactions without which processing could not take place. Theoretically, a function could be performed with only these activities and with absolutely no controls, although serious exposures may result. These activities were covered in chapter six of this book.

COMPLETING THE CONTROLS MATRIX
The auditor will refer to both the application documentation and the analytic flowchart in completing the controls matrix.

As a control over the preparation of the matrix, every process box, decision diamond, and transmittal line on the analytic flowchart should be numbered in sequence. All of the numbers should appear on the completed matrix as either controls or activities subject to control.

In the preparation, he will indicate across the top of the matrix those activities or items which should be subject to control. Down the left side, the preprinted form provides a comprehensive list of the controls that could be exercised. The presence of a control is indicated by placing a cross-reference number in the square that is intersected, both by the activity subject to control and by the preprinted control classification. Upon completion of the matrix, every

[1]STRATA is a widely used general purpose audit software system developed by Touche Ross & Co.

EXAMPLE OF STRATA PROGRAM LOGIC FLOWCHART SOFTWARE OUTPUT

TOUCHE ROSS & CO   STRATA FLOWCHART AND REFERENCE LISTINGS   05/29/73
STRATA/360   PAGE   134
VERSION 5.4C RUN 0445   A/R CONFIRMATIONS

LOGIC FLOWCHART OF CALCULATE STEPS IN PASS   1   CREATE CALCULATE

```
   CS10                          CS12                          CS14                          CS16
   ----                          ----                          ----                          ----
   **                            **                            **                            **
   **                            **                            **                            **
   **                            **                            **                            **
* W01-DISTRICT            * W10-CODE              * W09-AMOUNT            I  ADD    W03-DEPOSITS
* NOT EQUAL TO     *-CS12 * NOT EQUAL TO   *-CS14 * GREATER THAN    *-CS16 I  AND    W09-AMOUNT
* 01               * ---- * 0              * ---- * 0               * ---- I  GIVING W03-DEPOSITS
   **                            **                            **                            **
   **                            **                            **                            **
* W01-DISTRICT            * W10-CODE                 MULT   W09-AMOUNT          I  MOVE   Y
* NOT EQUAL TO     *-CS12 * NOT EQUAL TO   *-READ    BY               1-       I  TO     W20-CODE FIELD  -CS30
* 05               * ---- * C              * ----    GIVING W09-AMOUNT          I                        ----
   **                            **                            **                            I
   **                            **                            **                            I
* W01-DISTRICT            * W14-YR                 I  ADD    W03-DEPOSITS                     I
* NOT EQUAL TO     *-CS12 * EQUAL TO       *-CS18  I  AND    W09-AMOUNT                       I
* 07               * ---- * 72             * ----  I  GIVING W03-DEPOSITS                     I
   **                            **                            **                            I
   **                            **                            **                            I
                         * W15-MO                 I  MOVE   X                                 I
   THEN GO TO      -READ * EQUAL TO       *-CS20  I  TO     W20-CODE FIELD  -CS30            I
                   ----  * 12             * ----  I                         ----             I
                            **                                                               I
                            **                                                               I
                         * W16-DA                                                            I
                         * EQUAL TO       *-CS22                                             I
                         * 30             * ----                                             I
                            **                                                               I
                            **                                                               I
                            MOVE   F                                                          I
                            TO     W20-CODE FIELD  -CS30                                      I
                            **                     ----                                      I
```

Figure 8-3

APPLICATION CONTROLS MATRIX

TR & Co.
Schedule ______
date
Prepared by ______
Approved by ______

Client ______________________________

Application Area ______________________________

Audit Date ______________________________

ACTIVITIES SUBJECT TO CONTROL

CHARACTERISTICS WHICH CONSTITUTE CONTROLS

CONTROL FEATURE \ TRANSACTION/PROCESS																				
PREVENTIVE CONTROLS																				
Definition of responsibilities																				
Reliability of personnel																				
Training of personnel																				
Competence of personnel																				
Mechanization																				
Segregation of duties																				
Rotation of duties																				
Standardization																				
Authorization																				
Secure custody																				
Dual access/dual controls																				
Forms design																				
Prenumbered forms																				
Preprinted forms																				
Simultaneous preparation																				
Turnaround document																				
Drum Card																				
Endorsement																				
Cancellation																				
Documentation																				
Exception input																				
Default option																				
Passwords																				
DETECTIVE CONTROLS																				
Anticipation																				
Transmittal documents																				
Batch serial numbers																				
Control register																				
Amount control total																				
Document control count																				
Line control count																				
Hash total																				
Batch totals																				
Batch balancing																				
Visual verification																				
Sequence checking																				
Overflow checks																				
Format																				
Completeness check																				
Check digits																				
Reasonableness																				
Limit check																				
Validity check																				
Read-back																				
Dating																				
Expiration																				
Keystroke verification																				
Approval																				
Run-to-run totals																				
Balancing																				
Reconciliation																				
Aging																				
Suspense file																				
Suspense account																				
Matching																				
Clearing account																				
Tickler file																				
Periodic audit																				
Redundant processing																				
Summary processing																				
Labeling																				
Trailer label																				
CORRECTIVE CONTROLS																				
Discrepancy reports																				
Transaction trail																				
Error source statistics																				
Automatic error correction																				
Upstream resubmission																				
Backup and recovery																				

Figure 8-4

activity defined by a process box, decision diamond, or a transmittal line on the analytic flowchart should be categorized as either a control or an activity over which control is exercised.

The analytical flowchart will not normally indicate those controls which do not involve an activity or decision. Such passive controls are usually of a preventive nature, but their identification is still important. A thorough analysis using a control matrix will often assist the recognition and documentation of such controls.

The format and level of detail of a control matrix will vary, depending upon the complexity of what is being analyzed. Two examples of differing format and detail are shown in figures 8-5 and 8-6. Figure 8-5 describes a portion of a control matrix for the analysis of input edits in the accounts payable section. Note that in this case the "editing" activity across the top of Figure 8-5 includes each data field in a variety of types of input transactions to the accounts payable system. Figure 8-6 describes another level of matrix for the application system.

TOOLS TO VERIFY CONTROLS

Test Data Generators

One of the more recent attempts to improve the applicability of test data in complex systems and situations is test data generator software.

This type of software package employs various techniques to generate variable test data such as random values, constant values, values within specified ranges to be placed into fields within records, or data that are in error.

Tailored Computer Programs

In the past, auditors often had internal programming personnel or other EDP technicians write internal custom-designed computer programs for specific audit purposes. Alternatively, the auditor might possess adequate programming skills. Written in a conventional language, these programs could accomplish any audit task that could conceivably be performed by a computer. However, they were not without their *disadvantages,* which include:

- Relatively high development cost
- A requirement for the auditor to have sufficient specific technical capability in the programming language being used to perform them himself or to enable him to review the programs developed by others
- Unless prepared personally by the auditor, such programs must be verified or "audited" to assure that they perform the intended processes
- A high degree of obsolescence from year to year as file and record structures change

EXAMPLE INPUT EDIT CONTROLS MATRIX
FOR ACCOUNTS PAYABLE SYSTEM

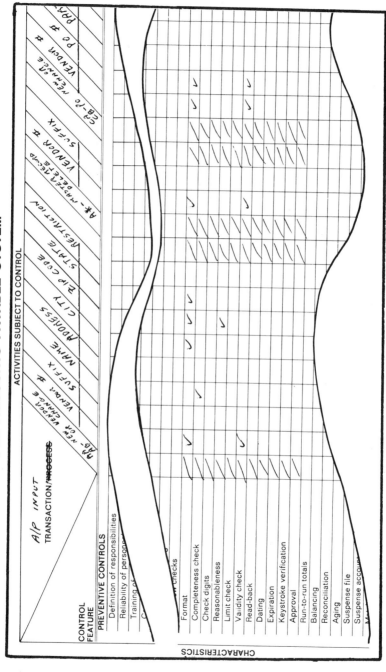

Figure 8-5

EXAMPLE OF APPLICATION CONTROL MATRIX ON SEGMENT OF ACCOUNTS PAYABLE SYSTEM

Client _____

Application Area _____

Audit Date _____

TR & Co.

Schedule _____

date

Prepared by _____

Approved by _____

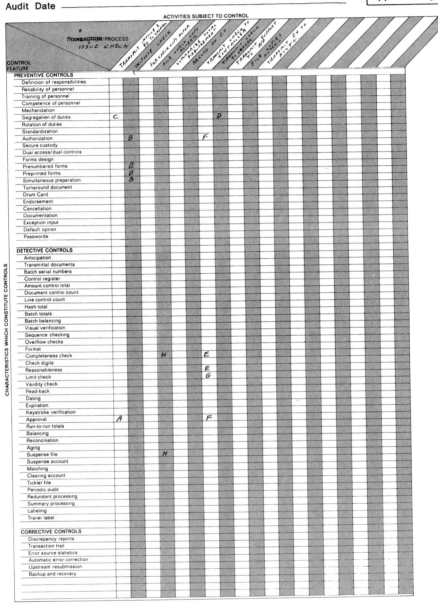

Figure 8-6

- Ongoing maintenance with associated technical assistance and cost

The primary advantage of custom-tailored programs is in place of audit software on those computers where nonstandard data file structures are used or where there is no available general purpose audit software (which will be described in the next topic). In the latter case, converting the client file from the native machine so as to run on another machine with audit software is a practical alternative.

Since the tailored program tool is usually implemented by using a programming language such as COBOL or RPG, it will not be covered in depth in this book. However, chapters in this book on systems design and development offer guidance to the auditor planning a tailored program.

In the event the auditor has tailored programs developed, the key points he must adhere to are:

- Technical proficiency is mandatory
- A long lead time for advance planning is often needed
- The auditor must be deeply involved in the planning and design of the program
- If internal personnel program the application, the auditor or independent personnel under his supervision must review the programs, determine that testing was adequate, and supervise the processing of the programs
- The final copy of the program run and related documentation must be kept under the control of the auditor

GENERAL PURPOSE AUDIT SOFTWARE

One of the prime tools for the audit function is general purpose audit software.

A number of general purpose audit software systems have been introduced. Though these have individual, unique features and characteristics, they tend to be similar in concept and purpose. Basically, general purpose audit software presents a method whereby written instructions covering audit activities may be converted into computer programs.

Audit software packages are specialized programming languages designed to meet the needs of the auditor. Audit software has, in effect, prefabricated or automated many of the common computer processing and "housekeeping" functions of tailored audit program preparation.

Example — The updating of computer files calls for application of a series of standardized decision rules and processing steps. Whenever an updating function is required in a conventionally written business data processing program, the programmer must design and write detailed coding instructions for each of a series of standard steps or alternatives. However, with a typical audit software approach, a single instruction, "update," can be written to call up the entire required sequence of processing logic.

A user of general purpose audit software will specify more processing with less program coding than tailored programs. Thus, this tool is far more productive in the use of programming time.

These principles of program prefabrication and automation have been applied similarly to tools which are known as programming aids, program generators, or data management systems. Characteristics and approaches are very similar.

General purpose audit software meets two specific needs of an auditor which are different from normal programming requirements:

- Computer programs developed by auditors are seldom used repetitively. A typical audit computer program will probably be subject to significant change in subsequent examinations because the application will have undergone modification. Thus, the auditor cannot afford the extensive costs of conventional program design and development.

- The auditor needs direct control of processing and logic of the programs prepared for application verification. Most other approaches to the preparation of audit computer programs have some drawbacks. For example, an EDP Department's own programmers may not have time for the preparation of audit computer programs. Even if they did, their assistance might jeopardize audit independence. In addition, auditors encounter persistent communications bottlenecks in attempting to deal with computer programmers.

Applications of Audit Software

General purpose audit software is applied in four broad areas:
- Detective examination of files
- Verification of application processing and controls
- Correction of file conditions
- Management inquiries

FILE EXAMINATION

Specific file examination techniques are discussed in the next chapter. Examination of files may be handled either manually or mechanically. If the size or complexity of an examination warrants mechanization, a computer should be used for the examination.

VERIFICATION OF APPLICATION PROCESSING AND CONTROLS

General purpose audit software may be used to verify application processing and controls through parallel simulation techniques. Parallel simulation is discussed in depth in the next chapter.

Another closely related technique is the use of audit software to perform "what-if" simulations. This approach is used to experiment with alternative methods for preparation of financial information rather than for verification. The auditor using this approach introduces changes in methods or principles of processing and notes the effect on results.

Example — Depreciation expense may be calculated on the basis of both straight-line and accelerated depreciation to see the impact of these alternative methods on net income and taxable income.

FILE CORRECTION

When an auditor identifies errors in accounting data, he is normally expected to suggest adjustments. These adjustments usually are applied to the general ledger. In addition, with advanced software systems, adjustments can also be made to detail computer files.

Example — A large institution had a file of unresolved input exceptions which was growing out of control. A team of accountants mechanized the resolution of many of the errors. The programs also matched many offsetting errors in the file. The audit software programs generated adjustments in the form of machine-readable transactions for resolving a major portion of the exceptions on the file. In such high-volume situations, error resolution was handled at far less cost than could have been done clerically

MANAGEMENT INQUIRY

The analysis and inquiry capabilities developed by auditors may have equal or greater value in developing management information. Audit software is particularly valuable where special reports must be developed on a timely basis. In such cases, frustration frequently results when a busy programming staff is asked to break off from other work for management reports. Managers experience difficulty in getting desired information as quickly as they would like. Programmers are hesitant about falling behind on long-range projects because of interruptions for special reports. With audit software, it becomes possible to develop inquiry or report routines without tying up the technical staff. Also, these special programs can be prepared quickly — frequently in a matter of hours.

Example — Management of a manufacturing company needed an aged report on outstanding freight damage claims. The time period covered by freight claims was such that normal 30-, 60-, 90-day aging programs were not applicable. Special programming was not justified due to the cost and time involved. With general purpose audit software, an application was prepared in 25 minutes. Processing was completed in about three hours.

Types of Audit Software

Virtually all audit software packages may be divided into two basic categories:

- COBOL preprocessors or generators
- Macrolanguages or interpreters

Preprocessor and generator systems generate COBOL program coding as their end product. This COBOL coding can then be compiled and processed like programs written directly in the COBOL language. An example of a preprocessor system is TRAP (Touche Ross Audit Package).

Macro and interpreter systems produce machine-language instructions for direct computer processing. STRATA (System by Touche Ross for Audit Technical Assistance) is an example of a table-driven interpreter.

COBOL PREPROCESSORS OR GENERATORS

In using a COBOL preprocessor, the auditor usually fabricates COBOL programs by either filling out skeleton statements or by using special shorthand statements. This package is the type most commonly used as an aid to programming productivity.

The greatest advantage of this approach is the ease with which a programmer proficient in the COBOL language can extend the capabilities of programs developed. This is done by adding standard COBOL statements to programs generated by the audit software package. This may be an important capability, since many preprocessors have relatively limited capabilities when used alone.

Another major advantage of COBOL preprocessors is that it is relatively easy to change programs from one make of computer to another when the coding is in COBOL. However, this advantage is limited because complete standardization of the COBOL compilers provided by the various manufacturers does not yet exist.

A disadvantage of COBOL preprocessors is that, on some major makes of equipment, COBOL programming cannot access all machine data formats which may be generated if an organization also has programs in other languages.

A second, but minor, disadvantage is that an extra processing step (the compilation) is required for COBOL programs.

MACROLANGUAGES AND INTERPRETERS

A major advantage of the macrolanguage approach is that data access limitations of COBOL may be avoided.

Another advantage lies in their "load-and-go" capabilities. It is unnecessary to go through the extra compilation step required for COBOL preprocessors.

A major disadvantage of macrolanguages is that they are usable only on the specific families of computers for which they are designed. Coding can seldom be converted for use on other computers, as can sometimes be done with COBOL preprocessors.

Another disadvantage is that many macrosystems cannot be expanded to accept the capabilities and speeds available in COBOL programs.

Common Characteristics

The method of coding used with most audit software packages is a series of standard fill-in-the-blanks specification sheets. Both STRATA and TRAP use this approach. A STRATA specification sheet is shown in Figure 8-8. A TRAP specification sheet is illustrated in Figure 8-7.

Audit Software Functions

The value of software packages to the auditor relates to the major processing functions which are available for specification. These functions are assembled in building-block fashion to create programs which perform the audit tests. The discussion which follows covers the major categories of audit software functions. These descriptions are an overview only. They are intended simply to provide a basis for understanding the audit techniques to be discussed later and to assist in evaluating audit software packages.

Because of the nature of this topic, some technical terminology is necessary in describing software functions. No attempt is made to define all terms used. An auditor attempting to use software tools should have enough bilingual capabilities to understand these terms. If any terms pose problems, a glossary is provided in the back of this text.

FILE ACCESS

File-access functions establish the capability to read computer-maintained files. Function descriptions should specify the specific types of file design or construction which the audit software can interrogate.

This is an extremely important capability in the construction of an audit computer program. The file-access function controls the availability of all other functions. Thus, a file-access function is an absolute necessity.

EXAMPLE OF TRAP SPECIFICATION SHEET

Client	Audit Date	Application		Prepared By	Date Prepared
Computer Control & Audit	5/1/76	*Receivables*		*NFM*	5/1/76

TOUCHE ROSS
AUDIT PACKAGE

∅ = ZERO

TRAP - A
FORM - 2

TRAP

DATA RECORD DEFINITION
FOR RECORD I.D. FIELDS (1) (2) (3)

CLIENT
NAME
76   80
`A C C R A`
Keypunch in each card.

CARD SEQUENCE NUMBER

```
1      6  8  9   12                                    26
0 5 2 0 1 0  0 1   C L I E N T S - F I E L D S .
```

1. DATA RECORD I.D. FIELD DEFINITIONS

CARD SEQUENCE NUMBER		I.D. FIELD LOCATION AND SIZE First Byte / Last Byte / Size		I.D. FIELD SIZE (4)
1 6	12	7 19 23 27 29	36	45 49
0 5 2 0 2 0	0 2	C L 1 7 2 6 8	P I C T U R E X (6 V 2) .	
0 5 2 0 3 0	0 2	C L 1 5 1 6 2	P I C T U R E X (2) .	
0 5 2 0 4 0	0 2	C L 1 3 1 4 2	P I C T U R E X (2) .	
0 5 2 0 5 0	0 2	C L 1 7 1 8 2	P I C T U R E X (2) .	
0 5 2 0 6 0	0 2	C L	P I C T U R E X ( ) .	

NOTES:

1. This form is not needed if all data records are to be processed in exactly the same way.

2. If some reoords are to be rejected, the record identifier field(s) must be defined using this form.

3. If this form is used, Card No. 030240, Item 3, on form A/2, Data File Definition, must be placed in proper sequence with the compile cards from the Data File Definition form (between Cards No. 030200 and 030300) if this form is not used, pull that card.

4. Columns 45—47 must contain numerics right justified with leading zeros. The total of all the numbers inserted in columns 45—47 must equal the number of bytes in the clients record.

COPYRIGHT © 1972
TOUCHE ROSS & CO.

A/2

OCTOBER 15, 1972

Figure 8-7

SPECIFIC FUNCTIONS

Individual audit software packages will vary in the types of file design and construction they can handle. File structures which fall within the capability of audit software packages include:

■ Sequential files
■ Index-sequential files

122

EXAMPLE OF STRATA SPECIFICATION SHEET

TOUCHE ROSS
STRATA

DATA FIELD SELECTION

FIXED SECTION OR REPEATING SECTION
(See Reverse for Continuation)

Sequence Number

F or R | F S 05
1   4

1 | 5

1 RECORD ID's TO BE SELECTED
Enter right justified 1 to 3 Record-ID specifications.
All criteria must be met for a record to be selected.

RECORD ID | SELECTION

	Location (1)	Length	Format	Criteria	Value
ID 1					
	6	9	10	11	12 13	14	18
ID 2					
	19	22	23	24	25 26	27	31
ID 3					
	32	35	36	37	38 39	40	44

2. DESCRIPTION OF REPEATING SECTION — ENTER ONLY WHEN USING FORM FOR REPEATING SECTIONS

Location (Number of Bytes preceding left most byte) of first repeating section of record.   Length of the record section that is repeated.   Maximum number of repeating sections.

45   48   49   52   53   55

3. DATA FIELD DEFINITION

LOCATION (1) OF DATA FIELD	SIZE OF DATA FIELD	F O R M A T (2)	DECIMAL PLACES IN NUMERIC FIELDS	DATA FIELD NAME (3) ALPHA-NUMERIC CONSTANT	NUMERIC CONSTANT	RECEIVING WORK FIELD (4)
5 6 9	10 12	13	14	15 21	28	29 31
2 18	8	P	2	BALANCE		W 05
2 14	2	C		TRANS MONTH		W 02
2		L			10	W 33
2 12	2	C		TRANS DAY		W 03
2		L			30	W 34
2 16	2	C		TRANS YEAR		W 04
2						W
2						W
2						W
2						W
2						W
2						W
2						W
2						W
2						W
2						W
2						W
2						W

(1) Number of bytes preceding the left-most byte of the DATA field.

(2) C for character
B for binary
P for packed (signed)
L for constant
U for unsigned packed
R for unsigned packed right
X for unsigned packed left

A for unsigned packed all
H for addressing bits
V for variable length fields preceded by 1 byte
D for variable length fields preceded by 2 bytes
*Do not use on RS

(3) Constants can be entered into a WORK field; by entering constant value here. Alpha Numeric Constant will be moved to work field from left, and Numeric Constant from right.

(4) Do not specify a numeric indicative WORK field as the receiving WORK field for more than one DATA field. Indicative fields are not summarized.

(5) If using more than one FSnn sheet to describe one DATA record the FSnn sequence numbers on each sheet are to be the same.

KEYPUNCH THIS SIDE	REVERSE SIDE	BOTH SIDES	KEYPUNCHED BY	VERIFIED BY

Figure 8-8

123

- Direct-access files
- Chained-reference files (data bases)
- Hierarchical files
- Fixed-length records
- Variable-length records
- Records with repeating segments
  In addition, media on which files reside include:
- 80-column punched cards
- Punched paper tape
- 96-character punched cards
- Magnetic tape
- Magnetic discs
- Special mass storage devices

EVALUATION

There is no general purpose audit software package yet available which can handle all of the file construction techniques and media listed above. In some cases, therefore, conversion to acceptable media is necessary. This frequently can be done through the use of manufacturer's utilities. However, access to punched card and magnetic tape and disc files, along with normal file structures used on these media, should be minimum requisites.

In addition, direct-access and chained-reference file structures are growing in importance. Chained-reference structures see particularly heavy use in systems utilizing data bases.

FORMAT ACCESS

Formats of data are based on various coding systems for representing data in computers. The format codes represent individual units of data, including characters, numbers, symbols, and so on.

The ability to read coded formats within records on computer files is another basic requirement for audit software.

SPECIFIC FUNCTIONS

Common data formats include:
- Character (BCD and EBCDIC)
- Zoned decimal
- Packed decimal
- Floating-point decimal
- Binary
- Hexadecimal (unsigned packed decimal)
- Individual bits

EVALUATION

The ability to access data in the character, zoned-decimal, and packed-decimal formats should be considered minimum requirements for an audit software package. The floating-point format is rarely encountered in business data processing and is, therefore, unnecessary.

The ability to access binary, hexadecimal, and individual-bit formats is frequently useful. This is particularly true in dealing with files generated by assembly language programs and in application packages provided by commercial software vendors.

ARITHMETICAL OPERATIONS

These functions automate the performance of arithmetical operations within programs developed by an auditor.

Arithmetical operations are essential to most processing of quantitative business data. Without arithmetical functions, audit software systems would be limited to mere report writing.

SPECIFIC FUNCTIONS

The basic functions are those of arithmetic itself: addition, subtraction, multiplication, and division. Some software packages have additional capabilities for rounding, percentaging, and exponential calculations.

EVALUATION

The basic arithmetical functions should be available as minimum requirements for any audit software package. Also, a fairly high limit should be available on the number of arithmetical operations which can be utilized. Some systems are limited to ten arithmetical operations per program. This is an extremely limiting factor on the scope of computerized audit examinations.

Rounding capabilities are so basic that they should be included automatically in audit software packages. Percentaging is a helpful feature which is desirable within packages. The only exponential function with a direct bearing on most business data processing is the square-root operation. There are cases where this is helpful.

LOGIC OPERATIONS

Logic operations compare values and direct decisions based on these comparisons. Some logic capabilities are required simply to acquire data from files. The variety and flexibility of the logic functions are major factors in determining the degree of processing sophistication an audit software system can attain.

SPECIFIC FUNCTIONS

Logic functions performed by computers are the same as those incorporated in Boolean algebra. These include: and, not and (exclude), equal to, less than, greater than, less than or equal to, greater than or equal to, and not equal.

More complex or efficient logic can be expressed by commands to execute subroutines, either within the general purpose audit software instructions or by exiting to instructions in a different language.

EVALUATION

At a minimum, an audit software package should have these capabilities: and, equal to, less than, greater than. The other functions may be constructed through combinations of these. However, if the other functions are included, they will improve preparation speed.

Whenever logic is performed, a program "branch" occurs. Depending on whether a true or false condition is sensed, processing will branch to a specific, programmed sequence. If the branch can be directed backward to a previous step in the logic, the auditor can build logic loops. These can be useful in economizing on computer operations and in applying sophisticated program logic.

RECORD-HANDLING OPERATIONS

Record-handling operations deal with the sequencing or consolidating of records in files.

Many audit tasks require that records be resequenced, combined, or that new records be added. Functions with these capabilities will bear upon the scope of the audit tasks which can be performed with any given software system.

SPECIFIC FUNCTIONS

Data handling operations sort, merge, or summarize records within files.

EVALUATION

The availability of these capabilities will substantially simplify or increase the scope of examinations which the auditor can perform. If sort or merge operations are not available, the auditor can use separate utility software with modest additional effort. A summarizing capability is useful in reducing the bulk of files for audit test purposes. By summarizing records, the auditor can apply tests to aggregate balances rather than to detail records.

UPDATE AND FILE COMPARISON FUNCTIONS

These functions permit the auditor to perform updating and comparison functions, using the contents of more than one file. Also, the content of one of the files may be altered or restructured on the basis of the content or conditions in another file.

This capability is usually essential to the preparation of audit confirmations, since names and addresses are commonly stored on files separate from account balance records.

126

Types of update and compare functions applicable to computerized auditing include:

- Update one file with the content of matching records in another
- Update one file with matching records and merge nonmatching records
- Update one file with matching records and drop nonmatching records in both
- Reject records from one file if they match with another
- Update master records with a series of matching transactions in another file

EVALUATION

The auditor will have difficulty preparing confirmations without some updating capability. Further, comparison of two files, which is a valuable audit procedure, requires these capabilities.

OUTPUT FUNCTIONS

Output functions control the production of the end products of programs developed by the auditor. These functions produce reports or files to be reemployed by the auditor in subsequent examination procedures. These outputs may be in forms readable by people, computers, or both.

The ability to produce end products specified by the auditor is the key function of audit software. Thus, output functions are essential. However, the variety and flexibility of outputs available through these functions are variable. Specific capabilities for outputting data may have a direct bearing on the uses to which audit software and processing results may be put.

SPECIFIC FUNCTIONS

Each audit software package must have some output capability, at least to produce reports. In addition, they may be able to produce output in one or more of the machine-readable formats described above under the file-access function. The number and type of machine-readable outputs available determines the flexibility of the software package.

EVALUATION

The ability to produce printed reports is a minimum requirement for all audit software packages. It is also desirable to have a capability for providing these printed outputs with identifiers, including page titles, column headings, editing symbols, and so on. Most audit packages provide columnar formatting for reports. Page-writing capabilities which allow free-form presentation of data will also enhance reporting. The auditor should also have reasonable control over the editing and spacing of printed output. Where such options exist, they should be provided with default options, minimizing the programming detail regularly required of the auditor.

The value of output functions to the auditor will also be affected by the number of reports which can be generated through a single processing of a file.

It is frequently helpful for the auditor to be able to reuse outputs of his programs for later processing. Therefore, it is desirable to have machine-readable outputs available. This will be particularly important where the auditor will use files generated through audit software more than once over a period of time. For instance, a file used in the preparation of confirmations may be subsequently used in the tabulation of replies.

Flexibility in the formatting of output may also be useful if the auditor wishes to produce machine-readable correcting entries or revised files.

STATISTICAL FUNCTIONS

These functions provide the capability for calculations which may be necessary for statistical applications. Statistical functions call for use of mathematical capabilities well beyond simple arithmetic.

Although other functions within audit software packages can eliminate some of the need for statistical analysis, availability of these functions will also facilitate more effective use of sampling techniques by the auditor. See chapter nine for further discussion of the role of statistics in EDP auditing.

SPECIFIC FUNCTIONS

Functions performed by the statistical elements within audit software include:
- Systematic selection
- Random selection
- Stratified random selection
- Selection proportionate to value
- Calculation of mean values
- Calculation of standard deviations
- Determination of attribute sample size
- ' Determination of variables sample size
- Analysis of attribute sample results
- Analysis of combined attribute/variable results (CAV)
- Analysis of variables sample results

EVALUATION

Because of the complexity of calculations required in statistics, it is desirable that the applications be prefabricated.

Mean and standard deviation calculations are performed through a series of arithmetical functions. If available, special operations are much faster to employ.

The determination of sample sizes and analyses of sample results involve calculations using exponential functions. Such functions will be helpful if the methods available coincide with the specific sampling requirements of a given engagement and auditor.

If audit software packages do not provide statistical sampling functions, the auditor may, alternatively, use time-sharing services for estimating sample size and evaluating results. When this is done, the audit software may still be called upon to accumulate the various parameters to be applied in the analysis.

MISCELLANEOUS FUNCTIONS

In addition to the functions described above, there are several others which are application oriented in nature. These are listed and described individually below.

Importance of these miscellaneous functions varies widely. Some are highly useful. Others are incidental to the performance of audits.

SPECIFIC FUNCTIONS

Miscellaneous functions of audit software packages include:
- Confirmation printing
- Automatic program testing
- Automatic job-control language
- Descriptive parameters to "snapshot" data
- Bar graphs (frequency histograms)
- Sequence comparison

EVALUATION

These functions are appropriate to specific types of audit tasks. Where they fit, they will be highly useful. In most cases, however, their use is largely a matter of convenience.

The most important functions of those listed above are the ability to prepare confirmations and to test the sequence of records.

HARDWARE AND SOFTWARE COMPATIBILITY

Hardware and software compatibility is the ability to function with specific computer models and operating systems. Audit software must be compatible with the equipment and operating systems of the installation where the audit applications will be processed.

SPECIFIC CAPABILITIES

Among the considerations which must be used in evaluating hardware and software compatibility capabilities are:

- Manufacturer
- CPU compatibility
- Peripheral compatibility
- Memory capacity
- Disc capacities
- Operating system software availability
- Multiprogramming requirements

EVALUATION

For an internal auditor, the most important consideration is that the software operate on the available in-house computer. If this equipment is other than IBM, the available software may be limited. Although off-premises use of audit software is feasible and is practiced by some auditors, it is seldom preferable.

The ability of audit software to run in a multiprogramming mode is an important factor in enabling the auditor to gain access to a computer. If a company uses multiprogramming capabilities, an audit software package which could not run in this mode would cause complete disruption. In addition, this ability makes it possible for an auditor to gain access to computers in more desirable parts of the working day.

The CPA must recognize the dominant position of IBM in the business computer market. To be broadly applicable, his audit software system should at least be able to operate on IBM System/360 and 370 equipment.

In most cases, magnetic tape files produced on equipment of other manufacturers can be converted for processing on IBM computers. However, certain manufacturers or data formats may present difficulties.

The configuration and capacities of the central processing unit and peripherals of any given computer will affect the ability to use general purpose audit software. Thus, audit software systems to be applied generally should recognize that a minimum realistic memory size for IBM System/360 and 370 computers will be 65,000 bytes. Also, IBM System/360 and 370 configurations can be expected to include at least two tape or disc units.

In the operating system area, a minimum requirement should be compatibility with IBM DOS. However, compatibility with O/S for large-scale computers is also desirable.

There is a wide variety of audit tools at the auditor's disposal. Whether gathering information, testing processing, or testing results, there are a number of alternative tools that may be employed. Each has its own particular advantages and disadvantages, and the auditor must be cautious to pick the one that fits his objectives best.

9
Application Audit Techniques

This chapter will discuss the primary techniques for determining the existence of and testing for controls.

The auditor can use a variety of EDP audit techniques in identifying and verifying application controls. There are two purposes for utilizing the various techniques described: *(1) to verify the manual and/or computer processing operations* and *(2) to verify the results of processing.* Figure 9-1 summarizes these, relates the various techniques to the application tool, and indicates the purpose of each.

SELECTING THE TECHNIQUE

Whichever technique or techniques the auditor selects, he must begin his audit of program-applied controls by identifying key processing steps and controls which will be verified. These identifications are derived from the analytic flowcharting and control-matrix documents discussed in the previous chapter. The advantages and disadvantages of each technique are also discussed so that the auditor may choose the one best suited for his needs.

TECHNIQUES FOR GATHERING INFORMATION
Program Listing Review

Review of program listings (also known as "desk checking" or "program code checking") provides information on computer processing through detailed analysis of program code listings. Under this approach, a member of the audit team reads and analyzes the detailed application coding written by the programmers. This technique requires a person trained in the principles of auditing and also extremely skilled in programming. He must have detailed knowledge of the specific programming language, operating system, and hardware being used.

SUMMARY OF APPLICATION AUDIT PURPOSES, TECHNIQUES, AND TOOLS

PURPOSE	TECHNIQUE	TOOLS
Gather information describing controls	Review program listing	
	Review logic flowchart	Flowcharting software
Verify processing	Audit around	
	Test data	Test data generator Audit software
	Integrated test facility	
	Parallel simulation	Audit software Tailored program
	S C A R F	
	Snapshot	
Verify results	Confirmation	Audit software Tailored program
	Comparison with file or physical	Audit software Tailored program
	Edit & reasonableness tests	Audit software Tailored program

Figure 9-1

Difficulties associated with this information-gathering technique apply principally in the skill level required. There simply are not many people sufficiently bilingual to perform this type of procedure. It is *also* extremely difficult to trace the program logic through code lists. Even the same programmers who wrote the programs will frequently encounter difficulty deciphering instructions that they wrote only recently. Also, with extensive applications involving multiple programs, time requirements for manual review of coding are apt to be economically unfeasible.

Nevertheless, source code listings may be the last resort for obtaining information. While the most difficult to interpret, source code will probably be the most current available reference. Neither should the difficulty be overrated. High-level language statements such as COBOL, which resembles English, may be intelligible. COBOL file description statements are quite easy to interpret.

Program Flowchart Review

Detailed information gathering may also be performed through examination of logic processing flowcharts. Most computers now accept commercial software routines which will generate processing flowcharts mechanically: The program source deck containing all appropriate program logic (directions) is converted into a flowchart which graphically depicts the processing which takes place. The main advantage of review through flowcharts is that it is considerably easier to comprehend the logic of a program in this way than from a code listing of the source program language.

The use of flowchartng software increases the likelihood that the flowchart the auditor examines will be current, reflecting processing as it is being done at the time of his review. This capability is important because manually drawn flowcharts are seldom up to date. As with the case of coding, a review of flowcharts still requires an expert in both auditing and data processing. This technique, too, is applied effectively only when the auditor knows what problems to look for.

TECHNIQUES FOR TESTING CONTROLS

Two major alternative approaches exist for the testing of the application controls. They are verified by:

- Testing the results
- Testing the processing

Testing the results provides an *inference* that, if the results are accurate, the essential controls must be functioning.

> *Example — If accounts receivable are confirmed at an interim date and if no significant exceptions are found, we may infer that adequate controls over the updating of the file for invoices and payments are functioning.*

When the actual processing is tested, key functions and controls are *individually* verified. Error rates that are detected in these functions and controls are then used to forecast the exposure.

> *Example — If sound credit limits are ignored in 7% of the cases when additional credit is requested, we may predict that 2% of the year-end receivables will be uncollectible.*

Each of these approaches has its advantages and disadvantages. Tests of results may allow the unjustified *assumption* that, simply because things are good now, they will stay that way. Individual controls are not directly tested. This allows a risk that unanticipated causes of exposure will occur that could have been predicted had controls been more closely verified. Testing of results is more reliable if the controls being tested are first specifically and explicitly identified. Then, tests of results *must be* applied *only* to those controls whose failure would be *clearly displayed* in the results.

Example — Confirmation exceptions are expected to clearly display the effects of a failure to apply check digit control whereby inaccurate recording of account numbers would result in payments updated against the wrong account. At the same time, however, confirmations would not reveal a defect in account aging controls.

Tests of the actual process provide a better awareness of the reliability of each individual, significant control. The main problem with this approach lies in converting the observed error rate into a quantified exposure.

Example — The determination that credit limits are ignored in 7% of the applicable requests for additional credit does not readily lead to the estimate of an exposure to 2% uncollectibles.

TECHNIQUES FOR TESTING RESULTS

Three techniques have been used extensively for many years in noncomputer audits of applications. They are used primarily as substantive tests and can be done manually or with the computer, using either custom designed audit programs or generalized software. The techniques are:

- **Confirmation** by direct correspondence with third parties to corroborate transactions or balances
- **Comparison** of files maintained by independent departments or with physical existence
- **Reasonableness and edit tests** of items *within* files

Confirmation of Items on a File with a Third Party

The most common example of testing results is confirmation of items from one organization's file with the records of another person or organization. The items may include the entire file or a representative sample. Typical examples of file testing through confirmation include cash deposits, accounts receivable, consigned inventories, accounts payable, and debt.

The successful confirmation of such items will normally provide strong assurance that the file being examined is updated accurately.

However, care should be taken not to presume that successful confirmation necessarily results in reliable testing of the value of the assets or liabilities represented in a file. For instance, the confirmation of a receivable balance is not an assurance of the ability or intention of the customer to meet his obligation.

Comparison of Items on a File to Another File or to Physical Existence

A second method is comparing records from one file with those of another file maintained independently within the same organization or with the materials represented by the records. A frequent example of this type of verification is the comparison of payroll files with personnel records. Similarly, records on a file can be compared to the physical items they represent: inventory, fixed assets, etc.

Edit and Reasonableness Tests on Items in a File

A third verification technique is the application of a wide range of reasonableness and edit tests to items within files which are not already provided as controls within the application. Frequently, such tests search for conditions that should not exist if prevention controls are effective.

If the auditor finds that meaningful edit and reasonableness tests can be applied for audit purposes, he should question whether they would also be useful as regular controls in the application. The need for this type of audit procedure frequently implies a corresponding control deficiency in the application.

The specific nature of reasonableness and edit tests can vary widely, depending upon the imagination of the auditor, his understanding of the data, and its relevance within the business organization.

We will not further discuss these approaches to testing of results, since the techniques are already well presented in existing audit literature.

TECHNIQUES FOR TESTING PROCESSING

Auditing Around the Computer

In auditing around the computer, the results of computer processing are tested manually against the source data entered into the computer. Verification takes place without direct involvement of the auditor in processing within the computer.

This type of testing is done on either a sampling basis or through a comparison of total balances. This technique is usually efficient as long as the documentation for external verification exists or can be readily created.

In implementing an audit around the computer, it is necessary to:

- *Determine that outputs exist* to facilitate the manual calculation of processes and controls under examination. At each major step in processing, there must be transaction listings and trial balances of the file being processed both before and after the file updating. Normally, the before-processing listing is the output from the previous processing cycle. In order to be effective, all transactions input to a processing or control step must be included on the computer-produced reports.
- *Develop methods for obtaining representative samples* of transactions. Sampling is usually necessary because the very presence of a computer indicates that volumes are too large for duplication of processing manually. Sampling techniques must also assure that representative and unusual transactions are tested. Therefore, a constraint to auditing around the computer lies in the audit resources needed to test the necessary variety of transactions.
- *Verify manually each control or processing step* which the auditor wishes to rely upon.

Advantages

One of the important advantages in auditing around the computer is that the audit staff needs little technical training. Examination is largely on a logical level. When this approach is feasible, the auditor is better able to judge the significance of his findings during the actual testing procedures than if he were using the computer in his testing and were required to design all reasonableness tests in advance.

Moreover, auditing around the computer is results oriented. End products are readily identifiable and may be used as a measure of processing reliability. Likewise, there are no logistical constraints associated with the data processing center. Documentation and techniques associated with this approach are easily understood by everyone.

Disadvantages

The larger the computer system, the less comprehensive will be the printed output. Therefore, the less practicable it will be to attempt to audit around it. Auditing around the computer requires detailed printouts at each processing step. Where actual printouts are exception oriented, thorough external testing may not be possible. Furthermore, when the variety or volume of transactions is large, the conditions to be tested may exceed the capacity of manual testing.

This may be true even when statistical sampling techniques are used to select transactions and output for verification. Where complex systems are implemented on large-scale computers, conventional sampling techniques may simply not be capable of providing for the testing of unusual situations. This may often be the case when applying reasonableness or limit checks.

When auditing around the computer, it is difficult to test the completeness of processing: to see what happened to all the records. The normal approach would be to verify batch controls, but this is difficult because many batch controls include such large quantities of transactions that it is not feasible to recalculate the processing manually.

Applying Around the Computer Techniques

In applying this technique, the auditor must do the following:

DEFINE THE PROCESSES AND CONTROLS TO BE TESTED

As in all audit situations, it is necessary to begin an around-the-computer audit by defining specific objectives. With this approach, the auditor has considerably more flexibility than with verification procedures utilizing the computer. This is because he retains complete personal control throughout testing. He can expand or decrease the scope of his tests based on interim findings.

SELECT TEST ITEMS

The auditor should begin by selecting the outputs to be tested. He then examines the related input in the application to determine the reasonableness and accuracy of the selected outputs. Where a number of inputs are processed to produce one output or where volumes exceed manual examination capacities, sampling is necessary. Each type of output of concern must be tested, including edit and error listings which indicate the effectiveness of many application controls.

Having identified outputs to be tested, the auditor must obtain related inputs. In auditing around the computer, it is desirable to test inputs back to the beginning of the manual processing portions. Thus, in auditing around the computer, it is possible to test both manual and computer portions of an application simultaneously.

REPROCESS THE TEST ITEMS

Next, having identified outputs and obtained corresponding inputs, the auditor is ready to perform the calculations of the application. This requires a detailed understanding of what should be done and what results should be attained. The auditor should be aware that the exact calculation techniques used by a computer do not necessarily correspond with those normally used under manual processing procedures. For instance, many calculations within clerical routines are set up to use tables instead of performing calculations for each transaction. With computers, however, it is usually more effective to perform specific calculations than to occupy the main memory with storage of tables.

Example — Authorized income tax withholding amounts differ according to whether IRS tables are used or the alternative "percentage method" is applied by computer.

Thus, results of calculations performed on a computer will not necessarily correspond precisely with table lookups. An auditor testing computer applications manually must simulate the exact calculation patterns followed under the application program. Therefore, a desk calculator would be a helpful tool for such verification procedures.

RESOLVE EXCEPTIONS

After testing is completed, if any exceptions in processing are identified, the auditor must follow up to determine the causes and establish whether they result from control weaknesses or incorrect processing routines. In many applications where auditing around the computer is appropriate, there is a comparatively high use of manual procedures. Therefore, exception testing may reveal types of errors normal for clerical processing. The impact of such exceptions should not be minimized as "merely clerical errors"; rather, the application programs and procedures should include edit and reasonableness tests to detect and report such errors.

TEST DATA

Test data, commonly called "test decks," are sets of input data which present a variety of transactions to the computer for verification through actual processing as a means of looking for invalid results. The ideal test data should present the application under examination with every possible combination of transactions, master file situations, values, and processing logic which could be encountered during actual operations. The quantity of transactions required for a comprehensive test may number in the thousands or even tens of thousands.

The auditor will experience some difficulty in identifying and capturing a comprehensive variety of combinations of file conditions and transactions to test all possible processing within an application. Therefore, test data are most feasible where the variety of transactions, processing, and controls is relatively limited. For test data verification to be feasible, highly reliable application documentation must be available. This should include thorough and comprehensive documentation of transaction formats, master file formats, processing terms, and controls.

One of the requirements of a system development project which creates a new application is the testing of programs prior to implementation of a new data processing system. Part of the application development effort calls for the creation of test data which can be used for debugging newly written programs. If such test data are retained, the auditor may find them suitable as a starting point. If test data are not already available, the feasibility of this technique decreases in proportion to the amount of effort necessary to devise new test data.

Availability of master file records is more critical by far than the availability of test transactions. The format and content of transaction records are usually relatively brief. Transactions usually take place in large volumes and should be designed for simple, regular, economic preparation and processing. In contrast, master file records which are affected by transactions may represent the accumulation of many cycles, even years, of transaction processing. Since master records may be established only infrequently, their replacement or creation may be comparatively difficult.

Should it be necessary for the auditor to create new master files for verification through the use of test data, two alternate approaches may be considered:

- Selected live records may be compiled as a test file
- Master file records may be especially created for this purpose by the auditor

The ability to select live records for test files is contingent on the existence of the desired conditions within some available file. In such cases, copying and using available records will require assistance from a computer and, possibly, the use of either programs written specially for this purpose or a general purpose audit software system.

To illustrate the process through use of general purpose audit software, the criteria for the selection of records can be entered on specification sheets. Automatically selected records can be written out in a format identical to the master file. The contents of a copy of the master file can also be altered under the control of the auditor to suit the needs of the test procedures more exactly.

If the auditor selects the alternative of designing master records from scratch, the greatest difficulty he faces is the conversion from master file specifications to a workable format within the computer. Frequently, this is done through the use of record-construction provisions within many applications provided for recovery from accidental destruction.

Finally, a test data generator software system may be used to create the required transactions and master records. If available, large quantities of data can be generated with relative ease.

If no such capabilities exist and if file design is relatively simple, the auditor may be able to construct his file on cards. This may be converted to the appropriate tape or disc media through the use of either utility programs or through the file generator capability of general purpose software. If the required program features or support software are not available, the use of test data may not be feasible.

Advantages

Test data can usually be prepared by persons with little technical background. However, a person preparing test data must still be very familiar with the mechanical details of the application program logic and the specific controls within it.

This approach provides a highly specific test of individual control features.

Disadvantages

It is impractical to expect the auditor to be completely familiar with all of the minute details of the application logic. As a result, it is practically impossible for a test data designer to anticipate all the circumstances which may develop in the processing of a computer application. This is true even when test generator software is applied, although this special-purpose software represents an improvement over manual design of test data.

The biggest single shortcoming of test data is that they are limited to testing "preconceived situations" and are likely to incorporate the same bugs or oversights which exist in the documentation of the application program; that is, the approach lacks objectivity in that the tests are oriented to documented controls only. *What will go wrong is what is not expected!*

Example — Test data were designed to verify the exception-reporting provisions of an installment loan application at a commercial bank. The test data verified that all edit features of the computer program were functioning as specified. However, a separate analysis uncovered the existence of a number of negative balances for accounts in the installment loan files: one in the amount of $30,000. Negative balances are improbable for installment loans. Therefore, no tests had been built into the application to report such situations.

Another major drawback is in proving the significance of the results. If the auditor finds some moderately subtle defect in the application logic, he is often met with the rebuttal that "it never happens." There may well be merit to such a rebuttal. Many times manual, preventive controls *do* keep particular situations from arising with significant frequency. However, at other times, the rebuttal may be presented just because the responsible persons haven't previously recognized the problem. The information provided by a test data verification cannot settle this question.

Finally, once a program is thoroughly tested, the auditor must still determine that the program he tested is actually the one used for regular processing. A different program could be fraudulently substituted for the "real" one to satisfy the auditor and appear to be proper. Even without a deliberate attempt to deceive, the "real" program could differ from the tested one due to maintenance changes, program "patches," or carelessness.

Applying Test Data Techniques

In applying the test data technique, the auditor does the following:

DEFINES THE OBJECTIVES

The requirement for formal definition of objectives, present for any audit test technique, applies at a higher level of formality for test data than for others. This is because of the specific nature of test data; they verify only those characteristics or controls which the auditor explicitly designates. Figure 9-2 shows a working paper for test deck objectives and characteristics.

PREPARES TEST DATA

The second step in the application of test data techniques is to obtain or develop the master file or files with proper characteristics. The acquisition or preparation of a master file which presents all conditions and features to be tested may be the most difficult technical aspect of utilization of the test data technique.

CALCULATES PREDICTED PROCESSING RESULTS

The next step in the work flow associated with test data is precalculation of anticipated results. This is done through the use of actual data included in the master records and related transactions which make up the test data. Based on an understanding of application logic, calculation methods, and control features, test data are calculated for comparison with the results of computer processing.

This step also presents a substantial obstacle. Manual processing of thousands or tens of thousands of items may overtax most normal audit resources. To implement these independent calculations, general purpose audit software routines may be developed.

PROCESSES TEST DATA THROUGH THE COMPUTER

The next point to consider is running the test data through all the programs in the application cycle. The auditor should anticipate that more than one class of transactions, and conceivably more than one master file, may be needed to accomplish test data verifications when different types of transactions are to be processed at different stages within an application.

COMPARES MANUAL AND COMPUTER-PRODUCED RESULTS
Following processing, the auditor compares actual results with those predicted on the basis of precalculations. All discrepancies must be identifed and analyzed for cause.

RESOLVES EXCEPTIONS
When test results indicate true discrepancies in the processing of application programs, the auditor must identify the precise cause of each and design additional procedures to quantify the effects of processing under fallacious programs.

WORKING PAPER SHOWING TEST-DECK
OBJECTIVES AND CHARACTERISTICS

Test ID Number	Objective	Description	Predicted Result	Actual Result
A	Verify department totals	Process hours worked for two employees in same department	Department 1 total equal 80 hours and gross pay of $200	Same
B	Verify regular gross pay	Process 40 hours worked for an employee on day shift	Gross pay of $100	Same
C	Verify gross pay with overtime	Process 48 hours worked for an employee on day shift	Gross pay of $130	Same
D	Verify gross pay with shift premium	Process 40 hours worked for an employee on night shift	Gross pay of $110	Same
E	Verify gross pay with overtime and shift premium	Process 48 hours worked for an employee on night shift	Gross pay of $140	Gross pay of $143
AA	Verify edit of over-limit hours	Process 96 hours worked for an employee	Rejected input	Same
AB	Verify edit of over-limit gross pay	Process 62 hours worked for an employee having $999 hourly rate	Edit Report No paycheck	Edit Report but paycheck drafted

Figure 9-2

INTEGRATED TEST FACILITY METHOD —
THE "MINICOMPANY" APPROACH

The integrated test facility (ITF) method is a further refinement of the test data approach. It permits the introduction of selected test inputs into a system together with, or as if they were with, "live" data and the tracing of the flow of these test transactions through the various functions in the system for comparison to predetermined results.

ITF involves the establishment of a "dummy" entity against which the data are processed: a division, employee, etc. After the entity is established, transactions are processed against this entity together with actual transactions. The auditor determines what checks he wishes to make such as overdue items, returned goods, etc., and compares the results to predetermined results.

Advantages

The advantages of using ITF are as follows:

- Little technical training is necessary
- Low processing cost since test data are processed with regular input
- Ability to test the actual system as it routinely operates
- Understood by everyone since the auditor utilizes the company's normal submission procedures

Disadvantages

The disadvantages of ITF are:

- The test data transactions must be removed from the company's control records (e.g., general ledger) by use of either manual journal entries or program modifications
- High cost if the application programs require modification to remove the effects of test data transactions
- Possibility of destroying files since transactions affect live files
- Difficult to identify all variations of exceptions to test the program
- The quantity of test data that is submitted by the auditor may be limited by the requirement to submit the data along with live data

Applying ITF Techniques

In applying the techniques of the integrated test facility, the auditor does the following:

DEFINES THE OBJECTIVES

The ITF method changes nothing with regard to the need to define objectives. The same approach as discussed for test decks may be applied to this situation.

ESTABLISH "DUMMY" RECORDS ON THE "LIVE" FILES

The auditor usually establishes separate master test records against which his transactions will be processed. The ITF method calls for establishing these records on the same file devices as the live records. However, some identification must be made of these records by specific account number, account number series, department number, branch number, etc. The approach to establishing this identification must be considered carefully, since it could create limitations in the testing procedures (e.g., interdepartmental transfers) or could allow the auditor to have unauthorized effects on records.

ESTABLISH THE METHOD FOR REMOVING TEST DATA EFFECTS

Since test master records are together with the other master file records and since test transactions will be submitted in the normal processing stream, some provision must be made to remove the effects of these transactions and records from the actual processing results. Several approaches exist:

- Manual reversal of transaction and record effects from reported results
- Programmed exclusion of transactions and records in control totals
- Use of insignificant values for transactions and records so that effects can be ignored

The manual reversal of the effects of ITF from application results is relatively inexpensive but somewhat unreliable. Some authorities having jurisdiction over regulated industries specifically prohibit this practice.

Programmed provisions to eliminate the effects require advance planning during development time. Otherwise, this may require potentially expensive program modifications. This circumstance increases the desirability for auditors to participate in the specifications of new applications. A second disadvantage of this alternative is that it automatically means that test data transactions are not being processed in exactly the same manner as live transactions. This may raise questions as to the validity and relevance of the tests.

The final alternative, use of insignificant values (e.g., $.01), avoids most of the drawbacks of the alternatives above but introduces a new one: It prevents testing of controls that apply to high-value transactions and balances. This may or may not interfere with the audit objectives.

CALCULATE PREDICTED PROCESSING RESULTS

This step is identical to that for the use of conventional test data. The auditor must determine, before or after the actual testing, what results should occur from the tests according to his understanding and audit objectives.

SUBMIT TEST DATA TO COMPUTER

Again, the ITF approach calls for the submission of test data along with live data. This does not mean that such data must actually be commingled with live data, but it must at least be submitted through identical procedures and processed at the same time.

COMPARE PREDICTED WITH ACTUAL RESULTS

This step is also similar to that for test data. Having predetermined the results that should be produced, the auditor must compare them with the actual results and resolve any discrepancies. This may lead to very time-consuming follow-up analysis.

REVERSE THE EFFECTS OF TESTS

The final step in this approach is to implement the measures provided to reverse the effects of the test on the output results. If this provision is programmed into the application, no further action may be necessary.

Conclusion

The integrated-test-facility approach is a useful audit technique but has many disadvantages. A common approach to implementing this technique is to develop it for the use of program maintenance personnel and utilize it for audit as the need arises.

SYSTEM CONTROL AUDIT REVIEW FILE

The *System Control Audit Review File* (SCARF) approach involves the incorporation of auditor-determined reasonableness tests into the normal processing programs. The results of these tests are reported to the auditor rather than the users for the auditor's review and possible investigation.

Implementing the SCARF Technique

The steps involved in this technique are as follows:

- The auditor provides his requirements to the systems development team during the user-specification phase of development.
- The auditor's selection requirements are implemented in the application programs along with the rest of the development of the application.
- Once the new application system is implemented, the auditor-specified detective controls function in conjunction with normal application processing, and exceptions to these audit tests are written out on a file.

- The file of audit exceptions is reviewed by the auditor using manual or computer-assisted techniques.
- The auditor takes the action he considers necessary based upon the exceptions he discovers.

While this technique may be quite powerful and innovative, the auditor rarely needs to repeatedly process detective controls that are not also of substantial interest to the users. *If the auditor-developed detective tests are good, the users should adopt them.*

Occasionally, the auditor may be unable to persuade the users of the importance of certain controls. In such cases, he may personally see that they are implemented. This should be considered an abdication of responsibility by the user and would imply many other significant user-management problems. Nonetheless, such occasions do arise, and the SCARF technique may be an effective way of compensating for them in the short run.

SARF

A *Sample Audit Review File* is somewhat similar to SCARF except the contents are selected randomly rather than as exceptions to any special edit or reasonableness test. The objective of this technique is to obtain a *representative* file for audit analysis (See SAMPLING, p. 147).

SARF is particularly appropriate for CPA's who are required to test controls or transactions throughout the year under examination. However, the technique is also appropriate for internal auditors who simply wish a representative sample.

Implementing the SARF Technique:

The steps involved in this technique are almost the same as SCARF:

- The auditor provides his requirements to the system development team during the user-specification phase of development.
- The auditor's selection requirements are implemented in the application programs along with the rest of the development of the application.
- Once the new application system is implemented, the random selection routine causes records to be written onto a file.
- The representative file of records is examined by the auditor using manual or computer-assisted techniques.
- The auditor takes appropriate action on his findings.

SNAPSHOT

The *snapshot* technique is a form of transaction trail provided only for selected inputs carrying a special code. This is often an effective approach in high-volume systems where a complete transaction trail of all inputs would generate an unusable profusion of information. If the capability is provided in the application system in advance, the attachment of a particular code to any input transaction can be made to generate a hard-copy transaction trail for that item following each step of application processing.

Implementation of the Snapshot Technique

The steps required to utilize the *snapshot* auditing technique are as follows:

- The auditor provides his requirements during the user-specification phase of development.
- The regular systems development project team implements the capability for a selective transaction trail during the remaining steps of the application system development.
- Following the implementation of the new application system, a special supplementary code may be added to transaction inputs without affecting any other aspect of the processing of that transaction.
- Throughout the processing of the transaction, reports are produced at predetermined points so as to reveal the impact of the "tagged" transaction on master records and subsequent calculations.
- The auditor receives the transaction-trail documentation.
- The auditor analyzes the transaction trail according to his audit objectives.

The use of a selective transaction trail is not only an effective tool to be utilized by the auditor but is especially useful to the systems development and programming staffs in localizing the cause of application-processing discrepancies. Furthermore, user management will share the same concerns as the auditor.

Accordingly, this technique is best implemented as a tool for debugging application computer programs by the programming staff. If the capability is available for the programming staff, the auditor and user may also employ it when desired.

SAMPLING

Computer-assisted audit techniques have a two-edged impact on the use of statistical sampling by auditors.

On one side, the availability of a computer for the auditor's use in analyzing masses of data eliminates the need to settle for partial samples. By merely preparing an audit software application that implements the logic of his audit analysis, the auditor can examine every transaction and record in little more time than it would have taken him to merely *select* items for manual testing. In such situations, sampling saves time but provides no other benefit to compensate for its uncertainties.

On the other side, the utilization of a computer is a tremendous aid in the selection of random samples and evaluation of their results. Computers may be programmed to select a truly random sample of transactions or records so as to eliminate the cumbersome manual task of employing random number tables. Many of the general purpose audit software languages provide simple user specifications that can perform the complex selection calculations with virtually no effort by the auditor. Even if such audit software languages are not available, commercial time-sharing services provide programs that will generate random numbers sorted into sequences and within specified ranges of values. These computer-assisted techniques in obtaining random samples allow the use by auditors of statistical evaluation techniques that would be virtually impossible on a manual basis.

Selecting a random sample is really a relatively unimportant first step in making a statistical evaluation. Sample sizes are merely guesses as to what number of items might provide desired reliability and precision, depending upon the conditions which are found. The real purpose of statistical analysis is to allow the auditor to measure the degree of precision and reliability that he is accepting by testing less than 100% of the items under examination.

Statistical analysis is a tool for audit quality control. It allows the auditor to estimate scientifically the range of results that he would probably obtain if he were to perform the same audit tests on 100% of the items under examination rather than on the sample. Judgmental sampling *may* produce results similar to that of statistical estimates, but it leaves the auditor unable to measure the degree of uncertainty occasioned by the use of samples. Samples selected judgmentally would normally be expected to contain a greater proportion of errors than would be found in the entire population. A trained auditor may instinctively, and quite unconsciously, allow his attention to be drawn by items that are unusual and most likely to be erroneous. Random sampling, without statistical evaluation, avoids unconscious biases in selection but omits a determination as to whether the sample size was adequate for the purposes of the results.

Time-sharing-based computer systems are most often used to assist in the evaluation of statistical samples. While the computations involved in these evaluations are not prohibitively difficult, if a simple calculator is available, the time-sharing assistance produces results slightly faster and is much easier to use for persons who are not familiar with the computations.

To implement certain advanced methods of sample selection and evaluation, the assistance of a computer is virtually essential. The selection of samples where the probability of selecting a particular record is proportionate to its dollar value is rather difficult to implement without computer assistance, particularly for reasonably large populations. This method of selection is required if subsequent evaluation is to be performed by using methods that apply attribute sampling concepts to the evaluation of dollar values.

Another advanced method is to subdivide the total population of items under examination into a large number (5 to 50) of strata (sub-populations). The relative homogenous values that lie within each stratum provide a number of small populations with extremely small standard deviations. Random samples may be taken of each of these strata and the results combined. This will provide a reliable statistical evaluation but a relatively small total sample size. Again, subdividing the population and selecting numerous small random samples within each stratum is extremely difficult to implement without computer assistance.

Summary

Statistical sampling has been, and is, an effective technique for testing controls and other characteristics of computerized information systems. The use of a computer in the acquisition and evaluation of samples is also an important technique of auditing *with* a computer.

PARALLEL SIMULATION

Parallel simulation consists of the preparation of a separate computer application that performs the same functions as those used by the actual application programs used for daily or other periodic processing. The simulation programs read in the *same input data* as the application programs, use the *same files,* and attempt to produce the *same results.* These results are matched with those from the live programs, providing a means for testing through comparison. This is the same basic concept as auditing around the computer except it is not dependent upon manual transaction trails or manual processing capacities.

Parallel simulation may be done in any programming language. However, the auditor is best served by general purpose audit software which makes it possible for nontechnical people to create the parallel programs with minimum effort.

Parallel simulation gets its name from the fact that the auditor can create a new set of application programs which process data in *parallel* with the operational processing programs. The *simulation* designation is appropriate because the program created for audit purposes performs the same processing functions as the regular application programs — but through a different means. Since computer programs will perform consistently (given identical circumstances), the auditor can derive a high degree of confidence that the same proper result will occur every time the same programs are used.

After the same files and transactions are processed by both systems, the results should be identical and directly comparable with respect to the application functions and controls selected for parallel simulation; that is, the parallel simulation technique need not reproduce applications in full. Rather, the auditor selects data and functions on the basis of their audit significance (relationship to materiality) to the application. He applies simulation techniques only to those areas.

The important characteristic of parallel simulation as an audit tool is that independent processing of relevant data takes place. The basic concept is the same as in auditing around the computer. Where the volume of transactions or the transaction trail of a system are beyond the capabilities of manual verification, general purpose audit software will mechanize the process.

The determination of whether parallel simulation is applicable to an audit depends on the nature of the application being examined. Simulation techniques are most effective when applied to application calculations, decisions, and programmed controls. Application functions which maintain and update files with transactions may also be simulated. However, confirmation or comparison techniques are often applied with less cost and more concrete findings. The internally initiated transaction, more than any other type, defies external verification techniques, as external techniques depend upon some kind of documented transaction trail.

As a further condition, the complexity or scope of the computer application should be beyond the reach of conventional, external summarized processing and balancing techniques. To illustrate, if the organization were using straight-line depreciation, it would be relatively simple for the auditor to verify balances by using summary calculations with a desk calculator. However, if depreciation were being calculated on a more complex basis, such as the sum-of-the-year's-digits or double-declining-balances, annual balance verification through manual techniques might not be practical. The auditor, then, is faced with the choice of sampling or computer recalculation. Recalculation on a computer through the use of general purpose audit software is more comprehensive and more reliable.

The choice between using parallel simulation for balance verification or for tests of internal control also depends on the quantity of transactions involved. For instance, the computer-processing demands of a depreciation account would be small enough to warrant a year-end balance approach; however, it would generally be impractical to rerun all of a company's payrolls for the entire year. So, in the case of a payroll, it is necessary to establish the reliability of the systems of internal control. Under parallel simulation, this is done by processing representative data at an interim date.

150

In audit assignments involving extensive computerized accounting operations, parallel simulation will serve as a broad, general purpose audit tool which fits conveniently into the working schedule of both the auditor and the audited organization.

Under the technique diagrammed in Figure 9-3, the audit software simulation processes transactions against file data, creating its own output files. It compares these with files generated by the actual application programs. The audit software application may include machine comparison between data produced by the actual application programs and those produced by the simulation. In such a case, the report delivered to the auditor includes only exception items.

From an auditing standpoint, the obvious benefit of this approach is that it is more thorough. The auditor is not restricted to the minimal transaction samples necessary when manual methods are employed. Therefore, since the results of parallel simulation can be confirmed through the computer, the application programs under which transactions are processed are considered validated.

Programming the parallel simulation through the use of general purpose audit software provides application simulation programs at a fraction of the cost which would be involved through conventional programming languages. This is because much of the functional housekeeping normally associated with the development of an EDP application is prefabricated with the audit software. This difference is important. The auditor using general purpose audit software does not code individual program instructions. Rather, he prepares data descriptions which build applications from the functional modules within the software as processing takes place. With this ability to operate at a functional level instead of a detailed level, an auditor can become proficient in the use of EDP audit techniques after as little as a few days of training in the use of general purpose audit software.

The computer is used directly for the performance of audit functions; therefore, the use of general purpose audit software, wherever it may be applied, usually accomplishes testing in less staff time and at a lower cost than is possible by using other techniques.

The functional relationships between computer applications and parallel simulation are represented in the flow diagram in Figure 9-3. This flowchart shows the direct parallel nature of simulation through use of general purpose audit software. As with the "live" application, the simulation software uses the actual computer master file and actual transactions which were entered into the system. The auditor must determine that the transactions processed under simulation are representative of the transactions which will be encountered for the period under audit.

PARALLEL SIMULATION PROCESS

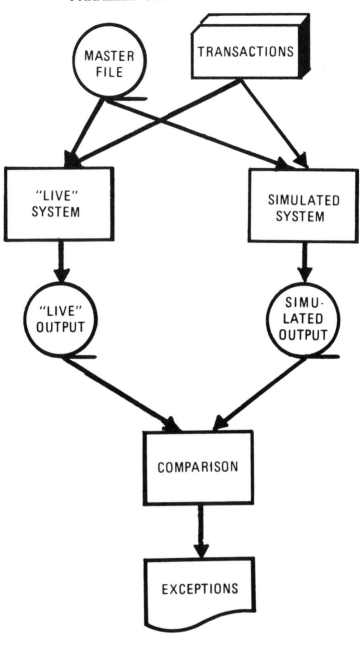

Figure 9-3

Applying Parallel Simulation Techniques

In preparing parallel simulation application through use of general purpose audit software, the auditor does the following:

DEFINES THE TEST OBJECTIVES

Problem definition from the auditor's standpoint is usually documented in an informal memo incorporated in audit working papers. The auditor describes which functions of the application are essential to the reliable operation of the application system. Three types of functions warrant verification:

- A *major processing function* such as the calculation of payroll withholding
- *Internally initiated transactions* such as automatic calculation of interest
- A *reasonableness control* function such as reporting of overdrawn checking accounts within a bank

OBTAINS DETAILED INFORMATION

The second step calls for obtaining a more detailed understanding of the application. The understanding does not need to be a comprehensive knowledge of all the logic in the computer programs but only that logic which is applied to the area of his concern and to the vast majority of situations. He should elect to omit from his parallel simulation complex logic that applies only to rare situations, and he should manually resolve any differences that are caused by this after-the-fact omission.

The detailed understanding must include:

- Accurate descriptions of records and transactions
- Meanings of codes used in the computer files
- Specific formulae or decision criteria used in the "live" application
- Number of decimal places to which calculations are carried

SPECIFIES THE LOGIC TO BE FOLLOWED

Next, the auditor specifies the logic to be followed, using logic-level flowcharts which sequence the functional operations to be performed within the simulation application. Under a system like STRATA, flowcharting for a simulation application is handled quickly with the flowchart taking as little as 30 minutes (see Figure 9-4).

CODES THE INSTRUCTIONS

Specification sheets must be developed for the functions performed within general purpose audit software. This coding technique minimizes the writing necessary by the auditor. The auditor simply enters abbreviated descriptions of the files to be processed and the functions to be performed. Figure 9-5 contains a specification sheet

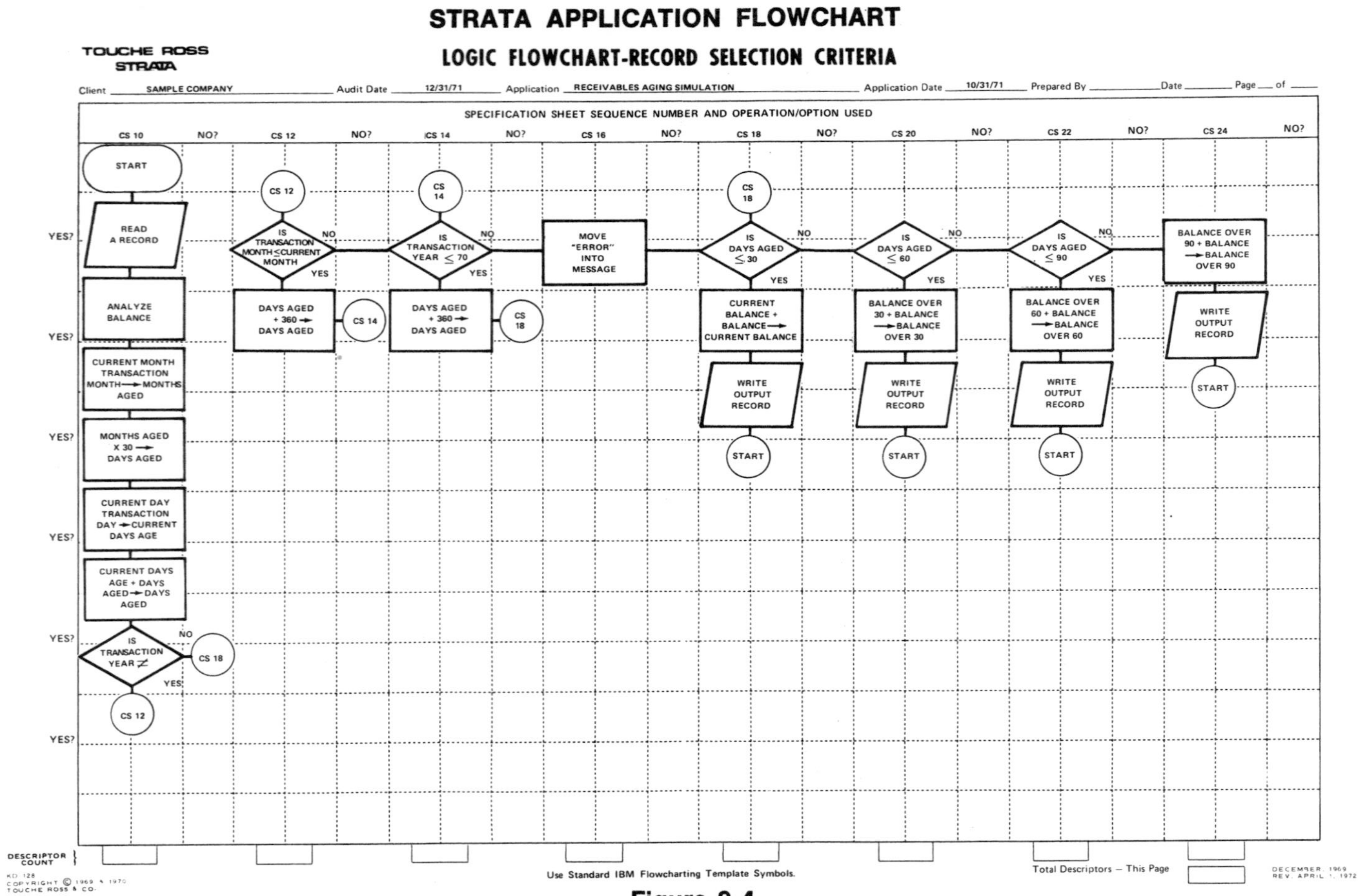
STRATA APPLICATION FLOWCHART
LOGIC FLOWCHART-RECORD SELECTION CRITERIA
TOUCHE ROSS
STRATA
Client SAMPLE COMPANY
Audit Date 12/31/71
Application RECEIVABLES AGING SIMULATION
Application Date 10/31/71
Prepared By
Date
Page of
SPECIFICATION SHEET SEQUENCE NUMBER AND OPERATION/OPTION USED
CS 10
NO?
CS 12
NO?
CS 14
NO?
CS 16
NO?
CS 18
NO?
CS 20
NO?
CS 22
NO?
CS 24
NO?
YES?
START
READ A RECORD
ANALYZE BALANCE
CURRENT MONTH TRANSACTION MONTH → MONTHS AGED
MONTHS AGED X 30 → DAYS AGED
CURRENT DAY TRANSACTION DAY → CURRENT DAYS AGE
CURRENT DAYS AGE + DAYS AGED → DAYS AGED
IS TRANSACTION YEAR ≠
NO
YES
CS 18
CS 12
IS TRANSACTION MONTH ≤ CURRENT MONTH
DAYS AGED + 360 → DAYS AGED
CS 14
IS TRANSACTION YEAR ≤ 70
MOVE "ERROR" INTO MESSAGE
IS DAYS AGED ≤ 30
CURRENT BALANCE + BALANCE → CURRENT BALANCE
WRITE OUTPUT RECORD
IS DAYS AGED ≤ 60
BALANCE OVER 30 + BALANCE → BALANCE OVER 30
IS DAYS AGED ≤ 90
BALANCE OVER 60 + BALANCE → BALANCE OVER 60
BALANCE OVER 90 + BALANCE → BALANCE OVER 90
DESCRIPTOR COUNT
KD 128
COPYRIGHT © 1969 & 1970
TOUCHE ROSS & CO.
Use Standard IBM Flowcharting Template Symbols.
Total Descriptors – This Page
DECEMBER, 1969
REV. APRIL 1, 1972

Figure 9-4

STRATA CALCULATE-STRATIFY SPECIFICATION FORM

TOUCHE ROSS
STRATA

CALCULATE-STRATIFY

SEE REVERSE FOR CONTINUATION PAGE

Sequence Number: C S 1 0

LINE NO.	FIELD A	OPERATION (1)	FIELD B	CONSTANT VALUE (3)(4) NUMERIC / ALPHA-NUMERIC	DEC. PL.	FIELD C RESULT (1)	GO TO (1)
0,5		ANL	W05				
1,0							
1,5	W33	SUB	W02			TO1	
2,0							
2,5	TO1	MUL		30	O	W35	
3,0							
3,5	W34	SUB	W03			TO2	
4,0							
4,5	TO2	ADD	W35			W35	
5,0							
5,5	W04	NE		71			CS18
6,0							
6,5							
7,0							
7,5							
8,0							
8,5							
9,0							
9,5							

CONDITIONAL OPERATIONS (1)

L - A less than B	LE - A less than or Equal to B
E - A equal to B	NE - A not equal to B
G - A greater than B	GE - A greater than or equal to B
RS - Random Selection of nn%. nn is a numeric constant from 01 to 99. For nn% of the records chosen at random, the condition is met.(3)	SC - Tests STRATA Code field of the WORK record. If equal to the two-digit Alpha-Numeric constant, the condition is met.(4)

EXIT ROUTINE — AVAILABLE IN O/S ONLY

XIT — EXTPROG3 — Allows exiting from STRATA to a user coded subroutine to act upon STRATA Work record. Enter "XIT" in Operation column and user exit member name in the constant value field.

MATHEMATICAL AND OTHER OPERATIONS (2)

ADD A + B → C MUL A × B → C

SUB A - B → C DIV A - B → C

ANL Analyze Field B
Optional — To obtain "Variance" of Field B with Analyze results, enter ANL in "Operation" column and "V" in column 17.
Available in 65K STRATA only.

MOV B → A, Moves Alpha-Numeric field B or Constant to field A.

COD Enters any two digit Alpha-Numeric Constant in the STRATA code field of the WORK record.(4)

EOP Enter EOP to stop all processing in that STRATA Pass.

GO TO OPTIONS (1)

END pass current WORK record to next STRATA function. (After Calculate/Stratify.)

READ reject current WORK record from any further STRATA function by getting the next record.

CSnn branch to page number nn.

EX CSnn
Perform steps on page nn and return. Put EX in "Operation Field" and CSnn in "Go To" field.

blank if any conditional operation fails, a blank "Go To" will cause a branch to the next page.

(1) In Conditional Operations
- if the tested condition is met the next sequential operation is performed.
- if the tested condition fails, STRATA takes "Go To" option.

(2) After performing a mathematical or other operation (except for EOP) STRATA performs the next sequential operation unless the "Go To" field is non blank.

(3) Enter Numeric Constants and Random Selection percent right justified in Constant Value field.
(4) Enter Alpha-Numeric Constants and two digit STRATA Codes left justified in Constant Value field.

KEYPUNCH THIS SIDE	REVERSE SIDE	BOTH SIDES	KEYPUNCHED BY	VERIFIED BY

Figure 9-5

for the calculate-stratify function of STRATA.

General purpose audit software may be used at a business-logic level and require comparatively little technical involvement of the auditor. The auditor will often complete all designing and coding necessary for a general purpose audit software application in a small percentage of the time required to handle the same program preparation under a conventional approach like COBOL.

OBTAINS REPRESENTATIVE FILES

Another important step is to acquire representative input master files and transactions as well as the resulting output files.

Obviously, a large set of input transactions and master record situations can be obtained directly from a live system. Care must be taken, however, to assure that the data include all of the situations that the auditor wishes to verify. In most cases this determination is readily satisfied by reviewing processing-control reports that list the quantity of transactions according to their type.

If the files for testing lack certain transaction types, the auditor has two alternative courses of action. He may "salt" the "live" files with additional transactions that he creates. This would produce a combination of parallel simulation and a test deck. Or he may accept the available files as suitably representative of the transactions which actually occur.

If certain transaction types occur rarely, verification of proper handling of these rare situations may not be necessary, since any errors would not be significant, even if processing were incorrect. Although a decision to ignore such situations must be made consciously and carefully, it is certainly valid to weigh one's audit tests toward those situations that would present the greatest potential frequency of error.

DEBUGGING THE PARALLEL SIMULATION APPLICATION

As with any programming technique, all general purpose audit software applications should be put through a trial run on the computer to identify "bugs." Debugging is facilitated under STRATA through the use of a feature which makes it possible to take a segment of the live file and to treat it as a complete file for the test purposes. Generation of separate test files is not required. During the debugging run on the computer, STRATA identifies errors or questionable items in the specifications. For each specification sheet completed by the auditor, the computer prints out an easily readable, narrative description of the processing performed and the files involved. Where errors in the data descriptions are identified during the test run, messages are also generated by the computer.

When all specification errors are identified and eliminated, the STRATA system develops its own application job stream, establishing processing sequences and application flowcharts to document the functions to be performed and the reports to be delivered. Computer time requirements are between five and ten minutes for testing STRATA specifications and generating machine instructions for the actual verification run. Successive test runs, after corrections are made, take a similar amount of time.

PROCESSING THE PARALLEL SIMULATION APPLICATION

Using general purpose audit software, the auditor is in complete control of the processing. An auditor who completes an adequate training program is capable of sitting at the console and operating the computer during the parallel simulation run. This does not mean that the auditor is an expert in operating a computer, but he does know enough to handle his own validation work independent of EDP personnel if necessary.

Time Requirements

Preparation time of the simulation process will depend on the complexity of the processes being simulated, the particular audit software or conventional language being used, and the quality of application documentation. In the experience of the authors, the preparation time for different applications, using the generalized audit software system "STRATA," may vary from 20 minutes to 100 hours. The average is less than a day. Another user of the technique who implements his simulations with COBOL finds a requirement of one-half hour to five weeks with a three-day average.

When embarking on the verification of an unfamiliar application, using parallel simulation with audit software, a reasonable minimum time requirement would be 40 hours. The information-gathering and evaluation-of-results phases require the greatest proportion of that time.

Where time requirements significantly exceed 40 hours, the reasons are usually that either the simulated functions are extremely complex or the detailed information which was gathered is incomplete or misleading. Unfortunately, this second problem is *quite common.*

The time required for actual processing depends directly on the quantity of data to be examined, the size and speed of the computer equipment being used, and the number of functions being performed.

Resolve Exceptions

The reports produced under general purpose audit software should contain all data necessary for the auditor to evaluate and to resolve apparent exceptions. To illustrate, the program might have calculated depreciation on an expense basis, whereas the auditor's simulation may compute the accumulated allowance balance. In such instances, there may be round-off differences which are not significant. These would indicate that there are no problems in the program. The simulation processing may also report items that are not true exceptions but, rather, reflections of specific types of special handling situations. These may be processed properly in accordance with the overall application but might not have been included by the auditor when the simulation program was designed.

> *Example — Employees requested a company to withhold pay in amounts in excess of legal minimums. The auditor's program tested for the normal deduction percentages without being aware of the exception cases. Such exceptions must be resolved but, obviously, do not affect internal control reliability.*
>
> *On another occasion, a STRATA simulation of a manufacturer's payroll program revealed that paychecks had actually been prepared for a number of employees whose identification codes indicated they had been laid off earlier. Resolution of this exception showed that the program, in fact, did not have a test of employee status before paychecks were generated by the computer.*

Common Problems

Detailed information which is incomplete or misleading is a result of inadequate application documentation. Program maintenance changes are often implemented without a corresponding revision of record layouts, code lists, and other essential items of application documentation. In anticipation of such discrepancies, the auditor should obtain a "dump" of the machine-readable files to the application and identify major discrepancies before further effort is wasted.

The auditor should also expect to run his simulation more than once. Experience indicates that, the first time the simulation is run, a large volume of differences generally result. Most often, this is because detailed information was provided that was incomplete or misleading, although, at other times, it is simply because the auditor spent insufficient time obtaining a clear understanding of the application.

A balance must be struck between preparation of detailed simulation logic and the volume of differences being generated due to the omission of simulation logic for unusual situations. Generally speaking, production of more than a few hundred such differences calls for revisions to the simulation logic to make it closer to the "live" application.

Skill Requirements

An auditor who uses the parallel simulation technique does not need to be a highly skilled EDP technician. However, he should be knowledgeable concerning the business significance of the application functions as well as proficient in the audit software system or conventional language used for the simulation. He should also be capable of reading record layouts, file dumps, and general application documentation and be able to communicate with EDP professionals. A facility for reading COBOL data divisions and procedures may also be useful.

The qualifications above are not particularly stringent. Only a moderate degree of technical expertise is required. This level may be reached with as little as two to three weeks of EDP audit instruction plus a general business and auditing background.

Recapitulation

To recapitulate the technique of parallel simulation, let's briefly list the steps involved:
1. Define the application functions to be verified.
2. Obtain a reasonable understanding of the processing logic for these functions.
3. Obtain and define the machine-readable inputs and outputs for the processing of a representative set of processing situations.
4. Prepare a computer program of the processing logic, using audit software or a conventional language.
5. Process the input data through the simulation application and compare the output to the output produced by the "live" application.
6. Identify differences attributable to situations and processes that you did not attempt to simulate.
7. Evaluate the consequences of the remaining discrepancies.

Points to Remember

While performing the steps above, the auditor should remain aware of the following factors:
- Application documentation often contains omissions or is actually misleading.
- Only those application functions which are both relevant to the audit objectives and which occur frequently need to be simulated.
- If the detailed logic of a particular application process is unclear or undocumented, you can usually simulate it by just using good business logic. Exceptions will be much more meaningful than if actual application logic is copied blindly.

- If the simulation produces large volumes of differences due to valid processing not included in the simulation, revise the simulation until the differences drop to a volume that can be readily resolved by hand.

CONCLUSIONS

The use of the parallel simulation technique to verify computer programs allows the verification of complex application processing in much less time than is required for any other except for the around-the-computer method. The auditor does not need to understand the processing logic comprehensively. He only needs to understand the functions with which he is specifically concerned. Often these functions can be adequately understood by simply understanding the nature of the business; that is, the auditor does not need to be overly concerned with the program logic that was used but only needs to be able to describe the logic that the user is relying on being used. Finally, the data that he processes, being from the actual system, are free from any biases that he may introduce according to his expectations of what kinds of errors "probably" occur. This combination of speed, business viewpoint, and objectivity make parallel simulation the most powerful tool available today to effectively examine the area of computer processing that is of greatest concern.

Based upon the practical experiences of the authors, parallel simulation seems to generally provide the best balance of reliability, resources, time, cost, and conclusiveness of all the alternative techniques.

10

AUDITING EDP APPLICATIONS

This chapter covers auditing of processes and controls in an application, the steps to be performed, and the role of application documentation.

OVERVIEW OF STEPS IN AN APPLICATIONS AUDIT

Steps that the auditor should follow in the audit of a computerized application are:

- Define objectives
- Obtain a basic understanding of the application
- Obtain a detailed understanding of the application
- Identify and evaluate critical controls, processes, and apparent exposures
- Design the audit procedures
- Test the critical controls, processes, and apparent exposures
- Evaluate the results of the tests and report on the results

These steps are illustrated in Figure 10-1 and are discussed in the remainder of this chapter.

If the steps above have previously been performed for an application that is currently under review again, the auditor may be able to substantially reduce his effort in gathering information, evaluating controls, and designing audit procedures. He should identify any modifications made since his last review, make any necessary changes in his evaluation and verification procedures, and emphasize testing and evaluation of results.

DEFINE OBJECTIVES

The general objective of an application audit is to verify those processes and controls necessary to make the application free from

FLOWCHART OF APPLICATION
AUDIT ACTIVITIES

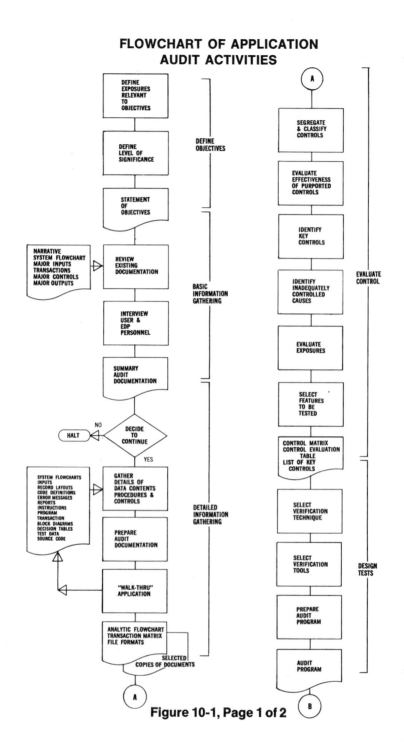

Figure 10-1, Page 1 of 2

FLOWCHART OF APPLICATION
AUDIT ACTIVITIES

Figure 10-1, Page 2 of 2

significant exposures. The specific nature of this general objective may vary by emphasizing certain exposures over others and by defining different levels of exposure as "significant."

Accordingly, a CPA's objective may emphasize accurate record keeping and appropriate accounting practices, whereas an internal auditor's may emphasize detection of fraud or limitation of costs. Furthermore, the CPA may consider 3% of net income to be "significant," whereas the internal auditor may consider ½% as "significant." Whatever the objectives and audit standards, they should be defined in advance.

OBTAINING A BASIC UNDERSTANDING OF THE APPLICATION

The auditor must obtain a general knowledge of the application from relevant application documentation and by interviewing key personnel. This general knowledge should be obtained prior to any final decision as to the scope of the audit.

A basic understanding may also be obtained through sources other than documentation and interviews. An experienced auditor may already be knowledgeable in key control practices common to the organization, within the same industry, or in similar applications in other industries. Whatever the source of information, the objective of this phase is to determine what general areas of control might be relied upon and tested.

Steps in Basic Understanding

There are generally three steps in obtaining a basic understanding:
- Review existing documentation that provides a general description of the application
- Interview responsible user and EDP personnel
- Prepare summary audit documentation of major features of the system

Depth of Basic Understanding

The depth of the basic information-gathering phase is best illustrated by typical questions that may be asked:
- What accounting entries result from the application?
- What management decisions result from the application?
- What types of inputs go into the system?
- What types of transactions are initiated within the application system?
- What major accounting, editing, and processing controls exist?
- How does this application affect the primary audit objectives?
- Where may further information be obtained to acquire a detailed understanding?

164

The source of this information will most commonly be interviews. To some extent, high-level documentation may also be suitable. Examples of such documentation might include:

- A general narrative description of the application
- A high-level system flowchart
- Copies of major input documents
- A table of transactions and affected master record fields (see Figure 10-2)
- A listing of major controls; e.g., descriptions of approvals, balancing procedures, etc.
- Copies of major output documents and reports

The main point to remember in basic information gathering is that it is intended to resolve questions as to the specific scope of examination. All efforts after the completion of this phase will be directed toward implementation of that scope. *Basic information gathering is a listening phase.* The auditor makes no evaluations of controls at this time but simply tries to learn enough to make sound judgments regarding the significant causes of exposure and controls that should be investigated further. In summary, the auditor attempts to learn enough about the application to make the initial decision as to whether or not it should be reviewed.

In some cases, the decision may be made that the application is not material to audit objectives and need not be reviewed further. Even in these cases, however, it may be wise to obtain corroborating evidence to verify that the computerized application controls do not actually impact the audit objectives and need not be reviewed.

Standard application audit questionnaires may be employed during basic information gathering. They may provide a useful framework for the general appraisal. However, their usefulness will rarely extend beyond this phase. Application systems may incorporate so many variables as to defy any conclusive evaluation based on the general inquiries provided by any standard questionnaire.

At the conclusion of this phase, the auditor must prepare working papers comprising the documentation that he has gathered, interview notes, and answers to important questions. Finally, he must declare his decision on further action and the basis for that decision.

Fulfillment of basic information gathering may satisfy the generally accepted auditing standards for CPA's with regard to proper study of existing internal control[1] if further audit procedures will *not* be reduced due to reliance on internal control. Further detail will normally be required if compliance tests are to be devised so that substantive tests may be limited.

[1]American Institute of Certified Public Accountants, *Statement on Auditing Standards No. 1*, paragraphs 320.01, .06, .50, .51, .53, .54; and *Statement on Auditing Standards No. 3 — The Effects of EDP on the Auditor's Study and Evaluation of Internal Control*, paragraphs 24-26.

MATRIX OF TRANSACTION IMPACT ON A PAYROLL MASTER FILE

Organization __ABC Company__

System __Payroll__

FISCAL YEAR ENDED 12/31/XX

T. R. & CO.
SCHEDULE _IC-36_
PREPARED BY _WS_ DATE _9/16/XX_
APPROVED BY _AB_ _0/6/XX_

P/R MASTER FIELD NAMES / TRANSACTIONS AFFECTING MASTER FILE Code Description	Y–T–D GROSS	CLOCK NO.	REG. HOURS	O.T. HOURS	PAY RATE	ADDRESS
500 - Labor - - Time Cards	No Affect	Match	Algebraic Add	Algebraic Add	No Affect	No Affect
510 - Adjustment Hours (Increase)	No Affect	Match	Add	Add	No Affect	No Affect
511 - Adjustment Hours (Decrease)	No Affect	Match	Subtract	Subtract	No Affect	No Affect
550 - Pay Rate Change	No Affect	Match	No Affect	No Affect	Replace	No Affect
590 - Address Change	No Affect	Match	No Affect	No Affect	No Affect	Replace

Figure 10-2

166

OBTAINING A DETAILED UNDERSTANDING
OF THE APPLICATION

Once the auditor makes the preliminary decision that the application must be reviewed in depth, he must obtain a more detailed understanding. This detailed understanding will concentrate on the specific controls and procedures that are directly relevant to the audit objectives. Procedures and controls that are not relevant may be noted but not reviewed in depth.

The primary source of this detailed understanding is application documentation. Documentation of the procedures and decision rules of computer application should be of such a quality that is clear and meaningful to a knowledgeable user of the system. One obvious value of this is that an auditor will also be able to make a meaningful evaluation of the application standards.

The auditor will encounter a tremendous variety of quality in application documentation he attempts to use. At one extreme, it may be so lavish that the auditor is swamped with detail. At the other extreme, the auditor may find there is virtually nothing available that is relevant to his concerns.

We will subsequently discuss, in Section III, the content and format of good systems documentation. Realistically, however, the auditor must be prepared to deal with documentation that is substantially different from the recommended quality. Accordingly, in this chapter, we will approach the problem according to what information the auditor must obtain, where he might obtain it, and what he should do if it is not available from the anticipated source.

Elements of Detailed Information

The major elements of detailed information that the auditor must gather are:
- Data contents
- Procedures
- Controls

Data contents are the most important element of information because all procedures and controls, whether actually implemented or desirable, are first dependent upon the nature of the data that are available to work with.

All of the *procedures* to which the data are subjected, both manual and programmed, comprise the business functions of the application system. These must be understood in detail in order to judge whether they are appropriate to the circumstances, efficient, and amenable to control.

The *controls* over the application will be subtly integrated with the procedures in the processing stream. They may be implemented manually or via computer programs. Controls may differ from procedures only in their purpose. While one mechanical calculation may be fundamental to the purpose of the application, a similar mechanical calculation may be primarily for purposes of control.

Example — A calculation of the number of days lapsed since a date may be required to calculate interest accumulated, or the same calculation of days may identify delinquent accounts.

While these three elements may sound simple in concept, their acquisition can be quite challenging.

Where the Auditor May Obtain Information

The information gathered must be selected and digested to facilitate the process of evaluation. Copies of certain types of application documentation may prove useful and may be copied for subsequent study and reference. Examples of such documents include:

- A *detailed system flowchart* of the computerized phases of the application
- A *detailed flowchart or* narrative description *of the paperwork flow* in the manual phases of the application
- Completed example copies of *each input document* used in the application
- *Record layouts of all* computer master files and transaction files
- Listings or *tables defining the codes* that are used in the records
- A copy of *all* of the *error messages* produced by input and processing edits of the application
- A copy of the first and last page of *all exception and production reports*

Detailed information gathering does not mean the reproduction of every item of application documentation with an office copier. A complete set of application documentation may readily fill a drawer of a file cabinet, and a large application system may even fill the entire cabinet. The auditor gathering detailed information should not be attempting to pass a test of sheer weight.

Other documentation will be found in addition to the items above but need not normally be reproduced by the auditor. Rather, he should study such documentation and extract those portions which are needed. If subsequent questions arise, he can always go back and reexamine the appropriate source.

The auditor need not study each item of documentation available. He need only examine those portions required to identify and to evaluate the processes and controls that are relevant to his audit objectives. The level of detail that he must acquire in this process is a matter of judgment.

The same information may be available with differing degrees of ease from various forms of documentation. These forms will be described below. Keep in mind, however, that he should obtain the necessary information from the *most convenient, reliable source.*

User Policy and Procedures Manuals

Hopefully, many of the major elements of information that the auditor will require may be available in a single *User Policy and Procedures Manual*. This manual may also be called the *User's Manual* or *Specifications Manual*. It is a document intended to communicate with and to guide users. Its contents usually include statements of systems objectives and of company or departmental policies for the operation of the system. The statements in the manual should have been developed and/or agreed to by users with regard to the scope and purpose of the application and the results to be realized.

A well-constructed, current user's manual is itself a strong internal control in that it helps to train users to prepare and to handle input transactions and error correction transactions properly. A typical user's manual may contain:

- A narrative description of the system
- A narrative or list describing major control features
- An overall, summary-level system flowchart
- A detailed flowchart of all clerical processes
- A copy of each input document completed as an example together with instructions for preparation
- A list of approvals required on each input document
- A copy of any batch control forms or other transmittal forms used together with instructions on their preparation and reconciliation to input batch edit reports
- A listing of computerized input and processing edits performed, the error messages that result therefrom, and instructions for correcting, resubmitting, and balancing the resubmitted items
- A copy of each edit report, working document, and other report produced by the system with a description of its purpose, the number of copies, and distribution thereof, including instructions for balancing output to original input
- A list of the retention periods for each input source document and output

As seen from the list above, many of the key elements of documentation of interest to the auditor should be readily available in a well-constructed user's manual. Accordingly, this should be one of the first items that the auditor requests.

Computer Run Book

Detailed documentation regarding the computerized phases of processing may be consolidated within one or more documents known as *Computer Run Book, Application Run Book,* or *Application Manual*. This should complement the *User Policy and Procedures Manual* by providing all information necessary for the EDP staff to operate, maintain, and troubleshoot the application.

Again, a well-constructed and current computer run book provides important control for guiding and instructing EDP personnel. A typical run book may contain:

- A narrative description of the system
- A summary-level flowchart
- Detailed computer system flowcharts
- Detailed specifications for individual programs
- Logic block diagrams and decision tables for single programs or subroutines
- Instructions for conversion of inputs from manual documents to machine-readable media
- Machine-readable record formats
- Documentation and approvals for program revisions
- Test-data specifications
- Source-code listings
- Interruption/recovery instructions
- Operating instructions

Descriptions of Documentation to Be Copied and Retained
COMPUTER SYSTEM FLOWCHART

Separate system flowcharts are commonly developed for the manual and computerized phases of processing. While we disagree with this practice (see further discussions in Section III), the fact remains that it occurs.

A computer system flowchart usually starts with the submission of documents for keypunch or other form of data conversion and ends with the distribution of computer-produced reports. It will usually follow standard flowcharting conventions prescribed by the International Organization for Standardization. These will show single blocks for individual computer programs (also known as "passes," "runs," or "job steps") and the input and output media. The descriptions of processing will be quite brief, and there will be no detail as to the contents of files (or data sets) directly on the flowchart.

PAPERWORK FLOWCHARTS

Paperwork flow documentation should show the handling and transmission of each document or form used within manual procedures. Usually, this documentation is handled best on a schematic basis with flowcharts using standard symbols to represent conditions and functions of processing. Such documentation should show each individual processing step, identifying documents or forms, the files in which they are included, the actions taken, the decisions made, the organization responsible, and so on. In addition, there should be short, associated phrases describing activities or status such as "price verified," "invoices extended," and so on.

In addition, paperwork flow documentation should explicitly show all batch controls applied to the documents processed.

From an auditing standpoint, elaborate sets of flowcharting symbols need not be applied rigorously. Clarity is the most important consideration. Standard symbols frequently facilitate understanding and minimize the requirement for narrative.

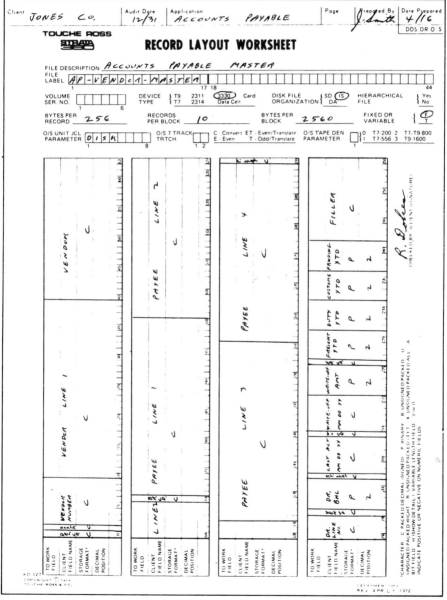

Figure 10-3

EXAMPLES OF EACH INPUT DOCUMENT

Audit documentation should include samples of significant forms used in the application. These should be complete with typical entries and cross-referenced against a set of notes describing field content, code interpretations, data sources, entry and edit procedures, and other elements. Such annotation or cross-referencing will normally have to be prepared by the auditor as it seldom exists in typical application documentation.

Control features built into forms should be described in greater depth than routine fields. Furthermore, any limits should be specifically described.

RECORD LAYOUTS

File documentation should include definitions of all files, records, and data fields. This should include header and trailer records and any summary control records. Normally, this information is acquired from a record-layout form, as illustrated in Figure 10-3. If this is not available nor current, the same information may be readily obtained from source-language listings such as in the data division of a COBOL program (see Figure 10-4).

A thorough understanding of each field on the record layout is essential to the auditor's accomplishing his review objectives completely. An annotated record layout is often a focal point of audit documentation.

TABLES DEFINING CODES

By itself, a record layout may often be useless without a supplementary document interpreting various codes stored within computer records. The use of codes to indicate status, classification, or record type is practically universal.

ERROR MESSAGES

Frequently, the only comprehensive documentation of programmed edit and reasonableness tests is a listing of the messages produced along with associated clerical instructions regarding resolution and correction.

If this is not available, the next best source may simply be copies of actual exception reports. While the actual reports will probably not provide a complete list, they should at least disclose the most common messages.

EXCEPTION AND PRODUCTION REPORTS

The auditor should obtain a copy of the first and last page of all reports. He should also determine the number of copies that are produced and to whom the reports are distributed.

FILE DESCRIPTION FOR DATA DIVISION OF AN APPLICATION PROGRAM WRITTEN FOR A COBOL COMPILER

COBOL DATA DIVISION

Line	Ref	Level	Field Description	Picture	Code
00112	C 01802	05	VM – DELETE – CODE	PICTURE X.	ALL 10001
00113	C 01803	05	VM – KEY.		ALL 10002
00114	C 01804		09 VM – SYSTEM	PICTURE 9.	ALL 10003
00115	C 01805		09 VM – VENDOR – NO	PICTURE 9(8).	ALL 10004
00116	C		09 VM – VENDOR – NO – R REDEFINES VM – VENDOR – NO	PICTURE X(8).	ALL 10005
00117	C				ALL 10006
00118	C	05	VM – VENDOR – LINE OCCURS 2 TIMES.		ALL 10007
00119	C 01807		09 VM – VENDOR – LINE	PICTURE X(30).	ALL 10008
00120	C 01808	05	VM – BROKER – CODE	PICTURE X.	ALL 10009
00121	C 01809	05	VM – PAYEE – LINE OCCURS 4 TIMES.		ALL 10010
00122	C 01810		09 VM – PAYEE – LINE	PICTURE X(30).	ALL 10011
00123	C 01811	05	VM – PAY – STATUS	PICTURE X.	ALL 10012
00124	C 01812	05	VM – DEBIT – LINE – NO	PICTURE 9(4).	ALL 10013
00125	C 01813	05	VM – VENDOR – PAY – CODE	PICTURE X.	ALL 10014
00126	C 01814	05	VM – DEBIT – BAL	PICTURE S9(7)V99 COMPUTATIONAL – 3.	ALL 10015
00127	C 01815	05	VM – STATEMENT – STATUS	PICTURE X.	ALL 10016
00128	C 01816	05	VM – LAST – ACT – DATE	PICTURE X(6).	ALL 10017
00129	C 01817	05	VM – LAST – ACT – DATE – R REDEFINES VM – LAST – ACT – DATE.		ALL 10018
00130	C 01818		09 VM – LAST – ACT – MO	PICTURE 99.	ALL 10019
00131	C 01819		09 VM – LAST – ACT – DY	PICTURE 99.	ALL 10020
00132	C 01820		09 VM – LAST – ACT – YR	PICTURE 99.	ALL 10021
00133	C 01821	05	VM – WRITE – OFFS.		ALL 10022
00134	C 01822		09 VM – WRITE – OFF – CODE	PICTURE X.	ALL 10023
00135	C 01823		09 VM – WRITE – OFF – DATE	PICTURE X(6).	ALL 10024
00136	C 01824		09 VM – WRITE – OFF – DATE – R REDEFINES VM – WRITE – OFF – DATE.		ALL 10025
00137	C 01901		13 VM – WRITE – OFF – MO	PICTURE 99.	ALL 10026
00138	C 01902		13 VM – WRITE – OFF – DY	PICTURE 99.	ALL 10027
00139	C 01903		13 VM – WRITE – OFF – YR	PICTURE 99.	ALL 10028
00140	C 019031		09 VM – WRITE – OFF – AMT PICTURE – S9(7)V99 COMPUTATIONAL-3.		ALL 10029
00141	C 01904	05	VM – ERROR – CODE	PICTURE X.	ALL 10030
00142	C 01905	05	VM – FREIGHT – YTD	PICTURE S9(7)V99 COMPUTATIONAL – 3.	ALL 10031
00143	C 01906	05	VM – DUTY – YTD	PICTURE S9(7)V99 COMPUTATIONAL – 3.	ALL 10032
00144	C 01907	05	VM – CUSTOMS – YTD	PICTURE S9(7)V99 COMPUTATIONAL – 3.	ALL 10033
00145	C 01908	05	VM – FORWARD – YTD	PICTURE S9(7)V99 COMPUTATIONAL – 3.	ALL 10034
00146	C 01909	05	FILLER	PICTURE X(14).	ALL 10035

Figure 10-4

Additional Documentation Not to Be Copied

Numerous additional items of documentation will normally be available. These should not normally be copied and incorporated into the working papers because the items are more detailed than the auditor needs or are simply too bulky. Rather, such documents should be reviewed on site and notes retained of important features. Common examples of such documentation include:

- Clerical instructions
- Individual program specifications
- Detailed input-transaction descriptions
- Descriptions of file maintenance transactions
- Description of EDP control group procedures
- Operator instructions
- Recovery instructions
- Batch control and transmittal procedures
- Document retention policies
- Logic block diagrams and decision tables
- Data conversion instructions
- Program revisions
- Test-data specifications
- Source-language listings

CLERICAL INSTRUCTIONS

Clerical instructions are the step-by-step, written directions on handling, evaluating, processing, or controlling documents or operations in the manual portions of EDP systems. Clerical instructions are illustrated in the discussion of standards in chapter 5. Any format is satisfactory, however, which clearly identifies job positions and describes each processing step or decision rule in the handling of forms or documents.

From the user's standpoint, the greatest value of clerical instructions is in the continuity and consistency of work performance. Clerical turnover is to be expected. Given instructions clearly written for qualified personnel to follow, control and quality can be maintained despite personnel changes.

For the auditor, clerical instructions provide a basis for evaluating the control designed into a system and for establishing tests to determine the extent to which specified controls are actually being applied.

The auditor should consistently be on the alert for instances where documentation of manual procedures does not exist. Where such situations are found, the auditor should attempt to immediately evaluate the exposures they create. For example, a missing code list may mean improper record coding, while a lack of edit descriptions or error list may mean that improperly corrected or uncorrected errors can enter the system, etc.

174

PROGRAM SPECIFICATIONS

A description of each individual computer program should be provided that describes the input files, the processes and controls that are performed, and the outputs that are produced.

INPUT TRANSACTION DESCRIPTIONS

The auditor needs to obtain descriptions of all input transactions having audit significance. This should include the type of document, initiator, codes, approval methods, methods of submission or transmission, frequency of submission, cutoff features, batching practices, and review procedures.

DESCRIPTIONS OF FILE MAINTENANCE TRANSACTIONS

The auditor must obtain a complete understanding of how master files are maintained. Listings of master file transactions and related transaction codes, together with forms related to such transactions and approvals and control procedures exercised over such transactions, should be obtained and reviewed.

DESCRIPTION OF EDP CONTROL GROUP PROCEDURES

A complete and comprehensive description of EDP control-group procedures is important to the audit of an application because the activities of the EDP control group are particularly significant. *Controls applied by this group primarily cover transmittals and balances.* They usually relate only to the computerized portion of processing within the application and seldom to the full processing cycle.

OPERATOR INSTRUCTIONS

Operator instructions are the counterpart to clerical instructions that are used by the computer operating personnel. They provide all necessary information for the operations of the programs in the application system but should omit other detailed information regarding input formats and processing logic that could conceivably compromise internal controls.

Operator instructions should normally contain an abundance of technical detail of little interest to the auditor. Examples of such information are job control language details, form alignment instructions, etc. The major information that will be of interest to the auditor will be any necessary operator responses to program options, any parameter cards that must be provided by the operator, and, most important, the procedures for recovery from machine or program malfunctions.

RECOVERY INSTRUCTIONS

Specific instructions should exist explaining the procedures and controls over recovery from minor and major processing interruptions. Normally, minor interruptions will be covered in the operator instructions to the extent that the procedures may be implemented quickly by the operator. Serious problems, such as the erasure or destruction of a critical file, should not be left to the operator to resolve. Additional recovery instructions should be maintained by the operations manager to assure the proper reconstruction and restart after an interruption.

BATCH CONTROL AND TRANSMITTAL PROCEDURES

The transmittal and balancing of input batches will involve users, data conversion personnel, and the EDP control group. Comprehensive instructions should be available and used by all involved parties so that everyone understands how responsibilities are allocated and coordinated.

DOCUMENT RETENTION POLICIES

Clear-cut procedures must be established and documented with regard to the disposition of original input documents, master and transaction files, and reports distributed to users. These policies should be formulated by top management after consideration of statutory requirements from taxing and regulatory authorities as well as business needs. The procedures must be incorporated into clerical instructions, operator instructions, and the procedures of the control group.

LOGIC BLOCK DIAGRAMS AND DECISION TABLES

Detailed flowcharts of program logic or decision tables may be incorporated in detailed computer program documentation. Experience clearly demonstrates, however, that manually drawn flowcharts are rarely revised for program modifications.

Decision tables provide logic rules in a more summary fashion but too often are not kept current. The auditor should view such documentation with skepticism, although his needs often do not demand use of such detailed documentation.

If information in such detail must be acquired by the auditor, he might have more confidence in the information he is obtaining if flowchart generator software were used to produce a detailed flowchart from the most current version of the source-language instructions (also see chapter 8).

DATA CONVERSION INSTRUCTIONS

The personnel in the Data Conversion Department (keypunch), key to tape, or key to disc) should maintain current instructions for the preparation of machine-readable inputs. Employee turnover in such departments tends to be fairly high, and such documentation is essential to properly instruct new employees.

Information of interest to the auditor in such documentation will generally be limited to the specifications for keystroke verification. Most verifiers have the capacity to skip fields selectively within a record being prepared. However, the punched card or other output may carry a designation that it has been verified with no indication that such verification was only partial.

PROGRAM REVISIONS

Modifications to operational applications is a highly error-prone activity. Procedures to control this activity will be discussed further in Section III. Within the application documentation, however, the auditor must be concerned with the nature of maintenance changes that have occurred since his last full review of the application.

The documentation supporting these changes may vary widely according to the extent of the change. At a minimum, however, there should be a brief narrative description of the modification with approvals of users and EDP management. There should also be an indication of the nature and results of the testing conducted of the system after the modification.

TEST-DATA SPECIFICATIONS

Each application, during development and after modifications, should be subjected to an extensive systems test as a part of sound system development controls. This phase of development will be discussed extensively in Section III. As a part of each application's documentation, however, there should be the specifications for test data and the location of where test data were retained.

The auditor may be interested in reviewing the test data for comprehensive situations, values, and combinations.

SOURCE-LANGUAGE LISTINGS

One of the few reliable sources for detailed information is the source-language listing. This is a printed list of the computer instructions at the source-language level. Although interpretation of these listings requires technical knowledge, high-level languages such as COBOL are often reasonably intelligible even to the layman.

The original developers of COBOL intended it to be self-documenting. The most common failure in attempts at self-documentation is a lack of descriptiveness in the data names. This is the method by which COBOL identifies fields within records. Because descriptive names are quite tedious to write out repeatedly, many programmers customarily abbreviate the names so that they are completely cryptic to the uninformed reader. However, if the data names are understood, the normal COBOL coding is a relatively clear English-language narrative. An example of a COBOL code data division is found in Figure 10-4.

Preference in Obtaining Information

File information is most readily obtained from record layouts. These should be accompanied by explanations of codes that are used. The only other source is usually the program source-language listings.

Processing should be described by one or more of the following sources listed in order of preference:

- Tables of transactions and codes
- Detailed programmed descriptions
- Decision tables
- Logic flowcharts
- Program source listings

Control descriptions may be obtained from the following documents listed again in order of preference:

- Detailed program descriptions
- Detailed systems flowcharts
- Descriptions of controls
- Descriptions of EDP control group procedures
- Listings of error and exception messages
- Copies of exception reports
- Program source-language listings

Note that the program source-language listings are a consistent alternative for obtaining information but are the least preferred. Program listings are usually the most detailed and, therefore, difficult to interpret. On the other hand, they are the most likely form of documentation to exist and be up to date.

What to Do When Documentation Is Inadequate

Upon attempting to obtain one or more of the sources of information listed previously, the auditor may find that it is inadequate in content, obviously out of date, or not even in existence. While he should always be able to obtain the source-language listings for the numerous programs comprising the application, they may be so time-consuming and difficult to interpret that it would be easier to create the missing elements of documentation from other sources.

The auditor may find that the people working with the system have created notes, descriptions, etc., for themselves to tell how the phase of the system works. The auditor may request the notes that users and others might possess. In this manner, he may often be able to fill in many of the otherwise undocumented gaps in the system.

If all else fails, the auditor may simply make assumptions as to how things work based upon usual business practices. He certainly can't rely on such assumptions, but he may be able to devise reasonable compliance tests on this basis. Ultimate reliance, of course, will depend on the results of the compliance tests.

The auditor must keep his audit objectives firmly in mind throughout this information-gathering phase. There will always be some aspects of information that the auditor does not find to be clearly documented in materials that are readily available. Before he pursues this information further, he must ask himself whether its lack will really hinder his evaluation of the system. Sometimes it is better to stop gathering information and start evaluating. Further documentation can always be sought when the auditor discovers a point in his evaluation that cannot be resolved. *Remember that the objective of information gathering is to facilitate the evaluation.* Excessive information gathering only delays the evaluation and obscures the primary issues.

Audit Documentation and Detailed Information Gathering

In completing his detailed information gathering, the auditor should document those aspects, and only those, which are relevant to his audit objectives. This documentation package should take the form of:

- A summary-level analytic audit flowchart which covers all *manual and computerized* phases of the system that are relevant to the audit objectives. An analytic audit flowchart is the first level of audit documentation. All other documentation is support to the analytic audit flowchart and should be cross-referenced to it. This flowchart may require several pages. If this becomes too bulky, two levels of analytic flowchart may be utilized: a single-page overview and a multipage detailed flowchart.
- A matrix of transactions and their effect on records, if not already available. This should be cross-referenced to the analytic audit flowchart.
- The best available descriptions of files, inputs, outputs, and processing. This will be application documentation previously obtained which is to be cross-referenced to the point of input, creation of the file, output, point of processing, etc., on the analytic flowcharts.

The auditor-generated papers and company-generated papers that are copied and retained must be prepared and selected with a clear objective in mind. The evaluation that must take place will require successive levels of summarization and classification. The evaluation process is digestive in nature. Too much bulk will probably hinder it.

This package is, however, not the end. The auditor must still verify that his understanding of the system is correct and that it works as described. Later, the auditor must evaluate whether the controls are adequate.

Verify the Understanding of the Application

In concluding the detailed information-gathering phase, the auditor may interview personnel, observe processing, inquire into exceptions to prescribed controls and procedures, and track a limited number of transactions through the system. This final approach is often called a "walk through" of transactions from the point of origination in the user's area through all phases of manual and computerized processing until completion and filing.

There are two key steps in verifying the understanding of the application:

- Verifying that the audit documentation collected and created reflects the system as described by users and others
- Verifying that the system does in fact work generally as described

Because many business systems are not adequately documented, a *significant* proportion of the application's documentation may have to be created or supplemented by the auditor from his interviews with users, supervisory personnel, management, data processing personnel, etc. Because interviewing does not always lead to completely accurate descriptions the first time, it is likely that the auditor's understanding of the system will not be correct the first time through. Any systems descriptions created by the auditor from interviews and sketchy documentation should be reviewed with the appropriate personnel *before* the auditor attempts to determine if the system works as described.

The same is true of the auditor's analytic audit flowchart. Experience shows that it is probably best to make a rough draft of this flowchart first and to develop a list of questions concerning apparent gaps in the flowchart. The rough draft and the questions should then be reviewed with users and other appropriate personnel to obtain the information necessary to finalize the draft of the analytic flowchart which *reflects the system as described* in interviews and in existing documentation.

When the auditor is satisfied with his draft of the analytic audit flowchart, his next step is to test briefly its accuracy and completeness as to *how the system actually works.* He does this by "walking through" the manual portions of the system and observing a limited number of examples of:

- Transaction working documents which were filled out
- Control logs or registers
- Other documentation available to establish that the flowchart represents the application accurately and that the auditor understands the processing which takes place

The auditor may occasionally find it desirable to observe actual computer processing of the application. He would generally do this only when he has reason to believe that existing application documentation may be either out of date or incomplete. Normally, however, observation of computer processing for flow-diagram verification is not necessary because the computer portions of applications are more formally designed and because considerably more effort is needed to change computer processing than to alter manual procedures.

IDENTIFY AND EVALUATE CRITICAL CONTROLS AND PROCESSES AND APPARENT EXPOSURES

In this step, the data gathered in basic and detailed information gathering are utilized to reach a conclusion with regard to the general quality of controls and the significance of particular controls. Evaluation of control strengths and weaknesses is a highly subjective process. No pat formula or procedures exist to give the answers or even to make it easy. This is the process which most requires professional skills of the auditor. Here the auditor must answer the following questions:

- Does the system appear to provide reliable results?
- Which controls should the auditor verify to substantiate his reliance?
- What investigations should be made of apparent weaknesses?

Evaluation Methodology

The procedures that we have described to this point have been consistent in both the general approach and in the specific techniques with numerous pronouncements in auditing literature. At this particular point, however, typical auditing literature indicates simply that the "auditor evaluates the controls" without elaborating much further.

As a matter of fact, the auditor customarily studies the detailed information that was gathered and then intuitively leaps to a conclusion. Such intuition is largely dependent upon the skills and experience of the auditor. The quality of the decision becomes quite suspect when the application system is sophisticated or unique.

Review of such conclusions may be approached in two ways. A reviewer may simply accept the judgment of the auditor, or he may restudy the detailed information gathered and reach his own independent conclusion. The first of these approaches requires a substantial amount of faith, and the second requires a substantial amount of time. Often neither approach is suitable or justifiable in the circumstances.

We believe that a third approach is feasible. The process of evaluating controls *can be* made into a formal, reviewable process supported by documentation. The steps in this process are as follows:

- Segregate and classify controls and activities subject to control.
- Subjectively quantify the effectiveness of purported controls over the various causes of exposure.
- Identify one or more key controls that should effectively act upon each of the potential causes of exposure.
- Identify those causes of exposure over which sufficient controls do not appear to exist.
- Subjectively quantify the business exposures that would result from an undetected occurrence of causes of exposure that lack adequate controls.
- Select application features to be tested.

On the basis of this selection, the auditor may devise appropriate auditing procedures.

Segregate and Classify Controls and Activities Subject to Control

As described previously in chapter 8, an application control matrix is a useful tool for distinguishing between the characteristics that constitute controls and the activities that are subject to controls and for classifying the controls. This tool should be utilized upon the completion of detailed information gathering as the first step in the evaluation of controls. It documents the controls that are supposed to exist in the application according to explanations from users and as determined by the documentation. One or more matrices may be prepared at both the level of the analytic flowchart and the matrix of transactions and effects. However, the preparation of an application control matrix is not, itself, an especially effective tool for the actual evaluation. Rather, it is a simple method by which controls can be identified and classified for meaningful, subjective analysis later.

Some preliminary impressions of serious omissions or redundant controls might be identified from the matrix and save time later. Specific controls may be related to specific activities subject to controls. A summary of these relationships appears in Figure 10-5. However, suitable compensating controls may well fall within a different control classification. This relationship is not readily apparent from a control matrix.

The controls exercised over each activity should be briefly reviewed for obvious omissions. To accomplish this, a template of Figure 10-5 may be used or a copy of the figure folded to align with the control matrix of the application under examination. The absence of an appropriate control does not necessarily indicate a weakness. It only raises a question of whether some information was omitted or whether an adequate compensating control will be identified later.

SUMMARY OF RELATIONSHIPS BETWEEN CONTROLS AND ACTIVITIES SUBJECT TO CONTROL

ACTIVITIES SUBJECT TO CONTROL — TRANSACTION/PROCESS

CHARACTERISTICS WHICH CONSTITUTE CONTROLS

CONTROL FEATURE	INITIATE	RECORD	TRANSCRIBE	CODE	TRANSMIT	COMPARE	CALCULATE	UPDATE	FILE MAINTENANCE	SUMMARIZE	SORT	REPORT	DISTRIBUTE	INQUIRE	WORKING DOCUMENT	REFERENCE REPORT	STORE
PREVENTIVE CONTROLS																	
Definition of responsibilities	✓	✓	✓	✓	✓	✓	✓	✓	✓	✓	✓	✓	✓	✓	✓	✓	
Reliability of personnel	✓	✓	✓	✓	✓	✓	✓	✓	✓	✓	✓	✓	✓	✓	✓	✓	
Training of personnel	✓	✓	✓	✓	✓	✓	✓	✓	✓	✓	✓	✓			✓	✓	✓
Competence of personnel	✓	✓		✓		✓	✓	✓	✓	✓		✓			✓	✓	✓
Mechanization	✓	✓	✓		✓	✓	✓	✓	✓		✓				✓	✓	✓
Segregation of duties	✓	✓						✓	✓			✓	✓	✓	✓	✓	
Rotation of duties	✓	✓						✓	✓			✓	✓	✓	✓	✓	
Standardization	✓	✓	✓	✓	✓	✓	✓	✓		✓	✓	✓		✓	✓	✓	
Authorization	✓							✓						✓	✓	✓	
Secure custody		✓	✓					✓	✓			✓	✓	✓	✓	✓	
Dual access/dual controls		✓						✓	✓				✓	✓	✓	✓	
Forms design		✓		✓								✓			✓	✓	
Prenumbered forms		✓		✓								✓			✓	✓	
Preprinted forms		✓		✓											✓	✓	
Simultaneous preparation		✓	✓												✓	✓	
Turnaround document	✓	✓		✓													
Drum Card			✓														
Endorsement		✓	✓		✓										✓		✓
Cancellation		✓	✓												✓		
Documentation	✓			✓	✓	✓	✓	✓	✓	✓	✓			✓	✓	✓	✓
Exception input	✓																
Default option	✓													✓			
Passwords	✓						✓	✓						✓			
DETECTIVE CONTROLS																	
Anticipation	✓	✓			✓							✓			✓		✓
Transmittal documents					✓							✓			✓	✓	✓
Batch serial numbers		✓			✓										✓	✓	✓
Control register															✓	✓	✓
Amount control total		✓	✓		✓			✓	✓						✓	✓	✓
Document control count		✓	✓		✓										✓	✓	✓
Line control count		✓	✓		✓										✓	✓	✓
Hash total		✓	✓		✓										✓	✓	✓
Batch totals					✓										✓	✓	✓
Batch balancing					✓										✓	✓	✓
Visual verification		✓	✓	✓	✓							✓			✓	✓	
Sequence checking							✓	✓	✓								
Overflow checks						✓											
Format		✓	✓	✓	✓												
Completeness check		✓	✓	✓	✓									✓			
Check digits		✓	✓	✓	✓												
Reasonableness		✓	✓		✓	✓	✓										
Limit check		✓			✓	✓	✓										
Validity check		✓	✓	✓	✓		✓	✓									
Read-back		✓			✓												
Dating		✓				✓		✓	✓					✓	✓	✓	
Expiration	✓	✓														✓	
Keystroke verification			✓														
Approval	✓													✓			
Run-to-run totals		✓	✓		✓		✓	✓	✓	✓	✓			✓	✓	✓	
Balancing	✓	✓	✓		✓	✓	✓	✓	✓	✓	✓			✓	✓	✓	
Reconciliation	✓	✓	✓	✓	✓	✓		✓						✓	✓	✓	
Aging	✓	✓	✓		✓	✓	✓	✓							✓	✓	
Suspense file	✓	✓	✓		✓	✓		✓							✓	✓	
Matching	✓	✓	✓	✓	✓	✓		✓						✓		✓	
Suspense account										✓						✓	
Clearing account										✓						✓	
Tickler file							✓	✓								✓	
Periodic audit		✓				✓	✓	✓				✓				✓	
Redundant processing			✓		✓		✓										
Summary processing							✓										
Labeling															✓	✓	
Trailer label							✓	✓	✓	✓							
CORRECTIVE CONTROLS																	
Discrepancy reports	✓	✓	✓	✓	✓	✓	✓	✓	✓	✓	✓	✓	✓	✓	✓	✓	
Transaction trail		✓	✓	✓	✓	✓	✓	✓	✓	✓	✓	✓	✓	✓	✓	✓	
Error source statistics	✓	✓	✓	✓	✓	✓	✓	✓	✓			✓	✓	✓	✓	✓	
Automatic error correction		✓		✓													
Upstream resubmission		✓		✓		✓	✓	✓							✓	✓	
Backup and recovery		✓						✓	✓								

Figure 10-5

Quantify Effective Control over Causes of Exposure

Upon completing the classification of controls, the control matrix can be used to develop a preliminary application control evaluation table. An application control evaluation table relates the exposures and causes of control as previously discussed in chapter 6 (see Figure 6-5) with the controls and causes of exposure discussed in chapter 7 (see Figure 7-2). An example of such a combined table is shown in Figure 10-6.

Using his knowledge gathered regarding the application system in conjunction with the completed control matrix, the auditor now proceeds to evaluate the effectiveness of each control classification over each cause of exposure which is of concern in the specific circumstances. If a particular cause is not applicable, the entire column on the table may be crossed out.

Example — The exposures and controls relating to internally initiated transactions would not apply if no such situation were a part of the particular application system.

If the specific controls within a particular classification are more or less effective than the typical situation, the numeric designation that applies to a typical situation should be altered.

Example — Visual verification of input media for missing data would not be considered even moderately reliable (a score of two) if the inputs were composed of massive volumes of small amounts. Humans would tire very quickly and become inattentive if required to visually scan masses of such data. A more appropriate rating would be one or zero.

Identify Key Controls

As explained previously in chapter 4, the most important controls are the detective type. These may measure the effectiveness of preventive controls and also exercise control over error corrections. Accordingly, the auditor should first review the detective controls on a control evaluation table as the most likely classification of controls which should be relied upon.

At the same time, and again as previously discussed in chapter 4, detective controls are not complete unless adequate provision is made for correction. Accordingly, the second most significant area for control evaluation is the corrective controls.

Lastly, some preventive controls over particular causes may be effective enough and sufficiently susceptible to testing to be reliable. Furthermore, the preventive controls will normally be the most important in recommending improvement since they are the easiest to implement and are essential if exceptions are to be kept to a level that can be effectively corrected.

APPLICATION CONTROL EVALUATION TABLE

APPLICATION CAUSES OF EXPOSURES

RELIANCE ON CONTROLS
3 — Reliably controls applicable cause
2 — Controls cause but should be accompanied by additional controls
1 — Useful but not especially effective
Blank — No significant contribution

EXPOSURES
Erroneous record keeping
Unacceptable accounting
Business interruption
Erroneous management decisions
Fraud
Statutory sanctions
Excessive costs/deficient revenues
Loss or destruction of assets
Competitive disadvantage

Legend (likelihood):
3 — Very likely to occur
2 — Likely to occur
1 — May occur
Blank — Generally little effect

PREVENTION CONTROLS	INPUT: LOST	DUPLICATED	INACCURATE	MISSING DATA	TRANSACTIONS NEVER RECORDED	BLANKET AUTHORIZE	INITIATED INTERNALLY	PROCESSING: WRONG FILE	WRONG RECORD	INCOMPLETE	INCORRECT	UNTIMELY	INAPPROPRIATE	FILE LOST	PROGRAM LOST	PEOPLE LOST	OUTPUT: IMPROPERLY DISTRIBUTED	LATE OR LOST	ERRONEOUS BUT PLAUSIBLE	OBVIOUSLY ERRONEOUS	EXCESSIVE ERROR CORRECTION	UNSUPPORTABLE	OTHER: SHADOW SYSTEM	UNLIMITED ACCESS	MANAGEMENT OVERRIDE
Definition of responsibilities	1	2	2	2	2	2	2	1	1	2	2	2	1	1	1	1	1	2	1	1	1	2	2	2	1
Reliability of personnel	1	1	1	1	1			1	1	2	2	2	2	1	1		2	1	2	2	2	2	2	2	1
Training	1	1	1	2	2			1	1	2	2	2	2	1	1	1	2	1	2	2	2	2	2	2	2
Competence	1	1	1	2	2	1		1	2	2	2	3	2	1	1	1	1	1	2	1	2	1	1	2	2
Mechanization	2	2	2	1	1	1		1	2	2	2		2	1		1		1	1	1	2		1	2	
Segregation of duties		2								2	2	1					2							2	1
Rotation of duties	1	2	1	2	1			1	1		2				2	1	2	1						2	1
Standardization	1							1	1			1	2	2	2	1	2	1				1	2	3	
Authorization	2	2	2	2	2			1						2	2		2	1				1		3	
Secure custody	1			1				2						2	2			1				1	2	3	
Dual custody			2							2															
Forms design		2		2																					
Prenumbered	2	2	2	2				1	1	2	2		1	1	1	2	1					1	1	1	
Preprinted	2		2	2				1	1	2	2		2	2	2	2				2	1	1	2		1
Simultaneous preparation	2	3	2	2						2	2	2		2	2										
Turnaround document			2	1	3							2		2	2	1					1	1	1	2	
Drum card			2	2						2	2	2													
Endorsement	2	2					2						2			2	2	2							
Cancellation	2	2		1								1											1		
Documentation	2		2	2			2	2	1	2	2	1	2	2	2		2	2	1	1	1	2			2
Exception input			1	1		1				2															
Default option			1	1		1				2												1			
Passwords		2	1	2	1	1	1	1	1							2						3	3		2
Erroneous record keeping	3	3	3	3	3			3	3	3	3	3	3	3	3	2	2	2	3	2	2	1	1	3	1
Unacceptable accounting	1	1	3	1	2	2		1	1	1	2	2	3	2	3	2	2	1	2	1	2	2	2	1	1
Business interruption	2	1	1	2	2	1		2	1	2	1	1	1	2	1	2	2	1	2	1	2	1	1	2	1
Erroneous management decisions	2	1	2	2	2	1	1	2	2	2	1	2	1	2	2	1	2	1	3	1	2	1	1	2	1
Fraud	2	2	2	2	2	1	1	1	1	1	1	1	1		1	1	1	1	1	1	2	2	1	2	1
Statutory sanctions	1	2	1	1	1		1	1	1	1	1	1	1	1	1	1	1	1	2	1	1	1	1	1	1
Excessive costs/deficient revenues	2	2	1	2	2		1	2	2	2	2	1	2	2	2	1	1	1	2	1	1	2	1	2	1
Loss or destruction of assets	2	2	1	1	1			2	2	1	2	1	2	2	1	1	1	1	2	1	2	2	2	2	1
Competitive disadvantage	1	2	1	1	1			1	1	1	1	1	1	2	1	1	1	1	1	1	1	3	3	1	1

Figure 10-6 (page 1 of 3)

185

APPLICATION CONTROL EVALUATION TABLE

APPLICATION CAUSES OF EXPOSURES

DETECTION CONTROLS	INPUT							PROCESSING									OUTPUT						OTHER		
	LOST	DUPLICATED	INACCURATE	MISSING DATA	NEVER RECORDED	BLANKET AUTHORIZE	INITIATED INTERNALLY	WRONG FILE	WRONG RECORD	INCOMPLETE	INCORRECT	UNTIMELY	INAPPROPRIATE	FILE LOST	PROGRAM LOST	PEOPLE LOST	IMPROPERLY DISTRIBUTED	LATE OR LOST	ERRONEOUS BUT PLAUSIBLE	OBVIOUSLY ERRONEOUS	EXCESSIVE ERROR CORRECTION	UNSUPPORTABLE	SHADOW SYSTEM	UNLIMITED ACCESS	MANAGEMENT OVERRIDE
Anticipation	3	2			3					3		1		2	2	2	3	3		3					
Transmittal document	2	2	2	1				2	1	2				3			2	2	3		2				
Batch serial numbers	3	3	2	1	2			2	2					2			2	2	2		1			3	
Control register	2	3	2	2				3	2	2	1	2					2	2	3		1				
Amount control totals	3	3	2					2	2	3	1						1	1	1	2	1			2	
Document control count	3	3						2	2	2	2						1	1	1	2	1				
Line control count	3	3	2					3	2	2	2						1	1	1	2	1				
Hash totals	3	3	2					3	2	1	1						1	1	1	2	1				
Batch totals	3	2	1					2	2	2	1			2	2		2	2	2		2				
Batch balancing	3	2	2	2					2	2	2						2	2	2		2		2		
Visual verification	2	2						2	2	2	2						2	2		3					
Sequence check			2					2	2	2				2											
Overflow check			2						2	2	2		1						1	2					
Format check			2	2	2			2	2	2	2		2												
Completeness check	2		3					2	2			1	2												
Check digit		2	2					2	2	2	2			2			2	2	3	2	2				
Reasonableness	1	2	2	2			2	2	1		2	1	2	2			3	3	3	1	2				
Limit check			2						2	2			2	1					1	1	2	2			
Validity check			3					1					2												
Readback	2	1			2			2	2				2						2						
Dating		2			2			2	1	1		2		2			1	1		1					
Expiration	2		2	1		1	1	1	1	1				1		1	1	1	1	1	1	1	1		1
Keystroke verification		2	2	2				2	1	2	2	1	1	2		1	2	2	3	1	2	3	1	1	1
Approval	1	2	2	2				2	2	2	2	2	2	2	2	1	2	2	2	1	2	1	1	2	1
Run-to-run totals			1	1	1			3	1	1	1	1	1	3	3		1	1	1	1	1	1	3	1	1

EXPOSURES

Erroneous record keeping	3	1	3	3	3	2	2	3	3	3	3	3	3	3	2	2	2	2	3	3	2	3	2	1	1
Unacceptable accounting	1	2	1	1	2	2	2	3	3	1	1	2	3	2	2	2	2	2	3	2	2	1	1	1	1
Business interruption	2	2	2	2	2	1	1	2	2	2	1	1	1	2	3	2	2	2	1	1	2	2	1	2	1
Erroneous management decisions	1	1	1	1	1	1	1	2	2	1	1	2	1	1	1	1	1	1	1	1	1	1	1	2	1
Fraud	2	1	2	1	1	2	1	2	2	1	1	1	2	1	1	3	1	1	1	1	2	3	1	2	1
Statutory sanctions	2	2	1	1	1	1	1	2	1	2	1	1	2	2	2	1	3	2	1	1	2	1	1	1	1
Excessive costs/deficient revenues	2	2	2	2	2	1	1	2	2	1	1	1	2	2	2	1	1	2	2	2	1	2	3	2	1
Loss or destruction of assets	2	2	2	2	1	1	1	2	1	1	1	1	2	2	2	1	1	1	1	1	1	1	2	2	1
Competitive disadvantage	1	1	1	1	1	1	1	2	1	1	1	1	1	2	1	1	1	1	1	1	1	1	1	1	1

Figure 10-6 (page 2 of 3)

APPLICATION CONTROL EVALUATION TABLE

APPLICATION CAUSES OF EXPOSURES

RELIANCE ON CONTROLS
3 — Reliably controls applicable cause
2 — Controls cause but should be accompanied by additional controls
1 — Useful but not especially effective
Blank — No significant contribution

DETECTION CONTROLS (continued) / CORRECTION CONTROLS

	INPUT							PROCESSING									OUTPUT						OTHER		
	LOST	DUPLICATED	INACCURATE	MISSING DATA	NEVER RECORDED	BLANKET AUTHORIZE	INITIATED INTERNALLY	WRONG FILE	WRONG RECORD	INCOMPLETE	INCORRECT	UNTIMELY	INAPPROPRIATE	FILE LOST	PROGRAM LOST	PEOPLE LOST	IMPROPERLY DISTRIBUTED	LATE OR LOST	ERRONEOUS BUT PLAUSIBLE	OBVIOUSLY ERRONEOUS	EXCESSIVE ERROR CORRECTION	UNSUPPORTABLE	SHADOW SYSTEM	UNLIMITED ACCESS	MANAGEMENT OVERRIDE
Balancing	2	2	2	1	2			3	2	3	2								2	3		2			1
Reconciliation	2	2	2	2	2			3	2	3	2	2	1									1		3	
Aging	2	2	1	1	1					2	2	2	1				2						2		1
Suspense file	2	2	2	2	2			2	2	2		2	1						2		2	1			
Suspense account	2	3	3	2	2			2		2	1	2	1								2	2			
Matching	3	2	2	2	2		3	3	3	2	2	2	1						2	3					1
Clearing account	2	2	2	2	2				2	2		2	1				2								
Tickler file	2	2	2	2	2							2	2				2	2							
Periodic audit	2	2	3	2	2	2	3	2	2	2	1	2	2	2	2	2	2	2	2	3	2	3	1	1	
Redundant process			2	2	1			3	3	3				2	2	2									
Summary process	2	2	2	2				2	2		1			2								3			
Label	1	1	1							3															
Trailer record	2	2	1	1				3	3	3		2	2	2	2									1	

CORRECTION CONTROLS

	LOST	DUPLICATED	INACCURATE	MISSING DATA	NEVER RECORDED	BLANKET AUTHORIZE	INITIATED INTERNALLY	WRONG FILE	WRONG RECORD	INCOMPLETE	INCORRECT	UNTIMELY	INAPPROPRIATE	FILE LOST	PROGRAM LOST	PEOPLE LOST	IMPROPERLY DISTRIBUTED	LATE OR LOST	ERRONEOUS BUT PLAUSIBLE	OBVIOUSLY ERRONEOUS	EXCESSIVE ERROR CORRECTION	UNSUPPORTABLE	SHADOW SYSTEM	UNLIMITED ACCESS	MANAGEMENT OVERRIDE
Discrepancy reports		2	2	2	2	2	2	3	3	2	2	2	2				2	2	2	2	3	2		2	1
Transaction trail	3	3	3	2	2	2	2	3	3	2	2	2	2	3	3	3	3	3	2	2	3	3	1	1	1
Error source statistics	2	2	2	2	2	1		2	2	2	2	1	1	2	2	2	2	2	2	3					
Automated error correction		1	2	2		1	1	1	1	2	1	2	2	2	2	1	2	2	1	2	1	1	1	2	1
Upstream resubmission	2	2	2	1	1	1	1	1	1	1	1	1	1	1	1	1	1	1	1	1	2	1	1	1	1
Backup and recovery	3	3	3	3				3	3					3	3	2		2	2	3	3	3	2	2	1

EXPOSURES
Erroneous record keeping
Unacceptable accounting
Business interruption
Erroneous management decisions
Fraud
Statutory sanctions
Excessive costs/deficient revenues
Loss or destruction of assets
Competitive disadvantage

3 — Very likely to occur
2 — Likely to occur
1 — May occur
Blank — Generally little effect

Figure 10-6 (page 3 of 3)

Identify Causes Lacking Sufficient Controls

The determination of when control is sufficient is subjective. It must be weighed in the light of the costs of implementing further controls balanced against the potential consequences. However, for the preliminary evaluation, a simple rule of thumb may be adopted for an evaluation of whether control is adequate over a particular cause.

One highly reliable control over a particular cause should be adequate. Such controls are designated by the numeral "3" on the control evaluation table. This does not mean that the control has to be perfectly reliable but, rather, that it would tolerate only an insignificant level of error.

Two or more controls of moderate strength (designated by the numeral "2") should be present if a strong control ("3") does not exist. Although useful, such controls would not be deemed sufficiently reliable by themselves.

A very large number of useful but not especially effective controls (designated by the number "1") would have to be available if there are not sufficient "strong" or "moderate-strength" controls. At some point, probably no quantity of weak controls makes any particular difference. This does not mean that controls that are useful but not especially effective should be completely discouraged since they will often reduce the error rates to levels that are more readily dealt with by the other controls. At the same time, they will seldom be of sufficient use to merit audit reliance or verification.

Causes of exposure that fail to meet the control ratings described above should be considered insufficiently controlled. This means that a reasonable probability exists that the cause would not be prevented from occurring, not detected, or not corrected when it occurs. Whether this is a serious problem depends upon the resulting exposures.

Quantify Business Exposures That Result

If adequate controls exist over specific causes, the business exposures that remain should be negligible. The evaluation of business exposures applies primarily to those causes which are not effectively controlled.

As previously discussed in chapter 6, the exposures listed on the control evaluation table should be tailored to suit the specific circumstances of the application under examination.

Example — If the application has no direct impact upon accounting entries, the exposure to unacceptable accounting would not apply.

188

Furthermore, the typical ratings shown on the example control evaluation tables should be adjusted to suit the particular industry and application.

Example — A bank might generally rate the exposures to fraud much higher than a manufacturer of rough castings. However, for the payroll application, there might not be much difference.

Finally, the magnitude of the application exposures must be estimated. This involves appraising the maximum plausible consequence in dollars that could result from a particular exposure. That amount may then be multiplied by the likelihood of its occurrence.

Example — A savings deposit application may contain $50 million. However, even the gradual fraudulent withdrawal of more than $5 or $10 million would certainly draw considerable attention. Furthermore, the probability of a major fraud occurring might be estimated at not more than 1%. The exposure could then be estimated as $10 million x 1% = $100,000.

Obviously, these estimates may be quite subjective and are often omitted in practice. While the subjectivity should be recognized, it should not be an excuse to avoid *any* estimate.

Points to Consider During Evaluation

Computer applications are more difficult to evaluate than purely manual systems. This is because they usually are larger, more complex, and incorporate a greater variety of alternative processing and control techniques. Below, we have listed some of the points that are peculiar to computerized applications that should be considered in the evaluation:

- File maintenance transactions
- EDP control group
- Absence of an EDP control group
- Evaluation of edits
- Unresolved errors
- Application backup and recovery
- Limitations of reliance on source code

FILE MAINTENANCE TRANSACTIONS

As discussed earlier, the auditor should challenge the decisions and procedures affecting the handling of file maintenance transactions. He should review the sample listings covering significant file maintenance transactions.

The auditor should also review controls over sensitive file maintenance transactions to determine that procedures monitor delivery of reports to the persons specified. These persons should be advised when no sensitive transactions are recorded during any scheduled processing cycle.

In most well-designed applications, the user has the capability to examine or to audit his important master files periodically. This will require preparation of complete file reference listings on either paper or microfilm which may be reviewed in detail, confirmed, or compared with other records by user personnel. These file-verification procedures may be virtually the same as those which the auditor might employ for the same purpose.

The auditor must still establish that the processing of the listings or confirmation selections is reliable. Techniques for performing such tests were covered in chapter 9.

In its examination of manual procedures, the auditor should determine the frequency with which file-verification listings are issued and supported by users. The auditor himself should review the results of the most recent verification activities.

EDP CONTROL GROUP

Of particular concern in the review of control group activities is the handling of out-of-balance conditions and input transactions that were rejected. Many applications provide a capability for excellent run-to-run and transaction-balancing controls only to find that this capability is wasted due to the absence of corrective controls needed to resolve the differences or exceptions. The control group should be responsible to account for and follow up on the resolution of errors. In some situations, the EDP Department takes the position that these are responsibilities solely of the user group. When the EDP control group relinquishes all accountability, a highly error-prone situation exists.

If the control group maintains accountability, the auditor must be concerned about the diligence with which unresolved items are tracked and resolved. Thus, the aging of error-control listings is critical in maintaining *accountability* for resolution of rejected input items. The auditor must review such aged reports and evaluate the impact of processing reliability in file balancing of the unresolved items.

Over and above determining that processing errors are resolved, it is important for the auditor to know *who* resolves them. Audit documentation should indicate the recipients of all error or rejected transaction reports. Furthermore, the auditor should investigate personally the number of copies of all such reports being produced and verify the actual distribution of all the copies to be sure that they go only to persons with legitimate needs. It is obvious that this last concern is one that the auditor should keep constantly in the back of his mind as it is crucial to many aspects of a properly supervised system.

The EDP control group should exercise rigorous control over the distribution of all reports and documents generated. For the auditor's review of report distribution, the audit documentation should indicate these distribution patterns. The auditor should challenge these practices to determine that reports and documents are being received only by those persons who need them. He should also determine that these persons include all the people who might need the information.

These concerns are particularly appropriate for voluminous, routine listings which could be replaced by either exception reports or summaries. While the auditor may find that little harm results from ineffective distribution of reports, review in this area provides an opportunity to make substantial contributions to the improvement of internal communications and to potential reductions in processing costs.

ABSENCE OF AN EDP CONTROL GROUP

In some cases, there may be no control group within the EDP Department. User organizations may apply the controls over processing normally handled by the EDP control group. Thus, in verifying processing by the computer, the auditor must first determine where, if at all, a control group exists.

If only the user is applying controls over computer processing, additional audit questions arise. The auditor should evaluate the nature and quality of the control information being provided to users by the EDP Department in light of:

- The controls required within the application
- The technical-comprehension levels of the user personnel

Example — If the auditor encounters an occasion where computer console logs are reviewed by the user rather than by an EDP specialist, he should question whether the user has the technical ability to understand the computer-generated messages. If not, the auditor should conclude that any controls intended for application in this matter are ineffective.

EVALUATION OF EDITS

Each field within important records should be reviewed in conjunction with transaction definitions, code tables, error messages, or edit lists to determine the answers to questions such as the partial list below taken from the "Detective Controls" section of the "Application Controls Matrix" discussed previously:

- If the field should always be numeric, is there an edit of the format?
- If the field should never be blank, is there an edit of completeness?

- If the field is numeric and should always be positive, is there a limit test?
- Is there a check on the existence of negative amounts?
- If a code table is used, is there an edit for invalid codes?
- If a numeric field should not exceed a certain amount, is there an edit for a field overflow during processing that could cause field capacity to be exceeded?
- If transactions are supposed to be entered in sequence, is there a sequence check on the key-control field?

UNRESOLVED ERRORS

All organizations using outputs of an application need some means of appraising the consequence of unresolved errors at any point in time. The auditor should review these procedures to see whether the capability for determining the potential impact of unresolved errors exists. He should also examine the handling of these outputs by user organizations. Accounting entries of the user organization should be reviewed to determine that reasonable accruals are provided for these suspense items.

Example — In a manufacturing company, all additions to the inventory account were accomplished by the use of a computerized accounts payable application. Receiving documents were entered into the system, matched with purchase orders, and the audited liability recorded and distributed to the several classes of inventory. Edits of the receiving transactions and the matching with purchase orders were quite stringent. In fact, they were so stringent that the quantity of exceptions exceeded the capacity of the clerical staff to resolve them. Furthermore, no accountability existed over the unresolved rejects.

When the company took its physical inventory, it was quite pleased with the exceptionally small inventory shrinkage which had occurred. Later that same year, it managed to clear up a large backlog of unresolved receipt exceptions. When it took its next physical inventory, the company was shocked to discover a huge shrinkage. Because it had not considered the large backlog of unresolved receipt exceptions when they took the first inventory, the book value was understated. The shrinkage discovered in the second year's inventory was the cumulative shrinkage for both years.

APPLICATION BACKUP AND RECOVERY

Backup and recovery controls may be addressed at two levels: (1) application or (2) information processing facility (IPF). At the application level, the evaluation must address itself to the significance of exposures to business interruption for the particular application, even though the causes of exposure may apply simultaneously to the entire IPF.

Example — A fire in the IPF may threaten loss of programs and files for all applications. When evaluating payroll application controls, however, thought must be given to the specific sensitivity and controls relating to payroll. These may be substantially different from the concerns over inventory files.

LIMITATIONS OF RELIANCE ON SOURCE CODE

The review of program listings cannot generally be considered as a program-*verification* technique. Even the programmer who prepares the source code frequently encounters difficulty in subsequently following the logical processes that he has not looked at for some time. For an auditor to claim that his review of such listings assures their accuracy is purely presumptuous. This is particularly true since the auditor will customarily have less practical experience with the particular source language than the individual who designed the program.

Neither is audit analysis of logic flowcharts likely to be a totally acceptable verification technique. While flowcharts do make processing logic somewhat clearer, that clarity is still not sufficient for general audit purposes.

Some cases may exist where an audit analysis of source listings or detailed program logic flowcharts will provide a clear and comprehensive understanding of the application. However, since the complexity of the code increases geometrically with the number of functions and controls that are provided, neither of these techniques can be effective with any application of substantial magnitude.

Even in such cases where it is found to be effective, the auditor must still perform additional procedures to determine that the code which he examines is, in fact, identical to the code which generated the object-language instructions that are actually being used by the computer. Making such a determination may be extremely complex and too time-consuming for the value received.

Select Application Features to Be Tested

Selection of the processing steps and controls to be tested is based primarily upon the factor of "exposure." The auditor selects the features within the application to be tested based upon:

- The relationships determined to exist between controls and causes
- The volume and value of the items being controlled
- The worst likely error rate to be expected without detection if the controls weren't there

If, in asking himself what would happen if a control did not exist, the auditor finds that no significant exposure would occur, there is no need to test that feature. On the other hand, if the exposure is potentially significant, existence of and compliance with the control should be tested.

If the auditor determines that a particular cause of exposure could exist undetected, he must assume that it *will* occur. He must also evaluate or test the impact of these undetected errors.

The auditor should use his analytic flowchart prepared earlier to evaluate the points at which these controls are exercised. Then he should determine if they are applied at the earliest feasible opportunity within the processing cycle.

If the controls are present but not exercised at the earliest possible point, effects are probably not serious. However, this positioning within the application may complicate the process of error correction and reduce its reliability.

Normally, applied editing and processing controls should also be executed for transactions correcting previously rejected items. Such transactions are so error prone that even more rigorous controls should be used. Thus, when the auditor analyzes the point where editing and validity controls are exercised, he should be particularly concerned that any capability to insert corrections subsequent to these control procedures might bypass them. Should such situations be uncovered, this should indicate a need for redundant edits at different stages in the processing.

Once detective controls are identified and evaluated, the auditor should then examine a selection of the reports of rejected transactions. He should know whether items are presented understandably. Error items should preferably be explained by messages rather than by codes which are difficult for a user to remember.

The auditor should also note the volumes of errors detected and consider these factors in his evaluation:

- If a significant quantity of the errors are serious, the auditor should determine whether this type of error is being resolved accurately and on a timely basis. Also, if errors of this type show a pattern of a particular type or source, the auditor should determine whether additional preventive controls are required.

- If large volumes of correction items are being generated, the auditor should determine whether these really warrant correction efforts or whether they are too insignificant. Where too many minor errors are being reported, the need for that intensity of detective controls should be challenged. Detective controls should strike a realistic balance between the potential damage from the errors themselves and the costs of resolving them. Consideration should be given to further prevention con-

194

trols or self-resolving routines which would automate the error-correction process.

The final product of the evaluation process should be a list of key controls upon which the auditor believes he may rely. These will the stronger or moderate-strength detective, corrective, or preventive controls discussed in the preceding section on identifying key controls. This list provides the basic input to the next phase of the audit.

DESIGN THE AUDIT PROCEDURES

The auditor, having developed his evaluation of the application, must now design his tests of the application controls which he identified as "key."

Steps in the Testing Phase

There are three steps in the test-design phase:
- Select the verification technique
- Determine whether use will be made of the computer or other tools
- Prepare the audit program

Select the Verification Technique

In general, two approaches can be applied in verifying controls and processing in an application:
- Testing results: Select one or more key files which are produced by the application and verify the accuracy of the results of the processing.
- Testing processing: Perform specific tests of critical processes and controls.

Successful verification of an important *file* is normally taken as substantial evidence that the updating which occurred during the application processing was complete and accurate. Furthermore, it provides assurance that all relevant updating transactions during the period tested were recorded in the file.

When the auditor verifies *processing,* he performs specific tests of important processes and controls applied by persons or computer programs. Care must be taken to apply such verification procedures to both representative transactions and unusual transactions of substantial magnitude.

The auditor may use either one or both of these approaches for testing. Selection will be based upon trade-offs between effectivness and the economics of each situation. Guidelines for this evaluation are provided later in this section.

Two principal functions within the typical business data processing application are significant in establishing the verification method:

- Maintaining and updating the files
- Decisions and processing which result from file conditions

Testing of file maintenance and updating requires determinations of the completeness of transactions processed. This is performed readily through a test of the file contents at some point in time.

Testing of decisions and processing which result from file conditions requires specific testing of those decisions and processes; thus, the auditor must approach it as a test of the processing method.

Verification of Results

Verification of results is usually performed by one of three methods:

- Confirmations by corresponding with outside parties
- Comparisons of files maintained by independent departments (e.g., personnel and payroll) or determining their physical existence
- Reasonableness and edit tests of items *within* files (credit balances, zero balances, excessive balances, etc.)

The implementation of these techniques was discussed previously in chapter 9.

Verification of results may be used to substantiate only specific controls whose absence or ineffectiveness would be clearly demonstrated in the test of the results.

Example — Confirmation replies could be relied upon to disclose a control breakdown over loss of cash receipts but would not reveal an improper aging of receivables.

Tests of results are tests for the undetected occurrence of causes of exposure. If no causing factor can be found to occur, the auditor *may* infer that the controls intended to act against each cause are effective. On the other hand, it may be that no causes occurred to test the controls. Of course, if causes are found through audit, they provide strong evidence that existing controls are less than perfect.

Although verification of results may not be the most reliable audit approach because it tests for the occurrence of a cause of exposure rather than explicitly testing a particular control, it may be sufficiently effective for the audit objectives and may be further justified by a comparatively low cost.

Verification of Processing

In verifying processing, the auditor performs his verification through specific tests of critical processes and controls, using the audit tools and techniques discussed in chapters 8 and 9.

196

SUMMARY OF APPLICATION AUDIT PURPOSES, TECHNIQUES, AND TOOLS

PURPOSE	TECHNIQUE	TOOLS
Gather information describing controls	Review program listing	
	Review logic flowchart	Flowcharting software
Verify processing	Audit around	
	Test data	Test data generator Audit software
	Integrated test facility	
	Parallel simulation	Audit software Tailored program
	S C A R F	
	Snapshot	
Verify results	Confirmation	Audit software Tailored program
	Comparison with file or physical	Audit software Tailored program
	Edit & reasonableness tests	Audit software Tailored program

Figure 10-7

These techniques are:
- Auditing "around the computer," using transaction trails
- Test data which provide a comprehensive variety of situations for application processing
- Integrated test facility which integrates test data with "live" processing
- SCARF where special edits are monitored by the auditor
- Snapshot which provides a selective transaction trail

- Parallel simulation where "live" transactions and records are independently reprocessed and compared with the original results

A summary of the alternative tools and techniques is shown in Figure 10-7.

VERIFICATION OF MANUAL AND COMPUTER PHASES OF PROCESSING

For convenience, verification of processing may be divided into verification of:

- Manual processing: verify manually or utilize the computer if the transactions are complex or voluminous
- Computer processing: through use of one or more of the computer-assisted audit tools and techniques previously discussed

Normally, the examination of manual procedures must be performed manually. Note that the computer phase of an application also usually contains many controls that are implemented manually. Testing is performed through examination of selected transactions or media which document the control. The auditor must presume that, unless documented evidence is available, control does not exist. Admittedly, in a few cases, effective control may exist without any direct documentary evidence. For instance, the absence of supervisory initials approving transactions would mean to the auditor that the approval did not take place, even though the approval might, in fact, have occurred and not been documented. However, the auditor may not rely upon such controls unless he obtains evidential matter to support their existence.

These verifications are performed for each control feature or critical processing function previously identified during the evaluation of controls. These procedures are performed on a test basis in virtually all cases for manual controls because transaction volumes are extensive. This is indicated by the very fact that the application is computerized. In the selection of transactions for testing, particular care must be exercised to assure that the documents to be tested are representative of the application as a whole, both in terms of quantity and types of transactions.

This selection of representative items may be determined by either statistical or judgmental sampling. Where statistical sampling is feasible, its use is preferred because of its greater inherent objectivity.

Tests of manually implemented procedures and controls should be spread throughout all or most of the period under audit. This is a generally accepted auditing standard for CPA's and is also suitable for internal auditors. The spread of tests should more readily reveal occasional control lapses due to sickness, vacation, personnel turn-over, etc.

In the verification of manual processing procedures, some error rate should always be detected due to the fact that humans make errors. Even in systems of comparatively high overall reliability, lapses are to be expected in the application of individual control features. Therefore, redundant, detective checks must be built into manual application processing. The auditor must satisfy himself that errors which slip through any individual clerical checkpoint will be detected by later compensating controls applied either manually or by the computer. If the presence of such detective controls cannot be verified, the auditor should conclude that there is a weakness in the system's design.

For the computerized phases of application processing, the applicable technique may be manual, computer assisted, or a combination. The selection depends upon the availability of transaction trails and other visible documentation, the volumes involved, and the relative costs.

Even if visible transaction trails are not readily available, they might be produced through a simple computer-programmed extraction routine from machine-readable media. *There is absolutely nothing wrong or archaic about using manual auditing techniques if they can be applied effectively and efficiently.*

Computer phases of processing differ from manual in two significant respects:

- Computer processing will occur with complete consistency under identical circumstances as long as the programs are not altered.
- Program alterations require formal controls that must be tested if the programs are to be relied upon.

Therefore, the auditor may be justified in placing reliance on programmed controls over a lengthy span of time if he can periodically verify the reliability of controls over changes to those programs. This is not true with manual controls, because people are subject to lapses, occasional errors, and informal revisions to procedures.

Determining Whether Computer-Assisted Techniques Will Be Used

The second step in the test-design phase is to determine if the computer will be used either for tests of results or for processing. The tools available, if the computer is used, are test data generators, audit software, etc., as covered in chapter 8.

The auditor must determine whether:

- Use of the computer is consistent with the nature of the control.
- Necessary files can be made available.
- Computer files that are available are also accessible.

- Computer time will be available.
- Use of the computer can be cost justified.
- Computer assistance would affect audit reliability.

Some controls might not relate to any feasible computer-assisted audit technique.

Example — Controls over loss of key people would not be likely to involve any computer-implemented controls. Neither would computer-assisted audit techniques apply.

The availability of appropriate computer files can be a major problem. Transaction files do not exist in some on-line applications (see chapter 20 for further discussion). Even where transaction files exist, their retention may be quite brief. The same holds true for retention of obsolete master files. The auditor must plan ahead to have files available after their customary retention.

Even files that are retained may be organized or contain data formats that are not compatible with the particular general purpose audit software system available to the auditor. These file-access considerations were discussed in chapter 8.

Furthermore, the auditor must have access to adequate time on an appropriate computer configuration. This may present a particular problem during the period when fiscal year-end processing must be handled in addition to normal daily processing.

Usually, the first time the computer is used in auditing, there will be additional learning costs. However, with proper planning and supervision, these additional costs can be kept to a minimum in the first year and reduced to a favorable position in subsequent years.

In addition, audit reliability is generally enhanced due to a more thorough examination of details when the computer is used.

Example — The auditor may use statistical sampling or some other method to manually test the extensions of a voluminous, priced inventory. If the computer is used to verify extensions, it can be readily done on a 100% basis.

Preparing the Audit Program

A formal audit program of test procedures should be prepared in all cases. There are three reasons for this:

- Structure the auditor's own planning
- Guide audit assistants in performing planned procedures
- Provide audit documentation for review and reference

The use of audit programs is a well-established practice among all auditors. An example of an audit program for a computerized application is shown in Figure 10-8. Since a substantial amount of professional literature already exists on this subject, we will not discuss it further here.

AUDIT PROGRAM FOR COMPUTERIZED APPLICATION

	DONE BY	DATE	W/P REF.
3. Review the Bank's policies and procedures to determine that they are stated in this program.	WM	12/14	memo
4. Obtain the undisbursed funds sheets on mortgage loans as of the examination date. Determine if there are any abnormal or large amounts outstanding.	WM	1/4	M-3
5. Determine the amount and nature of any outstanding mortgage loan commitments. Determine that such commitments do not represent an abnormal risk or any inconsistency with present lending policies.	WM	1/4	M-4
6. Obtain detail analyses of all miscellaneous accounts assigned to the mortgage department. Prove their mathematical accuracy and trace the totals to the examination date's statement of condition. Discuss the nature of the account's activity with the department personnel and, on a test basis, support the account makeup.	WM	1/5	M-5
7. Mortgage income:			
a. Run the STRATA parallel simulation application computing interest income on a daily basis and accrued interest receivable at month's end.	WM	1/8	M-6 Run 373
b. Trace the control totals per the STRATA application to the general ledger. Follow up on any exceptions.	WM	1/8	M-6

Figure 10-8

201

PERFORMING THE TESTS

Using the tools and techniques as planned, the auditor next performs such compliance tests as are required in the circumstances to verify that the controls previously identified as "key" for the application are, in fact, working properly.

One important aspect of this step, especially if use is made of the computer, is to run tests of computerized audit procedures to assure that the computer audit programs accomplish anticipated objectives. Too often, an audit procedure is run to completion only to discover that there was an error in audit logic and that the test was incorrect, resulting in a loss of valuable audit time and money.

The auditor should examine reports and control statistics provided after each processing step. The precision, completeness, and adequacy of this information should be documented. Then the auditor should examine whatever documentary evidence exists of reconciliations or follow-up actions applied by the control group to verify balances throughout the computer-processing segments of the application. Implementation of these procedures should be evidenced on logs maintained by the control group and by reconciliations and endorsements on the face of the transaction control documents. If such controls are not documented, although the organization contends that they exist, the auditor should still not rely upon them.

The items, controls, and procedures involved in each test must be thoroughly documented in audit working papers. These are required as evidence of compliance with sound auditing standards and as the medium for audit review.

Upon completion, the audit working papers should be reviewed very carefully to insure that all objectives were met. The auditor is now ready for the final step.

EVALUATE RESULTS OF THE TESTS

The objective of the final evaluation phase is to resolve the degree of reliance that the auditor can place upon the internal control. This evaluation is based upon the auditor's knowledge of the procedures and controls obtained during the previous phases.

Documentation of Evaluation

Documentation of the auditor's final evaluation should include:

- Identification of weaknesses in the system of internal controls and a measure of their impact, if any
- Evaluation of the application based upon all controls proven to exist
- Substantive audit procedures selected as a result of the testing and evaluation process (primarily for CPA's)

Relating Results to Audit Scope

During the final evaluation phase, the same procedures and tools utilized in the preliminary evaluation of controls may be used to provide guidance. We briefly recapitulate these below:

- Requantify the verified effectiveness of key controls over the respective causes of exposure.
- Identify those causes of exposure over which sufficient controls do not exist.
- Revise or redraft the preliminary application control evaluation table to reflect the above.
- Perform additional procedures to verify alternative controls or to quantify resulting exposures.

Two significant differences exist between the preliminary evaluation that followed detailed information gathering and the final evaluation that follows actual testing:

- The auditor now *knows* whether the controls are implemented effectively.
- Adverse conclusions may call for additional audit procedures to test compensating controls or to measure the actual effects of identified weaknesses.

Eventually, after the auditor thoroughly evaluates the results of his tests and additional procedures, if any, he is ready to report.

Reporting on the Audit Results

The auditor should prepare a constructive letter of comments to be given to management. This will discuss the results of his examination and his recommendations for improvements. Some helpful hints regarding the letter of recommendations are provided as a guide.

LETTER-OF-RECOMMENDATIONS FORMAT

The proven format for the letter of recommendations is to present each weakness as follows:

- The objective and scope of the examination
- The nature and extent of the tests performed
- A general description of the control weaknesses or improvement opportunities found
- One or more examples supporting each finding
- Explanation of why the control improvement or change is desirable
- A recommended action to be taken

There are three major parts to an audit: (1) collecting and documenting information, (2) evaluating and testing that information, and (3) reporting on the results of the examination. Management sees or understands very little about the first two parts. Their impression of the work performed and the conclusions reached will depend almost entirely upon the third part, the report. Consequently, the importance of good reporting cannot be overemphasized. Also, a critical examination of the EDP function may be a new experience for management and EDP personnel as well as a new venture for the auditor. It is very important, therefore, to consider some basic hints and to apply plenty of good, common sense in preparing the report.

In preparing the report, the auditor should always keep in mind that no EDP activity is ever perfect. Accordingly, he should not only keep points in proper perspective but should also exert every reasonable effort to encourage middle management to take corrective action. The auditor should not be satisfied with just reporting on deficiencies in the EDP area but should strive to approach the subject so that the problems will be resolved. A follow-up plan is a proper conclusion to the EDP review and, in many cases, should lead to a continuing amiable relationship.

Steps in Completing the Report and Determining Required Follow-Up

Because of the technical nature of an EDP audit, several additional review steps are normally required before the report should be issued. The auditor should bear in mind that the EDP manager will almost inevitably be required to respond to the report. Therefore, the technical accuracy and relevancy of the report's contents are extremely important.

The major steps the auditor should follow are:

- Prepare preliminary findings and conclusions.
- Review the findings and conclusions with technical consultants. This review should be mandatory if the auditor does not have a strong background in data processing or if unusual technical issues or significant EDP management disputes exist.
- Review them next with the EDP manager. If he disputes any item, recheck the facts and reevaluate the conclusions.
- Prepare points for the report in a sequence which will give emphasis to the most significant issues being reported.
- Review the final report with the EDP manager. If he disputes any items at this point, reverify the facts. If the point is still valid, report the dissenting position of the EDP manager.
- Prepare the final report.
- Submit the report for review by audit management and quality control personnel.
- Present the report to the appropriate company officer.
- Establish a plan of auditor's follow-up.

To be effective, the report on EDP examinations must be more than a critical list of deficiencies found in the EDP activity. It should include specific recommendations for correcting the defects and should suggest priorities for the steps recommended. The entire report should be helpful and constructive. A good philosophy to adopt is to try to establish an objective, factual reading on the current condition as a base for recommending corrective action and for measuring improvement. Placed in this context, the EDP personnel may be less defensive and more willing to cooperate. Often the defects the auditor identifies and reports are already problems for the EDP personnel, but they have been unable to gain management's attention or support for necessary improvements. The auditor serves in such instances as a catalyst to get EDP problems resolved. Furthermore, this approach will give the auditor an objective base by which to evaluate the EDP Department at a later date to determine if improvements have been made.

In many instances, the EDP Department is deluged with complaints and bad internal publicity. If the auditor establishes his position firmly, but within reason, he can persuade the EDP manager that good controls and well-documented application systems are also in the EDP manager's best interest. With the proper rapport, the auditor's job will be much easier; his findings will be more thorough and accurate; and he will provide real assistance.

Section III
SYSTEMS DEVELOPMENT

11

Systems Development Activities

Systems standards are an essential factor for controlling the systems development process. The advent of a formal process has facilitated the auditing of computerized procedures in two ways:

- Documentation standards serve increasingly as the basis for both financial and operational audits.
- As generalized process for developing systems becomes more accepted, the auditor will find it easier to determine what his role should be.

This chapter discusses one proven method which has been used successfully in the development of many EDP systems in many organizations and in establishing repeatable phases and activities appropriate to virtually all systems projects. The project structure will be shown as the basis for application development as well as for documentation which serves as a basis for controlling and auditing ongoing EDP applications.

This chapter should help the auditor understand that standardized system development techniques exist and are feasible within any organization making significant use of EDP capabilities. Controls over the systems development process implemented by or within the EDP Department are covered in chapter 12. Chapters 13 and 14 cover control and audit procedures appropriate to the systems development process.

EMERGENCE OF PROJECTED TECHNIQUES FOR DEVELOPMENT OF EDP SYSTEMS

One of the factors which has inhibited effective development of EDP systems in the past was a lack of structure, standards, and documentation (in general, a reliable method for the *process of* systems development). Until the late sixties, management and financial con-

208

trols were largely absent because of a prevalent tendency to treat systems development almost entirely as a technical process.

The traditional, technical orientation of computer systems development led to a distorted emphasis on the role of programming. For many years, the terms "programming" and "system development" were considered by many as synonymous. In retrospect, this is both understandable and regrettable.

The emphasis on programming resulted largely from the emergence of EDP systems from punched-card processing techniques. During the punched-card era, systems development consisted chiefly of drawing rudimentary flowcharts, designing cards and forms, and wiring boards which would direct the machines through individual operations. Emphasis was on jobs rather than on systems.

When computers entered the scene, most programming efforts picked up where plugboard wiring left off. The newness, technical nature, and complexity of programming led to a mystique associated with the programming process. Programming was at once unmanageable yet necessary to management. The concentration on programming led to a distortion of the systems development process.

The anxiety to create program coding frequently led to insufficient attention to the more critical requirements for understanding business problems and their environment and for designing systems to meet user needs. It took so much effort to computerize individual jobs that there could be little concern with integrated systems.

Management was the chief missing ingredient in the systems development process in most companies. By the middle sixties, horrible examples of cost overruns in systems development abounded. Ultimately, the combination of loss of control, increasing costs, and growing management requirements for application of computers made it mandatory that control techniques be developed. In large measure, the EDP control methodologies, which emerged in the late sixties, were derived from project methods already proven in industry. Companies associated with defense programs, for example, found similarities between EDP systems planning and development and the planning and development of new aerospace systems.

SYSTEMS DEVELOPMENT EXPOSURES

The development of new application systems is subject to all of the general business exposures that we have discussed previously. Most of these exposures arise when a new application is implemented and is found to contain features that permit many application exposures.

Accordingly, systems design personnel may implement *unacceptable accounting policies* or make unauthorized changes to existing policies. The resulting application may readily tolerate or even promote *inaccurate record keeping*. The *business may be interrupted* — either temporarily or permanently — through the implementation of an application with many types of design inadequacies. Similarly, such design errors may also provide information that is inaccurate or incomplete and which results in *erroneous management decisions*. The ability to commit *fraud* may be designed into the application accidentally or deliberately during its development. The implemented application may violate mandatory statutes or regulations, leading to *legal sanctions*. Design decisions may force the application to operate at *excessive costs*. And, finally, an application may be designed so that subsequent revisions to meet *competitive* situations require excessive effort or time.

In addition to the exposures that arise from design errors which are not found in an application until after its implementation, additional exposures exist during the systems development process itself. Feasibility decisions regarding the design of new systems may include errors. These errors may lead to the design of systems that fail to respond adequately to *competitive demands* or lead to decisions not to develop systems when competitive demands actually justify them. Some organizations have developed a theory that all systems development projects will *overrun their budgets*. Such assumptions usually assure the expected results. Finally, *management decisions* regarding the project may be *erroneous* due to a lack of information, misinformation, or outright absence of management involvement.

TASK DEFINITION

Under sound systems development methods, the overall system to be developed is broken down into a series of comparatively small tasks. The intent is to render the entire project predictable by breaking the work into units which are small enough to be analyzed, evaluated, and budgeted at the outset of the project. With work units broken down this way, unknown state-of-the-art elements of a project may be given appropriate attention. Quality may also be monitored continuously on an incremental basis. Controls may be reviewed and evaluated as the system develops.

Since cost and time estimating for tasks becomes more predictable, management is no longer asked to underwrite "blank-check" commitments for the total development of a system. Rather, commitments are made at predetermined review points under an approach which has been referred to as a "creeping commitment." Management's authorization is sought for individual, comparatively small steps. Within this process, realistic emphasis is placed on previously neglected functions such as evaluating the economic feasibility of a system, developing output specifications, setting work schedules and responsibilities to meet user requirements, and so on.

Perspective on Programming

Some idea of the relative importance assigned to programming and other aspects of systems development under modern project techniques is seen in Figure 11-1. This table[1] shows that:

- Programming is important, but it represents only about 30 percent of the total cost and time commitments of a typical systems development project.
- Programming does not begin until 40 percent of the total required resources have already been expended.
- Programming is not undertaken until studies of the business problem, environment, and solution indicate that there is 80 percent certainty of the success of the project.

The commitment concept illustrated in Figure 11-1 is just one of a number which have proven workable for the development of EDP systems in different organizations. The principles involved are general enough so that a person familiar with the structure discussed here can readily appreciate alternative structures. He should be able to adapt his control or audit activities readily to the needs or the situations encountered in virtually any company using a structured project approach to systems development.

THE SYSTEMS DEVELOPMENT PROJECT: AN OVERVIEW

A project structure for the development of EDP systems is diagrammed in Figure 11-2 (see footnote, Shaw and Atkins). This depicts systems project activities as a series of steps. The project begins with an initial investigation of ideas for potential EDP systems and culminates, after defined activities and appropriate management decisions, with an implemented system subject to continuing, ongoing maintenance.

Projects are divided into three major phases: planning, development, and implementation. The arrows in Figure 11-2 placed above the steps at the conclusion of each of the first two phases indicate major review points. Project activities are evaluated, and decisions are made whether to continue the allocation of resources and scheduling.

A basic ingredient of the project technique lies in its heavy orientation to the application. One of the requirements is clear documentation which serves as a basis for communication between EDP

[1]For a fuller discussion of the table — especially for persons actively involved in planning, scheduling, and directing engagements involving operational audits of the system planning process — see *Managing Computer Systems Projects,* Shaw and Atkins, McGraw-Hill Book Company, 1970, in the Touche Ross management series.

THE CREEPING COMMITMENT

PROJECT ACTIVITY	Degree of Risk of Proceeding to Project Completion Without Further Checkpoints	Degree of Organizational Commitment to Project	Cumulative Expenditures
SYSTEM PLANNING			
Initial Investigation	100%	0%	0%
Preliminary System Study	90	10	5
System Planning Study	75	25	15
DEVELOPMENT			
User Requirements	50	50	25
Technical Specifications	40	60	35
Implementation Planning	20	80	40
Programming	15	85	70
User Procedures and Training	15	85	75
System Test	10	90	80
IMPLEMENTATION			
Conversion	5	90	99
Postimplementation Review	0	95	100
Ongoing Maintenance			

Figure 11-1

and user personnel. This documentation establishes clear-cut standards and procedures to achieve them. Experience has shown that there is a direct correlation between user participation in application specification and design and the ultimate success of developing the application, implementing it, and realizing the initially-predicted results.

212

MAJOR STEPS IN THE SYSTEMS
DEVELOPMENT PROCESS

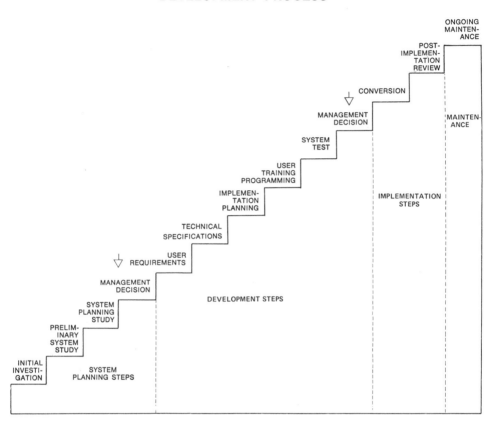

Figure 11-2
PROJECT STRUCTURE FOR THE DEVELOPMENT OF EDP SYSTEMS

With the recommended approach, planning and development are handled by a project team composed of user and EDP personnel. User personnel play a critical role in establishing requirements and identifying benefits for each new application. EDP people serve as project coordinators or leaders and as technical support. They make commitments in the systems design, programming, and operations areas for fulfilling the requirements stipulated by users. Thus, project techniques make a joint-venture approach to systems development possible. Such a project structure helps assure the development of adequate documentation as a basis for communication and agreement between user and technical personnel. The relationship of internal auditors is discussed in chapter 13.

213

SYSTEM PROJECT STRUCTURE

System projects are structured as cumulative efforts; each stage or activity relies heavily on the preceding one. The process has been likened to the peeling of an onion with system project teams peeling away at layers of a problem as they add to their knowledge and orientation. The creeping-commitment concept helps assure that the allocation of resources at each succeeding stage of a project will be commensurate with results to date, prospective values, and probabilities for success.

In the paragraphs which follow, the project structure is reviewed at summary level. Then, in separate, succeeding sections, individual activities with audit implications are covered in greater depth.

Each of the areas in the systems project structure is summarized in Figure 11-3 as to its scope and purpose, level of detail, skills required, and control considerations. Since each area has its own unique documentation, Figure 12-9 summarizes the documentation requirements for each.

System Planning

The initial activities identify the scope and the objectives of a project. Also developed are preliminary cost, benefit, and design presentations. To the level necessary, any required capital budgeting decisions are also made. As indicated in Figure 11-1, these planning activities usually average 15 percent of the total costs of developing and implementing a major application.

The system planning portion of the project is accomplished by:

- Studying existing procedures within the organization
- Determining opportunities for improvement
- Identifying applicable EDP methods
- Evaluating the practicability of computer techniques for the application under study
- Identifying and quantifying projected costs and benefits

The system planning portion of a project corresponds roughly with what used to be identified as a "feasibility study." The system planning designation fits more appropriately as a description of the continuing, cumulative effort represented by project techniques.

System planning for a large project may be broken up into as many as three steps: initial investigation, preliminary system study, and system planning study. In other cases, all three activities may be compressed into a single effort. The extent of activities will depend on project scope, EDP maturity of the organization, and other factors. Because of the high degree of risk involved in system planning, on-the-spot judgments must be applied to determine the extent or depth of efforts or expenditures to be committed. As would be expected in comparable capital budgeting efforts, tasks associated with the planning of systems projects should be performed by senior-level

214

SYSTEM PLANNING	USER SPECIFICATIONS	TECHNICAL SPECIFICATIONS	IMPLEMENTATION PLANNING	PROGRAMMING
Scope and purpose: Establish project, scope, objectives, economics and feasibility to level necessary for management's decision on resource allocation and priority	Establish detailed specification of new system for the user's viewpoint Confirm economics	Develop technical-level decisions and documentation Transition from business to technical solutions or problems	Review development progress Plan for balance of implementation of new system Reassemble project team as working unit following technical planning	Prepare detailed logic, write coding and test programs
Level of Detail: Depends on Significance of costs and benefits Impact on other EDP operations Degree of technical stretch required Place in overall systems development activity of company	Prepare full documentation of present and new system from user's viewpoint	Final, detailed design and documentation for computer portions of new application Programs specified to module level for coding and control Programming schedules developed	Develop specific plans and schedules for Conversion System test User training Review and validate programming plan, revising as necessary	Deliver operating programs which have been tested and documented
Skills Required: Business and technical management participation at senior level	Systems analysts User business orientation	Almost entirely technical at supervisory level	Full range of project skills Management review and approval	Activity is entirely technical Programming management and supervision set up work modules for programmers
Control Considerations: Review control concept Carry systems planning report forward for later review Limited audit effort	Requirements documentation serves as primary source for review of controls specified for new system	Controls imbedded in technical specifications Processing logic specifications include controls Control review frequently postponed to next activity	Major control review point, since all controls have been specified for conversion and ongoing operation Review guides audit participation and examination after implementation Audit test can be specific	

Figure 11-3 (1 of 2)

SYSTEMS DEVELOPMENT ACTIVITIES

	SYSTEM TEST	CONVERSION	POSTIMPLEMENTATION REVIEW	ONGOING MAINTENANCE
USER PROCEDURES AND TRAINING				
Scope and Purpose: Performed concurrently with programming Users are trained to operate new system User manuals are prepared	Tests complete, integrated system Certifies readiness for use	Implement new system for ongoing use Achieve targeted benefits	Determine how well system met objectives Measure and evaluate benefits realized	Change system as necessary to meet external requirements or to enhance value
Level of Detail: Full user staff must be trained	Test: Programs Computer operations User activities Control group	Users take possession of system EDP operations and control personnel begin regular duties	Auditor and supervisory or management personnel participate	Generally carried out by EDP technical personnel
Skills Required: Users primarily Systems analysts support and monitor	Users perform final functions EDP personnel operate computer functions Systems analysts and programmers note and deal with exceptions	All user, systems analysis, and EDP operations personnel are active	Management and supervision of user, EDP, and audit	User supervision and EDP technical personnel
Control Consideration: Control reviews of: Procedures manuals Functional job descriptions	Control interests: Test results Documentation and handling of exceptions Approvals	File conversion control documents Initial operating reports on new system Operating approval or "buy-offs"	Operational audit?	Assure continuing control and documentation

Figure 11-3 (2 of 2)

managers. These persons must have the maturity and judgment to evaluate opportunities and deal with uncertainties. They must also have enough stature so that their recommendations to develop or abort the project will carry weight with decision-level management.

For instance, a project which shows high promise at the outset may turn out to be untenable or undesirable after a few days of investigation. Conversely, new opportunities or a broader scope may be projected after a study begins.

User Specifications

The user specifications activity is oriented toward development of a statement of business problems and specifications for their solution.. The activity is performed through joint efforts by users and systems analysts as members of a project team. The systems project team examines all related manual procedures and computer processing. The relationships between the application under development and others adjacent to it are also studied.

Documentation created during the user specifications activity has the stature and effect of a contract between users and EDP people. It covers both one-time development commitments and performance within the implemented, ongoing system. Thus, this documentation must be complete in identifying:

- Actions the user is to take
- Decision rules which will be applied
- Services to be performed by the EDP Department
- Methods and schedules for interactions between users and the EDP Department

Since the activity is business-problem oriented, the major efforts are expended by users and systems analysts. The programming supervisor or manager is consulted on technical feasibility and estimates of programming time and cost requirements; but the technical specifics of hardware, software, and application programs are not yet treated in depth.

Technical Specifications

The technical specifications activity bridges the gap between the business and the technical levels of project activity. The project is carried to a point where the processing and file logic required for the computer and for the programmer are generated. End products of this activity include documentation covering a series of technical and operational constraints on the system. The tasks within this activity are performed by senior-level specialists or managers in hardware and software areas of the EDP Department.

The results of this phase should be a comprehensive set of specifications that could be adequate for complete development of all detailed program and user instructions.

Implementation Planning

Once the technical specifications have been completed, a separate implementation-planning activity is advisable, particularly on large projects. This serves to combine all the resources and cumulative knowledge on the project to prepare for the final thrust needed to implement the system. This is a joint EDP and user activity.

The implementation planning activity results in a detailed planning document which includes:

- A recommitment to objectives, scope, benefits, and costs for the new application
- Implementation schedules and responsibilities
- A progress report to and a final preimplementation review with users and management

As indicated in Figure 11-1, there should be few uncertainties remaining upon completion of this phase. Failure to take the time to perform this important activity is probably the major reason for disappointments and failures on large systems development projects.

Programming

Programming is a totally technical activity initiated on the basis of documentation carried forward from technical specifications. This activity results in completed application programs which have been compiled from the programming language into machine language *and tested.* Other end products include the operating instructions necessary to run the programs and linkage between application programs and associated elements of system software, including utility routines and the operating system.

User Procedures and Training

Concurrent with the programming activity, user procedures and training materials are prepared for converting to and operating the new application. Maximum user involvement is sought to ensure that users understand the application and are prepared to carry it forward as specified.

System Test

On a planned basis, all functional elements of the new application — programs, clerical procedures, test files, and personnel — are combined for test of the full application. The objective here is to place heavy stress upon the system in an attempt to make it fail. Any shortcomings are then analyzed for corrective actions.

As noted previously, experience has shown that virtually all systems will still contain "bugs" after they have gone through the testing activity. However, a concentrated test, during which the system is consciously overloaded, maximizes the number of "bugs" which surface.

Conversion

The conversion activity takes in the transition of all equipment, files, and manual procedures from the old application to the new. The magnitude of this may vary widely. In many cases, conversion will require a major effort with special data acquisition and computer programs. Failure to recognize the amount of effort involved in conversion and to sequence and to schedule the tasks carefully will seriously jeopardize the success of the overall project.

Postimplementation Review

After a new data processing system is implemented and running, it should be an established practice to perform a review aimed at comparing accomplishments with plans. The objective at this point is both to measure project performance and to use this activity as a learning experience. Practice of postimplementation reviews serves to:

- Sharpen systems development skills
- Identify possible areas for modification or improvement to systems development methods
- Suggest possible project control techniques to minimize problems encountered in past efforts

The postimplementation review is frequently performed about three to six months after conversion. Based on the results, it may be desirable to schedule a second review to ensure that any open items are resolved.

Ongoing Maintenance

As a last point, specifying an activity and a mechanism for ongoing maintenance of an EDP system recognizes that change is a constant in this environment. Therefore, each project should produce documentation and build in the capability for modification of the implemented application as requirements change.

SYSTEM PLANNING

In discussing those elements of the project approach which are of special concern in the area of documentation, control, and auditing, the first item should be systems planning. The purposes of the system planning activities include establishing the scope and objectives of a proposed project. Attendant facts and logic are developed to the level necessary for management review and evaluation as part of a capital budgeting process.

Level of Effort

The level and extent of effort expended in system planning should be highly dependent on the nature of the project. Project factors affecting the scope of planning activities include:

- Projected benefits and costs
- The degree to which the proposed project affects other applications in operation or under development
- The degree of technical knowledge required versus what is available
- The overall status of the total systems development picture within the company

Figure 11-1 indicates that the system planning activity may involve 10 to 15 percent of the total project effort and may be divided into up to three activities. Such an activity breakdown would be particularly appropriate when a new system promises major impact on overall company operations and when the probability for going ahead with development is proportionately high. Under these assumptions, formal planning activities may be extended knowingly to substantial parts of the tasks usually performed as part of user specifications. Conversely, where a project is technically trivial and the users are well versed in computer applications, system planning may be scaled downward into a single, short activity not exceeding five percent of the overall project expenditures.

In effect, the systems development structure should provide effective, flexible guidance commensurate with situations encountered and skills available.

Skills Required

The results of system planning activities are as good as the mix of business and technical management which goes into them. Typically, the most critical judgments are made early in the life of a project. The 80/20 rule of relevance applies. That is, 80 percent of the relevance and management concern within any given system will center on 20 percent of documents and efforts. An inadequate level of management and technical judgment at this point may lead to a high degree of waste. Perhaps more important, a degree of confusion and disenchantment that makes it difficult to complete a valuable and otherwise viable project may also result.

The full spectrum of disciplines associated with the future of the project must be represented. In particular, middle- and upper-user management, together with key personnel in systems analysis, programming, software, hardware, and operations, should place their judgment and commitment behind any decision to proceed with the extensive development effort that follows.

Results

Planning activities produce two closely interrelated results: a system planning report and a management decision on whether to proceed with the project. If the project is approved, development priorities are assigned.

The system planning report, which results from these activities, should be consistent in format and content with other reports which support other investment decisions. Thus, each planning report should include the recommendation of the system project team on whether to proceed with or drop the project.

USER SPECIFICATIONS

Objectives

One of the important objectives of the user specifications activity is the development, by the analyst, of a thorough familiarity with the user environment and the present user system. Analysts must understand the user's responsibilities, constraints, and problems as well as the procedures being performed. This understanding must be recognized by the user as a basis for placing confidence in the subsequent recommendations of the analyst. When the user is satisfied with the analyst's understanding, he will communicate his own needs.

A second objective of user specifications is the development of a detailed manual describing the new system, what services and processing will be performed by and for the user, and what performance criteria will be met. This manual is one of the basic sources of information for an auditor examining the systems development process or performing an application audit as well as a major factor in establishing a commitment to and the specifics of the quality measures to be applied to operations and controls.

A final objective for user specifications is the establishment of responsibility for the implementation and operation of the new system. To this end, literal, formal requirements documentation is a major factor in establishing an understanding of the responsibilities as well as of the data processing concepts which form the basis for the application under development.

Work Plans

The work plans for user specifications start with flowcharting of the existing system as shown in Figure 11-4. The flow begins with the system planning report, a good example of the principle of cumulative documentation. As new staff members are added to the project, this report provides excellent background. Also, in cases where there has been a time lapse between system planning and user specifications, a review of the report serves as a refresher for the project staff.

Figure 11-4 presupposes little or no prior documentation of present procedures beyond the planning report. Therefore, the logical starting point within the work plan is a study and documentation of present systems as they are applied within the user group

221

USER SPECIFICATIONS WORK FLOW (PRESENT SYSTEM)

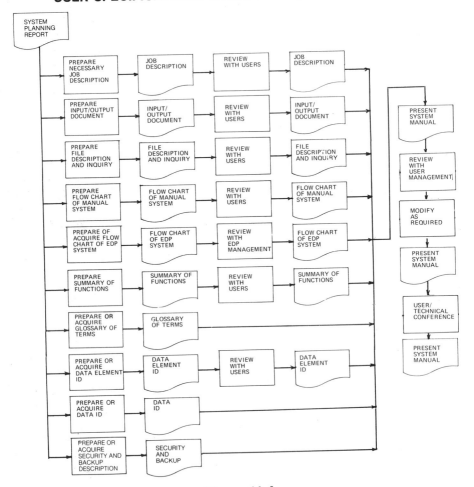

Figure 11-4

222

and, if applicable, in the EDP Department. In documenting a current system, the study begins with describing each person's job and then the source of input data and flows through the system to the conclusion. Obviously, if the present system is a revision of work done by a previous system project, the existing documentation is used as a starting point and is tested and updated as necessary. Much of this work is done in a clerical or first-line supervisory environment within the user organization. As appropriate, understandings developed at this level may be confirmed with successively higher levels of user management. In addition, sessions with user management will provide an opportunity to discover plans or potentials for changes which may affect the application under study.

Hopefully, the thought processes associated with the development of the new application are continually active among the analysts and other members of the project team. However, time and effort should not be devoted to documentation of a proposed new application until there is mutual agreement with user management that the present system is fully documented and understood.

Documentation of requirements for the new system shown in Figure 11-5 follows a work flow which is the reverse of that used in documenting the existing procedures. The plan to this point is tailored to the fact that systems analysts and users are gaining an understanding of exactly how and why things are done. Members of the team have spotted areas where improvements can be made in capturing, processing, or reporting.

In documenting the new system, it is advisable to begin with tentative decisions on the end results desired. Work starts with a determination of what information will be reported and what decisions will be affected. Content and layout specifications are developed for the reports, forms, or displays to be generated. From there, the team follows the structure upstream toward the beginning. The study determines and documents the data content which will be necessary in computer files to generate the required outputs. These data elements are then traced back to the source to determine whether they may best originate. Overview-level design specifications are established for working documents, file content, and procedures.

This work flow is illustrated in Figure 11-5 as proceeding on a straight-line basis. In actual practice, however, system requirements is a reiterative learning process. A single cycle through present and new procedures is seldom sufficient. In effect, the development of requirements for the new system involves playing a game of "what if," projecting different approaches and alternatives. These creative exercises may take place at any point in the requirements process. They should not be discouraged by project and activity structures. Rather, these structures should provide a basis for guidance and management without encumbering creativity.

DEFINE REQUIREMENTS OF NEW SYSTEM

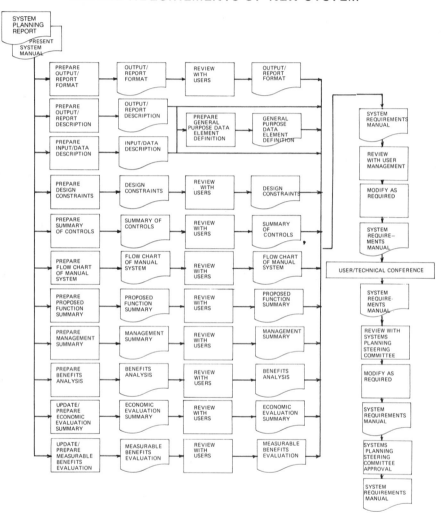

Figure 11-5

224

COMMON STUDY FEATURES

When completed, the documentation for the current system and the proposed new system bear a direct resemblance to each other. The new document also resembles its predecessor, the system planning study. The greatest point of comparison between the documentation of the system planning and user specifications activities lies in their end-product orientation. All planning and requirements documentation stresses application results. These representations are then supported by descriptions of work flows, files, controls, working documents, procedures, and costs.

The intent (and value) of such standard documentation is obvious. There is direct comparability for both working continuity within the project and management decisions on comparative benefits, costs, and consequences of developing the new system to replace the present one.

The clarity of communication implied by continuity of documentation reviewed by users and EDP people is important because one of the main objectives of user specifications is to establish documented standards which the users can understand and "buy." User approvals are necessary for every functional and logical element of a new system, including clerical procedures, file content, decision logic, controls, source transaction documents, working documents and end-product reports.

One objective of the piecemeal agreement and approval procedures used in the user specifications activity is to establish a series of formal meetings between key people in the user organization and the EDP Department. This provides assurance that both user and EDP technical people will discuss and understand the same documentation.

PRESENT SYSTEM DOCUMENTATION

At a minimum seven key elements of documentation required on present applications are:

- Clerical functions
- Input-output document descriptions
- File descriptions
- A flowchart of the present system (both manual and EDP phases)
- A summary of functions performed
- A detailed description of data (records) and elements (fields)
- Present security and backup

An illustration of *clerical functions required for each position* in the present application is shown in Figure 11-6. The form shown is completed to a depth necessary to analyze work volumes and flows for a typical clerical position supporting a payroll application. Note that the position described is a control-oriented job.

This is the type of functional description on which users and EDP people should agree in their evaluation of benefits and opportunities for a proposed system. This is also part of their presentation requesting management's allocation of resources to develop a new system. For less important clerical positions within a system, commensurately less descriptive detail is necessary.

Discretion is also important in describing documents associated with the present application. The intent is to select and document all forms which are significant in terms of the recording, processing, and reporting of data or the exercising of controls. Each document description form should be accompanied by a sample of the document described. There should be typical entries in all appropriate fields of the sample documents.

Job and document descriptions should be tied together on analytic flowcharts like those discussed earlier. A typical *flowchart detailing activities* of the present system is shown on Figure 11-7. There is an obvious similarity between this system development activity and the initial procedures of an audit. This helps demonstrate that uniform documentation during the system development process serves both to improve the reliability of controls built into applications and also to improve effectiveness of audits.

Additional user specifications documentation may be necessary where transaction volumes or processing complexity will be a factor in designing a new application or determining its economic feasibility. In such cases, the analytic flowchart of the present procedures should be supplemented with detail similar to the clerical-functions form in Figure 11-6.

In documenting an existing application, definition of the records and data elements to be processed is necessary. For every project, for example, the need for consistency in documentation suggests that some sort of *glossary of terms describing data elements or fields* within the application be developed (see Figure 11-8). In addition, an inventory of data elements for an existing system serves as a control to be sure that all data are carried forward from the old system to the new one.

As additional, standard documentation of present applications in the user specifications activity, *each data element or field* according to logical grouping for processing or file content may be identified and described on a form as shown in Figure 11-9. As can be seen, the purpose of each element of data necessary to an application is given on the form. The depth to which such definition forms are executed within a user specifications activity will depend on the complexity and scope of the application. Content will also relate to the need or potential value of such documentation in furthering communication among user organizations and EDP people.

CLERICAL FUNCTIONS

CLERICAL FUNCTIONS

TOUCHE ROSS

☒ JOB DESCRIPTIONS

☐ SUMMARY OF FUNCTIONS

☒ PRESENT SYSTEM

☐ NEW SYSTEM

ORGANIZATION A B C Company
Accounting
SYSTEM Labor Distribution
USER REP J. Doe

PAGE __1__ OF __1__
PROJECT NO. 123
PREPARED BY W. Smith
REVIEWED BY J. Jones
DATE 2/24
PHASE User Area

FUNC-TION NO.	HOURS PER DAY	HOURS PER WEEK	HOURS PER MONTH	VOLUME		N/D	FUNCTION DESCRIPTION
1	2			1,000		D	Receive Labor Transactions from Timekeepers, Sort to Employee sequence within Department
2	2			1,000		D	Post to Control Sheet by Employee
3	1					D	Foot Control Sheet and Balance to Totals Produced by Timekeeper
4							Foward Labor Transactions to Payroll
5		12				D	Extend Regular and overtime Hours by Hourly Rate and Post to Labor Distribution Report by Employee and Department
6		3					Balance Totals of Labor Distribution Report to Control Sheets
TOTAL	5	15	—				
TOTAL PER MONTH	108	65	—				COMMENTS: Performed by Accounting Clerk
% TIME AVAILABLE			173				

COPYRIGHT 1973 FORM NO. 70
TOUCHE ROSS & CO.

Figure 11-6

227

FLOWCHART OF MANUAL SYSTEM

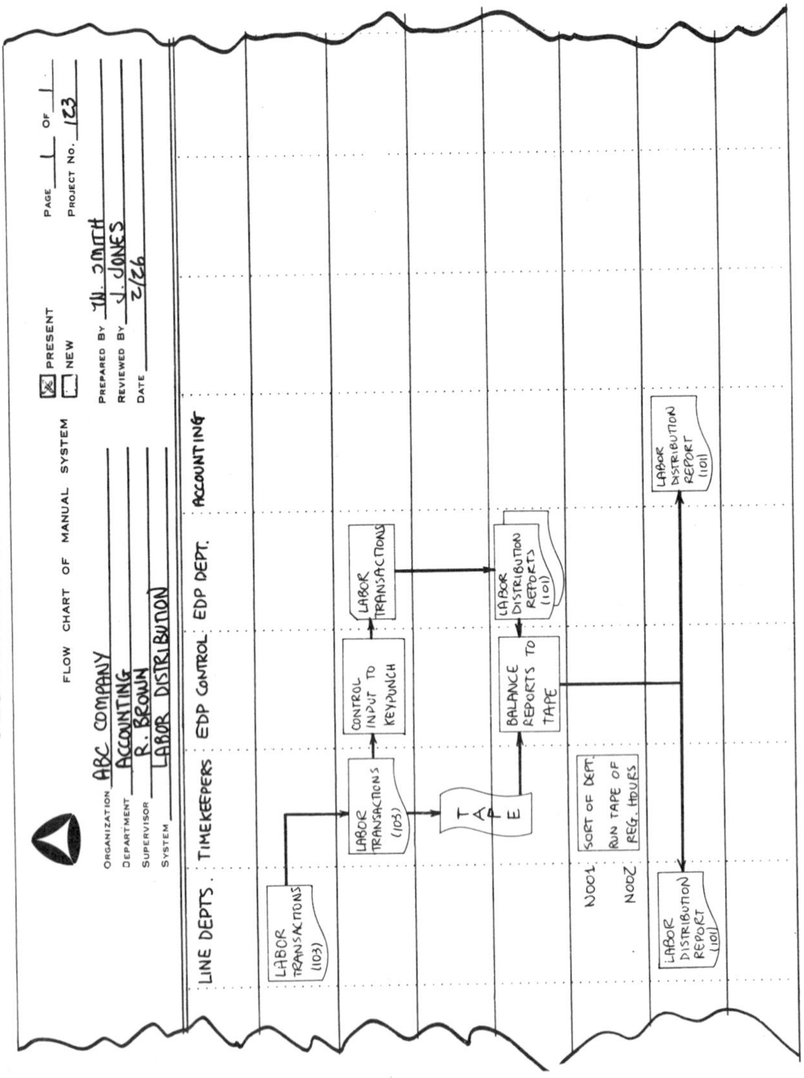

FLOW CHART OF MANUAL SYSTEM
PRESENT
NEW
ORGANIZATION ABC COMPANY
DEPARTMENT ACCOUNTING
SUPERVISOR R. BROWN
SYSTEM LABOR DISTRIBUTION
PREPARED BY W. SMITH
REVIEWED BY J. JONES
DATE 2/26
PAGE 1 OF 1
PROJECT NO. 123
LINE DEPTS.
TIMEKEEPERS
EDP CONTROL
EDP DEPT.
ACCOUNTING
LABOR TRANSACTIONS (103)
LABOR TRANSACTIONS (103)
CONTROL INPUT TO KEYPUNCH
LABOR TRANSACTIONS
TAPE
BALANCE REPORTS TO TAPE
LABOR DISTRIBUTION REPORTS (101)
N001
N002
SORT OF DEPT.
RUN TAPE OF REG. HOURS
LABOR DISTRIBUTION REPORT (101)
LABOR DISTRIBUTION REPORT (101)

Figure 11-7

GLOSSARY OF TERMS DESCRIBING DATA ELEMENTS

GLOSSARY OF TERMS

PAGE _1_ OF _1_

PROJECT NO. _/ 23_

▲ **· TOUCHE ROSS**

ORGANIZATION _A BC Company_

Accounting

SYSTEM _Labor Distribution_

USER REP _J, Doe_

PREPARED BY _W. Smith_

REVIEWED BY _J Jones_

DATE _2/26_

PHASE _User specs_

TERM	MEANING
Clock No.	Number Assigned to an Employee for Reporting Hours worked
Dept. No.	Operating Groups within Company
Regular Hours	Hours worked ≤ 8 Monday - Friday
Overtime Hrs.	Hours worked > 8 Monday - Friday And All Hours on Sat, Sun And Holidays
Shift Bonus	Premium for working 4-12 shift or 12 - 8 shift

COPYRIGHT 1973   FORM NO. 10
TOUCHE ROSS & CO.

Figure 11-8

DATA ELEMENT DEFINITION

TOUCHE ROSS

ELEMENT DEFINITION

PREPARED BY ___W. Smith___

APPROVED BY ___J. Jones___

DATE ___2/26___

Element
Number

DATA ELEMENT NAME	Unit of Measure	PICTURE	SOURCE
Overtime - Rate	$	Z ZV 99	Personnel

DESCRIPTION

Labor Overtime Rate: Defines the wage Rate for Hours worked in Excess of 8 Monday through Friday, and All Hours on Saturday, Sunday and Holidays.

EDIT CRITERIA

Positive Numeric with value between 4.35 and 8.50, and Greater than Regular-Rate, Reject if fails the following: $1.4 (Regular-Rate) \leq Overtime - Rate \leq 1.6 (Regular-Rate)$.

CONTROL Edit and Security Specifications

SYNONYMS

None

DATA DEPENDENCIES

None

SECURITY CONSIDERATIONS Internal Confidential - Inquiry Limited to Personnel, Accounting, Direct Supervisors. Update Limited to Personnel.

STATUTORY or POLICY CONSIDERATIONS

Security only

CODING ATTRIBUTES (Over) Table of Initial Overtime-Rates by Labor Class

COMMENTS

Update Annually as Result of Contract Re-Negotiations

COPYRIGHT 1973 FORM NO. 11
TOUCHE ROSS & CO.

Figure 11-9

230

NEW SYSTEM DOCUMENTATION

Similar, comparable documentation should be prepared during the user specifications activity to describe the content and processing associated with the proposed new application. Minimum documentation standards include:

- An output report format using standard data processing layout sheets. In effect, this is a rough draft showing the content of documents and reports to be produced under the computerized portions of the new application. A *typical report layout* is illustrated in Figure 11-10.

- An output report description which serves as a design guide. Specifications on this document should cover data sources, computer print specifications, handling of the report or document in the EDP control group, and distribution.

- An input data description form which specifies what each record will look like as it is presented to the EDP Department for data conversion and processing. An example of an *input data description* associated with the documentation of a proposed system is shown in Figure 11-11.

- Data fields associated with each report or document to be produced under the new application should be specified (see Figure 11-12, record/document contents).

- For each output to be generated by the new system, a table *form indicating the processing steps* which should be taken under varying conditions of data content should be developed. Such a general purpose form is shown in Figure 11-13. This table is designed to relate processing functions to the conditions which will trigger them. The simplicity of this processing functions table fits in well with its role as a means of documenting specifications stipulated by users for processing to be performed.

- *Decision tables* (Figure 11-14), or their equivalent in block-flow diagrams, should be prepared to cover all logic to be applied in computer processing. In the example given, specifications are drawn for the testing of data elements within input records for the existence of predetermined conditions. Decision rules are established and based on the sensing of these conditions. Actions to be taken by the computer are outlined. Files to be used in the processing are identified on the table.

- Any *constraints* to be applied to the design of the new application should be specified in terms of scheduling and timing, policies, and preliminary identification of technical feasibility or requirements constraints.

- All *controls* to be applied within the new application should be identified and separated according to the location of their implementation.

REPORT LAYOUT

ORGANIZATION ABC Company
DEPARTMENT Accounting
SYSTEM Labor Distribution

PREPARED BY W. Smith
REVIEWED BY J. Jones
DATE 2/26

SEQUENCE	DATA ELEMENT
DEPARTMENT	
CLOCK NO.	

LABOR DISTRIBUTION REPORT

DEPARTMENT	CLOCK NO.	REGULAR HOURS	OVERTIME HOURS	SHIFT BONUS HOURS	REGULAR DOLLARS	OVERTIME DOLLARS	TOTAL DOLLARS
GENERAL LEDGER DEPT. NUMBER	NUMBER ASSIGNED TO EACH EMPLOYEE	HOURS WORKED DURING 1 DAY =<8; OR 1 WK. =<40	HOURS WORKED DURING 1 DAY >8; OR 1 WK. >40	HOURS WORKED BETWEEN 5PM AND 7AM	REGULAR HOURS X HOURLY RATE	OVERTIME HOURS X 150% OF HOURLY RATE	SUM OF REGULAR $ + OVERTIME $ + SHIFT $
TOTAL BY CLOCK NO.	(SUM THIS COL)	(SUM THIS COL)	(SUM THIS COL)	(SUM THIS COL)	(SUM THIS COL)	(SUM THIS COL)	(SUM THIS COL)
TOTAL BY DEPT.	"	"	"	"	"	"	"
TOTAL AT END OF REPT.	"	"	"	"	"	"	"

DEPARTMENT	CLOCK NO.	HOURLY RATE
(SEE ABOVE)	(SEE ABOVE)	RATE OF PAY FIXED PER EMPLOYEE

Figure 11-10

232

INPUT DATA DESCRIPTION

▲ **TOUCHE ROSS**

MANUAL DOCUMENT SHEET

☒ CURRENT SYSTEM
☐ PROPOSED SYSTEM

PAGE _/_ OF _/_
PROJECT NO. _/ 23_

ORGANIZATION _A BC Company_
Accounting
SYSTEM _LABOR Distribution_
USER REP _J. Dee_

PREPARED BY _W Smith_
REVIEWED BY _J Jones_
DATE _2/26_
PHASE _USER specs_

_142_ DOCUMENT NUMBER		COPY ATTACHED Y ☒

FORM NAME: _LABOR TRANSACTIONS_   FORM NUMBER: _H-3_

PRESENT INPUT FORM:

PUNCHED CARD ☐	MAGNETIC TAPE ☐	MEMO ☐
PREPRINTED FORM ☒	OTHER _____ ☐	DOES NOT EXIST ☐

DOCUMENT CONVERTED TO:

CARD ☒   DEMAND INQ. ☐   MAGNETIC TAPE ☐   OTHER _____ ☐

MANUAL PROCESS AND EDIT STEPS	Performed By
Receive And check off TRANSACTIONS	_Timekeeper_
RUN Adding Machine Tape of TRANSACTIONS	_''_

DISTRIBUTION FLOW	
1. _Accounting Department_	
2.	
3.	
4.	
5.	
6.	
7.	

CONTROL	Performed By
Tape of Total Regular Hours	_Timekeeper_

VOLUME / KEY STROKES

PERIOD	FREQ.	MIN.	AVE.	MAX.	Strokes	Period Sept-July	Ave-Sept		
Aug - Sept	_Daily_	_500_	_700_	_1,000_	PUNCH	_15,900_	_10,600_		
Sept - July	_Daily_	_1,000_	_1,200_	_1,500_	VERIFY	_15,900_	_10,600_		
					TOTAL	_31,800_	_21,200_		

COMMENTS

Figure 11-11

RECORD/DOCUMENT CONTENTS

RECORD/DOCUMENT CONTENTS RD /0 3

TOUCHE ROSS

RECORD/DOCUMENT I.D. _____

TITLE _Labor Transactions_____

PAGE __2__ OF __2__

PROJECT NO. _/23_____

ORGANIZATION _ABC Company_

Accounting

SYSTEM _Labor Distribution_

USER REP _J. Doe_

PREPARED BY _W. Smith_

REVIEWED BY _J. Jones_

DATE _2/26_

PHASE _USER REQ_

SUPPORT OF DOCUMENT NO. | 0 3 NAME _Labor Transactions_

ELE. NO.	DATA ELEMENT	ID	LENGTH	USAGE	PICTURE	FD LEVEL	
001	Department No.	Lt	4	N	9999	05	
002	Clock No.	Lt	4	N	9999	05	
003	Regular Hours	Lt	3	N	S99V9	05	
004	Overtime Hours	Lt	3	N	S99V9	05	
005	Shift Bonus Hours	Lt	3	N	S99V9	05	

Figure 11-12

PROCESSING CONDITIONS TABLE

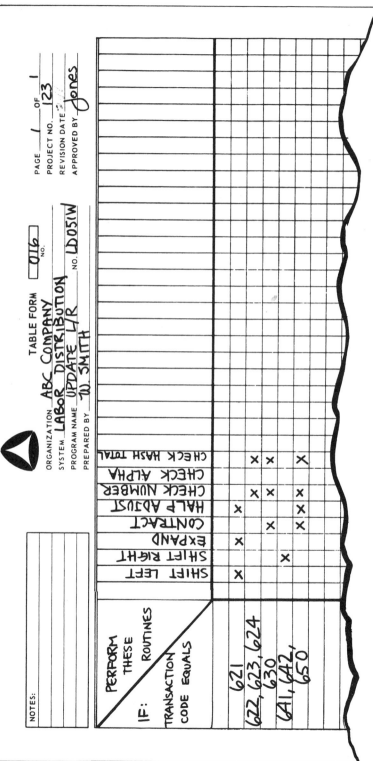

TABLE FORM `016` NO.

ORGANIZATION ABC Company

SYSTEM LABOR DISTRIBUTION

PROGRAM NAME UPDATE L/R NO. LD051W

PREPARED BY W. SMITH

NOTES:

IF: TRANSACTION CODE EQUALS	PERFORM THESE ROUTINES	SHIFT LEFT	SHIFT RIGHT	EXPAND	CONTRACT	HALF ADJUST	CHECK NUMBER	CHECK ALPHA	CHECK HASH TOTAL
621		X		X		X			
622, 623, 624, 630			X		X		X		X
641, 642, 650			X		X	X	X		X

Figure 11-13

36-037

235

DECISION TABLE LDCI NO.

ORGANIZATION: ABC COMPANY
SYSTEM: LABOR DISTRIBUTION
PROGRAM NAME: LABOR DIST PRINT
PREPARED BY: W. SMITH   DATE 2/26
NO. LD01   APPROVED BY: J. Jones

PAGE 123 OF 1
PROJECT NO.
REVISION DATE 2/26

TABLE NAME:

LINE	CONDITION ACTION	RULE → 1	2	3	4	5	6	7	8
1	IS REGULAR HOURS PUNCHED	Y	-	-	-	N	Y	N	N
2	IS OVERTIME HOURS PUNCHED	Y	-	N	Y	Y	N	Y	N
3	IS SHIFT BONUS HOURS PUNCHED	Y	-	Y	N	N	Y	Y	N
10	REGULAR DOLLARS = REGULAR HOURS * (HOURLY + .005)	X	X				X		
11	OVERTIME DOLLARS = OVERTIME HOURS * 150% (HRS. + .005)	X	X		X			X	
12	SHIFT DOLLARS = SHIFT BONUS HOURS * $.10	X		X			X	X	
13	ERROR; NO SHIFT OR O'T WITHOUT REGULAR	X	X	X		X	X		
14	NEXT RECORD					X	X	X	X

NOTES: THE ERROR MESSAGE AT LINE 13 SHOULD BE DISPLAYED IN THE "DOLLARS" AREA OF THE REPORT, TO THE RIGHT OF A DUMP OF THE 501 RECORD.

GO TO — F (FUNCTION), R (RULE, SAME TABLE), T (TABLE)

Figure 11-14

31–037

- An *analytic flowchart,* separated according to functions, should be prepared to cover the clerical portions of the proposed new application (similar to the ones discussed above and illustrated in Figure 11-7).
- A *summary of functions* comparable to the one shown in Figure 11-6 should be prepared for the new application. This should tie in with the documentation of logic decisions, assuring that all processing steps required in the new application are spelled out and agreed to between users and EDP people. In effect, this

represents a commitment by user management for the work to be performed within their organization.

- A *management summary* covering recommendations for the feasibility of and general benefits from the proposed new application. At the end of the user specifications activity, this report will serve as an introductory cover section for the documentation which will be considered in determining whether to proceed with the development of the new application and, if so, what priorities to assign.

- A separate *summary of benefits* forecast for the proposed new application. The user organization should associate itself closely with this document.

- A specific *economic evaluation* of the impact of the proposed new application upon operations within the user department. Where feasible, it should show actual budget reductions which will be experienced in the user department if benefits from the proposed new application are realized.

Optionally, data elements and data files or tables should be described for the new application in much the same manner as was recommended for the present one in the discussion covering figures 11-9 and 11-12.

The set of forms used in this chapter should be viewed as an *example* of what should be expected in the way of content of standard documentation. Any format of documentation is adequate if it is consistently used, complete in content, and provides clear communication between user and EDP people. *In this area, the existence of effective documentation is more critical than its specific format.*

Activity Results

The primary product of the user specifications activity is a detailed, bound manual with contents and documentation stated in terms of the needs, policies, and expectations from the planned application by the user organization. This user specifications manual should be complete enough so that, if amplification is required, it will be primarily in the area of detailed instructions. These instructions are, by design, prepared later in the project. Also, in many cases, clerical instructions are prepared only at a draft level during a system development project and are refined following implementation and operational experience. Subsequent changes should be accumulated separately.

TECHNICAL SPECIFICATIONS

Objectives

The major objectives of the technical specifications activity are the development of technical-level decisions and documentation for the computer processing portions of an EDP application and associated operating functions within the EDP Department. This technical documentation is in substantially greater detail than any prepared during earlier activities. It provides directions to be followed during the programming activity. Similarly, this same documentation will be vital to maintenance changes after conversion and implementation of the application. Depending on the results of this effort, it may become necessary to do some modest reevaluation of earlier decisions and documentation covering processing and work flows within user or data-source organizations.

An additional objective of this activity is the development of a detailed plan and schedule for the preparation of application programs. This objective can be met realistically only if a proper mix of senior-level skills is used.

Work Plan

The work done during the technical specifications activity is heavily dependent on documentation accumulated from the user specifications activity. Additional tasks and end items added to the results of the earlier activity include:

- Final, detailed design and documentation for the computer portions of the new application should be developed as a logical starting point within the work plan. This will break the computer processing into modules or programming segments.
- Programs and modules, once they are identified and specified, must be related to the files which will support the application. This involves determination of how files will be organized logically and physically for processing: index sequential, random access, data storage (packing) density, record sizes, and so on. Also to be considered are the physical equipment and storage media which must be allocated for the most efficient use of equipment and materials in support of the application. In dealing with files during the system planning and user specifications activities, technical evaluations were at a feasibility level only. These earlier reviews were intended to identify file content, response characteristics, and costs. User-EDP interaction may be necessary within this technically oriented activity to the extent that technical considerations uncover requirements for modifications in specifications or procedures established previously with the user. For example, new technical developments

may make another technique of data conversion or input desirable. Where such situations arise, they should be explained fully to the user and concurrence obtained. Final user approval should come during the next activity: implementation planning.

- A series of other technical considerations must be dealt with. These include selection of programming languages and operating system software. Technical personnel must also develop standards for operations-center handling of the application. These include operator controls, file retention schedules, operator actions in case of program interruptions, provisions for processing backup, and restart procedures.

- Development of a programming schedule. Programming represents 30 percent of the expenditures in time and cost for the typical system project. Its realistic planning, budgeting, and scheduling represent an important area for effective management within a system project.

IMPLEMENTATION PLANNING

Implementation planning is the last planned point for evaluation, analysis, and change to the application under development prior to actual development of the new system. In the activities immediately following implementation planning, the project moves concurrently along two separate paths in that (1) final application programs are written and user training is carried out and (2) work begins on establishing master files to support the computer processing portions of the new application.

The implementation planning activity is, in a sense, a turning point within the project structure. Some 60 percent of the time and cost expenditures are still to be made, but the most creative portions of the project are substantially over. In addition, most applications of management philosophy and control have already been exerted. Once implementation planning is completed, the project takes a strong turn toward the mechanical.

Objectives

Three main objectives exist in the implementation planning activity:

- Detailed plans must be developed for the remaining activities in the project.
- Full utilization must be made of the knowledge accumulated and experience gained in earlier project activities.
- Full and complete user and management review and approval must be obtained.

Detailed planning of the remaining activities becomes feasible only at this stage of the project because of the information accumulated to this point. Planning is also important at this point because the degree of overlap in the remaining activities of the project is greater than that which existed in the preceding activities.

The objective of securing a complete review by user and management is obviously vital because of the strategic position of the implementation planning activity within the project's structure. Further steps without full approval usually result in disappointments.

Work Plan

The plan of work for the implementation planning activity is highly end-item oriented. Each major segment of the activity is aimed directly at producing a specific set of planning documents (the documents and the task needed to create them should be closely related). Three specific set of end-item documentation can be identified for the implementation planning activity:

- User procedures and training plan
- System test plan
- Conversion plan

USER PROCEDURES AND TRAINING PLAN

A plan for user training is likely to be the last of the three major documents completed during the implementation planning activity, basically because the nature of the interaction between activities being planned is such that final detailing in user training depends on decisions made about the conversion and system test activities (see the checklist for the user training plan in Figure 11-15). User training functions are dependent on finalized specifications for procedures, equipment, and so on. This listing also indicates that the user training activity will include planning for three separate training elements. Users must be trained to operate the implemented, ongoing application as well as the system test and conversion activities.

SYSTEM TEST PLAN

The scope and content of a system test plan are illustrated in Figure 11-16. This serves to demonstrate that the system test activity is a point of convergence for the results of most preceding activities within the project.

As can be seen from the entries on the form in Figure 11-16 on page 242, the idea employed is to bring together and test increments of a finished application until all elements are operated and tested as a unit. Thus, programs which have been tested both individually and in groups are brought together as designed for final use within the application. Similarly, manual procedures in departments or groups which act as users or data sources will be tested on an interactive basis.

USER PROCEDURES AND TRAINING PLAN CHECKLIST

USER PROCEDURES TRAINING & CHECK LIST   PAGE _/_ OF _2_

TOUCHE ROSS

PROJECT NO. _123_

ORGANIZATION _ABC Company_
Accounting

PREPARED BY _W Smith_
REVIEWED BY _J Jones_

SYSTEM _Labor Distribution_

DATE _2/26_

USER REP _J, Doe_

PHASE _IMPL. PLAN_

DESCRIPTION OF ACTIVITY	INDIVIDUAL RESPONSIBLE	ORGANIZATION RESPONSIBLE	START DATE	COMPLETION DATE	APPROVED BY
1. USER PREPARATION	—				
2. INTERNAL NOTIFICATION					
EXECUTIVE ANNOUNCEMENT	R. Roe	Plant Mgr	4/1	5/15	
EMPLOYEE ANNOUNCEMENT	J. Doe	Acc ty.	4/1	5/15	
3. EXTERNAL NOTIFICATION					
CUSTOMER CO-ORDINATION					
VENDOR CO-ORDINATION					
PUBLIC RELATIONS					
OTHER					
4. POLICY CONSIDERATIONS					
CORPORATE	J Doe	Acc'ty.	4/1	5/1	
DIVISIONAL	J Doe	Accty.	4/1	5/1	
5. PROCEDURES					
CONTENT PLAN	J. Jones	Systems	4/15	4/20	
MANUALS	J Jones	Systems	4/15	5/1	
PUBLICATION & ISSUANCE	J. Doe	Accty.	5/1	5/15	
6. JOB OUTLINES	J. Jones	Systems	5/15	5/30	
7. FORMS					
DESIGN	J. Jones	Systems	6/1	6/15	
INTERNAL PRINTING	—				
EXTERNAL PRINTING	J. Jones	Systems	6/1	6/15	
8. TRAINING AND ORIENTATION					
PROGRAM PLAN	J. Jones	Systems	6/1	6/15	
PROGRAM INSTRUCTORS MANUAL	J. Jones	Systems	6/1	6/15	
PRESENTATION	J. Jones	Systems	6/1	6/15	
OTHER	J. Doe	Acctg	6/15	6/30	
9. SPECIAL EQUIPMENT & FIXTURES					
DETERMINATION OF REQ'MTS.					
ENGINEERING DEPARTMENT					
SUB CONTRACTORS					
10. OFFICE EQUIPMENT REQ.	J. Doe	Accty	6/1	6/15	
11. FLOOR SPACE & LAYOUT					
12. SUPPLIES	J. Doe	Accta.	6/1	7/1	
13. PERSONNEL					
RECLASSIFICATION	—				
HIRING	J. Doe	Accty.	6/1	7/1	

APPROVED BY: _W. White_
              SYSTEMS GROUP   _Q. Jones_ PROJECT LEADER

Figure 11-15

Example — For an application being developed to handle order entry, invoicing, and accounts receivable, the manual and computer portions of the system might be interrelated in three or more stages. These could cover the writing of orders, the issuing of invoices, and the posting of accounts receivable. Then, as a separate test increment, procedures for posting of cash receipts might be conducted with manual and computer portions of the application interrelated.

241

SYSTEM TEST CHECKLIST

△
TOUCHE ROSS

ORGANIZATION *ABC COMPANY*
ACCOUNTING
SYSTEM *LABOR DISTRIBUTION*
USER REP *J. DoE*

PREPARED BY *W. Smith*
REVIEWED BY *J. Jones*
DATE *2/26*
PHASE *Impl Plan*

MODULE NO.	MODULE NAME	SCHEDULED START DATE	ACTUAL START DATE	SCHEDULED COMPLETION	ACTUAL COMPLETION	PROJECT LEADER
		7/1		9/15		

DESCRIPTION OF ACTIVITY	INDIVIDUAL RESPONSIBLE	ORGANIZATION RESPONSIBLE	START DATE	COMPLETION DATE	APPROVED BY
1. COMPUTER TEST PLAN	J. JONES	SYSTEMS	7/1	7/15	
2. TEST PROCEDURES					
USER ORGANIZATION	J. DoE	ACCTG	7/15	8/1	
DATA PROCESSING OPERATIONS	S. JAMES	D.P. OPNS.	7/15	8/1	
SYSTEMS & PROGRAMMING	W. WHITE	SYSTEMS	7/15	8/1	
DATA PROCESSING CONTROLS	K. DAVIS	CONTROL GP	7/15	8/1	
3. FORMS					
INPUT TEST DATA	J. DoE	ACCTG	8/1	8/15	
FILE CREATION & MAINTENANCE	J. JONES	SYSTEMS	8/1	8/15	
4. CONTROLS					
USER ORGANIZATION	J. DoE	ACCTG	7/15	8/1	
DATA PROCESSING CONTROLS	K. DAVIS	CONTROL GP.	7/15	8/1	
5. EQUIPMENT					
AVAILABILITY	S. JAMES	D.P. OPNS.	7/15	8/1	
EMERGENCY SERVICE	S. JAMES	D.P. OPNS.	7/15	8/1	
6. MANPOWER					
USER ORGANIZATION	J. DoE	ACCTG	7/15	8/1	
DATA PROCESSING OPERATIONS	S. JAMES	D.P. OPNS	7/15	8/1	
SYSTEMS & PROGRAMMING	W. WHITE	SYSTEMS	7/15	8/1	
DATA PROCESSING CONTROLS	K. DAVIS	CONTROL GP.	7/15	8/1	
7. SUPPLIES					
AVAILABILITY	S. JAMES	D.P. OPNS	8/1	8/15	
8. DATA					
CREATED & VERIFIED	J. DoE	ACCTG	9/1	9/15	
CONTROLLED	K. DAVIS	CONTROL GP.	9/1	9/15	
9. FILES					
CREATED & VERIFIED	J. JONES	SYSTEMS	9/1	9/15	
CONTROLLED	K. DAVIS	CONTROL GP	9/1	9/15	
10. MISCELLANEOUS	J. JONES	SYSTEMS	8/1	8/15	

Approved by

J. Doe
USER ORGANIZATION

W. White
SYSTEMS GROUP

S. James
DATA PROCESSING OPERATIONS

J. Jones
PROJECT LEADER

Figure 11-16

OTHER WORK PLAN ELEMENTS

The programming plan, completed just prior to implementation planning during the technical specifications activity, may be affected by some of the decisions or commitments made in the development of plans for conversion or system test. If so, a review of the programming plan should be included as part of the implementation planning activity. At a minimum, assurance should be developed that the programming plan coordinates with the other plans developed during implementation planning for the carrying out of the remainder of the activities in the system development project. And, as a final element in the work plan for this activity, a complete, overall plan for the balance of the project should be prepared for a highly crucial review and approval by users and management. At this point, management should receive and expect adherence to realistic budgets and schedules for the remainder of the project.

CONVERSION PLAN

The scope of the conversion plan and the extent of the activities needed to create it are illustrated in Figure 11-17 on page 244. As shown, it is necessary to plan for a series of closely related, one-time tasks which call for assembly of data and materials from users and the EDP Department. All of these documents and materials must be brought together in a position of readiness for inclusion in the ongoing application. Activities involved include:

- Acquisition of data
- Identification of sources
- Development of final procedures
- Formalization of specifications
- Development of any special programs which might be needed to convert files from a present computer system to a new one
- A control plan to assure that the new files provide an appropriate starting point

One of the objectives present is to establish schedules and commitments for the people and equipment needed to implement the conversion. The conversion plan must also spell out exactly under what conditions conversion will be considered complete and successful. These definitions and specifications are needed both for the increments of parallel processing and for final conversion.

PROGRAMMING

Within a structured system development project, most of the evaluations and decisions affecting programming are made before the formal activity called "programming" actually begins. As indicated earlier, supervisory and senior members of the programming and technical-services functions were involved in these decisions. These persons might have spent significant time calculating various technical alternatives. At this point in a project, however, programming consists chiefly of the production-type tasks of writing code and testing and debugging of modules.

CONVERSION PLAN CHECKLIST

▲
TOUCHE ROSS

ORGANIZATION _ABC. Company_
Accounting
SYSTEM _Labor Distribution_
USER REP _J. Doe_

PREPARED BY _W. Smith_
REVIEWED BY _J. Jones_
DATE _2/26_
PHASE _IMPL PLAN_

DESCRIPTION OF ACTIVITY	INDIVIDUAL RESPONSIBLE	ORGANIZATION RESPONSIBLE	START DATE	COMPLETION DATE	APPROVED BY
1. CONVERSION PLAN	J. Jones	Systems	5/1	6/1	
2. FILE DATA ACQUISITION PLAN	J. Jones	Systems	5/1	6/1	
3. MANPOWER & EQUIPMENT PLAN	J. Doe	Acctg	5/1	6/1	
4. FILES					
PURIFICATION OF RECORDS	J. Doe	Acctg.	5/15	7/1	
CODING REQUIREMENTS	J. Doe	Acctg.	5/15	7/1	
CONTROL	J. Doe	Acctg	7/1	7/1	
CONVERSION	J. Jones	Systems	6/1	7/1	
MAINTENANCE	J. Doe	Acctg.	7/1	—	
5. FORMS					
DESIGN					
INTERNAL PRINTING					
EXTERNAL PRINTING					
CONVERSION					
6. PARALLEL PROCESSING					
PROCEDURES	J. Jones	Systems	5/1	6/1	
VERIFICATION REQUIREMENTS	J. Doe	Acctg.	5/1	6/1	
SCHEDULE	J. Jones	Systems	5/1	6/1	
7. CONVERSION SEQUENCE					
ORGANIZATIONAL SEQUENCE	J. Doe	Acctg.	5/1	6/1	
SCHEDULE	J. Jones	Systems	5/1	6/1	
8. CONVERSION PROGRAMS					
DEFINITION	J. Jones	Systems	4/1	5/1	
SPECIFICATIONS	J. Jones	Systems	5/1	6/1	
PROGRAMMING	W. Smith	Prog.	6/1	7/1	
9. INTERFACE WITH OTHER SYSTEMS					
FILES					
DATA					
PROGRAMS					

APPROVED BY:

J. Doe   _W. White_   _S. James_   _J. Jones_
USER ORGANIZATION   SYSTEMS GROUP   DATA PROCESSING OPERATIONS   PROJECT LEADER

Figure 11-17

Objectives

The objective of the programming activity is to reduce all user and technical specifications to operational machine language. This includes compiling, testing, and modifying the source program modules as necessary to make them fully operational. The activity should produce programs which are in documented, maintainable form. Finally, documented instructions for computer operators should be developed for the running of the new application.

Work Plan

The work of the programmer begins with the preparation of a series of highly detailed logic tables and processing diagrams. These expand upon the programming specifications initiated during the technical specifications activity (see Figure 11-18). The example given outlines a form designed for the detailing of functional descriptions of specifications for a program module. This form may be supplemented with further detailed logic tables or program flow dia-

PROGRAMMING SPECIFICATIONS

TOUCHE ROSS

PROGRAM FUNCTION SHEET
PROGRAM ID _LD05IW_
PROGRAM TITLE _UpDAte L/R File_

PAGE _/_ OF _/_
PROJECT NO. _123_

ORGANIZATION _ABC Company_
Accounting
SYSTEM _Labor Distribution_
USER REP _J. Doe_

PREPARED BY _W Smith_
REVIEWED BY _J. Jones_
DATE _4/26_
PHASE _Tech spec_

FILES USED

FILE NO.	FILE NAME	MEDIA	ORGANIZATION	ACCESSING	OPENED
1	Daily Transactions	T9	seq	seq	I
2	Labor / Rate	T9	seq	seq	I
3	Error File 1	T9	seq	seq	O
4	Labor / Rate	T9	seq	seq	O
5	Labor Distribution Report	PRTR	—	seq	O

FUNCTIONS PERFORMED

FUNCTION NUMBER	DESCRIPTION OF FUNCTION	SUPPORT SHEETS
1	Compute Record counts for input And output files	MPF 1
2	Update the Labor/Rate file	DT, TF 1
3	Print Labor Distribution Report	PS 1
4	Print All record counts At EoJ -See Standard Layout	

COMMENTS: _This program will update the Labor/Rate file And print the Labor Distribution Report. Any Input Errors Detected by the program will be processed, but written on An output Error file._

COPYRIGHT 1973   FORM NO. 32
TOUCHE ROSS & CO.

Figure 11-18

grams. The degree of documentation effort depends largely on the experience of the individual programmer and also on the degree of complexity of the specific module. On relatively straightforward modules, the programmer may decide to begin coding directly from the logic and flow documentation prepared during the technical specifications activity. This may depend in part on the programming language used (COBOL, for example, provides good self-documentation for short, simple programs).

Following the documentation of logic and processing flow to the satisfaction of the programmer, actual coding is written in a source language such as COBOL. The source program module is then compiled, converting the programmer's source coding into machine-language instructions for subsequent execution by the computer. For this operation, the computer functions under control of a software system known as a "compiler" or "assembler." The resulting set of machine-language coding is usually referred to as the "object program." Certain errors in program coding are identified by the compiler with error messages printed to help the programmer in the preparation of correct coding.

The preparation of test data for use with the programs under development, the next step in this process, is best performed concurrently with the detail logic design and coding. It may also be necessary to arrange for additional software for program testing. Typically, system software — such as sort or merge routines or file handling software — will be required in order to run the new application. This software preparation is frequently done concurrently with the tasks associated with program design or coding.

Also to be developed before program testing are error messages and operating instructions. The specific error or status messages to be generated by the computer when problems arise in processing the finished program will identify problems or requirements specifically. They will contain or refer to recovery instructions for the steps to be followed in restarting the program under any conditions which might cause a processing interruption.

Operating instructions should also be prepared at this time. Where testing is remote, these instructions are prerequisites. Remote program testing, an increasing practice, is the running of tests by computer operators without the programmers present.

Testing and debugging of programs, then, takes in all of the programming elements described above. The concluding tasks within the programming activity necessitate technical and operational reviews. The technical reviews deal with program logic compatibility, with programming standards, with error recovery procedures, with acceptability of file-handling techniques, and with maintainability of the system. In addition, EDP operations people must also accept the operational characteristics of the system and the documented instructions for running it.

The end product of the programming phase is a completely programmed application system that the programming staff believes to be fully operational.

USER PROCEDURES AND TRAINING

The user procedures and training activity usually runs concurrently with programming. Although these activities are relatively independent of each other, both must follow implementation planning and must be completed before the system is implemented.

Objectives

Two separate objectives can be identified for the user procedures and training activity:

- The users are trained to handle conversion, testing, and operation of the new application on an ongoing basis.
- Procedures must be prepared, perhaps in a draft status, for continuing training and reference.

Work Plan

The tasks which make up the user procedures and training activity are specified in the checklist in Figure 11-15. Each of these tasks should be considered essential to the activity. Even though some may appear routine, all of these points must be checked before any computerized application becomes operational.

Two of the items, however, are of comparatively long duration and great importance. These are items five and eight:

- Development of written manual procedures
- Training and orientation

Development of procedures will frequently be handled in two stages. The first stage should conclude with the preparation of a comprehensive draft concentrating on technical and instructional content of clerical activities associated with the application. In many cases, it is desirable to use this draft as a basis for user training, postponing a final version of procedural standards to a specified future date. This is because changes or revisions to procedures almost invariably result from the initial exercising of the system. In some cases, particularly with large or complex applications, it is both economically and functionally better to wait until a system is implemented before finalizing procedures. It is good discipline, however, to specify when the final procedures will be prepared and to provide the resources to complete them.

In brief, training efforts must bring users to a point where they can perform their work normally and effectively so that procedures can be evaluated and changes made realistically during system test, conversion, and ongoing operations.

SYSTEM TEST

The purpose of the system test activity is for the *users* to test all facets of an application as a unit, including:

- Programs
- Computer operations
- User activities
- Control group functions

These tests should be performed under realistic conditions. Obviously, the final purpose is to make any revisions necessary to prepare the application for implementation and ongoing use. These tests should be developed and conducted by the user personnel. The systems analysts and programmers should participate only to correct discrepancies discovered. They should also encourage the user personnel to introduce every conceivable situation that could occur to *make the system fail.*

Objectives

The first objective of the system test activity is to identify and correct as many deficiencies as possible. The final, paramount objective is to bring the application to a state of readiness for implementation.

Work Plan

The actual tasks associated with the system test activity are shown back in Figure 11-16. As can be seen, this activity is designed to encompass all facets of the new system, to keep track of the timing and completion of each task, and to secure approval from users or responsible EDP people as work is completed.

One of the important parts of the system test activity is to maintain a log, in some level of detail, for all tasks performed (see Figure 11-19). In addition, for each discrepancy uncovered during the testing process, a separate discrepancy report (illustrated in Figure 11-20) should be prepared. This report should be designed for use as a control as well as a reporting document. Typically, three copies of each report would be prepared. One would be kept by the initiator for follow-up. Two copies would be given to the systems section of the EDP Department of which one would be used for control by the manager or supervisor and the other would go to the analyst or programmer assigned to do the work.

Also, vital in the system test activity is the documentation of approvals for each test performed. At the conclusion of this activity, both user and EDP personnel must register approval for every element of the new application.

SYSTEM TEST-RESULTS LOG

	SYSTEM TEST ☒	RESULTS LOG	PAGE _1_ OF _1_
▲ TOUCHE ROSS	IMPLEMENTATION ☐		PROJECT NO. _123_

ORGANIZATION _ABC Company_
Accounting
SYSTEM _Labor Distribution_
USER REP _J. Doe_

PREPARED BY _W. Smith_
REVIEWED BY _J. Jones_
DATE _2/26_
PHASE _SYS TEST_

DATE OF TEST	TIME OF TEST	MODULE NO.	OPERATOR RESPONSIBLE	ANALYST RESPONSIBLE	√	RESULTS
6/1	0800	01	N. A. W.	W. Smith	✓	Processed to EOJ. Overtime Dollars Wrong for All Employees

COPYRIGHT 1973   FORM NO. 50
TOUCHE ROSS & CO.

Figure 11-19

CONVERSION

During the conversion activity, the new application comes into its useful life. Depending on the conversion plan, existing systems are either gradually or suddenly discontinued; and the new application is implemented.

Objectives

The prime objective of the conversion activity is to realize an operational system. Achieving the benefits and cost performances

DISCREPANCY REPORT

TOUCHE ROSS

PROBLEM/REQUEST CONTROL SHEET

NUMBER ___3___

SYSTEM _Labor Distribution_

COMMITMENT DATE ___6/2___

COMPLETE? ☒

PAGE _1_ OF _1_

SYMPTOM REQUEST
Overtime Dollars INCorrectly Calculated for All Employees
Q. Doe   SUBMITTED BY   _6/1_ DATE

PROBLEM/REASON
Hours over 8 not Extended by 150% of Hourly Rate - using 15%
W. White   DIAGNOSED BY   _6/2_ DATE

SOLUTION/DISPOSITION
Correct Program LiteRAL
W. White   SOLVED BY   _6/2_ DATE

CHANGE REQUEST(S) ISSUED

NO.	ITEM TO BE CHANGED	ASSIGNED TO	DATE REQUIRED	DATE OF ACTUAL COMPLETION
1	Overtime Multiplier Literal Program LDOSIW Module 01 Labor Distribution Report	W. White	6/2	6/6

Q. Doe   APPROVED BY   _6/2_ DATE

COPYRIGHT 1973   FORM NO. 33
TOUCHE ROSS & CO.

Figure 11-20

predicted at the outset of the project and reaffirmed at several points is also significant.

Work Plan

The activities associated with conversion are shown on the conversion checklist in Figure 11-17. Three of these tasks are particularly worth noting in terms of their audit relevance:

- *File conversion approvals* are the beginning points for the operation of the new application. It is critical that file conversion operations be accepted, that files be controlled and balanced, and that results be approved by the user. All of this should be documented.

- *Operational approval* of the new application must be based on a previously determined number of operating cycles. The experience level should assure that the conversion has taken place in full and to the satisfaction of user and EDP personnel.
- *Discrepancy notices* must be evaluated and corrective actions scheduled accordingly. At this point, users may realize that the system can operate with identified discrepancies, possibly using temporary compensating controls. Corrective actions should be scheduled and implemented as part of ongoing maintenance for the new system.

POSTIMPLEMENTATION REVIEW

Completion of the conversion activity represents the beginning of the life of the application as an ongoing system. Full implementation also signals the need to schedule another important milestone within the system development process: a postimplementation review activity.

Need

At least one formal review following implementation should be part of the activity cycle for each project. This review should be regarded as necessary for consistent improvement of project techniques.

Since project performance is a factor affecting all parties involved in system development, each group should be represented in the review activity. Participation should be aimed at deriving lessons and guidelines to improve system development capabilities.

Scope

The review activity should focus on a comparison of planned and actual benefits from the implemented system. This is best done by waiting until the new system reaches an operating status which is considered normal. That is, the rate of change should be about what is expected for a mature application. Critical problems should have been resolved. However, this activity should not be delayed until the system is in a state approaching stagnation or until persons who were active on the project have forgotten what took place. Experience has shown that an effective review may usually be performed profitably about three to six months after the conclusion of the conversion activity. Studies and recommendations during a postimplementation review activity should fall into two broad categories:

- The ongoing system should be reviewed and evaluated.
- The prior structure and activities should be reviewed and evaluated for lessons which may be applied to future efforts.

Application Review and Evaluation

In the review of the application, concentration should be on a comparison between planned and actual results. This should include both benefits and costs. Comparisons should also be made between the planned and actual scope of the implemented system. Generally, review efforts will concentrate on project documentation accumulated through the completion of the implementation planning activity. In particular, the documents examined should include figures on costs and benefits as they were updated at the time of implementation planning.

Further documentation of the ongoing system reviewed at this point includes:

- Budgets of user departments reflecting the impact of the ongoing application
- Operating cost data of the EDP Department which apply to the new application

In addition, data are gathered on the performance of the new system, including schedule adherence and response time in delivery of results to users. Actual cost and performance figures are then compared with predicted costs and benefits. In particular, comparisons should be made between operating results and user forecasts of benefits during the user specifications activity.

Discrepancy notices, changes, and error logs prepared since the system was implemented should also be reviewed. This would include disposition and promptness in handling discrepancies, documentation of changes according to standards, and possible patterns of errors which could point to problems in application logic.

Additionally, there should be a comparison between actual controls operating within the application and those which were planned in project documentation. This review may be coordinated with the development of audit programs for ongoing use in examinations, a requirement which may be met conveniently at this point.

Project Management Review and Evaluation

The project effort should be reviewed and evaluated concurrently with the ongoing application. The organizations which participated in the project should be able to derive valuable lessons from this phase of the review. As emphasis is on methods for improving project management techniques, participants in this phase of the review should, if possible, be at a supervisory or management level.

The project review and evaluation can be best initiated with a team effort which tracks actual conditions back through the key activities documented during the development project such as system planning, user specifications, and implementation planning. At each of these points, there should be comparisons between plans and results. In the course of these reviews, the project structure should be studied and challenged. *The essential goal here is to use these observations for guidance in future projects.*

A particular area for attention is identification of ways in which coordination may be improved and responsibilities established more effectively. It is far more important to study the project structure than the performance of individuals. Performance reviews for individuals are the responsibility of line management in the various participating departments. The project team should always leave such evaluations of personnel performance to responsible line managers.

Another element of the project structure review is an internal, technical evaluation of performance of the functions within the EDP Department. This phase of the review should be carried out by EDP people. Other organizations may be aware of the results of this review; however, they do not usually have the technical background to participate in this specialized study.

ONGOING MAINTENANCE

Long before an application is implemented, dynamic forces come into play which precipitate change. These forces emerge from both the nature of the company and from developments in the computer industry. Thus, a basic part of the project, approach provides for revision of all implemented EDP systems on an ongoing basis. These revisions are characterized as maintenance efforts when their scope falls short of requiring new projects for replacement of existing systems.

Reasons for Changes

Reasons for modifying implemented information systems may be classified according to two broad categories: *mandatory changes* and *enhancements.*

Mandatory changes in existing applications are usually initiated for one of two reasons: Either discrepancies or bugs are uncovered in the application as it was originally implemented, or requirements of the business demand modifications. Discrepancies will come to light through the exercise of controls built into the application or through incidents which make it apparent that errors have occurred.

Mandatory changes to meet business requirements result chiefly from government regulations or from changes in other adjacent applications, as in payroll deduction rates. These changes usually carry a high degree of urgency which may lead to a shortcutting of controls and documentation procedures. Thus, the level of control which was considered mandatory during development may be compromised.

Enhancements to ongoing applications stem from the same basic reasons which led to the development project for the application itself. That is, opportunities appear for improving the application to render better service, operate more effectively, or achieve greater efficiency. One reason for application enhancement is that the user becomes accustomed to operating in an EDP environment. Then, as is common in any other area of human activity, the user applies creativity to come up with better methods. Maintenance requests aimed at system refinement are to be expected as users gain sophistication.

A second reason for application enhancement lies in modifications which keep up with or take advantage of new hardware or software developments. In general, however, enhancements will not carry the same degree of urgency as mandatory changes. Concern should be to make sure that controls are applied in implementing and documenting changes.

Extent of Change

The primary difference between maintenance and development projects are the extent of changes involved. In a system development project, every aspect is subject to change. In a maintenance project, on the other hand, the size of maintenance changes should probably be restricted to modest alterations of existing applications. However, even though they are small, maintenance changes will tend to occur frequently. In some organizations, maintenance requirements may evolve to a point where they represent as much as 20 percent of total application development efforts. While this degree of effort may seem minor, application maintenance is a special situation — a good illustration of the appropriateness of the 80-20 rule.

Management attention must reflect the fact that, every time the operating structure of an ongoing application is opened up and modified, there is an exposure to errors and control problems. This exposure doesn't permit the luxury of treating as unimportant projects which may be minor in scope and cost.

Controlling Maintenance Changes

Exposure in maintenance of applications is significant enough so that methods for managing change must be structured. Though necessarily simple, these structures and methods should place great emphasis on quality control. Controls applied to each change in an application must provide assurance that there has been no degradation of quality in the application as a result of the modifications. In a system development project, emphasis is at a management level with objectives chiefly economic. In a maintenance project, management controls are replaced with tighter, more technical screening techniques for approval and control of changes.

One method of applying quality control during maintenance projects is the change batch control in which all ongoing applications within an installation are divided into groups. Barring emergencies, all applications within a group become eligible for maintenance modification on a rotating basis.

Maintenance requirements which emerge, provided they are not urgent, are accumulated. Then, by handling all change requirements in a batch, control measures would be more effective than if attempts were made to handle all modifications individually. In addition, a single, comprehensive set of tests covering the entire application will serve to verify all changes.

Acceptance of enhancement changes on a continuous "demand" basis will usually inhibit adequate testing of the revised application. Who can afford an extensive system test every week, particularly when the modification only requires 15 minutes of effort?

Minimum documentation standards must also be set up and applied to maintenance projects just as they are for system development efforts. One important addition, however, would be a *program-change log* set up for each program within every application including some indication of what changes have been made, when, why, and by whom.

Program-change documentation must continue to be comparable to that resulting from the programming activity. *Every time a program is modified, new documentation should be generated.* This should include complete program source and object lists, technical specifications for coding, and documentation for any changed decision rules. Of course, any changes should be accompanied by documented user and technical approvals. Also included in the documentation of a maintenance project should be the original request for modification.

This chapter has described one proven approach for the application of project techniques to information systems development. Although there will be many variations, some formal structure of this type should be in place and in use in any organization making effective use of EDP techniques and capabilities. In each case, the auditor should study and understand the systems development techniques being used. This understanding will allow the auditor to work more effectively with the resulting systems and documentation. Familiarity with the concepts and techniques for managing system projects will facilitate the auditor's participation on such projects. This is an increasing requirement as applications become more complex and exposure to loss of control becomes more unacceptable.

12
Systems Development Controls

NATURE OF PROJECT CONTROLS

A system development project, as described in the last chapter, *should be a finite, predefined, structured set of activities for the attainment of specific goals.* Based upon its own definitions, each project has a definite starting point, definable intermediate tasks, and a clearly understood conclusion. Project management is a method for planning and controlling the process of system development. Specific techniques for management of the system development process should be aimed at:

- Delivering a quality application system on schedule and within the budget
- Communicating an understanding of the status throughout the duration of a project
- Identifying problems before they develop as well as detecting and correcting problems which are unforeseen

Specific reasons behind the emergence of management techniques for system projects, some of which have been cited previously, include:

- Projects are increasing in size and number as companies accelerate application of information systems.
- Applications are becoming more complex.
- Individual applications are crossing geographic and organizational boundaries.
- Projects are costing more because larger systems require more advanced and greater quantities of resources for completion.
- Demands for rapid completion of projects are increasing.

CAUSES OF EXPOSURE RESULTING FROM SYSTEMS DEVELOPMENT

Having seen uncontrolled applications and the monumental costs that have resulted from many systems development efforts, the auditor must ask "how on earth did we get into this mess?" The exposures that we find in applications and systems projects do not arise out of a vacuum; each is caused. These causes range from incompetent personnel to a system approach that does not suit the needs. A list of the more common causes of exposures in systems development include:

- Incomplete economic evaluation
- Management abdication
- Inadequate specifications
- Systems design errors
- Incompetent design personnel
- Technical self-gratification
- Poor communications
- No project "kill points"
- Temptations to computer abuse
- Unmaintainable applications
- Incoherent direction

Incomplete Economic Evaluation

Many economic evaluations use the crystal-ball approach to systems planning. Instead of substantiating planned benefits, the planners may try to predict the effect of proposed systems without hard facts or with facts so meager that adequate capital budgeting decisions cannot be made. *Excessive costs* may result when unjustified systems are developed. Conversely, justified systems may not be developed. This may be just as costly. Incomplete economic evaluation may also put the company at a *competitive disadvantage* if application systems are not developed which are needed to meet the changing market requirements of the company. Following a preliminary economic evaluation, additional reevaluations may be necessary as questions are resolved and further information becomes available.

Management Abdication

Frequently, senior management abdicates its responsibilities and its decisions-making role over the systems development process. In so doing they abdicate much of their responsibility for control of the future of the organization. Systems development projects affect both the short- and long-range operations of the entire organization. Decisions that have such implications are clearly the responsibility of management. Abdication with the excuse that it is "too technical to understand" is tantamount to admission that management is not competent to manage. Abdication by senior management often results in *competitive disadvantage* and *excessive costs.*

Inadequate Specifications

User and technical specifications must be developed by both user and technical personnel. Inadequate specifications are those which exclude any important requirements, present the requirements inaccurately, or overstate the required capabilities. The resulting application may thus include any or all of the application exposures that were discussed previously. Within the systems development process, inadequate or overstated requirements will result in *excessive costs.*

Systems Design Errors

Even given adequate specifications, design personnel are still human and subject to errors in judgment. This can occur no matter how competent or well informed the people are.

Incompetent Design Personnel

The success of a systems development effort depends, to a large extent, upon the competence of user management, systems analysts, and programmers. Since effective systems design requires clear and rational thinking, no application system will ever reach effective implementation if the personnel involved are severely lacking in these capabilities. Accordingly, incompetent personnel performing essential functions may cause any of the exposures in either system design or application operations.

Technical Self-Gratification

This is a frequent cause of exposure. Systems analysts are often tempted to design a system to exercise their own creative impulses and to incorporate "state-of-the-art" techniques. Systems analysts and programmers view themselves primarily as creators. However, the application systems being designed are for the use of the users, not the designers.

Systems analysts sometimes come to believe that they understand a particular user's business needs better than he does himself. At other times the analyst seeks to satisfy the user's needs by creating an application that is beyond the capabilities of the user to operate. Such conceit usually results in a system that doesn't work at all, forces the user into continuing a "shadow system," and is generally nothing more than a waste of development money.

Poor Communications

Inherently, the process of successful systems design depends upon the effective communication of application requirements to those who will implement those requirements. Any significant weaknesses in communications between the project development team, user departments, and top management will readily result in any or all systems development and application exposures.

No Project "Kill Points"

Once started, some systems development projects roll on inexorably to their implementation, no matter what obstacles arise. Once the wheels are rolling, they may continue without regard to new cost estimates, changes in the organization's needs, or even new external regulations. Some way must be devised to stop projects when it becomes apparent that the benefits no longer justify the costs. The exposure that exists if no such kill points are allowed is *excessive development costs.*

Temptations to Computer Abuse

Opportunities to implement fraud, embezzlement, mischievous "bugs," or the malicious destruction of the whole project or application system may present themselves during systems development. If such opportunities are allowed to exist, the organization will eventually be hurt by someone who cannot resist these temptations. Depending upon the nature of the transactions being performed by the application, a programmer could use an inconspicuous section of program logic to evade other application controls and divert assets for his benefit. Such a programmer need not have subsequent access to either the application programs or data files. Accordingly, controls which are designed to prohibit the programmer's access to computer operations provide no real certainty that data will not be manipulated to the benefit of perverse programmers.

Unmaintainable Applications

An unmaintainable application is a system which cannot technically or economically be modified to meet the changing requirements of the organization. Such an application system freezes the whole organization in the status quo. Since a change in requirements could conceivably allow the emergence of any type of application exposure, virtually any application exposure could be an ultimate result from an unmaintainable system.

Incoherent Direction

When numerous individuals are involved in the design and implementation of a new application, each one of them may form a slightly different conception of what they are to accomplish and how they should go about it. Their efforts will diverge unless some unifying force continually guides them in a common direction.

RESULTING EXPOSURES

Only four of the normal business exposures would actually result within the systems development project. However, many of the causes of exposure resulting from weaknesses in systems development may result in any or all of the exposures found in applications if the application is implemented. Two levels of exposure — one for the projects and one for the applications implemented — are related to their causes in Figure 12-1.

APPROPRIATE METHODOLOGY

In the past, system project management approaches and techniques tended to follow a "town-hall-meeting" pattern. Typically,

SYSTEMS DEVELOPMENT CAUSES AND EXPOSURES

INCOMPLETE ECONOMIC EVALUATION	MANAGEMENT ABDICATION	INADEQUATE SPECIFICATIONS	SYSTEM DESIGN ERRORS	INCOMPETENT DESIGN PERSONNEL	TECHNICAL SELF-GRATIFICATION	POOR COMMUNICATIONS	NO PROJECT KILL POINTS	TEMPTATIONS TO COMPUTER ABUSE	UNMAINTAINABLE APPLICATION	INCOHERENT DIRECTION	EXPOSURES
											Application Exposures (if project implemented)
	2	3	3			3		2	2	3	Erroneous record keeping
2	2	2	2			2		2	2		Unacceptable accounting
	1	1	1			1	1	1		1	Business interruption
3	3	2	3			2		2	2	2	Erroneous management decisions
	1	1	1			1		2		1	Fraud
1	1	1	1			1	1		2	1	Statutory sanctions
2	3	3	3	3	2	2			1	2	Excessive costs/deficient revenues
	1	1	1			1		2		1	Loss or destruction of assets
2	2	2	2	1	2	1			2	2	Competitive disadvantage
											Project Exposures
	3	3	3	2		3				3	Erroneous management decisions
2	2	3	3	3	3	3	2		3	3	Excessive costs
2	2	2	2	2	1	2	1		2	2	Competitive disadvantage
	2	2	3	2	2				2	3	Business interruption (delay timetable)

IMPACT OF CAUSES

3 — Very likely to occur

2 — Likely to occur

1 — May occur

Blank — Generally little effect

Figure 12-1

groups of management, EDP, and user people would sit around a conference table in periodic sessions for open-forum-type discussions. Detailed activities and tasks were assigned. The meeting served to communicate what had been accomplished and what was being done. Shortcomings of these early approaches have identified some specific requirements which serve as a basis for meeting objectives of individual projects and of system development programs as a whole. These include establishing discrete work units which, in turn, help to measure results and outline progress. Also, predetermined quality control review points must be interspersed throughout the project structure. It is no longer feasible to attempt to change a system the day before it is to be implemented. Today, project schedules must include more than target dates for final completion.

These needs are based on corporate experience patterns which show that EDP application development efforts have expanded in size — becoming more complex and taking in more departments or organizations. It is these multiple factors of quantity, complexity, and interdepartmental scope of system development projects which demand new management approaches and techniques. A company in the simplistic status of developing only small systems, a few at a time and on a crash basis, might conceivably be able to handle its project management requirements on an informal, town-meeting basis. Personnel would have to be sufficiently experienced to work informally.

If the advantages of controlled, predictable systems development are to be realized, certain supporting commitments must be made at all management levels within an organization. These include:

- **Supportive commitment from top management.** These commitments should include allocation of necessary resources and assurance of continuing top-management participation in the project management process.
- **Leadership and credibility** on the part of project managers. They must be comfortable in a multidiscipline environment. Both the individuals and the managers to whom they report must recognize the stand-or-fall importance of project leadership.
- **A definitive modular structure** which breaks the project into known increments. This modularity is necessary for planning and directing activities as well as for measuring and evaluating performance.

SYSTEM DEVELOPMENT CONTROLS

In the preceding chapter on systems development standards, we described a number of activities and features that provide control over the systems development process. They included:

- **The methodology** with defined activities and end products
- **Project management** which plans and monitors the project activities
- **Staff hiring and training** which provides a staff capable of implementing technically demanding application systems
- **Checklists** of essential tasks
- **Technical review and approval**
- **Management review and approval**
- **Audit** participation
- **The entire systems test** phase
- **The postimplementation review** phase, which somewhat resembles an audit
- And, most important, **DOCUMENTATION!**

In the balance of this chapter, we will examine the properties of each of these controls. Most of the emphasis will be on controls that were not fully described in the prior chapter as a part of systems development standards, especially:

- Project management
- Staff hiring and training
- Reviews and approvals

An entire chapter will be dedicated to the control provided by audit participation in the development of individual applications. We will also summarize the significant aspects of other controls already discussed in detail.

PROJECT MANAGEMENT

Project management at a detailed level is implemented in two phases: *project planning* and *project supervision.*

A *project plan* is a formalized statement structuring a project for orderly implementation. The plan reflects the statement of objectives and scope of the system planning study and defines this structure in terms of units of work to be done. These work units are related to each other, to schedule dates, and to performance responsibilities.

The *project supervision* phase of project management covers the execution of project activities. It monitors progress, evaluates, and initiates revisions or corrective actions as necessary. Management controls of a project follow this general path:

- Schedules are reviewed
- Work is assigned
- Work performance is recorded and monitored
- Progress is measured against schedules and objectives
- Status and discrepancies are reported on a regular basis
- Corrective action is taken

Project Planning

It is usually desirable to have the people who are assigned to the project assume responsibility for its planning. Obvious benefits of this assignment approach include familiarity with and commitment to the project by participants. Reliance on system planning documentation is particularly heavy in cases where there is a substantial interval between completion of planning activities and the initiation of development activities. Project planning activities will usually pick up, review, and accept the statements of objectives and scope established in the system planning study. Major elements of the project planning include:

- *Project guidelines* documented in greater detail.
- *Work breakdowns* prepared for each development activity and task.
- *For each work unit, start and completion dates* are set. These schedules are based on the level of skills and the facilities committed to the project. It is usually not necessary to assign specific individuals to the work units at this point.
- *Plans and schedules* are reviewed and approved. Formal commitments are obtained for their fulfillment. At this point, project planning documentation becomes a yardstick against which all subsequent activities within a system development project are monitored and measured so that variances may be reported.

The following analysis will cover each of these four elements of project planning more specifically.

PROJECT GUIDELINES

Formal development of project guidelines will frequently seem an unnecessary overhead item. Persons straining to get into the specific procedural or technical activities will be impatient with efforts to develop guideline statements. Partly because of this attitude, this is probably the point where more mistakes are made than in any other single area of system development.

Guidelines are necessary because they plot the course for complex, expensive, interactive efforts. They help establish a project's objectives, its scope, and procedures as well as the desired products to be delivered.

Clearly, when applied diligently, guidelines will serve to establish a basis of agreement on what work is to be done and what costs are to be incurred. Disappointments with new application systems result primarily from a lack of understanding of the results to be achieved. Management-approved guidelines eliminate misunderstandings and minimize disappointments. However, care should be taken to be sure that documented guidelines do not get buried in files and forgotten. It should be clear to all persons affected that these statements are to be used and followed. Users, in particular, should understand that stated guidelines represent limits of work to be done and budgets available. Once a project moves into its implementation phase, efforts are limited to those activities, schedules, and resources specified in the project guidelines. Any material alterations of scope and activities will lead only to cost overruns or possible aborting of the project.

WORK BREAKDOWNS

The objective of work definition is to break personnel assignments down into consecutive units which are small enough to be managed. As much as possible, this process should reach a level where work units become predictable enough to be assigned to individuals for completion. Work definitions should be made according to the levels of skill for individual assignments. *Each work unit should have tangible end products which can be reviewed and evaluated.*

Activities are major units of work required to complete a project. Frequently, the activities of a system development project will provide the first step in the project planning breakdown. Within an activity, multiple tasks are established. These are usually based on end items specified for project activities, as discussed in the last chapter. It is desirable to establish tasks at a level where they may be assigned to individuals. Task breakdowns should be made according to applicable skill. Subtasks may be required to break large tasks into work units requiring a single skill and manageable duration, generally not exceeding two man-weeks.

A work breakdown in an orderly sequence is essential to effective project control. Carrying the breakdown to the level suggested eliminates most of the problems inherent in other methods which try to accomplish similar results. Typically, these other methods handle scheduling and reporting on a percentage-of-completion basis. As an alternative, percentage of completion may have to be used when work units run two to three months. However, when it is used, direction and measurement are less certain; and estimates frequently lack credibility.

After the work breakdown is completed, personnel requirements are summarized according to skill. Based on these summaries, time requirements are estimated for each major activity and for the project as a whole. These should be summarized from the lowest level upward. This approach generally corresponds with the personnel structure within the system project team. The critical point in scheduling work assignments will be allocating the time of qualified supervisors. Summaries of skill levels will facilitate both definition and scheduling of assignments.

At best, work-requirement summaries at this point will only be approximations. The degree of accuracy in estimating work assignments will, obviously, depend partly on project management experience within the organization. With each passing project, systems analysis personnel should become more skilled in estimating activity work requirements. In any case, however, the individual project team might still not have accumulated the wisdom for exactness in work specification at this point in a project.

WORK UNIT START AND COMPLETION DATES

Even if time estimates cannot be made exactly, there should be no compromise in the detailing of work descriptions down to a sub-task level. As long as specific work requirements are defined, a later point in the project can be specified for providing time requirements. This is feasible because of the checkpointing built into project structures.

PLANS AND SCHEDULES

The scheduling phase of the project management process begins where the work definition phase ends. Beginning documentation of the scheduling phase calls for a buildup of all work units from the subtask to the task, to the activity, to the full-project level (see figures 12-2, 12-3, and 12-4).

Figure 12-2 is a task listing for a series of subtasks associated with the design of the new procedures of an accounts receivable system. This new application will be part of an overall management information system under development for a company. Most of the subtotals referred to are specified as end items of activities in the discussion found in the previous chapter.

Figure 12-3 is an activity listing built from the tasks which make up the full accounts receivable system. The design of the new system is the second task on this list. This corresponds with the activity code on the form in Figure 12-2.

Figure 12-4 summarizes all activities for the project. On this form, the accounts receivable system is the fourth item. This designation was picked up in the identification fields of figures 12-2 and 12-3 respectively.

This level-by-level work breakdown and the work units will be basic to all subsequent efforts in scheduling, evaluating, and reporting.

A typical technique for handling work assignments at this point is illustrated in Figure 12-5. This shows a general purpose personnel planning form which is used to create a matrix of activities and work assignments. Space is provided for entry of days of effort, start dates, and completion dates for each assignment. The column at the far right is used for budgetary controls and provides spaces for entering data on assigned days and the rates for the skill involved. At the bottom of this column are cumulative totals for man-days and budget dollars for the personnel assignments covered.

WORK DEFINITION – TASK LEVEL

WORK OUTLINE FORM

PROJECT LIST ☐
ACTIVITY LIST ☐
TASK LIST ☑

DATE __1_/_1_/_1_
PAGE __1__ OF __1__
JOB CODE _3_
PROJECT CODE _04_
ACTIVITY CODE _002_

WORK LEVEL _DESIGN NEW AIR SYSTEM_
ORGANIZATION _ABC CORPORATION_

No.	WORK DEFINITION	RESPONSI-BILITY	PERSONNEL TYPE	MAN DAYS REQUIRED	BUDGET	START DATE	TARGET DATE
001	DESIGN OUTPUT FORMATS	ABC + TR & CO.	ANALYST	05		5/20/-	5/24/-
002	DEFINE INFORMATION FILES		ANALYST	05		5/20/-	5/24/-
003	DEFINE INPUT FORMATS		ANALYST	05		5/27/-	5/31/-
004	PREPARE PROCESS RUN-TO-RUN FLOW CHART		ANALYST OR PROGRAMMER	05		5/27/-	5/31/-
005	DEFINE RUN FUNCTIONS		ANALYST	02		5/29/-	5/31/-
006	ESTABLISH INPUT/OUTPUT AND PROCESS CONTROLS		ANALYST	04		5/31/-	6/6/-
007	SELECT PROGRAMMING LANGUAGES FOR RUN		CHIEF/LEAD PROGRAMMER	01		6/6/-	6/6/-
008	IDENTIFY NEW CLERICAL PROCEDURES		ANALYST	03		6/6/-	6/10/-
009	FINALIZE SYSTEM SAVINGS AND OPERATING COSTS		PROJECT LEADER	02		6/6/-	6/7/-
010	REVIEW SYSTEM WITH AUDIT STAFF		PROJECT LEADER & ANALYST	02		6/10/-	6/11/-
011	REVIEW SYSTEM WITH ABC		PROJECT LEADER & ANALYST	02		6/12/-	6/13/-
	MANAGEMENT					5/20/-	6/13
	TOTAL MAN DAYS THIS ACTIVITY			36			

TASK LEVEL ONLY

PREPARED BY _W. Williams_
APPROVED BY _R. Johnson_

COPYRIGHT 1967
TOUCHE ROSS & CO.   102 - 028

Figure 12-2

WORK DEFINITION — ACTIVITY LEVEL

WORK OUTLINE FORM

PROJECT LIST ☐
ACTIVITY LIST ☑
TASK LIST ☐

WORK LEVEL _ACCOUNTS RECEIVABLE SYSTEM_
ORGANIZATION _ABC CORPORATION_

DATE _1/20/_
PAGE _1_ OF _1_
JOB CODE _3_
PROJECT CODE _04_
ACTIVITY CODE

No.	WORK DEFINITION	RESPONSI-BILITY	PERSONNEL TYPE	MAN DAYS REQUIRED	BUDGET	START DATE	TARGET DATE
001	DEFINE SYSTEM REQUIREMENTS OF NEW A/R SYSTEM.	ABa + TR a QO.	—	21			
002	DESIGN NEW A/R SYSTEM		—	36			
003	PREPARE PROGRAMMING SPECIFICATIONS		—	20			
004	DESIGN PROGRAMMING LOGIC		—	20			
005	WRITE A/R PROGRAMS		—	60			
006	PERFORM A/R SYSTEM TEST		—	10			
007	CONVERSION PLANNING		—	10			
008	PREPARE NEW MANUAL PROCEDURES		—	20			
009	FILE SET UP AND CONVERSION		—	10			
010	PLAN AND IMPLEMENT TRAIN-ING PROGRAM		—	10			
011	CONVERSION PILOT A/R SYSTEM		—	06			
012	CONVERSION A/R SYSTEM		—	10			
	TOTAL MANDAYS THIS PROJECT			(233)			

PREPARED BY _W. Williams_
APPROVED BY _R. Johnson_

TASK LEVEL ONLY

Figure 12-3

267

WORK DEFINITION – PROJECT LEVEL

WORK OUTLINE FORM

PROJECT LIST ☑
ACTIVITY LIST ☐
TASK LIST ☐

DATE ___1__/__15__/__1__
PAGE __1__ OF __1__
JOB CODE __3__
PROJECT CODE _____
ACTIVITY CODE _____

WORK LEVEL _DISTRIBUTION AND SALES ENGAGE-MENT_
ORGANIZATION _ABC CORPORATION_

No.	WORK DEFINITION	RESPONSI-BILITY	PERSONNEL TYPE	MAN DAYS REQUIRED	BUDGET	START DATE	TARGET DATE
01	ORGANIZATION AND PROJECT PLANNING		1	30			
02	DEFINITION OF PRESENT DIS-TRIBUTION AND SALES SYSTEM		1	30			
03	INVOICING SYSTEM		1	270			
04	ACCOUNTS RECEIVABLE SYSTEM		1	233			
05	INVENTORY MANAGEMENT AND CONTROL			500			
06	ACCOUNTS PAYABLE SYSTEM			125			
	TOTAL MAN DAYS THIS ENGAGEMENT			1188			

PREPARED BY _____
APPROVED BY _____

TASK LEVEL ONLY

COPYRIGHT 1967
TOUCHE ROSS & CO.   102 - 028

Figure 12-4

Obviously, entries for job assignments on this form are based on work unit sequences and personnel availabilities. This type of working form provides another upward step in the building of a schedule for the development and implementation phases of the system development project. In addition, this documentation remains as necessary support for project implementation schedules.

For communication purposes, schedules are generally shown at the activity level, using Gantt charts like the one illustrated in Figure 12-6. This schedule, in effect, is a graphic, time-scale representation of the data listed in Figure 12-5. This chart is intended to display the general relationships between work-unit completion dates. It is often modified to reflect status.

The schedule and work assignment documentation are used to initiate the planning document illustrated in Figure 12-7. Similar documents will be prepared for each project level. These documents represent the formal plan and commitment against which accomplishments and status are reported. Changes in plans or budgets are authorized only when displayed on a document like the one in Figure 12-7.

PERSONNEL PLANNING FORM

PERSONNEL PLANNING FORM

DATE 1/30/-
PAGE 1 OF 2

JOB NUMBER ABC CORPORATION
PROJECT NUMBER DISTRIBUTION AND SALES ENGAGEMENT
PROJECT NAME ACCOUNTS RECEIVABLE SYSTEM

[X] TR & CO. [ ] HOURS
[ ] CLIENT [X] DAYS
[ ] OTHER

ACTIVITY/DESCRIPTION	224 WHITCOMB	360 JONES	224 SMITH	160 WEARLY	192 DAVID			TOTAL EFFORT
001 DEFINE SYSTEM REQUIREMENTS	5/6 – 5/17 10							10 / 2240
002 DESIGN NEW A/R SYSTEM	5/20 – 6/13 18							18 / 4032
003 PREPARE PROGRAM SPECS.			6/3 – 6/28 20					20 / 4480
004 DESIGN PROGRAM LOGIC				6/14 – 6/31 10				10 / 1600
005 WRITE A/R PROGRAMS				7/1 – 7/15 10	7/1 – 7/15 10			20 / 3520
006 PERFORM A/R SYSTEMS TEST								
007 CONVERSION PLANNING			7/15 – 7/26 10					10 / 2240
008 NEW MANUAL PROCEDURES	6/14 – 7/15 20							20 / 4480
SUB-TOTALS	48		30	20	10			10.8 / 22,592

PREPARED BY J Brown
APPROVED BY H. Cone

NAME

START END
DAYS/HRS.

105-028

Figure 12-5

ACTIVITY SCHEDULE

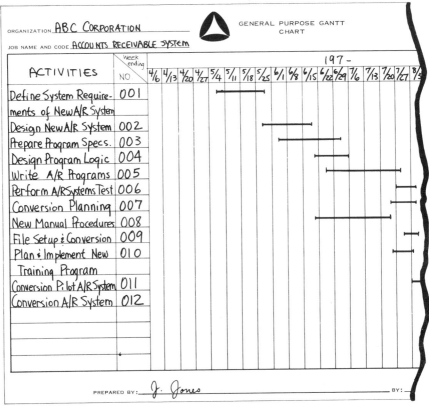

Figure 12-6

Project Supervision

Project supervision is a process for assigning, measuring, evaluating, and redirecting the performance of a project. Three basic elements are involved: *short-term scheduling, work assignment, evaluating and reporting status.*

SHORT-TERM SCHEDULING

Prior to the initiation of each activity within a project, particularly on a large project, a review should be made of preceding activities and accumulated documentation. There should be assurance that prior activities were completed and that personnel are available as planned. This is also a good time for the project leader to reaffirm the scope, objectives, and budget for the project. Any changes in the project plan or planned variances from the original plan should be approved and documented at this point.

STATUS REPORT

STATUS REPORT

△

DATE 6/7/—
PAGE / OF /

WORK LEVEL *ACCOUNTS RECEIVABLE SYS.*

ORGANIZATION *ABC CORP*

JOB NO.	3
PROJECT NO	04
ACTIVITY NO	

PROJECT [✓]
ACTIVITY [ ]

NO	ACTIVITY PROJECT NAME	ORIGINAL END DATE	PLAN HOURS	PLAN COST	REVISED END DATE	PLAN HOURS	PLAN COST	Earned Hours	Hours to date	Remaining to do	Performance Variance This Week	Performance Variance To Date	Schedule Variance This Week	Schedule Variance To Date
001	Define Sys. Req of New A/R System	5/17	168	4400				168	154			14		(14)
002	Design New A/R System	6/13	288	7600	6/13	296	8100	208	236	64	(4)	(4)	6	(4)
003	Prepare Prog Specs	6/29	160	4500						160				
004	Design Prog Logic	6/31	160	3600						160				
005	Write A/R Prog	7/19	480	10,800						480				
006	Perform A/R System Test	7/26	80	2,000						80				
007	Conversion Planning	7/26	80	2800						80				
008	Prepare New Manual Prog	7/15	160	4500						160				
009	File Set up + Conversion	7/16	80	2,000						80				
010	Plan & Implement Training Program	7/23	80	2800						80				
011	Conversion Pilot A/R Sys	8/5	48							48				
012	Conversion A/R Sys	9/9	80	2000						80				
013	Project Mtg.	9/9	160	7200				24	24	136				
	TOTALS		2024	54800		2032	54700	400	414	1608	(4)	10	6	(18)

PART A
PREPARED BY *J. Davis*
APPROVED BY *P. Brown*

PART B
COPYRIGHT 1966 TOUCHE ROSS & CO.
PREPARED BY *J. Davis*
APPROVED BY *L. Alter*

Figure 12-7

WORK ASSIGNMENT

Actual work assignments are extensions of the short-term scheduling activity. Assignments are made as personnel complete performance of earlier tasks and have their work reviewed. Work assignment documentation should include full descriptions of all tasks to be performed. These should be reviewed with assigned personnel. There should be assurance that each individual knows what to do, how long it is to take, and exactly what he must achieve. Furthermore, he should be aware of precisely how his performance is to be evaluated.

EVALUATING AND REPORTING STATUS

Reporting for system development projects should concentrate primarily on progress against the .plan and analysis` of variances. Information on completion of all subtasks, tasks, and activities should be available on a summary, level-by-level basis as approved in the project plan. This complete documentation should be available for reference. Reports to management should show only the top level plus those areas where there are problems.

Status reports should be issued according to two main categories: by levels of work units and by people. Reports on the completion of work modules should summarize both planned and actual times for the project to date. Variances should be reported at the subtask, task, and activity levels according to type:

- Planning variances will occur when the original plans and estimates were inadequate or if they have been proved incorrect in light of work experience. Such variances should be expected as an organization develops its project management skills.
- Performance variances represent work taking more or less time in man-hours or elapsed time than indicated on original plans.
- Schedule variances cover shortages or advances in the level of effort compared with what was planned.
- Variances should also be analyzed by individual to determine whether they result from on-the-job training, poor direction, or other causes.

STATUS REVIEW

Status reports on a project should be reviewed periodically by users and others responsible for approving the project. These review sessions should cover status, problems, and alternative solutions.

EARNED HOURS REPORTED

One commonly used technique which has proven to be appropriate in project control is reporting on a basis of earned hours. Typically, work units on system development projects are assigned specific numbers of hours. These hours are earned only when the work unit is completed, reviewed, and accepted. Earned hours are expressions of scheduled work units which were completed.

Time might have been spent on an assignment which is not completed. Since there will be no earned hours until completion, actual hours spent until the point of completion will be variances. When work units are completed, actual hours worked may be more or less than earned hours. However, large variances would indicate problems, either actual or potential. Conditions brought to light by large variances between earned and actual hours may mean actual performance is taking more time than planned or a significant amount of time has been spent on work units which were started and not completed. Either condition may point to performance variances. The second, however, reflects a potential handicap for task completion. Such variances could indicate inadequacies in resources or direction.

An example of a working document for recording and appraising accomplishments and variances is illustrated in Figure 12-8, an activity history sheet. Each task on an activity is listed in terms of planned hours of work. Earned and actual hours are listed in adjacent columns.

Actual work performance is recorded by week in the example shown. For each week, there are separate columns for planned and actual hours. In addition, there is a third column used for reporting "remaining-to-do" work. This may be an important item when significant variances are projected. Adding the estimate or work remaining to the actual performance provides a running figure for projected variances for each activity down to the work-unit level.

The primary project status report for management is the one shown in Figure 12-8. This report brings together results of all the thoughts put into the initial planning of the project. It reflects actual performance on the same basis.

ACTIVITY HISTORY SHEET,
APPLYING EARNED-HOURS CONCEPT

ACTIVITY HISTORY SHEET

ACTIVITY NAME DESIGN A/R SYSTEM   JOB NO. 3   DATE 2/15/ –
PREPARED BY WHITCOMB   PROJECT NO. 04   PAGE 1 OF 1
APPROVED BY JONES   ACTIVITY NO. 002
ORGANIZATION ABC CORPORATION

TASK NO.	TASK DESCRIPTION	SKILL CODE	PLAN HRS		EARNED HRS.	ACTUAL HRS.	5/20 P	A	RTD	5/27 P	A	RTD	6/3 P	A	RTD	6/10 P	A	RTD	P	A	R		P	A	R		P	A	R	RTD
001	Design Output Formats		40	v	40	40	40	40	–																					
002	Design Info File		40	v	40	40	40	40	–																					
003	Design Input Formats		40	v	40	40				40	30	10	0	10	–															
004	Prepare Process Run to Run Flow Chart		40	v	40	40				40	40	–																		
005	Define Run Functions		16	v	16	16							16	16	–															
006	Establish I/o and Process Controls		32	v	32	32							32	32	–															
007	Select Programming language for Runs		16										8	8	8	8														
008	Identify New Clerical Procedures		24										24	20	8															
009	Finalize Sys. Savings and Operating Costs		16													16	16													
010	Review Sys. with Audit		16													16	16													
011	Review Sys. with ABC Management		16																											
			296				80	80	–	80	70	10	80	86		64	56													

007 Revised 8 ADD'L HRS.

COPYRIGHT 1968
TOUCHE ROSS & CO.   100-028

Figure 12-8

STAFF HIRING AND TRAINING

Competent systems analysts and programmers are not born; they must be developed. The only acceptable alternatives in obtaining such people are to train them after hiring or to hire only persons already trained. This decision may differ for different levels of skill.

However, training cannot be limited to only the professional and technical body of knowledge required of systems analysts and programmers. The organization's standards for the conduct of systems development projects must also be provided.

As noted previously, the evaluation and decision requirements within the systems development project prevent detailed instruction standards. Only policies and guidelines are feasible. However, the guidelines may still be quite extensive and call for formal instruction.

Continuing technical training may be either internal or external. Highly advanced topics will usually require use of some external training resources.

CHECKLISTS

The detailed systems development standards described in the preceding chapter included checklists for completion of the following development phases:

- User training and procedures
- System test
- Conversion

Checklists lend control to these particular activities because of the relatively consistent nature of the tasks included in these phases. The use of checklists helps assure that no significant task is forgotten. However, checklists cannot be considered a very strong control, since they have no effect on the quality or content of the tasks that are completed.

TECHNICAL REVIEW AND APPROVAL

The supervisors of the systems analysts and programmers must review the results of each phase before submitting it to management and to users for approval. This review should not only involve the normal daily supervision but also a final page-by-page review of everything. The supervisor's initials and date should be placed on each page of the phase documents as an indication of his approval.

MANAGEMENT AND USER REVIEW AND APPROVAL

One of the strongest controls over the logical contents of the end products of most of the development phases is the review by top management and/or users.

They should review the results of each phase except for programming. This review must occur in adequate time to allow incorporation of their revisions in the next — more detailed — phase of development.

Although delay of the next phase while awaiting user approvals may not always be practical, top management and users must take the responsibility for halting further development if serious deficiencies exist in the results produced to date.

AUDIT PARTICIPATION

The auditor (usually the internal auditor) should also review the results of each development phase. This *may* serve in lieu of review by top management for the more detailed phases. Following his review, the auditor should sign off as evidence that this review was performed. This also forces him to *commit himself* on the effectiveness of the proposed application controls.

Auditors sometimes resist appearing to "approve" the end products of development phases out of concern for compromising their independence or because they cannot be as confident of the eventual outcome as when an application is completed. Whether they like it or not, however, the auditors must also approve the interim phase end products — just like the users and others — and comment as to their satisfaction, subject to specific recommendations, with the project to date.

We will cover in more detail the role and specific concerns of the auditor's participation in the development of individual application systems in the next chapter.

SYSTEM TEST

A comprehensive acceptance test directed by the users is the last opportunity to detect and correct deficiencies in an application system before it is implemented. Since the system test is the last line of defense, it is extremely important.

The operation of the system test was described in detail in the previous chapter. Of the procedures described, the most important to control is the handling and resolution of reported discrepancies.

POSTIMPLEMENTATION REVIEW

By the time this phase is performed, the application system has been operational for some time. Serious discrepancies in the new application will have already done their damage. Therefore, the postimplementation review should not be relied upon as the first warning of significant exposures. Although it may provide such a warning, if nothing else has, this phase is more properly a control to detect excessive application operating costs; to reveal minor application defects; and, particularly, to help analyze the causes of any of the project exposures which resulted from the project.

DOCUMENTATION

Documentation, as a control over system development projects, can perform all three functions of control. A summary of the documents that should be produced by each phase is in Figure 12-9.

The very act of preparing documentation will provide a preventive control over incomplete economic evaluations or inadequate specifications. It will facilitate communications as well as subsequent modifications. Finally, its presence will reduce temptations to defraud.

In its detective capacity, documentation provides the medium for effective review by management, users, technical supervisors, and auditors after each phase, in system test, and in postimplementation review. Such reviews are particularly important for detection of design errors due to either lapses in judgment or incompetence.

Finally, documentation is essential to the effective correction of design errors and for system maintenance.

While the need for documentation is emphasized throughout this book, it is here in system development that it plays its most important role.

We have tried to indicate the controls appropriate to a system development project and to show that control depends on the establishment and implementation of a structured sequence of activities for the completion of a project. With the combination of a structured project and an accompanying control methodology, the system development process can be rendered predictable and manageable. The process will be as reliable as budgeting procedures elsewhere in a well-run company. For the manager, these techniques indicate that system development can, in fact, be predicted and controlled accurately. For the auditor, there are dual meanings. The first is that a structured system development process within a company provides an opportunity to monitor procedures for building controls into data processing applications. The second is that an interest in this area, particularly on the part of the internal auditor, provides an opportunity to impact the efficiency of an important segment of company activity.

A summary of the relationships between these controls and the causes of exposures is found in Figure 12-10.

276

SYSTEMS DOCUMENTATION SUMMARY

SYSTEMS PLANNING	USER SPECIFICATIONS	TECHNICAL SPECIFICATIONS	IMPLEMENTATION PLANNING
A System Planning Study Report, covering:	A Systems Requirements Report, containing:	A Technical Specification Report, covering:	An Implementation Plan, consisting of:
· Executive Summary · Introduction (background, terms) · Objectives and scope · Functional Descriptions · Performance Specifications · Design Specifications · Feasibility Analysis (technical, economic) · Acceptability Analysis (user, legal) · Supporting Documentation · For Present System: Functions, documents, manning chart, file elements, flow chart, constraints, controls, costs · For Proposed System: Functions, files, documentation, flow chart, constraints, controls, manning chart, file elements, inputs, outputs, flow charts and costs for non-computer and computer parts, development project plan, Gantt or PERT chart, cost comparisons, tangible and intangible benefits	· Job Descriptions · Input/Output Documents · File Description and Inquiry · Flow Chart of Computer System · Summary of Functions Performed (volume, times) · Data Element Description · Data Description · Glossary For Proposed System: · Management Summary (General description, benefits, processing cycle, system outputs) · Output Format · Output Description · Input Data Description · Data Element Catalog · Design Constraints · Controls · Flow Chart of Non-Computer Systems · New Manual Functions · Benefits Analysis · Economic Evaluation (updated) · Tangible Benefits Evaluation (updated)	· Output Layout · Input Layout · Data Flow Diagram (of processing steps) · Master File Definition · Processing Flow Chart and Volumes · Run/Module Definitions and Volumes · Constraints (refined or updated) · Controls (refined or updated) · Back-Up Procedures and Security · Tangible Benefits Evaluation (updated)	· Job/Run/Module Flow Charts · File Definitions & Labels · Input Definition · Standard Program Requirements (form headings, tables, run controls) · Run/Module Requirements (Functions, decision tables, logic charts, matrix tables, printer specification and support, merge or sort macro specifications, file controls) · Operating System Requirements (Job stream assembly, JCL) · Programming Schedule and Costs	· Project Plan (updated) · User Training Checklist · User Training Plan · System Test Increments · System Test Checklist · Computer Test Plan · Conversion Plan (Parallel processing, sequence) · File Data Acquisition Plan · Manpower and Equipment Plan · Tangible Benefits Evaluation (updated)

Figure 12-9 (Page 1 of 2)

SYSTEMS DOCUMENTATION SUMMARY

PROGRAMMING	USER PROCEDURES AND TRAINING	SYSTEMS TEST	CONVERSION	POST IMPLEMENTATION REVIEW
· Source Listings · Object Listings · Supervisory Parameters (JCL, etc.) · Utility Parameters · Program Test Plan · Test Data · Test Results · Console Messages and Operator Responses · Computer Center Instructions : ·· Console ·· Library · Restart Procedures · Logic Documentation ·· Logic Diagrams ·· Decision Tables	· Modified User Training Plan · Policies · Procedures · Job Outlines · Forms · Notifications · Training Plans · Training Schedules · Training Manuals · Training Aids · Equipment and Facilities Requirements	· Revised Systems Test Checklist · Revised Computer Test Plan · Test Data · Systems Test Results (approved by user or IPC) · Systems Test Discrepancy Notices (acted upon) · Systems Acceptance · Updated Systems Project Plan	· Modified Conversion Plan · Implementation Results Log · Implementation Discrepancy Notices (acted upon) · Implementation Results Approval · Project Termination Notice	· A Post-Implementation Review Report, including: · Management Summary · Interview Schedule · Related Systems · Service Requests or Initial Investigation Summaries · Implementation Discrepancy Notices · Interview Summary · Actual Staffing Requirements · Actual Non-Computer Cost Summary · Actual Computer Cost Summary · Systems Development Cost and Schedule Performance Summary · Actual Benefits Analysis (Narrative) · Actual Tangible Benefits Evaluation · Planned versus Actual Economic Evaluation Summary

Figure 12-9 (Page 2 of 2)

RELATIONSHIP OF SYSTEMS DEVELOPMENT CONTROLS TO CAUSES OF EXPOSURE

	CAUSES OF EXPOSURE										
	INCOMPLETE ECONOMIC EVALUATION	MANAGEMENT ABDICATION	INADEQUATE SPECIFICATIONS	SYSTEM DESIGN ERRORS	INCOMPETENT DESIGN PERSONNEL	TECHNICAL SELF-GRATIFICATION	POOR COMMUNICATIONS	NO PROJECT KILL POINTS	TEMPTATIONS TO COMPUTER ABUSE	UNMAINTAINABLE APPLICATION	INCOHERENT DIRECTION
PREVENTION CONTROLS											
Appropriate methodology	2	3	2				2	2			2
Project management		2			2	3	3				3
Staff hiring and training	1		2	2	3	1				2	
Checklists	2		1	1	1						
Documentation	2		2				3		2	3	1
DETECTION CONTROLS											
Technical reviews and approvals			2	2	3	2	2	2	2	3	3
Management and user reviews and approvals	3	3	2		2		2	2	2		2
Audit participation	3	2	2	2	2		2	2	2		3
System test			3	3	3		2		2	3	3
Post-implementation review	2	2	2		2	2				2	3
Documentation					3	2					3
CORRECTION CONTROLS											
Documentation					2	1				3	

RELIANCE ON CONTROLS

3 — Reliably controls applicable cause

2 — Controls cause but should be accompanied by additional controls

1 — Useful but not especially effective

Blank — No significant contribution

Figure 12-10

279

13
Audit Participation in Systems Development

OBJECTIVE

One of the major controls over the development of new application systems is the participation of an auditor on the development team. Although the auditor will be concerned with all aspects of the new system — control, efficiency, management information, and security — he is particularly expert in evaluating application controls. Accordingly, his primary contribution is to assure that newly implemented computer applications include sound and reliable control features.

At the same time, participation in systems development should not be the sole function of the internal auditor. He must realize that he, as well as the others involved in the development, cannot anticipate every possible situation that the implemented computer application may encounter. Accordingly, participation in the development of new systems does not eliminate the necessity for examination of existing application systems. What it does, in an overall sense, is to help prevent the implementation of application systems having significant exposures.

AUDIT TECHNIQUES

The auditor participates in the systems development process by reviewing and approving the documentation produced as the end products of certain systems development activities. By "approving" we do not mean that the auditor authorizes the development process to continue or that he provides any absolute guarantee that no exposures have escaped his notice. Rather, we simply mean that the auditor must *make a decision* as to whether the documentation end products are or are not adequate. All members of the team — designers, users, management — must make *similar commitments.* The auditor will lose his credibility if he does not also stand up and be counted.

At the same time, the auditor must remain independent, be aware that his review has limitations, and continue to report any significant exposures which he detects. His role does not depend upon whether the systems development process involves a purchased or an internally developed system. It is the same in all cases.

DEVELOPMENT CONTROLS MUST EXIST TO BE AUDITED

All of the following material regarding the appropriate role of an auditor in systems development is predicated upon the assumption that sound standards for systems development exist in the first place. If the systems development methodology and the controls over it differ substantially from those we have described in the previous chapters, the auditor's role must change appropriately. In such a situation, his response may vary from initiating the implementation of sound development controls to his assuming various development control functions which would not normally be his role. In many cases, both roles may be assumed. The first role would provide a long-range solution to the development of well-controlled applications which may be attempted in the future, and the second role may provide short-range protection with regard to the development projects that are under way.

Preferably, the auditor's role will be that described on the next several pages.

SYSTEMS PLANNING

Systems planning determines the project's scope, objectives, cost and benefits, and feasibility in the manner of a capital budgeting decision.

Most systems development projects call for limited audit involvement during the planning activity. The auditor's review of the systems planning documentation does not include any evaluation of controls, since they are much too vague and general at this time. His primary concern is to become familiar with the nature and impact of the project and *to plan and to schedule his future involvement.* His role is generally quite similar to that of basic information gathering for the examination of an application that had already been implemented.

The systems planning report which results from this phase should be retained by the auditor, since information on the objectives and benefits provides important references for the rest of the project. In addition, the preliminary control concepts that are described should be reviewed by the auditor for any gross omissions.

In planning and scheduling the auditor's future involvement, one of the first considerations that often arises is that of acquiring the necessary knowledge to deal with any new technical concepts or methods that are planned for the new application. Since this is a problem that also faces the systems development staff, the auditor should arrange to include himself or an assistant in the same technical training that is being provided the systems analysts.

USER SPECIFICATIONS

User specifications is a statement in nontechnical but detailed terms answering the questions:
- *What does the system have to accomplish?*
- *What is the problem to be solved?*
- *What is the solution (in nontechnical language)?*

Since the documentation produced by the user requirements activity fully describes all aspects of the application from the user's perspective, the auditor should perform an intensive review. As stated, the user requirements activity documents and describes in detail all of the application's manual processing as well as the general system of computer processing. Based upon this, the auditor should expect that all controls except those which specifically depend upon technical specifications will be defined at this stage. Figure 13-1 provides an application control matrix with X's indicating the major control classifications that should be defined within user specifications.

The most typical weakness encountered in this phase is failure to specify that *all* parties who will be affected, particularly secondary users, must participate in stating the application requirements, approving those requirements, and specifying controls. "Users" must include not only the obvious primary users but also secondary users such as the Accounting Department. Unilateral development of systems by data processing personnel will frequently produce applications which omit controls or processing capabilities required by some users.

The Auditor as a User

The internal auditor may also have requirements of a system that must be introduced during the user specification phase in order to provide him with effective application audit capabilities at a later date. Particularly, the auditor's user requirements might involve a capability to generate confirmations, to reverse transactions initiated through an integrated test facility, or to implement a system control audit review file (SCARF) or snapshot audit capability. Accordingly, the auditor must consider some of the potential application audit techniques that he may desire to use at a later date (see chapter 9).

APPLICATION CONTROL MATRIX INDICATING THE MAJOR CONTROL CLASSIFICATIONS THAT SHOULD BE DEFINED WITHIN USER AND TECHNICAL SPECIFICATIONS

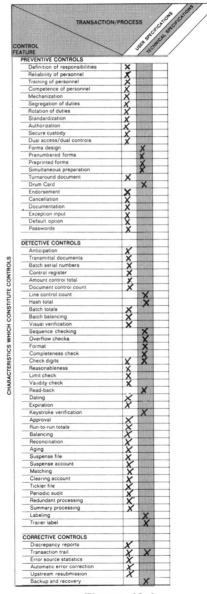

Figure 13-1

While the internal auditor must consider his own future needs as a potential user of computer applications, he must also be particularly mindful of certain risks and disadvantages inherent in his having any significant dependence upon application capabilities that are devised by the very people that he will subsequently audit. *The systems development staff should not be allowed to develop any audit capabilities that could possibly present a conflict of interest at some future date.* Whether improperly motivated or not, the one thing that an auditor may depend upon, if he allows his computerized audit routines to be developed by the same people who develop the application to be examined, is that these routines will not include examination of any elements that the development people do not believe should be examined. Furthermore, if the auditor feels additional controls, audit review files, or selective transaction trail documentation are desirable, then these things are probably at least as desirable to the systems development and user people. Accordingly, such recommendations should be implemented as much for programming and user personnel as for the auditor. The auditor may then direct his attention to verifying that these and other essential controls function properly.

Nonetheless, in certain situations the auditor will need particular capabilities programmed into the application system in advance, but he may not be able to convince user and systems development personnel that such capabilities are also in their best interests. In other situations, the implementation of computerized audit techniques by the auditor will exceed his technical capacity. He must then seek the assistance of data processing professionals. In such situations, *at a minimum,* the systems and programming personnel who implement these audit features should be independent of the individuals developing the application.

TECHNICAL SPECIFICATIONS

This phase is a translation of problem-and-solution statements from business to technical language at the level necessary to communicate with the programmers.

All remaining controls should be defined by the completion of the technical specifications.

The auditor's evaluation of these specifications, together with those produced in user specifications, should provide him with a comprehensive view of all controls to be implemented in the new system. Together, the auditor's review of user specifications and technical specifications is very similar to detailed information gathering of an implemented computer application. If a good job is performed by everyone up to this point, the remaining audit effort should be limited to a verification that the promised controls have, indeed, been incorporated.

By the same token, any serious deficiencies which exist after this review through either error or omission will be implemented and remain undetected at least until the systems test phase.

The technical specifications resulting from this activity include a number of items of interest to the auditor. However, the auditor may opt to review these items within the context of the next activity: implementation planning. That phase marks the completion of the systems design phases of the project and is a major review point for everyone involved, particularly top management. On the other hand, if the projects are large or the implementation planning is delayed, the auditor may prefer to perform an extensive review upon the completion of technical specifications. The choice between these alternatives is not particularly important.

Particular audit attention should be paid to modifications made to the user specifications during the development of technical specifications.

The final file content specifications will also be of special concern, particularly if the auditor plans to use general purpose audit software for subsequent testing. In addition to the obvious application concerns, the auditor should note whether all relevant information is included and whether a provision exists for making additional information available should changing circumstances require it.

IMPLEMENTATON PLANNNG

Following the preparation of detailed specifications in both user and technical languages, the balance of the implementation of an application may be planned with a significant degree of reliability.

This should be a *major control review point* for both the auditor and top management. While the auditor is interested in the entire implementation planning activity, he should be particularly interested in the controls being planned over conversion and implementation. The auditor's review at this point will serve as a guide for the balance of his audit participation as well as his examination after implementation. As noted previously, the auditor may also elect to delay his review of technical controls until this time.

Implementation controls include those controls associated with the creation of new master files as well as conversion of old master files to new. These may encompass a variety of edits and balancing controls as well as controls over the corrections of errors.

If the conversion is to require a significant span of time, additional controls may be necessary to convert the effects of transactions that occur during the conversion period. In some cases, the conversion activity may require significant programming activity to produce a conversion application that will be used only once. The management of the conversion activity can also present a significant challenge if the organization cannot abruptly terminate the old system and must operate under both systems during a transitional period.

Example — A conversion of a customer billing system may require the simultaneous operation of both systems to process payments received on invoices issued under both the old and new systems. This would be particularly true if the new system featured a turnaround document that was not utilized in the old system.

PROGRAMMING

This step converts the technical specifications to an operational, tested computer language with operating instructions. Programming should begin only after all of the design phases have been completed and approved.

Two major problems arise during computer programming. First, errors and misunderstandings may arise in the preparation of source language code from the technical specifications. This is quite natural and should be corrected by the supervisory controls available within the programming activity. However, the second problem may not be corrected by such supervision.

If user and technical specifications have not been prepared in adequate depth, the programmers may be called upon to make decisions with regard to processing that are beyond their authority or capability. Decisions as to the functional logic of processing must be made by management and the users, not by the programmers.

The auditor's role in the programming phase of development will depend, in part, upon the degree of his technical expertise. If he is qualified in the programming language and operating system being used, he may *occasionally* wish to verify the implementation of sound programming standards as well as the implementation of adequate application controls by examining the programming documentation.

Example — One way of verifying that field sizes have been defined to be large enough to accept the largest possible value is to look at the Data Division of a COBOL language program.

However, if sound controls over the programming activity are being exercised, the auditor should generally be able to rely upon such controls to the extent that is necessary at this phase.

Preliminary programming efforts will always include a significant number of defects in processing logic and controls. The programming activity is a highly error-prone activity. Before the programming activity is considered complete, these discrepancies must be detected and corrected by the programming staff and its supervision. *The testing of programs by the programming staff is not the same as the systems test phase of the development.* The programming phase is not complete until the programming staff and their direct supervisors are satisfied that all programs and sets of programs function in the manner specified in the user and technical specifications. Possible improvements to those specifications which may become apparent during the programming must not be implemented without the approval of those who approved the original specifications.

The primary control available to verify the correctness of the completed computer programs is the systems test. Normally, the auditor will be more effective by becoming involved in systems test rather than in programming.

USER PROCEDURES AND TRAINING

This phase includes the preparation of procedures for the conversion to and operation of the new system. The preparation and training are performed by the users themselves to assure that they fully understand the new system.

The user procedures and training activity result in the establishment of procedures for the manual phases of an application. This includes data acquisition, data consolidation, resolution of exceptions, and disposition of outputs. With the exception of error resolution, manual activities specified during user specifications and training will generally be simpler than under predecessor systems. The primary audit concern usually lies in control over the resolution of exceptions.

Like programming, the auditor need not normally become involved in detail with this activity. The functions and controls to be performed by the users have already been specified in the users specifications phase, which the auditor has already reviewed. Given that everyone else is doing his job reasonably well, the auditor may limit his activity to reviewing the detailed procedures to verify that the controls specified in the user requirements have been properly defined in the user procedures and training materials. These materials will include procedures manuals and the job descriptions for clerical activities.

SYSTEMS TEST

This is the "make-it-fail" stage of extensive testing. Care should be exercised to assure that an appropriate range of valid and invalid transactions are tested and that results are properly evaluated.

The systems test is an *acceptance test* by all users of the system, including the auditor. The auditor should be prepared to recommend to top management that implementation not proceed if he finds that significant application exposures exist due to oversights in original specifications or due to discrepancies in the implementation of those specifications. *The final decision to implement a computer application belongs to top management.* However, as the eyes and ears of top management, the internal auditor should provide the information to top management that they need to make an informed decision.

The systems test activity functions as a detective control over the preceding phases of the project. The systems test should not be expected to build quality into a system that has reached this stage of completion.

In the systems test, the auditor should insure that the *users* are actually performing the test, that the test data and procedures are comprehensive, and that the controls specified are actually working as intended. The auditor should also review all test results and be sure that significant discrepancies are corrected and retested before conversion of the system.

The systems test is the last line of defense against the implementation of an application with major exposures. Therefore, the *auditor's participation in this activity is essential,* even if he participates in no other phase. However, waiting until this phase to show any participation is highly undesirable because substantial commitments to the implementation of a project exist by this time. As a rule of thumb, 80% of the total project costs have been incurred upon the completion of systems testing, whereas only about 35% would normally have been invested by the completion of technical specifications. The auditor will be more effective and the systems development process far more efficient if the auditor were to participate throughout the earlier planning and development activities. However, it is imperative that he participate at least in the systems test if application exposures are to be avoided.

Three end items of the systems activity are of major interest to the auditor:

- Documentation of tests performed
- Documentation of discrepancies reported and corrective actions
- User approvals

Documentation of tests performed is significant because these records will indicate the adequacy of the testing. Furthermore, test materials used during this activity may be retained by the auditor for later revision and use as test data in subsequent examinations of the implemented application. Reports on discrepancies and corrections are also valuable because they indicate the nature of errors encountered and provide evidence that corrective actions were, in fact, taken. Finally, approvals are important because they indicate that the users have taken an active role and have specified corrections which they approve.

CONVERSION

This is the conversion of data, equipment, procedures, and personnel to the new system. It must be performed within a carefully planned and controlled environment to prevent a breakdown and to assure that the implemented system yields satisfactory operating results.

The quality of conversion and implementation procedures provide control effects separate and in addition to the other project activities. The process of conversion may be more complex than all the preceding activities combined. Of particular concern to the auditor is the maintenance of file integrity and the consistency of data affecting accounting reports.

Participation by the auditor in the conversion activity will vary substantially according to the effort involved in that activity. If special computer applications must be utilized simply for the conversion, the auditor will want to review them in much the same manner that he reviews the programs to be used in the ongoing application. On the other hand, if the conversion is relatively simple, the auditor may limit his participation to merely ascertaining that necessary tasks are completed in an orderly manner.

Parallel processing is frequently used during the conversion process and may constitute a simultaneous systems test. The feasibility of parallel processing depends upon two characteristics:

- The existence of a previous application system that provided results with identical content.
- Having sufficient organizational resources so that both old and new application systems can function simultaneously.

Example — Parallel processing would not be feasible if the new application system provided a perpetual inventory where none existed before. Neither would it be feasible if all of the previous inventory clerks were now retrained and employed as keypunchers.

Whatever the degree of involvement required, the auditor's objectives should be to assure that planned conversion controls are properly implemented, that exceptions and discrepancies are properly resolved, and that the conversion will allow effective comparison of the application results both before and after the conversion.

Three documentary end products of the conversion activity are important to the auditor:

- Edit documentation should indicate that the file conversion has achieved a satisfactory level of quality. Application control totals should indicate that all of the previously existing files have been converted.

- Documentation of operating results should reveal the volumes of processing, volumes of discrepancies, and indicate that the application is capable of handling existing levels of processing and error correction.
- All application documentation reflects the system that was ultimately implemented with proper approvals by user and EDP management.

POSTIMPLEMENTATION REVIEW

A review should be made by users and systems personnel after the new system has been operating for a period of time to assure that all functions of the system are operating as intended and that the systems development methodology was effective.

The auditor should actively participate in the postimplementation review. He should work *with* the users and systems development management to verify that the benefits planned by the new system have actually been achieved. This includes verifying that all manual systems have been discontinued and that operating problems are being resolved. A frequent cause of excessive costs is the continued operation and staffing of both the old and new application systems. The auditor may frequently act as the independent third party to resolve disputes relating to the discontinuance of the old methods.

Depending upon the degree of auditor participation in the earlier phases of the systems development project, some organizations prefer to have a different internal auditor participate in the postimplementation review. This philosophy is also common for later examinations of ongoing applications. The intent is to reduce any questions as to the independence of the auditor with regard to the effectiveness of controls recommended or omitted during the design and testing phases of the project.

ONGOING MAINTENANCE

Ongoing maintenance is the common term applied to any continuing work on the application after the implementation phase is complete.

Many organizations apply thorough efforts to the documentation of applications during the systems development projects. However, documentation and testing of maintenance changes often fall below acceptable levels.

At a minimum, the auditor should be informed of all planned modifications to the programs of the application system. He may then judge for himself what modifications might create significant exposures and determine the degree to which he should become involved.

Just as in the development of a major application system, ongoing maintenance should be controlled, first, by the preparation of adequate specifications and, second, by the adequate testing of the completed revisions. The auditor's involvement in these activities should parallel his involvement in similar activities found in a full-scale development project.

The auditor should be extensively involved in the review of the end product of the users requirements, technical requirements, implementation planning, and systems test phases. In these activities, he is primarily concerned with the development and implementation of adequate application controls. His participation in the system planning, user procedures and training, and programming phases should, in most cases, be limited to a general monitoring. Involvement in the conversion phase will vary according to the extent of the conversion procedures required. Subsequent to implementation, the auditor should actively participate in the postimplementation review and ongoing maintenance activities.

While these generalizations will vary according to the reliability of the systems development process within various organizations, a pronounced need to deviate from this general pattern should be indicative of deep-seated control weaknesses over that systems development process. This may lead the auditor to the subject of the next chapter: "Auditing the Systems Development Process."

14
Auditing The Systems Development Process

REASONS FOR AUDITING THE DEVELOPMENT PROCESS

The principal effect of a company's systems development mechanism on audit activities lies in helping to prevent omission of adequate controls during the development of new applications and during the application maintenance process. In total, the systems development process constitutes a preventive control. Systems development controls should assure compliance with design standards and protect against the implementation of any application with major control weaknesses.

TWO AUDIT ROLES EXIST IN SYSTEMS DEVELOPMENT

Prior to discussing the auditing of the systems activity, the auditor must clearly understand that the audit of the *systems development process* is different from participating in the development of a *particular application.* When the auditor participates in the development of an application, he is principally concerned with application controls (described in chapter 7). The controls that are under examination during an audit of the systems development process are those which were discussed in chapter 12. While gathering evidence to support the existence of controls over the development process may require the examination of application documentation, the objectives differ.

STEPS IN THE REVIEW OF THE SYSTEMS DEVELOPMENT PROCESS

Steps in the review of the systems development process are presented in Figure 14-1 and are summarized here:

292

Basic Information Gathering — Obtain an initial understanding of the systems and programming activities and evaluate them in relation to audit objectives to set the preliminary scope.

Detailed Information Gathering — Examine documentation in each of the four major areas of the systems and programming activities to determine whether policies and practices are being adhered to and supplement these findings by interviews with various personnel as necessary.

Evaluation of Control Strengths and Weaknesses — Identify and evaluate the critical controls in the systems and programming activity and prepare a list of them.

Design Audit Procedures — Prepare an audit program for the systems development function which consists of a list of applications to be reviewed and individuals to be interviewed.

Testing — Perform a review of the systems development controls by selecting certain applications for review and performing the tests as planned.

Evaluate Findings and Report — Evaluate the results of the work and prepare a report on the findings.

BASIC INFORMATION GATHERING

General background information should be gathered to indicate the level of activity and magnitude of the systems and programming functions. Some situations that may limit the auditor's concern include:

- No applications are planned which affect audit objectives.
- Consistent system design standards are lacking.

Except in the situations above, the auditor should always be concerned about testing the systems development process. While this audit activity is one that may be new to many auditors, its importance is gaining widespread recognition.

The first thing the auditor should request is the manual documenting the systems development standards. If none exists, the audit is terminated at this point. Although standards may exist without being documented, the likelihood that they are being implemented with any consistency is so small that any further effort would be a waste of time.

Even if standards have been documented, the auditor should quickly review them to determine whether they are in use and if they are revised regularly. A set of beautiful standards with virgin pages and dated five years previous probably bears little resemblance to actual practices. The audit should continue only if real, operating standards exist.

STEPS IN AUDIT OF SYSTEMS DEVELOPMENT PROCESS

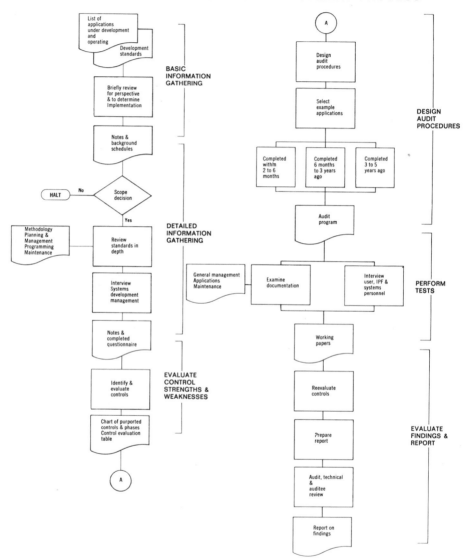

Figure 14-1

294

DETAILED INFORMATION GATHERING

The systems and programming activities should be governed by well-documented, current statements of policy, standards, procedures, practices, etc., in each of the four following segments of activity:

- Systems development standards (methodology and control)
- Systems planning and management
- Programming standards
- Application maintenance

The auditor should obtain documentation on each of these areas and review it to obtain an understanding of the policies and practices in the respective activities. The primary documentation will normally be a systems and procedures manual (or similar written policy statement) which contains the policies and standards for:

- Organization
- Project planning
- Project management
- Systems design and development steps
- Programming conventions, procedures, and documentation
- Flowcharting conventions
- System controls
- Application documentation
- Application conversion and implementation
- User interface
- Application maintenance

Interviews with management, user, and systems personnel may be required to complete the understanding of the policies and practices, depending upon the level of detail included in the documentation. As interface with activities outside the systems development group is not often included in such documentation, interviews with management and users, to determine the level of their interaction with the systems staff, will often be needed. During these interviews, the auditor should also determine the level of satisfaction of users and management with the systems development function.

EVALUATE CONTROL STRENGTHS AND WEAKNESSES

Once he obtains an understanding of the systems and programming functions and their relationship with activities outside their departments, the auditor may select those controls which could have a significant impact on the reliability of applications being developed. These controls were previously discussed in chapter 12.

Many of the systems development controls are exercised on each development phase, whereas others apply only to certain phases. The controls and the phases to which they apply are provided in Figure 14-2.

CONTROLS AND DEVELOPMENT PHASES TO WHICH THEY APPLY

CONTROLS	PROJECT ACTIVITIES										
	INITIAL INVESTIGATION	PRELIMINARY SYSTEM STUDY	SYSTEM PLANNING STUDY	USER REQUIREMENTS	TECHNICAL SPECIFICATIONS	IMPLEMENTATION PLANNING	PROGRAMMING	USER PROCEDURES AND TRAINING	SYSTEM TEST	CONVERSION	POST-IMPLEMENTATION REVIEW
Appropriate Methodology											
Project Management											
Staff Hiring and Training											
Checklists	■	■	■	■	■		■				■
Technical Review and Approval											
Management Review and Approval							■				
User Review and Approval							■				
Audit Participation	■						■				
System Test	■	■	■	■	■	■	■	■		■	■
Post-Implementation Review	■	■	■	■	■	■	■	■	■	■	■
Documentation											

Figure 14-2

The most important control over a systems development project is thorough review and approval at well-defined project checkpoints. Each project must have a specified end product which is subjected to review and approval by all concerned parties before the next phase commences. If the organization has such defined checkpoints and end products, compliance can be readily verified through examination of the written approvals. If no such definitions exist, other controls are not likely to compensate; and further compliance tests may be fruitless.

The auditor's primary concern should be the quality of and control over the application systems which result from the system development process. Secondarily, he should be concerned with the various project exposures which may occur separate from and in addition to those of implemented applications. A control evaluation table to assist in this process is provided in Figure 14-3.

DESIGN COMPLIANCE AUDITING PROCEDURES

Compliance with the controls over the systems development process may be tested by examining the following two classes of documentation:

- *Administrative reports* covering project planning and management
- *Application documentation* prepared during development

Administrative Reports

The following types of reports should be located and reviewed for compliance with the following systems development controls:

- Project management
- Staff hiring
- Staff training

This documentation should be readily available as it provides the primary tool for effective supervision by the management of the systems development function. The following types of documents may indicate these controls:

- Long-range plans
- Gantt chart of projects
- Detailed budgets for projects
- Reports of actual versus budgeted project costs
- Written explanations for project deviations
- Personnel records of training
- Personnel evaluations of development staff

Application Documentation

The documentation packages produced in the development of individual applications should provide evidence of the following systems development controls:

- Systems methodology
- Activity checklists
- Technical reviews and approvals
- Management reviews and approvals
- User reviews and approvals
- Internal audit reviews and approvals
- Systems test results
- Postimplementation review findings
- Documentation of application functions and controls

SYSTEMS DEVELOPMENT CONTROL EVALUATION TABLE

RELIANCE ON CONTROLS*
3 — Reliably controls applicable cause
2 — Controls cause but should be accompanied by additional controls
1 — Useful but not especially effective
Blank — No significant contribution

*Warning — Typical values preprinted must be tailored for specific use

EXPOSURES

Application Exposures (if project implemented)
- Erroneous record keeping
- Unacceptable accounting
- Business interruption
- Erroneous management decisions
- Fraud
- Statutory sanctions
- Excessive costs/deficient revenues
- Loss or destruction of assets
- Competitive disadvantage

Project Exposures
- Erroneous management decisions
- Excessive costs
- Competitive disadvantage
- Business interruption (delay timetable)

IMPACT OF CAUSES
3 — Very likely to occur
2 — Likely to occur
1 — May occur
Blank — Generally little effect

CAUSES OF EXPOSURE:
1. Incomplete economic evaluation
2. Management abdication
3. Inadequate specifications
4. System design errors
5. Incompetent personnel design
6. Technical self-gratification
7. Poor communications
8. No project kill points
9. Temptations to computer abuse
10. Unmaintainable application
11. Incoherent direction

Controls / Rows	Inc. econ. eval.	Mgmt abdication	Inadeq. specs	System design errors	Incompetent personnel	Technical self-gratif.	Poor communications	No project kill points	Temptations comp. abuse	Unmaintainable appl.	Incoherent direction
PREVENTION CONTROLS											
Appropriate methodology	2	3			2		2	2	2		2
Project management	1	2		1	3	1	3				3
Staff hiring and training	2		2	1	1				2		
Checklists	2		1					2	2	3	1
Documentation	2		2				3			3	
DETECTION CONTROLS											
Technical reviews and approvals			2	2	2	2	2	2	2	3	3
Management and user reviews and approvals	3	3	2	2	2		2	2	2	2	2
Audit participation	3	2	2	3	3	2	2	2	2	3	3
System test			3	3	2		2		2	3	3
Post-implementation review	2	2	2		2	2				2	3
Documentation				3							
CORRECTION CONTROLS											
Documentation	2		2	2	1		3	1	2		3
IMPACT OF CAUSES			2	2	3	3	2	1	1	2	2
Application Exposures											
Erroneous record keeping			1	1			1		1		1
Unacceptable accounting			3	2	3		2		2	2	2
Business interruption			1	1	1		1	1	2	2	1
Erroneous management decisions			1	1	1			1		1	
Fraud			1		3	3	2	1	2		2
Statutory sanctions				1	1	2	1	2		2	1
Excessive costs/deficient revenues			2	1	3	1	2		2	1	2
Loss or destruction of assets				1	1	3	1	1	2		1
Competitive disadvantage		2				2				2	2
Project Exposures											
Erroneous management decisions	2	3	3	2	2	3	3	2		3	3
Excessive costs		2	1	2	3	2	3	1		2	3
Competitive disadvantage	2	2	2	2	2	2	2			2	2
Business interruption (delay timetable)	2	2	2	2	3					2	3

Figure 14-3

METHODOLOGY

The implementation of an appropriate systems development methodology should be pervasive in the application documentation. Since each development phase is marked by the preparation of specified end products, the auditor need only obtain and examine those end products. In doing so, he may also verify many other controls.

CHECKLISTS

Certain phases, as discussed previously and illustrated in figures 11-15, 11-16, and 11-17, include a standard set of tasks that may be controlled by means of a checklist.

REVIEWS AND APPROVALS

Evidence of review and approval by technical supervisors should be found throughout the application documentation. Preferably, each page should be initialed and dated by the individual who prepared it and the one who approved it. At a minimum, all reviewers should indicate their approval on a lead sheet that accompanies each set of development phase end products. These approvals should include all primary and secondary users, top management, where applicable, as well as internal audit. Modifications requested by users and recommendations made by auditors should be examined in conjunction with the systems end-product documentation. In most cases, such items will be maintained separately.

SYSTEM TEST

The evidence of an adequate systems test should be provided by the end-product documentation of that phase. Of course, this should also contain appropriate approvals.

POSTIMPLEMENTATION REVIEW

Reports of findings from postimplementation reviews should be available for each application system that has existed for at least six months. Findings should be accompanied by action plans for correction and by support showing that the corrections had been achieved.

DOCUMENTATION

Documentation of the application functions and controls should exist in the form of the end products from several development phases. To reiterate, this documentation should include:

- A narrative description of the application
- A current system flowchart
- Instructions for computer operators
- File specifications and record layouts for all records in all files shown on the system flowchart

- Listings of all transactions and status codes used together with explanations of their meanings and their impact upon records
- Descriptions of all input and output documents and machine-readable media indicated on the system flowchart
- Detailed documentation of program logic using logic flowcharts or decision tables. If flowcharting software is available, this may serve in lieu of keeping logic-level flowcharts on hand.
- Program specifications for all jobs on the application flowchart
- Lists of edits, error messages, and other controls
- A current set of source code listings for all application programs or program decks which can be converted readily to provide such listings.

The purpose of thorough documentation, with regard to control, is to provide a medium for supervisory review and approval. In addition, it facilitates accurate logic, simplifies programming, and assists future maintenance. Without effective supervision, the quality of the application system becomes largely dependent upon the care and ability exercised by the individuals engaged in the development project. Such reliance may not be justified.

PERFORMING COMPLIANCE TESTS

The procedures discussed above should be applied to a selection of representative applications. In selecting the applications to be tested, the auditor should utilize a representative cross-section of ongoing, implemented applications such as:

- An application which has recently been implemented: in the range of the past three to six months.
- A mature application: one that has been implemented for six months to three years.
- A third application should be approaching the end of its useful life: three to five years.

The selection criteria above are only guidelines and must be evaluated in relation to the audit objectives and the level of development activity.

Systems Development Audit Techniques

The two primary verification techniques appropriate for the systems development audit process are:

- Examination of selected documentation to support compliance
- Supplemental interviews of users, management, *auditors,* and information processing facility personnel to verify compliance where such is not documented and to determine their involvement in the various development phases, since this is often not documented

300

In conjunction with these techniques, the auditor has two proven tools to help guide him through the verification process. These are standardized audit questionnaires and the proven EDP management techniques described in *Managing Computer Systems Projects* by Shaw and Atkins.

Documentation

The auditor should conduct his examination of application documentation to produce a general evaluation of controls over documentation rather than of their specific contents. Again, remember that the objective of this type of compliance auditing is to verify compliance with the controls listed as *systems development controls*, not application controls.

In reviewing application documentation, the auditor ascertains the existence, content, and timeliness of the documentation for a representative selection of applications being processed. Weaknesses in application documentation affect control principally by increasing the potential for design and programming errors. Thus, if deficiencies in documentation of systems development and ongoing maintenance are encountered, the auditor should develop a commensurate degree of skepticism regarding the quality of design and programming within all applications. He should consider increasing the scope of his application verification procedures accordingly.

As indicated earlier, weak or deficient application documentation is the auditor's most common and most serious problem in an EDP environment. In such instances, one alternative is to attempt to measure the degree to which programming defects might have been introduced and exposures created because of inadequate application documentation.

The auditor should also visit the Data Conversion Department within the information processing facility and review the instructions for key entry and verification. He should determine if such documentation is current and readily available. Failure to have such documentation accessible will substantially increase the probability of format errors in the preparation of inputs. Lack of such documentation should also alert the auditor to devote particular attention to the quality of input edit routines within application controls. Documentary evidence of the nature and extent of such input problems may be provided through a review of the nature and number of exceptions being listed on application edit reports.

Documentation of application maintenance should be regarded as even more important than documentation supporting initial application development, because *maintenance is much more error prone.* The maintenance activity requires heavy reliance upon the quality of documentation end products of the systems development process. The auditor *may* find that a competent programmer was able to develop high-quality, well-controlled application programs without extensive, formal documentation. He should recognize that, in such situations, different programmers will generally be involved in application maintenance. Thus, the auditor should hold that the only reliable means of communicating the necessary depth of information on application functions and controls is through adequate end-product project documentation. The quality of application maintenance which may be expected depends directly upon the quality of initial application documentation.

Application maintenance documentation examined by the auditor should include:

- Narrative descriptions of application changes
- Statements giving reasons for and effects of changes
- Dates on which changes were implemented
- Signed approvals of changes
- Numerical control over the changes made
- Documentation of tests performed before implementation of changes
- Appropriate revisions to all previous documentation affected by application changes

This documentation should be examined for each of the representative applications selected for review. During this examination, the auditor should determine whether changes had been affected through alteration of source code instructions with attendant recompilation of machine instructions or by direct patching of the machine instructions. Use of patching introduces a higher probability that logic errors have been introduced through program maintenance. Note, however, that successful patching becomes quite difficult to perform under most of today's high-level compilers and relocatable program libraries. It is principally found in second-generation (1401) language programs and is generally not of concern in modern operations.

The test data used in program maintenance activities should also be reviewed. Preferably, the entire application should be tested rather than the individual programs or modules which were modified. At a minimum, the tests should include all programs that are "down stream" (those programs that accept, as input, the output from the modified programs). The easiest way to assure such testing thoroughness is for standards to call for the retention of all test data, although in some cases this may be impractical. This will apply to both the original systems test phase and for all successive application modifications. If testing of program modifications is not applied to the complete application, the probability of the introduction of logic errors may increase.

In examining application maintenance documentation, the auditor should also note whether users have indicated, where appropriate, their approval of the test procedures used. These approvals, should extend to the results of testing.

The auditor should interview users and discuss program maintenance of the representative applications selected. He should determine whether users are satisfied with responsiveness to their needs for change. This should apply to changes required by either business conditions or by the increased awareness of users of the advantages of EDP.

In the course of such interviews, the auditor should identify and review programming changes to selected applications. If documented approval is not included for these recent changes, the auditor should note whether users are aware of the changes which were made. In addition, he should cover the nature of the changes made in his discussions with users and note whether modification procedures have conformed to the organization's accounting policies, systems development standards, and internal control requirements.

One technique for determining whether there were changes to application programs is for the auditor to maintain an independent control copy of the program. Periodically, he should compare his control copy to the copy maintained in the information processing facility. In larger organizations, this procedure may be limited to certain highly sensitive programs. This comparison may be manual, or the auditor may employ special purpose software which can compare the two program decks and list differences. There is also software available, which is normally resident on the operating system, to continually monitor programs and automatically produce change listings, dates of changes, etc. The auditor should investigate the use of these additional tools and employ them if circumstances warrant it.

Finally, the auditor should interview the systems development manager and discuss all the changes effected during the period under examination. Any applications which are found to have sustained major changes or indications of user dissatisfaction should be considered carefully for possible inclusion in the auditor's application verification scope.

EVALUATE FINDINGS

The Control Evaluation Table (Figure 14-3) may again be consulted in the final evaluation of the effectiveness of controls whose implementation has been verified. However, rather than accept the typical "effectiveness ratings" that are printed in Figure 14-3, the auditor may insert his own scale of ratings based upon the actual quality of implementation.

Quality of control implementation is the major factor in the final evaluation of findings. This must be a subjective measure made by the auditor. Unlike applications, observed error rates are not normally applicable.

Example — The auditor will not normally find that documentation is missing in 10% of his tests but, rather, must determine whether the quality of the documentation will provide control over the various causes of exposure.

The quality, rather than frequency, of implementation will determine the effectiveness of all of the various system development controls with the possible exception of the checklists. For this reason, the auditor must possess a higher level of technical expertise than is necessary for evaluation of application controls.

The most common quality problems that will be encountered include the following:

- Methodology — missing complete phases
- Project management — insufficient definition of tasks
- Training — not done prior to attempting unfamiliar designs
- Technical reviews — not done in detail
- Management and user reviews — don't understand development plan or role
- System Test — not controlled by users
- Postimplementation review — not done
- Documentation — not summarized nor revised for changes

Identification of any of these deficiencies in control implementation should reduce or eliminate the auditor's reliance.

A structured approach to systems development is new for many companies which have utilized electronic data processing for many years. Auditors should recognize that this activity has a critically important impact on the quality and reliability of computerized applications. Because of this, the auditor should include the systems development process within the scope of both his interest and his examination activity.

Section IV
INFORMATION PROCESSING FACILITY

15
IPF Activities

This section deals with the computer information processing facility (IPF) as a separate entity.

Chapter 15 describes the activities generally found in the IPF but does not deal with computer concepts since substantial professional literature on that subject already exists. Accordingly, this chapter is relatively brief and merely summarizes the activities that are subject to control and the causes of exposures within an IPF.

Chapters 16, 17, and 18 deal with the three major categories of control within an IPF: operations, hardware and software, and security.

Chapter 19 describes the procedures and concerns necessary in auditing the IPF.

IPF ACTIVITIES

The operations of an IPF are no more (or less) complex than those of a comparable-sized factory. The basic objectives of the operations are to produce a high-quality product at minimum cost. Competent businessmen are fully capable of understanding the operations of the IPF without becoming technicians, just as they can understand the operations of a factory they manage without being engineers.

Although the operations of the IPF are part of the application processing of each computerized application, all applications are generally treated in a similar manner. Therefore, the activities, causes of exposure, and controls of the IPF apply to every computerized application that is processed.

The principal functions of the computer IPF are:
- Data conversion
- Computer operations
- File and program libraries
- Output distribution

Data Conversion

The most common machinery used for data conversion is the keypunch. These machines, which produce the standard 80-column punched card, currently (1975) account for about 80 percent of the data conversion devices in use. However, this proportion is declining rapidly as keypunches are replaced by key-input devices that have a higher productivity. These include:
- Key-to-tape cassettes
- Key-to-"floppy" discs
- Key-to-conventional tapes and discs

The most obvious advantage of these replacement devices is the elimination of the unnecessary conversion from a punched card to a magnetic tape or disc, which is commonly performed before high-volume processing commences. An additional benefit occurs when minicomputers are used as components of such systems and provide the capacity to perform limited editing and balancing so that many errors can be efficiently corrected before the input is submitted to the central computer.

Other popular major data conversion devices are optical character recognition (OCR) and magnetic ink character recognition (MICR).

Optical character recognition may accept documents inscribed with stylized type fonts, conventional type, or handwriting. The rate of unreadable characters and documents varies substantially according to which of these alternatives is used as well as the quality of the actual inscribing.

Magnetic ink character recognition (MICR) systems dominate the banking industry but are rarely found elsewhere. Bank identification and account numbers are preprinted on checks and other input documents. Amounts must be entered on the documents, using key inscribing equipment. Once inscribed, high-volume reading and physical sorting can be performed.

The choice of data conversion devices is generally an economic decision rather than one of capabilities or controls. The key-to-tape and key-to-disc conversion systems eliminate the additional effort of transcribing from cards to tape or disc media. OCR and MICR make use of turnaround documents with preprinted information.

The variable information on OCR inputs may be handwritten or typed on conventional typewriters; however, the rejection rate of unreadable data is commonly quite high: 10 to 60 percent. Accordingly, even when OCR is employed, it is generally supplemented by more conventional key-input devices for correction of rejected items. OCR has not yet achieved widespread acceptance in low-volume operations because of its high fixed cost, the problems inherent in using stylized types, and the cost of maintaining a supplementary input system to handle the "unreadable" items. However, as all other alternatives involve an essentially redundant clerical transcription of data, major technical advances will almost certainly lie in optical recognition cost reductions and improved reject correction techniques.

The duties and responsibilities of a key-input-device operator are to simply transcribe source documents that are provided onto a machine-readable medium: cards, tapes, or discs. The operator is subject to normal typographical errors like inversion of digits, hitting the wrong key, and misaligning data according to its magnitude or nature. In addition, the operator is responsible for processing all materials. This applies to the collection of punched cards and the consolidation of tape cassettes or "floppy-disc" onto high-speed magnetic media.

Since the data conversion function tends to be labor intensive, it is normally one of the activities representing a major cost in any information processing facility.

Computer Operations

The actual operation of the computer is a fairly simple task, as most of the complex tasks are automated within an operating system. The physical activities required of a computer operator consist mostly of the following, depending on the operating system, in order of descending proportionate time:

- Mounting and dismounting data files
- Loading paper in the printer
- Aligning forms in the printer
- Loading programs
- Responding to decisions requested by the operating system
- Responding to decisions requested by the application programs
- Maintaining accounting records
- Performing routine maintenance
- Responding to equipment failures

The time required to perform these tasks on a large batch-oriented machine, processing multiple programs, may keep two men occupied constantly. The greatest value of the operators may be in the judgment exercised in maintaining an efficient mix of concurrent programs to maximize the throughput.

The central element in the communication between an operator and the computer is the console. This is a typewriter, printer, or cathode-ray tube with a keyboard similar to a conventional typewriter.

The console may display information messages, messages describing discrepancies in the data or equipment operations, or requests for actions to be performed regarding the various peripheral devices.

As succeeding generations of computers have provided greater capacity and sophistication of operations, many of the previous routine, as well as judgmental, tasks of the computer operator have been automated. The software which perform these operating functions are known as "operating systems," "supervisors," or "master control programs." The exact functions performed by operating systems vary widely according to the vendor, the capacity of the computer, and the particular options selected by the IPF management. Some of the operating functions which may be found in various operating systems include:

- Assignment of programs to core memory partitions
- Assignments of peripheral devices to programs
- Editing of input data for format or parity
- Editing of programmed operations
- Monitoring of device performance
- Storage of language translators or compilers
- Storage of general purpose utilities
- Job accounting

The assumption of operating control functions by software has been a distinct trend in the development of operating systems. Unfortunately, there is such a profusion of operating systems and options within those systems that no comprehensive study presently is available which even lists the control features available, much less evaluates them. The authors consider this to be a major gap in the information available to managers and auditors who are concerned with control. Research on this subject has been initiated, and an analysis of the results will hopefully be available in a future edition of this book.

The truly competent computer operator is capable of far more than merely mounting magnetic tapes on their drives. Depending upon the operating system and IPF standards, he or she may be called upon to make processing decisions for recovery from hardware or software errors, to delve deeply into the efficiency of computer operations, and to maintain a fairly extensive knowledge of the inner workings of the computer. The technical requirements of operation of some of today's computers may provide the operators with fulfilling career progression into technical services.

Management and auditors must become familiar with the specific operating duties of the computer operations and information processing facilities they are concerned with. Since these duties will vary widely according to the operating system, equipment, configuration, and organization, we will make no further generalizations of duties here.

Data and Program Libraries

Application data files are maintained either "on-" or "off-line." On-line files generally reside on magnetic disc or other mass storage devices. Off-line files are normally on magnetic tape or removable disc packs. Files which are on-line reside on peripheral devices of the computer during normal operations. They can be immediately accessed by any program, subject to various controls. Off-line files are normally retained in a library adjacent to the machine room. Such files must be physically obtained from that room and mounted upon a peripheral device before application programs can access them.

Programs are maintained in two distinct forms: source and object code. The object, or machine-level, program instructions are customarily retained on a special disc file controlled by the operating system. Such programs can be executed whenever requested through the operator's console or by control cards submitted to the operating system by the operator, a programmer, or other person setting up the work flow. Changes to the programs may be made in two ways. First, the source code may be changed and recompiled into new object code. Second, the old object code may be directly patched.

Source-language program statements may either be maintained in another disc file under control of the operating system or off-line on punched cards or magnetic media. Such off-line program files may be either in the custody of the programming staff or in the library with the data files.

Some of the functions of the program library may be automated. The software which performs these functions is known as "library software." Such systems generally maintain control files of program source-language statements. The automated functions that they may provide include:

- Updating of source statements
- Renumbering of source statements
- Retention and identification of prior program versions
- Limited edits over program statement format and content

Library software may also distinguish production programs from obsolete and test versions. This facilitates control of the programming process and allows processing of production files only by those programs approved by management as having production status.

Programs, in any machine-readable form, are physically identical to data files and, without proper control, on-line libraries can be accessed and altered by any technique also suitable for data files. At the same time, maintenance of the source statements on-line allows utilization of library software to manage revisions.

The operation of the library of computer files and programs exists primarily as a control function to segregate the custody of information assets from those who process them. It also has major productivity implications in larger organizations since the procurement of the appropriate files and programs by computer operators can consume a significant amount of time.

Output Distribution

Finally, the hard copy and other products of computer processing must be distributed to their proper recipients. Before this can occur, multiple-part paper and forms must be decollated and burst apart into individual documents. Other operations that may be required include folding, stuffing, and mailing. These various functions may be additional duties of existing IPF personnel, of the input-output section, or of the Mail Department.

In the course of these activities, opportunities exist to damage, mutilate, or misroute the appropriate outputs. The waste carbon paper and other scrap also constitute a fire hazard.

CAUSES OF IPF EXPOSURES

The causes of exposures within the computer operations activity fall into four major categories:
- Human errors
- Hardware/software failures
- Computer abuse
- Catastrophies

Human Errors

Computers are operated by humans. Like all others, these humans are subject to accidents, lapses of memory, errors of judgment, etc. Generally speaking, however, the major categories of human errors are in the following areas:
- Data entry
- Console entries
- Use of wrong data files or programs
- File damaged in handling

Data-entry errors are simple clerical errors in keystroke conversion of input documents. *Console-entry* errors are in response to operating system messages which require a human decision. Computer file and program media are virtually identical in their exterior appearance. Controls can be used to distinguish them; however, without these, they may be readily confused and the *wrong one used.* The computer media are also subject to *physical damage.* Tapes can easily be stretched, creased, scratched, or burned. Computer discs can be scratched and bent. Any of these causes will bring about the destruction of information.

Hardware/Software Failures

Although the computer hardware and the associated software are extremely reliable when compared to humans, they are not infallible. They are dependent upon constant supplies of power and are readily subject to *interruption* of operations due to mechanical or power failures. Their failure can also cause the *loss or destruction of data.* Finally, although the least common, subtle malfunctions can occur, causing their *logical processes* to be incorrect.

Computer Abuse

Computers can be the object, tool, or symbol of an act of abuse as well as constitute the environment in which such acts occur. The computers and their time can be stolen or be the vehicles to *steal* something else. If this theft involves a position of trust, it is normally called *embezzlement.* The computer can also be used to deceive in a *fraudulent* manner. It can be the object of *corporate espionage* or *invasion of personal privacy.* And, finally, it can be the object or instrument of acts of *mischievousness or maliciousness.* These problems are discussed in greater detail in Section V.

Catastrophies

The major catastrophies that may befall an information processing facility are fire, water, wind, and civil disorder. Computers are particularly vulnerable to *fire,* since some of their components and recording media may be damaged at temperatures as low as 120° F. *Water* from burst pipes, leaks, floods, or firefighting efforts can cause short circuits or deposit residues that are impossible to remove. *Winds,* principally in the form of hurricanes and tornadoes, have been responsible for the physical destruction of buildings in which computers reside. Finally, major acts of *civil disorder* have occasionally been directed toward computers or the buildings in which they reside, causing their physical destruction as well as destruction by associated fire and water.

Rates of Occurrence

No one really knows the probability of the various IPF causes of exposure occurring. To predict the impact of controls, one should know the occurrence rate under a complete absence of control. Such situations rarely exist. Since many of the IPF causes of exposure actually occur rather seldom (fire, embezzlement, etc.), any estimates of their probability in individual cases may be viewed as either pure judgment or speculation.

At least one collection of judgments of occurrence rates has been published by James Martin in *Security, Accuracy, and Privacy in Computer Systems.* These estimates of the IPF causes of exposure appear in Figure 15-1.

CAUSE OF EXPOSURE	ESTIMATED OCCURRENCE RATE
Human Errors	
Data Entry	10 Times per Day
Console Entries	Once per 10 Days
Wrong File or Program	Once per 4 Years
File Damaged in Handling	Once per 4 Years
Hardware/Software Failures	
Interrupt Operations	Once per 10 Days
Loss of Data	Once per 10 Days
Logic Error	Once per 10 Days
Computer Abuse	
Theft	Once per 4 Years
Embezzlement	Once per 100 Days
Fraud	Once per 4 Years
Espionage	Once per 4 Years
Invasion of Privacy	Once per 100 Days
Maliciousness	Once per 4 Years
Mischievousness	Once per 100 Days
Catastrophe	
Fire	Once per 40 Years
Water	Once per 40 Years
Wind	Once per 40 Years
Civil Disorder	Once per 40 Years

Adapted from *Security, Accuracy, and Privacy in Computer Systems* by James Martin, Prentice-Hall, 1973.

Figure 15-1

EXPOSURES

Most of these causes will have varied and widespread effects. The exposures that result may range from a minor increase in costs to the complete ruin of the business. The exposures that typically result, with an indication of the magnitude of their likelihood, are summarized in the table in Figure 15-2. This table is intended as an illustration of typical relationships. It should be revised to reflect the specific environment before it is used to evaluate any particular IPF.

In this chapter, we have briefly reviewed the activities performed within the information processing facility. We have not attempted to provide comprehensive technical instruction on all areas of IPF activities, since this is generally the subject of a text on computer science. While the effective manager or auditor must have a sound comprehension of the areas they are examining, a thorough technical comprehension is beyond the scope of this book. If further information on this subject is desired, we recommend that the reader acquire one of the many excellent texts on computer concepts (see "Recommended Readings" in this volume).

RELATIONSHIP OF IPF CAUSES OF EXPOSURE TO EXPOSURES

IMPACT OF CAUSES
3 — Very likely to occur
2 — Likely to occur
1 — May occur
Blank — Generally little effect

CAUSES OF EXPOSURE

EXPOSURES	HUMAN ERRORS				HARDWARE/SOFTWARE FAILURES			COMPUTER ABUSE							CATASTROPHE			
	DATA ENTRY	CONSOLE ENTRY	WRONG FILE OR PROGRAM	FILE DAMAGED	INTERRUPT OPERATION	LOSS OF DATA	LOGIC ERROR	THEFT	EMBEZZLEMENT	FRAUD	ESPIONAGE	INVASION OF PRIVACY	MALICIOUSNESS	MISCHIEVOUSNESS	FIRE	WATER	WIND	CIVIL DISORDER
Erroneous record keeping	2				1	2	1	1					1	1				
Unacceptable accounting		1	1		3	2	1						1	1				
Business interruption	2			2	2	2	1	1					3	1	3	3	2	3
Erroneous management decisions				1		2	1					3	2	1				
Fraud	1								3	3			2					
Statutory sanctions	2										2	3						
Excessive costs	2	2	2	2	2	2	2	2	3	2	1		3	1	3	3	2	3
Loss or destruction of assets	2	2	2	2	2	2	1	2	3	2			1	1	3	2	2	3
Competitive disadvantage			2					1			2				2	2	2	2
Occurrence	10 per day	1 per 10 days	1 per 4 yrs	1 per 4 yrs	1 per 10 days	1 per 10 days	1 per 10 days	1 per 4 yrs	1 per 100 days	1 per 4 yrs	1 per 4 yrs	1 per 100 days	1 per 4 yrs	1 per 100 days	1 per 40 yrs	1 per 40 yrs	1 per 40 yrs	1 per 40 yrs

Figure 15-2

16
IPF Operating Controls

This chapter will deal with considerations in the people activities of the information processing facility (IPF).

These are the controls that particularly require clear standards for their consistent daily implementation.

PUNCHED-CARD HERITAGE

The genesis for many of today's major computer facilities was in punched-card installations or early-generation computers. Punched-card installations expanded rapidly in the late 1940's and early 1950's. First- and second-generation computers came into general use during the middle to late 1950's and early 1960's.

During this era, systems and operations reflected their punched-card origins. Jobs were broken down into a series of individual tasks which were treated as individual machine steps for card-processing functions. Work modules included sorting, collating, calculating, summarizing, and printing.

While machines were performing their functions, the operator was providing the linkage to the next process as well as performing most of the library functions. Frequently, he also applied whatever balancing controls were performed.

Error processing had disturbing characteristics:

- Error rates were high.
- Operators resolved many errors personally. They could decide whether each error was significant, whether they could bypass it, or whether correction was required. If so, they could make data corrections on the spot.
- The operator frequently had whatever system and programming documentation existed. As with data errors, programs could

also be modified. Delays for the resolution of errors by independent persons were generally regarded as luxuries which most data processing facilities could not afford.

OPERATING SYSTEM INFLUENCE

Operating controls improved noticeably in the mid-sixties with widespread installation of third-generation computers. By 1970, all computers and their accompanying software provided operating controls of greatly improved reliability. Hardware and software introduced during the seventies provided improved operating reliability supported by more sophisticated operating controls.

Processing of individual jobs gave way to integration of work into continuous job streams established and supervised automatically by operating system software. Integration of hardware and software assumed several new dimensions:

- Computer operating tasks were integrated into continuous streams. The operator was no longer pressed with the decisions on mechanics associated with individual jobs. Rather than being intimately involved in operating details, the operator was instructed through the console on what to do.
- The operator was discouraged from attempting to diagnose and solve programming problems at the console (the environment encourages separation of responsibilities for programming and operations).
- Error handling underwent major changes in approach. Most jobs are now designed either to run to completion despite errors or to be aborted automatically without the operator's decisions or interference.

These factors were combined to make for a more controllable environment in IPF's. However, in many IPF's, the full extent of control capabilities of hardware, software, and application programs has been realized only partially. Still, IPF's are now in a position to establish and to apply a comprehensive, reliable set of control objectives.

STANDARDS

Standard operating procedures for IPF's are becoming more important in supporting the policies and objectives of an organization as a whole. *Formal statements* of procedures are a prerequisite to the basic processes of management. These include:

- Planning for operations
- Performance of planned services or functions
- Evaluation of results
- Review and improvements of procedures

316

In the IPF area, standard procedures, in addition to meeting basic requirements, should provide efficient, effective, and proper use of resources.

Reports which are generated and used within the daily activities of competent management personnel are probably the most important controls that are needed within an IPF. *Planning, supervision, and reporting* within an IPF department provide the primary evidence indicating the quality and sophistication of management controls.

A well-run EDP facility will have formal scheduling and reporting structures. Scheduling and reporting would account for all the uses of equipment and data. Both should indicate, by job, the amount of running time and the time of its occurrence. Scheduling and reporting should be explicit in describing the use of programs, software, files, and transactions for computer operations.

Management reporting on IPF operations should include:

- Daily, weekly, or periodic operations schedules preauthorizing computer use in advance
- Processing logs
- Reports on completed jobs processed
- Reports of uncompleted jobs (with reasons)
- Reports on nonproductive machine time
- Summary performance statistics based on detail reports listed above
- Payroll and overtime reports
- Operator rotation and vacation schedules
- Budgetary results: forecast to actual

Reporting of this caliber should be complete enough that an experienced reviewer can determine that applications are being run in the proper order and with reasonable utilization of computer resources. Any deviations, such as reruns or unauthorized processing, may then be pinpointed. Absence of schedules and reporting systems on the use of specific files will indicate control weaknesses. Such weaknesses could result in situations where files are used in wasteful or unauthorized ways.

For all management reports, there should be signed or initialed evidence of *supervisory reviews* (and planning in the case of preauthorization of computer-time use), particularly those which show variances from the plan or expected norms indicating that each report was accepted and approved. Absence of either reports or approval evidence may indicate ineffective control over operating costs, unauthorized activities by computer operators, inappropriate production capacities, and/or general lack of discipline with the IPF.

From management's standpoint, it is impossible to exercise supervisory responsibilities without some regular reporting of operating statistics as guidelines. Past history (operating statistics) is only part of management's responsibilities. There should also be evidence of management's short- and long-range planning. Such planning should cover hardware as well as systems development and should include participation by user departments and be subject to top-management review and approval.

PERSONNEL CONTROLS
Job Descriptions

Job descriptions identify responsibilities for work to be done and the resources to be used. They also describe qualifications for personnel and relate the positions to each other.

In effect, formal *definitions of duties* reflect the hierarchical structure of responsibilities, including the segregation of duties and the providing of adequate supervision and resources essential to effective operations and control.

Personnel Evaluations

A continuing and formal evaluation of personnel performance in comparision with position descriptions is an essential and obvious element in a formal organizational plan. The objective of performance valuation is to assure that the staff performs in a *competent* and *reliable* manner. While candid and realistic formal evaluations are always difficult to obtain, they are particularly important in larger facilities where personnel staff contacts with EDP management are limited.

SEGREGATION OF IPF DUTIES

The first control consideration normally associated with the organization of an IPF is *segregation of duties*. In assigning work responsibilities, care must be taken to avoid incompatible duties and conflicts of interest. For example:

- Data processing should be independent of operating departments that initiate or authorize transactions and should be prohibited from initiating general or subsidiary ledger entries.
- Systems and programming should be independent from computer operations, and both should be independent of the file library and the input/output controls functions.
- Programmers should not be allowed to operate the computer for tests, assemblies, or other purposes unless production programs and data files have been physically secured from accidental or intentional manipulations.
- Computer operators should not have access to the file library and program documentation, nor should they perform I/O control functions.
- The EDP librarian should be independent of computer operations.

- Data processing personnel should not have asset custodianship functions, nor should they have indirect access to company assets.
- Computer operations should be rotated on sensitive applications.
- Data processing personnel, particularly computer operations and input/output control function personnel, should be required to take vacations.
- Computer operators should not attempt the detection or the correction of errors in application programs. If errors are detected, they should be turned over to the systems function for corrective action.

As shown in the organization charts in chapter three, the section supervisors report in parallel to the head of the information processing facility.

Additional segregation is accomplished by *restricting knowledge* of applications, programming, and documentation to only those facts necessary for operations. Only qualified personnel within the system development and technical functions should possess knowledge of program logic or record formats based on their "need to know." These technical personnel should then be *restricted from access* to data files or the computer.

Job rotation is a standard control technique to augment segregation of duties. It applies to computer operations personnel equally as well as to any other function where financial information is processed. In a small facility, job rotation may be difficult to apply continually. However, at a minimum, it should be a standard practice to require vacations.

The basic principle in this area of the segregation of responsibilities is that excessive access only creates, not solves, problems!

EDP LIBRARY

The EDP library should establish accountability controls and maintain physical possession of files when they are not scheduled for processing. The librarian may report to the IPF manager but not to any person directly involved in running the computer.

Authorization for the release of files from the library to the computer operations staff is contained in the operating schedule for each shift. Similarly, return of files from the computer operations staff to the library should conform to preestablished schedules or authorizations. The library should be accessible only to approved personnel. In particular, it should not be accessible to console operators and programmers.

In addition to physical custody, the librarian should maintain two sets of records on file usage:

- *A log which lists files* according to file content or label. This should be used to insure that proper file backup is available at all times.
- A tape and disc log should control the physical file media. This should contain a *history* of each use of every disc pack or tape reel.

For each *file* maintained in the library, the current log should include:

- The present location or person holding the file
- The formal name of the file, as used and checked by the operating system
- The volume identification for the individual file
- The date the file was created
- The date the file will be available for reuse or scratching
- The serial number of the physical tape reel or disc on which the data are stored
- Remote storage location of the file for backup

The second set of records regarding the physical files are designed to provide a control over the quality of this information asset. Perhaps, equally important, controls over the peripheral devices also help assure the quality of recording media. These records should be retained by the serial number of each file unit. For each unit of media, records should show every use, including a history of all errors. The records should reflect cleaning and recertification. If errors persist, the unit should be withdrawn from service.

In small EDP organizations, library records will generally be maintained manually on card files. In large facilities, the records may be maintained on the computer.

File retention policies must be specified and implemented not only to allow recovery but also to support processing results. This policy should consider the Internal Revenue Service's Ruling 71-20, which calls for retention of selected computer files for support of tax deductions.

If controls over the EDP library are weak, there may be no limitations to the use of the files. This could cause serious concern with regard to the integrity of data for specific applications.

COMPUTER OPERATOR PROCEDURES

The quality of many of the procedures performed by computer operators applies to control as well as working efficiency within an IPF. Several types of controls used to direct computer operators can affect an IPF's ability to prevent accidental destruction of information assets and the enforcement of many input controls.

Both internal and external *labels* are essential to assuring that the proper files are utilized at the proper times. External labels are affixed by an adhesive to the outside casings of files to indicate their identification number, contents, date produced, density, etc. Internal labels are additional data records that may be read by the application programs or operating system software. Their function is described in the next chapter.

Tape files can be protected against accidental erasures or overwriting by *protect rings*. Normally, these rings are plastic and approximately four inches in diameter. They can be inserted in a recess on the back of all standard magnetic tape reels. When inserted and loaded upon a tape drive, they depress a switch that allows the drive to write upon that particular reel. Thus, protect rings protect only when they are absent. The rule to remember is "no ring, no write."

Some disc devices also provide a *read-only* switch that acts somewhat like a protect ring. If a disc file is not to be written upon during normal operations (the disc holding the operating system), the operator may "disable" that drive from writing at the time he loads the disc. However, since discs may hold more than one file and since nonsequential access methods may write upon the same file they read, a disc "read-only" feature cannot be applied in many cases.

The *cleaning* of the read/write heads of tape drives will be important to the reliability of operations as dirt accumulates rapidly and causes processing interruptions.

Operator activities should be conducted in an efficient and orderly manner regardless of whether such obvious factors are specified in IPF standards. Furthermore, just as with any activity associated with the processing of financial information, the staff should be competent. Significant deficiencies will promulgate a variety of operator errors. Particularly likely are the processing of obsolete programs, incorrect files, and failure to take proper action following equipment malfunctions or errors in loading data.

Available documentation on controls of operator procedures is usually limited to operator logs and reports of error conditions. Other activities by the computer operator rarely produce documented evidence of the application of controls.

CONTROL GROUP FUNCTIONS

Input-output controls should be separated from computer operations in the same way and for the same basic reasons as the library. The library controls computer-produced files. The control group has responsibility for control and balancing of transactions being processed by other groups within the IPF. The control also provides representation and accountability to users.

In its capacity as a gateway for the IPF, the input-output control group primarily applies detective controls. These are designed to keep improper transactions from entering or leaving the IPF and to identify and to deal with errors in transactions and operations in the processing cycle respectively.

The I/O control group should maintain a *control log* of anticipated and received batches of inputs. Control totals that accompany these inputs should be summarized and reconciled to interim and final output totals.

The control group should also perform or supervise the distribution of outputs, *visually scanning* them before distribution for general propriety and quality.

This same group may also maintain the quality control records. These would include tabulations of the *sources* of various types of *errors* as well as logs supporting their disposition.

Properly staffed and supported, the control group is in a particularly good position to monitor all phases of operations, including emergencies or periodic "cold starts" (initializing the on-line program library from an off-line master). When it is necessary to patch production files on-line or to cold start (IPL), the potential exists to make improper changes either accidentally or intentionally. The nature of these activities make them difficult to review after the fact.

HOUSEKEEPING

Neat and tidy maintenance of the IPF not only indicates a generally organized approach to processing but also reduces the likelihood of using incorrect files and lessens the hazard of fire. Files awaiting processing should be clearly segregated and stacked neatly. Files available to be written upon should be segregated and marked appropriately. Output files and reports should be stacked in a third location and also be segregated. Waste materials should be deposited in containers and cleared away frequently. Foods, beverages, and cigarette ashes should be discouraged and, at a minimum, kept away from ventilated cabinets and peripheral devices. Cleaning personnel should be supervised in their use of cleaning materials and warned about the possibility of contaminating the equipment.

> *Example — A cheese sandwich was left on top of a central processing unit and the heat caused some of the cheese to run onto the upper surface. Conscientious cleaning personnel then attemped to remove the hardened cheese with steel wool. The steel fibers entered the cabinet and necessitated the replacement of the entire central processing unit.*

KEY VERIFICATION

The principal control over the data conversion process is key verification. The exact devices employed vary according to the specific key-input devices employed. The most common device used in conjunction with keypunches is the key verifier. This device appears almost identical to a keypunch. However, when its keys are depressed, it reads the card rather than punch it. If a character it reads is different from that which was keyed in, a red light comes on and the device locks. A notch will also be cut in the upper edge of the card above the offending column. The error must then be investigated and a new card punched if necessary.

Key verification for key-to-tape, key-to-disc, and key-to-on-line entry devices is somewhat easier. While the process is the same, corrections can be made directly to the machine-readable media. Key verification is not normally employed with OCR or MICR devices if input control can be exercised by batch-balancing and computer edits.

TRAINING

Competent computer operators do not simply obtain their knowledge by osmosis or even on-the-job training. Formal training is necessary until they have gained experience and whenever new devices or systems software are introduced.

Furthermore computer operating personnel should have only *supervised* access to software utilities. One method for applying this control is to have all access to and use of software utilities listed on the computer console log. This log is then reviewed daily for appropriateness of software access.

OUTPUT DISTRIBUTION

Control over the distribution of outputs is a vital activity of an IPF. Many activities in the company are affected seriously by the timeliness and quality of computer outputs. Sensitive documents (savings bonds, checks) are of particular concern. Special care should also be exercised to see that error reports are delivered reliably and promptly and only to those people who have a valid need for them.

Failure to maintain adequate distribution controls may have radically unpredictable results: Major accounting entries may be omitted; serious exceptions may go unresolved; or negotiable outputs may be misappropriated. Also, unwarranted management decisions may be caused by lack of proper information.

Distribution control is complicated by the unpredictable timing and nature of breakdowns in service and the difficulties associated with implementing detective controls.

As part of the control over output distribution, some final *visual scan* should be made to catch any gross errors in the form or content of reports. Persons handling decollating and bursting activities should have instructions on actions to be taken if they discover unreadable copies or similar, obvious discrepancies.

An IPF should maintain *distribution schedules* of report due-dates and frequencies as well as *distribution lists* of recipients which cover all copies of each report. Preferably, a substantial portion of such controls may be incorporated in transmittal documents that accompany the outputs, signed by recipients, and maintained in files within the IPF.

SUPERVISION

Supervision of IPF operations is an operating control appropriate to *any* IPF. Supervision (and the term is used here generally rather than specifically in terms of actual title) responsibilities should include:

- *Approving* the computer operations schedule prior to each working shift
- *Monitoring* actual operations for adherence to standards
- *Observing* activities that occur during pauses in the console logs due to shutting down and then reinitiating the hardware and software
- *Signing* off on the console log
- *Reviewing* the daily operating report prepared by the computer covering the previous day's operations and the responsibility to identify and explain all the variances from the daily schedule

When no management reporting procedures for EDP operations exist, continuous observation becomes the only feasible supervisory technique. Except in the smallest IPF's, the quality of management which can be applied through direct observations will never be adequate.

The EDP operations supervisor is the "production manager" of the IPF "factory." He is responsible for quality and efficiency and must see that all of the innumerable tasks of personnel administration, etc., are carried out. Supervision plays a key role in efficient, well-controlled operations. Supervisory personnel should be able to *observe* the computer room and should review operating practices periodically to verify adherence to prescribed operating policies and procedures.

UTILIZATION, SCHEDULING, AND REPORTING

To begin with, the unauthorized use of a computer can be prevented and detected by defining, in advance, what constitutes *authorized* utilization. This is most effectively done through tight, specific scheduling of computer operations.

Scheduling procedures are built around the fact that most computer utilization (more than 80 percent in most IPF's) can be preauthorized. Thus, it becomes feasible to establish computer operating schedules on a long-range, monthly basis. In the short range, it is necessary for an IPF to be able to react to such utilization requirements as:

- Additional user demands
- Reruns of programs
- Reprocessing of files
- Testing
- Other unforeseen problems

All jobs, long or short range, should be authorized in advance. Even when emergencies arise, as happens when reruns or special processing is required, the work should be authorized by someone other than the console operator. In large EDP facilities, this might be the operations supervisor. In a smaller department, the data processing manager may handle such authorizations himself. If the data processing manager is unavailable, authorizations should be provided by someone at a supervisory level who does not have actual console-operating responsibility.

To make scheduling effective, there must be formal review of all variances from authorized schedules. This is accomplished through consistent comparison of schedules and authorized modifications of schedules with data on actual computer operations. Computer operating data should be available from two separate sources:

- There should be a console log prepared by the computer on the basis of actions by operating system software and by the computer operators. Console logs should be examined daily by operating supervisors within the IPF.

  In cases where the processing volume prohibits effective manual review, the console message should be recorded on machine-readable media and edited by a program designed for that purpose.
- Equipment-utilization reports should be prepared regularly. Reports should cover each use of the computer, giving the exact time and the duration of time required. Report content should also show scheduled as well as actual time for each job.

The level of detail in computer utilization reporting should be sufficient for any analyses which may be required of IPF operations or budgets. In general, five categories are identified and discussed below:

- Assembly or compilation
- Test
- Rerun
- Maintenance
- Production

In addition, three additional aspects of utilization reporting, to be discussed further on, are:

- Time and volume data
- Hierarchy of utilization reporting
- Size of IPF

Assembly or Compilation

Assembly or compilation is the computer process for converting coding written by programmers to machine language for processing. Each assembly or compilation run on a computer is related to the programming phase of a system development or system maintenance project. The specific program segment and project should be identified on schedules and reports of computer operations for accounting and analysis.

Test

Testing includes both program and system testing for maintenance and for new applications. The project to which the test is related should be identified and accumulated for project accounting and analysis.

Rerun

When processing must be redone, reruns occur. This represents a variance from plan and carries attendant concerns for inefficiencies and controls. Reruns are required for four different reasons, which should be recorded on schedules and operating reports:

- Machine failures in either a central processor or peripheral.
- Operator failure — For example, an operator may mount the wrong file on a peripheral device or enter an improper command. In either case, the processing run may be aborted by detective controls within the application program or operating system.
- Failures in either application programs or operating systems.
- Input errors resulting in a file of unacceptable results.

Whatever the cause, rerun time should be watched closely as an index of the effectiveness of IPF management. Excessive rerun time could indicate problems with equipment reliability, operator training, or inadequate input procedures. Each is accompanied by its own exposure concerns.

Reruns should also be watched from a security standpoint. Since a rerun requires the use of files, there should be accompanying evidence of authorization for and controls over the utilization and protection of files. In particular, it is crucial that the correct generation of the master file be used in the rerun.

Maintenance

Computer maintenance efforts fall into two broad categories: preventive and remedial. Preventive maintenance programs involve inspections, tests, and routine replacements of components at regular intervals. Remedial maintenance, on the other hand, is applied when something goes wrong. This is generally performed on an emergency basis, interrupting processing schedules.

Generally, maintenance is performed by an outside vendor: either the equipment manufacturer or an independent service organization. Record keeping and reporting on maintenance activities are facilitated if arrangements are made to secure copies of all the maintenance reports prepared by service personnel. Detailed records should be kept, and information reported should include:

- Computer time used for maintenance purposes, according to type of maintenance, should be reported according to both elapsed time and computer time utilized.
- Downtime — periods during which the equipment is out of service due to failure.
- Cumulative maintenance records for each unit of computer equipment. This information should be used to develop an estimate of exposure to loss of files and processing capabilities.

Production

Production, the last of the group, will, hopefully, represent the primary use of computer time. This includes all running of applications, jobs, or special reports where results are delivered to users. In reporting, all production runs should be identified according to the application and the program processed.

Time and Volume Data

For each utilization category, it is desirable to record and report both clock time and meter time. Clock time is the elapsed time during which processing took place. Meter time is the actual CPU processing time.

Also, some measure of volume for each unit of work performed should be reported. This measure may be generic to the type of work done on printed output reports. For instance, the measure might be in the lines of listing; in program assembly, a suitable measure might be the number of source instructions processed.

The importance of these information elements should be considered in the design of reports on computer processing.

Hierarchy of Utilization Reporting

Concurrently, computer utilization reports should be reviewed on a bottom-up basis. That is, reviews should begin at a base level in terms of both reporting detail and organizational level of personnel. The lowest-level report, for example, should be based on daily production from manual of software-created records. These should be compared with the console log daily by the shift supervisor, and any exceptional items should be explained.

Only someone with close knowledge of computer operations is in a position to sift through and give meaning to a report at this level of detail. Furthermore, daily review is the only feasible way to give full perspective to a chronological list of events which rapidly lose meaning in a high-volume computer shop. Subsequently, reporting on EDP operations for control and audit purposes should include a detailed listing according to each of the five preceding categories. Within each category, entries should be listed by program or project and chronologically. A report of this type would typically be produced on a monthly basis.

The report would show job classification, date and hour, clock and meter time, and volumes. With all processing information brought together for a full month, any variances in performance stand out immediately. These reports represent a significant operating control. References back to the lowest available level of operating documents will provide a useful insight into daily operating practices.

Size of IPF

Lastly — and realistically — the size and capacity of computers used may impose limitations on computer utilization reporting capabilities. In general, the more complex the system, the more difficult it may be to report on processing times for individual applications. In small and medium-sized computer facilities, the chief requirement for implementation of an operational reporting system may simply be a management decision to have one. Once this determination is made, scheduling and reporting of usage are implemented in the same general manner as for any other production unit in a manufacturing company.

In working with larger-scale computers, actual techniques are somewhat more troublesome. This is particularly true for IPF's where several jobs are processed concurrently on the same CPU. Some computer hardware and software for implementing multi-programming systems are capable of reporting only elapsed-time utilization of individual programs. In such cases, meter readings are not available for actual computer usage for each of the jobs being processed. As a result, a complex program may be run with several other simple jobs in, for example, an hour of elapsed time. Later, the same job, run concurrently with other complex jobs, would receive more contentions for CPU time. Elapsed time might be two hours.

Without reporting of meter readings by jobs, operating controls and possible audit controls are marginal at best.

INTERDEPARTMENT CHARGES

The information processing facility will incur substantial costs in servicing the requirements of many corporate departments. Many benefits may be derived from charging these departments for the services rendered. On the other hand, an unfair method of charging may create more problems than benefits.

Users should be charged for service provided on a basis that includes only those actual costs over which the user has an influence. Costs of reruns or idle time are not properly the responsibility of the users. Rather, the IPF should be responsible for such costs and hold them within predefined performance limits.

The cost to a user should be a function of the resources used and the time required for processing. This should normally be a function of the CPU usage, the amount and type of storage required, response time (real-time versus days), and the volume of inputs and outputs. Accordingly, the user may reduce the cost of his services by performing the processes manually, by reducing the volumes of transactions and reports, or by deleting unnecessary master records from the files. He can also reappraise the cost of a fast-response system as opposed to the real benefits provided.

Implementation of a fair cross-charging system in a small batch-processing IPF is relatively simple. The problem only becomes difficult when multiple applications and departments share common data-base files and processing hardware.

Example — When multiple programs are processed concurrently (multiprogramming), the lapsed time required for individual applications is not only a function of the complexity and volume of that application but also of the degree of conflict for available resources.

System software must then be utilized to identify the proportion of actual processing time being utilized by the individual application programs. Such software may be costly and may also reduce performance.

The most sophisticated systems for controlling and allocating costs within IPF's resemble a standard costing system for a factory. Operating efficiency may be measured by comparing planned versus actual performance. This performance must encompass all elements of costs, including idle time, wasted production, general overhead, etc.

At the same time, care must be exercised with regard to the level of precision that is attempted with these measures. The costs of multiple applications within a common facility become increasingly arbitrary (and of decreasing utility) as higher and higher degrees of cost allocation are requested.

If operations are to be managed rather than experienced, plans must be established; standards must be set; tolerance limits must be determined; and a reporting system must be created to record deviations. Volume, efficiency, price variances, and prudent levels of idle capacity should be recognized by the system. Users may then be charged a standard rate based upon transaction volumes, size of master files, and utilization of special devices. Direct and indirect overhead costs may be included as burden. The actual charges to the user may be the standards themselves or include a return on investment for the IPF according to preferences of management.

Pure processing efficiency must not be allowed to be the only motivator for the IPF management. Control must also be motivated by holding the IPF responsible for user satisfaction. Unacceptable production must be reprocessed by the IPF without additional cost to the user.

The benefits of this approach are to provide general motivation to utilize the computer facilities for only those tasks which are justified on the basis of costs and benefits. Users are measured on the basis of the corporate services they actually consume, and the IPF management may be evaluated on its relative efficiency in providing the services demanded.

While the benefits of this approach may be substantial, so may the costs of establishing an adequate cost system. Where it is desirable to establish this level of operating control, the evaluation and testing of general IPF operating controls may be greatly enhanced. While the primary intent of cost charging is to promote efficient use of resources, it also provides a general level of accountability control over the IPF. Even if cross-charging were not adopted, the IPF management should still be held responsible for meeting operating *budgets.*

Like any system of internal control, IPF control depends upon people. These people must be organized and aware of their duties. Operations may then be managed by using a reporting system that compares actual operations to standards and plans.

17
IPF Hardware/Software Controls

CONTROLS APPLIED BY
HARDWARE AND SOFTWARE

Important controls within any IPF lie in the built-in capabilities of equipment and vendor software. Technical controls applied by hardware and software should be understood by the system designer and auditor as separate from those controls applied by people and application programs or incorporated in procedures and standards. The discussions following will limit themselves to the controls applied by hardware and software which are made available automatically to all applications. As a basis for building an understanding of these controls, this opening section will describe and define the elements of computer equipment and IPF software which perform control functions.

Computer Equipment

In referring to computer equipment within an IPF, the terms "equipment," "hardware," and "computer" are used frequently. Although often used almost synonymously, they have different shades of meaning.

"Equipment" and "hardware" are inclusive terms, generally taking in all the working equipment within a computer facility, including items which are not part of the computer such as discs and tapes, storage facilities, data conversion and transmission equipment, and protective devices.

"Computer," when used in its precise sense, refers to an interconnected group of equipment modules which function together for the processing of data. These modules consist of a central processing unit or CPU and a group of connected devices known generically as "peripherals." The CPU is the unit within the computer configuration where arithmetic and logic processing take place and movement of data is controlled.

Peripherals serve two general purposes within a computer: input/output (I/O) and data storage. Peripherals, in an inclusive sense, take in disc and tape drives, drum storage units, card read/punch units, printers, console typewriters, on-line terminals, and other remote devices for communicating with the computer.

The input and output functions are largely self-explanatory. There are important differences, however, among various input and output peripherals (basically in terms of varying capacities, costs, and capabilities for interaction with the CPU). Peripherals, in general represent a lower-cost method of maintaining programs and files for use by the computer. Obviously, it is important to balance the capacity and speed of storage peripherals with the capacity of the main memory.

IPF Software

IPF software consists of the programming routines designed to control and to support the processing function of the computer for execution of application programs. Because of the close interaction of these programmed routines with the computer equipment, the term "system software" is generally used. Historically, system software has been continually increasing its "housekeeping" scope as application programs concentrate more and more on user problems. System software elements have a common use in processing all applications within an IPF.

The most basic level of software used to control application processing is referred to by various vendors as "operating systems," "control programs," "executives," or "supervisors." Different operating system versions are designed for particular equipment configurations or functions.

An operating system controls the functioning of all elements of a computer configuration. It can implement techniques for multiprogramming — the interleaved, concurrent processing of two or more programs through automatic allocation of CPU and peripheral capacities. Operating systems also control multiprocessing techniques under which coordinated processing of data takes place in two or more CPU's.

Also included under the general category of system software are processing utilities and compilers or assemblers to support programming languages used with individual computer makes or models.

A *utility* is a program or set of programs developed to provide commonly encountered data handling functions: sorting data, merging files, reading data from cards and tapes, output to cards, or tapes. Today, most manufacturers and software vendors provide comprehensive libraries of such utility programs. Individual standards within an IPF determine which utilities will be made available and when they will be used.

Compilers and *assemblers* are automatic language translators which accept coding written by programmers and convert it to machine language for processing by the computer. Programming languages are generally described as being at different levels, depending on the degree of detail required of the programmer and the operating and time factors involved in their use. The selection of programming languages and appropriate assemblers or compilers for the programming of applications is a matter of management decision and standards within each IPF.

Increasingly, as file structures have become more and more complex, particularly in IPF's implementing data-base concepts, specialized file management software known as *data management systems* has been developed by a number of manufacturers and independent vendors. Designed specifically for handling and integration of files, data management systems may either operate in conjunction with existing operating system software or incorporate their own operating systems.

The on-line interface between a central CPU and a remote terminal may be handled by *terminal management* software.

Sources

IPF software is acquired from three general sources. The first is the computer manufacturer. All leading computer manufacturers support their equipment with operating system, file management, utility, and language software. The second source is independent companies which provide a range of software packages in competition with computer manufacturers. The third source of software lies within the IPF. In larger IPF's, particularly, technical services specialists may develop standard routines which become part of the software library for use in applications.

The functions performed by and reliability of software may be expected to vary significantly among sources and among versions provided by the same source.

HARDWARE/SOFTWARE INTERACTION

Both hardware and software apply controls to the processing of data within a computer system. As a general trend, the emergence and increasing sophistication of operating system software have led to the delegation of increasing numbers and types of control functions once performed by computer operators and application programs. This is particularly true in such areas as the control of peripherals and the scheduling and sequencing of processing jobs. Comparable improvements in hardware have led to a trend in which a number of the most repetitive software functions are being absorbed by hardware.

In large measure, then, the implementation of controls within a computer system results from an interaction of coordinated functioning of hardware and software. Consequently, the following discussion recognizes that the auditor is apt to encounter automatically applied controls in either hardware or software. His basic requirement is to determine the existence and reliability of the controls, regardless of how they are applied.

CONTROL OBJECTIVES

Four specific objectives are important to a discussion of hardware and software controls:
- Detection of errors
- Prevention of unauthorized access to and use of data and equipment
- Recording of activities performed with the IPF
- Supporting effective utilization of the computer

Detection of Errors

Hardware and software controls are designed to detect three types of errors:
- Errors generated by the hardware system — Here detective controls are designed because processing errors occur within computers as a result of malfunctions, interference, worn out parts, electrical irregularities, etc.
- Errors within application programs or system software — Here detective controls deal primarily with the identification and handling of files.
- Clerical-type errors within the IPF — Generally, these will be made either by computer operators or data librarians and will involve either improper console instructions or the mounting of incorrect files on peripherals.

The logic for these detective controls is generally applied through a combination of hardware and software features.

Prevention of Unauthorized Access to and Use of Data and Equipment

As indicated earlier, authorizations for access and processing are included in the design of computer files and transactions. The role of hardware and software is significant where on-line terminals are used, since the computer plays a critical role in authorizations.

Recording of Activities Performed Within the IPF

Each use of the computer should be recorded. The hardware and software within the larger systems should log all activities performed. Larger systems, as described here, are those which perform multiprogramming regularly. Concurrent processing of multiple jobs usually precludes effective manual reporting of computer usage.

Supporting Effective Utilization of the Computer

As noted above, much of the scheduling and allocation of equipment and jobs are now determined automatically. In this situation, an important aspect of control lies in determining the effectiveness at which these hardware and software features are functioning. Thus, identifying specific equipment, software modules, and jobs with each other provides a basis for both measurement and improvement of utilization of EDP resources.

Environmental Controls

The computer hardware, recording media, and paper-output stock are sensitive to deviations outside of a relatively narrow range of temperature and humidity. Certain plastic components of a computer may deform at 120°F. This temperature may be reached on a warm day augmented by equipment-generated heat. Low temperatures can also affect components but not as readily.

High humidity may cause condensation within electrical components and upon media. The biggest problem may be swelling and distortion of punch cards and paper stock. Low humidity will allow buildup of static electricity, attracting dust onto the surface of magnetic media and causing attraction between paper products.

Accordingly, most facilities require corrective controls such as *air conditioning* usually controlled separately from that of the building in general. A *humidifier* may also be necessary. However, beware of humidifiers that allow distribution of metalic impurities in the water supply.

> *Example — After installing humidifying equipment to reduce static electricity and thereby reduce problems with dirty tapes, one IPF actually encountered increased problems. Eventually, the cause was identified as being metalic dust that was being sprayed out from the "hard" water used in the humidifier.*

Detective control of temperature and humidity is often provided by a cylindrical *recorder.*

UNINTERRUPTABLE POWER SOURCES (UIP's)

Hardware failure may be caused by increases or decreases in the specified voltage of the external power supply. Different items of equipment vary, but tolerances are typically around ±10%.

Momentary increases (spikes) in the voltage may be prevented from affecting the hardware by using voltage regulators. These are fairly inexpensive and only deal with momentary voltage increases.

Sustained voltage increases usually require shutdown of the hardware. This is almost always provided automatically through built-in circuit breakers.

Brief reductions or absence of power may be corrected by storage batteries. Similar to automobile batteries, these may sustain operations only a few minutes, enough to permit an orderly shutdown of the processing.

Sustained "brown-outs" or complete outages can only be corrected on site by the use of a complete generating station. This is extremely expensive.

The level of UIP control that is needed by a specific IPF depends primarily upon the level and the performance of the power utility. Occasional interruptions due to lightning, fallen power lines, etc., can usually be accepted, given a moderate recovery capability and no application which is extremely sensitive.

Manufacturers Controls

Hardware controls are applied by the equipment manufacturer:
- In the *design* of equipment elements
- In the complete *testing* of configurations of equipment before they are put into use
- By extensive *preventive maintenance* programs
- By field *replacement* of parts or components which prove troublesome

Hardware controls insure that (1) data are read and recorded accurately by computer peripherals and that (2) errors will not be caused by flaws in the central processing unit, memory, or other hardware.

Procedures applied by manufacturers or contract service organizations have resulted in high levels of hardware reliability. Service in this area has been marked by continuing improvements.

Preventive controls in the preparation and distribution of software have proved more difficult to implement. It is common to find bugs or deficiencies in early release versions of software packages. However, both manufacturers and independent software vendors have improved their skills and increased their diligence extensively in the application of preventive controls to the preparation of software packages.

PARITY

The *parity-check* technique calls on the computer to create an additional bit within each character processed. This bit is used to detect errors in the use and handling of its associated character. This control applies throughout computer processing and in the storage of data on magnetic tapes or disc packs (see Figure 17-1).

DIAGRAM SHOWING AN EXAMPLE OF PARITY BITS ON 7 CHANNEL TAPE

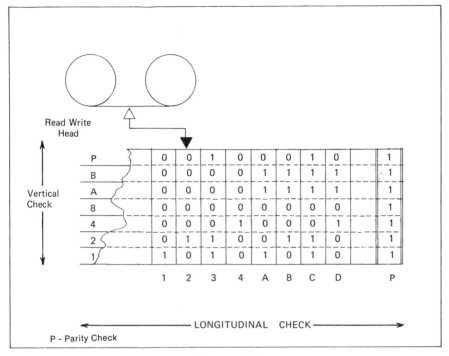

Figure 17-1

(The figure shows odd parity for each character and each channel.)

This technique is used for a number of data coding structures. The most common formats consist of six or eight bits representing the data with a parity bit added. Validation is done by hardware in initially setting and subsequently counting the number of bits in each character and determining whether their total is odd or even. Data processing equipment is set up for either odd or even parity checks. On odd-parity equipment, for instance, the check bit will be set initially as required to create an odd parity. Subsequent losses or additions of one or more bits, for example, may create an even parity and signal an error.

Different peripheral devices may have their own formats for recording and moving data. Most disc and tape units work in either seven- or nine-bit (or channel) formats. In these devices, six and eight bits are data bits with one parity bit in each character.

Parity-bit techniques may also be used on a longitudinal or bi-directional basis in which characters or units of data are recorded in "frames" across the width of the tape. Each frame consists of eight data bits and one parity bit; longitudinally, (see Figure 17-1) as they

337

are recorded in sequence, the frames form nine channels. As a record is written, the number of bits is determined for each channel within the record. A separate frame is then recorded at the end of the record containing the appropriate configuration of bits to establish parity longitudinally for each channel within the record. Thus, parity checks are applied on a bidirectional basis. In this way, any given bit of data in an entire record which is not read or recorded is pinpointed laterally through the *longitudinal parity check* and vertically through the parity check on each frame.

VALID CHARACTER CHECKS

Another method for hardware validation of each unit of data is *valid character checking.* Under this technique, patterns are established to identify and to accept each valid combination of bits. When nonconforming characters are detected, an error condition is created.

Among peripherals, this technique is particularly appropriate for card readers or printers. For instance, a total of 256 characters may be derived from all combinations available through an eight-bit character code. However, the total number of data characters available for a specific printer (i.e., the character set on the print chain) may be limited to only 64. Thus, the printer control hardware would be set up to accept only the 64 valid bit combinations and would treat all others as invalid. If invalid, either a character may not be printed or another character will be substituted.

Both valid character and parity checking make for an extremely high probability that processing or transferring within a computer system will be accurate and reliable. Neither checking technique, however, will detect an error when one valid character is recorded improperly in place of another at the source.

FILE DATA CONTROLS

Additionally, software detective controls can be applied to data files through two separate techniques:

- With file *header labels,* system software can determine that the file being used for processing is the correct one for the application being run
- With *trailer labels,* the software can determine that files are processed in their entirety and that records were neither lost nor added

Figure 7-2 diagrams the format of a tape header record. This is the first data recorded on a magnetic tape file. Similar techniques are used by most other types of peripherals used for data storage.

Three data elements of the tape header label are used in the file data controls before processing can begin. First, the title of the file is listed on the label. This label will be compared with a control field associated with the application program. A failure to match will result in a discrepancy notice printed on the console log which must be resolved by the operator before processing is continued.

Also included in the header label is a sequence number indicating the volume sequence of the file. The number is advanced automatically as the file is processed, and a new file is created. This number is checked by the software before processing can begin, assuring that the file organization will be maintained.

A third field in the header label is the expiration data. This tells when the file is no longer needed for backup or recovery. This expiration date is compared with the current processing date before the computer permits the tape to be reused for writing over with another file.

At a minimum, each trailer record contains the number of blocks written on the file or volume of a multiple-volume file. This total is created when the file is originated. Every time the file is read, each block is counted; and the total of blocks read is compared with the number indicated in the trailer record. This process will detect whether a block is dropped or added. The control totals in a trailer record are frequently expanded by the application program to include control totals of records, dollar balances, transaction quantities, etc.

Both header and trailer control capabilities are available as standard features on most operating systems. However, the use of these features is optional.

ACCESS CONTROLS

Hardware and software controls can be developed which protect against improper or unauthorized accessing of reserved or restricted portions of storage, including CPU memory and storage peripherals.

This *isolation* protection is applied primarily through the recording of codes, or keys, entered in predetermined positions of restricted memory and peripheral devices. Any processing against the restricted areas must contain these access keys in their initial records, or an error condition will be reported.

This particular control may be used when a CPU is operating in multiprogramming mode, processing two or more application programs concurrently. In such case, it is necessary to keep one program from interfering with the files or processing of other programs. Similar techniques are used to restrict access to files from remote terminals. Keys correspond with identifications for terminals, individual users, or both. Access to files and processing are limited to inquiries or processing requests which contain acceptable identifying keys in their initial transmissions. Hardware and software features also contain the ability to identify and report on the occurrence of restricted-access transactions. In particular, where a given terminal has repeatedly attempted to access files and transactions have been rejected, these reports are essential for supervisory follow-up.

MAINTENANCE DIAGNOSTICS

On another level, *maintenance diagnostic programs* are run on the IPF computer during periodic service inspections by the manufacturer or contractor. The maintenance diagnostics used are programmed tests applied to all components within the IPF and compared with established standards.

CONSOLE LOG

A running log of all activities performed should exist in order to monitor processing. It should contain:

- Job identification
- Inquiries and instructions between the operating system and the operator
- File labels processed
- Balancing of trailer labels
- Indications of each malfunction or error detected
- Application operating messages

To assure the validity of this control measure, a qualified person should review *console logs* regularly to determine that they do, in fact, reflect activities of equipment and software, that they are complete, and that no spurious activities have been conducted. One way of assuring continuity and completeness for console logs is to have them prepared on continuous paper with *prenumbered sheets.* Another method is to *enclose* and *lock* the paper supply and printing section of the typewriter. This provides stronger assurance that nothing will interfere with the printing of all operating system messages, but it can also interrupt operations by delaying the replacement of the console paper stock. The log should also be compared with computer utilization reports to insure the integrity of both records.

Messages on console logs should be simple in format and directly related to hardware and software functions. Deviations from standard control messages tend to add confusion and to diminish the value of console logs as controls. See Figure 17-2 for an illustration of a typical console log created on a medium-range IBM System/360 computer, utilizing multiprogramming operating system software. These obviously represent only a scattered selection of typical log entries.

In large IPF's, the volume of console messages may effectively prohibit manual review. The solution is to record these messages on some machine-readable medium and to perform the review by using a computer application. Some vendors of operating systems provide the option to magnetically record such messages, and a few even provide programs for the analysis.

340

```
BG
BG   // ASSGN SYS005,X'01E'
BG   1A14D  CONFLICTING I/O ASSIGNMENT.
BG   // assgn sys005,x'00e'
BG
BG   G0771 GRASPCTL 2.4 27.113 ABM 809 73061 CPU=060430
BG   IF NOT RERUN HIT EOB ELSE ENTER OFFICE & CODE NNN-N
BG     AWAITING REPLY
BG   330-2
BG   PROCESSING DATE IS 04/25/73
F1   79051    RCD IN 0009940, OUT 0009940, ESTIMATED 0001000
F1   72011    END MERGE PH
BG   EOJ UT921
     DATE 05/01/73,CLOCK 16/44/24,DURATION 00/02/03
F1   79051    RCD IN 0009940, OUT 0009940, ESTIMATED 0001000
BG   1C00A  ATTN. 0 0B.
BG
F1   73021    END OF SORT/MERGE
BG 0P08A      INTERV REQ SYSRDR=00B
F1   EOJ SRT005
     DATE 05/01/73,CLOCK 16/44/52,DURATION 00/03/46
F1   // JOB FA005,A=F1          PRODUCTION EDITS
     DATE 05/01/73,CLOCK 16/44/58
BG   // JOB UT921,A=F1
     DATE 05/01/73,CLOCK 16/45/07
BG   // ASSGN SYS004,X'01B'
BG   1A14D  CONFLICTING I/O ASSIGNMENT.
BG   // assgn sys004,x'00b'
BG
BG   // ASSGN SYS005,X'01E'
BG   1A14D  CONFLICTING I/O ASSIGNMENT.
BG   // assgn sys005,x'00e'
BG
BG   IF NOT RERUN HIT EOB ELSE ENTER OFFICE & CODE NNN-N
BG     AWAITING REPLY
BG   330-1
BG   PROCESSING DATE IS 04/25/73
BG   EOJ UT921
     DATE 05/01/73,CLOCK 16/46/36,DURATION 00/01/28
```

Figure 17-2

Media Controls

To a substantial degree, the auditor can rely on controls built into equipment by manufacturers to detect machine malfunctions or failures. However, activities to assure the reliability of file media require greater effort within an IPF. An organized, documented maintenance plan should exist for the periodic *recertification* of magnetic tapes and to provide for scheduled *inspection* of disc packs. The cost of correcting minor tape defects may be considerably less than the cost of replacement. Of course, eventually, deterioration will require replacement; but this may often be postponed with substantial savings.

Discs are inspected under software programs processed by the computer on which they are used. This software is provided by computer vendors and may be run easily within the IPF.

Failure to maintain these controls over file media may generate wasteful or inefficient utilization of equipment or repeated needs for implementation of recovery procedures for file reconstruction purposes.

Complete records should be maintained within the IPF covering utilization, cleaning, and recertification of individual tapes and discs.

Transmission Controls

Many controls over electronic transmissions are embedded within the multiple levels of system software that accompany such equipment. Most of these controls are specified by the software vendor, and additional controls may be difficult to implement by management or auditors within individual using organizations. This subject is so extensive and specialized that we will not attempt to cover it in this comparatively brief discussion. For additional information, refer to the "recommended readings" section of this book.

Reliability of equipment and files available today has considerably more impact on efficiency than on control. Control considerations relate to possible loss of data and to the bypassing of other controls with processing shortcuts due to the time lost because of breakdowns. The problems of reliability are more substantial in the area of productivity. Such operating problems as machine halts and system downtime result in loss of EDP services for the duration of the interruption. Frequently, they also involve further losses for reprocessing of the interrupted jobs.

Computer hardware and software control capabilities are extensive and are increasing continually. It is important that the manager and auditor understand these capabilities and limitations in order to assist them in evaluating reliability of controls and in determining which manual procedures are necessary to apply control to the operation of a computer.

18
IPF Security and Recovery

Security measures are mandatory for any information processing facility where vital financial and operational data are processed and stored. Some aspects of security requirements are specialized and technical; others can be dealt with by managers and auditors familiar with company operations and the consequences of loss of information assets.

In this discussion, EDP security will be separated into the three areas covering the functions of control:

- Prevention from loss
- Detection which allows the minimization of loss when accidents or disasters occur
- Correction through:
    - Recovery from loss
    - Insurance to cover the costs of losses and recovery measures

Discussions of these elements will touch on associated considerations of causes and operating considerations. Our purpose will be only to provide a perspective for security controls as they should be viewed by management and auditors. An abundance of technical literature is available on the subject for study in greater depth (see "recommended readings").

Methods applied in the prevention of loss and protection of EDP facilities and data depend upon the potential cause of damage and the resources exposed. However, many of the controls that apply to accidents and the violent forms of computer abuse also apply to "natural" catastrophies.

ACCIDENTAL AND ABUSIVE CAUSES

Accidental damage may result from many causes including defective software, faulty hardware, computer operator actions, or from the actions of any other persons with access to the computer center. Accidental damage primarily affects data. Media on which data are stored and other EDP resources may also be affected, but the exposure is minor compared to the loss of data.

Abusive actions include situations where information or files are stolen or misused. Stealing involves theft of machine-readable and printed data or accessing on-line files through illicit use of terminals. Misuse includes manipulation of files, programs, equipment, or input/output for personal gain or for malicious reasons. As is the case with accidental actions, the affected resources are primarily data with secondary effects on media used to store affected data; e.g., tapes and discs.

Preventive Measures

Preventive controls against the damaging actions of people can be divided into four major areas: *responsibilities, facilities, access* and *individuals.*

RESPONSIBILITIES

Important security measures in an IPF involve the standards previously discussed, particularly restricting access to data. Detailed job descriptions should be prepared with data security in mind. They will minimize confusion resulting from unclear statements of responsibilities of personnel. Similarly, specific instructions on handling of data, software, and equipment are needed to minimize accidental destruction.

FACILITIES

The physical location and construction of the IPF should be planned so as to avoid hazards. While the geographic location may be dictated by the general business premises, many organizations establish separate computer operations centers. Within the structure, the IPF should avoid locations that are subject to carry abnormal fire or water hazards such as those adjacent to the kitchen or in the basement. Finally, the IPF should be *"containerized";* that is, be bounded by sturdy and resistant walls that limit the spread of fire and allow control over access.

ACCESS

Some measures for prevention of loss through human activities apply only to data processing facilities themselves. Emphasis in this area should be to make access available only to authorized persons as they need to enter the facility and limit all other entries.

A low profile should be sought for the IPF. Locations of a computer room and EDP library need not be listed in company directories or on directories in building lobbies. Entrances should be *inconspic-*

uous. There should, for example, be no (or minimal) external signs in halls or doors pointing to computer facilities. This may require coordination with fire or other emergency forces to insure that they can readily locate the computer facilities if necessary.

Limiting the number of avenues of *access* is also important. The principle here is simple: the fewer the access opportunities, the easier it will be to protect the facility.

Avenues of access considered in security programs should include the *less obvious* such as the case which arose when a bomb was left in a public lavatory adjacent to a computer room. All entrances or corridors contiguous to EDP facilities should be considered as avenues of access.

Each entrance should have some form of restriction on access. Such restrictions may be applied through a variety of devices and techniques including:

- Keys
- Magnetic cards
- Voice or hand print identification systems
- Security personnel

INDIVIDUALS

Preventive measures relating to individuals should apply to both employees and outside service personnel with regular access to an EDP facility. In each instance, there should be a program of *security checks* on individuals. These may range from simply checking references with past employers prior to hiring to regular, extensive security and other checks.

Clearly, such preventive measures should be determined with specialized, expert assistance. The only principles which apply at the level of the manager or auditor are those which assure that formal programs exist and are applied on a continuing basis; that is, security investigations applied at the time of employment without subsequent follow-up are inadequate. Individuals must, with their own advance permission, be subjected to periodic security checks to evaluate their reliability.

Protection against loss from individual actions is also inherent in a program of employee *bonding.* Although bonding is primarily a corrective measure, preventive benefits accrue through investigative activities of bonding companies. These often exceed the measure of investigation done by employers.

Detective Measures

Detective measures are those designed to minimize the impact of damage which occurs despite preventive techniques. Detective controls against accident and abuse consist primarily of early *detection of unauthorized access. Application controls* (discussed in chapter 7), rather than IPF controls, are needed to detect the effects of nondisruptive incidents. Early detection through detective controls should limit the amount of losses that occur.

CATASTROPHE CONTROLS

Disaster prevention and protection measures apply to damage from fire, water, earthquakes, malicious acts, and riots. Preventive, detective, and corrective measures are all appropriate in such cases.

Preventive Measures

Preventive measures against disaster consist primarily of *construction* techniques and the selective *location* of facilities. The choice of location should avoid obvious exposure to natural disaster. Computer facilities, for example, should not be located in low-lying river basins or floors subject to flooding; neither should facilities be situated near known geologic faults subject to earth tremors, at the entrance to canyons subject to severe winds, and so on. Furthermore, locations should be at sites with minimal prospects of human intervention in case of riot or civil disturbance. Natural disaster may strike anywhere. But prudent judgment should be applied to avoid the more likely dangers.

Construction techniques are more substantive in disaster prevention. Construction materials and methods should provide a fireproof and waterproof facility. At the same time, provision should be made to minimize secondary effects of water damage. For instance, care should be taken to protect the facility from seepage of water used to extinguish fires above or from bursting pipes during cold weather. Similarly, drainage in the computer room should be sufficient to draw off water which might evade other preventive efforts.

Obviously, construction materials and techniques should also attempt to provide resistance to other natural phenomena such as hurricanes, tornadoes, etc.

SECURE STORAGE

Selection of resistant storage devices such as vaults or safes should provide security against unauthorized access as well as heat and water.

The level of protection required will depend on the media selected for storage and the type and location of storage facilities. For example, magnetic discs and tapes have lower tolerances for withstanding heat and humidity than paper records. Therefore, greater protection is necessary. Typically, magnetic media must be stored in vaults or safes with Underwriters' Laboratories ratings.

Secure storage considerations should also include provision for remote storage of backup files. Vaults or safes at remote locations should also be rated in accordance with the structures in which they are located and media to be protected.

Detection Measures

The objective of detection devices is early recognition of unauthorized entry or dangerous levels of smoke, heat, fire, or humidity. Hopefully, this recognition will take place early enough so that corrective actions may be initiated before data and other resources are exposed to extensive damage.

In the selection and placement of *fire detection devices,* there is considerable variety of opinion among experts on which methods and locations are best and most reliable. Different devices and techniques call for placement in open areas, under floors, in air conditioning ducts, etc.

The manner of detection also varies. Devices can detect smoke, temperature, infrared radiation, or combustion by-products.

Correction Measures

Water or certain gases are the most common *extinguishing agents* for fire. Even though water can damage computer equipment, it still has its advocates as an extinguishing agent.

The strongest advantage of water extinguishing systems is their low cost. Overhead sprinkler systems are frequently installed when the building is constructed. Water will usually do little damage to tapes or discs and even only limited damage to electronic gear. The relative costs and risks may justify such systems.

The gases that are used are either carbon dioxide (CO_2) or Halon, the trademark for a complex fluoride gas. Carbon dioxide extinguishes by suffocation, which works as well on people as on fires. Halon gas reacts with the fire, extinguishing it and forming a poisonous by-product. While the use of carbon dioxide requires evacuation of the area before discharge, Halon may be released (in suitably low concentrations) while people are still present. The poisonous by-product is usually in such minimal quantities that the danger is limited and quickly removable. However, the cost of these agents, particularly Halon, is relatively high. The cost of the distribution system for any agent may also be high.

Recovery Plan

The key to the capability of an IPF to correct the effects of damage or disaster is the existence of a proven, operational recovery plan which should provide for a range of incidents from a casual operator accident to a major disaster. Each recovery plan should be *formal, modular,* and *tested.*

FORMALITY

The recovery plan must be fully *documented.* Responsibilities and activities of each section and affected individual should be spelled out specifically.

The plan should be supported by effective analysis covering uses of resources. This analysis should cover levels of protection and procedures necessary to assure a readiness to recover critical data and resources and to restart operations at some predetermined minimum level.

CONTENTS

The plan should be dated and include the following topics:

- Data: Listing all off-premises master files — their date, location, and procedures for updating
- Hardware: Giving the precise specifications of each item of equipment and source of short- and long-term replacement
- Software: Giving location and arrangements for off-premises backup
- Personnel: Listing names and home phones of company executives, data processing personnel, and vendor representatives
- Supplies: Listing special forms and supplies stored off-premises, procurement contracts, and specifications
- Documentation: Listing off-premises copies of source code, application run manuals, and operator manuals
- Facilities: Describing space and support services such as telephone lines

MODULARITY

The recovery plan should cover several levels of disruption, including minor operator or hardware errors as well as major or total destruction of a facility.

For each level or module, the plan should provide for recovery to predetermined operating levels. In this aspect, the plan should recognize that all applications and elements of a facility are not equally critical. For some applications, plans should call for restoration of EDP services at the earliest possible moment with almost no concern for cost. Other applications can wait for restart, depending on availability of reinstated resources.

TESTING

Each element of the recovery plans should be tested through some type of simulated emergency. The degree to which a plan is tested determines the reliance which may be placed on its workability.

Typically, testing of a recovery plan is carried out in some type of *emergency drill.* One medium-sized company offers a good case in point.

Example — Perhaps twice a year, the financial vice president notifies personnel at the close of business that they are re-

quested to be at their offices early the next morning for a drill. The previous evening, the vice president tours the facility to set the situation. Different colored cards are placed on file and equipment to indicate the degree of availability or damage. Given the conditions they find, personnel are asked to simulate execution of recovery procedures which they would implement in the situations indicated. Memos are prepared and consolidated, and plans and procedures are modified based on findings.

Recovery Methods

The sections which follow cover recovery methods according to type of resource: *data, equipment, software, personnel, input and output materials, recovery documents,* and *space.*

DATA

Data form the first and most important resource of a recovery plan. The recovery plan should deal with all files associated with each computer application, including machine-readable, manual, and various stages of in-process documents. The plan should be based on an analysis made of each file. The analysis should include:

- Usage
- Relative importance of information
- Consequences of loss
- Speed with which restoration must be accomplished
- Sources of information for recovery operations
- Methods for recovery
- Cost of recovery

In establishing priorities for protection and recovery plans, a classification plan recommended by the National Fire Protection Association (NFPA) and the Federal Fire Council (FFC) should be considered. These organizations recommend three classifications, numbered in order, for critical, important, and useful records.

Class 1, or critical records, are those which are necessary for operating continuity of the company and which would require more than one week or a predetermined, substantial level of effort to restore if destroyed. These records are also used at weekly or more frequent intervals. It is relatively difficult both to duplicate these records and to keep the duplicates updated.

Class 2, or important records, are similar to Class 1 records but are used less frequently than once a week or are easier to replace and to maintain updated duplicates.

Class 3 records are characterized as useful for continued operation. Their loss would cause inconvenience rather than complete disruption of services. Furthermore, copies of data may readily be maintained or data restored within an acceptable amount of time or effort.

The analysis must provide for considering the files according to use or application. Since there is some limit to the amount of backup and recovery costs, priorities should be set among the applications. When any reconstruction is required, the use of file copies should require serious review and approval at a higher level. The more serious the loss, the more complete the analysis to insure that fatal damage is not done to the recovery copies of data.

EQUIPMENT

The chief ingredients for equipment recovery will be provisions for *alternate premises.* For critical on-line systems, this may include multiple power and data communications cables through independent substations.

Equipment manufacturers generally promise full cooperation with priority delivery of actual computer hardware. Obtaining an adequate location for the equipment is often the greater problem.

For most companies, planned recovery will consist of agreements for the use of compatible backup facilities at other locations. These should be detailed and in writing, even if the alternate facility is operated by the same company. Where outside organizations are involved, there should be appropriate contracts. However, cooperative agreements should be expected to provide only brief continuation of the most critical applications. Virtually no host facility will have such excess capacity as to provide the visitor with accustomed response or convenience.

The backup plans should be applied to each unit of equipment within a facility; that is, where there are multiple computers at a single location, backup arrangements should be established for each. Similarly, it is becoming accepted practice to establish separate protection for each computer, including fire walls between systems, separate air conditioning systems, fire extinguishing devices, and so on.

Where remote storage is used for media, it is ideal to have a supplemental computer at the same site. One approach is to store media in the vault of a bank and contract for backup use of the bank's computer. No matter what recovery is planned, however, testing of applications should be made on the alternate equipment. Periodic testing assures that modifications which might have been made to either computer configuration do not impede backup capabilities.

It should be readily determined whether the alternate computer will be available only for limited time periods to cover emergency processing. Where this is the case, further provision should be made to cover the possibilities of extended damage to the physical facilities. This would include provision for normal operating time and also for what may be extensive computer recovery time. For many IPF's this will require duplicate facilities with unlimited use. Presumably, for current generation equipment, this is available from the computer manufacturer.

SOFTWARE

Software recovery is closely related to equipment recovery. Full *backup* and *recovery plans* should be made for all software — operating systems, utilities, and application programs (object and source code). Care should be taken to be sure that the generation of software stored in the backup facility corresponds with stored data files; that is, when it becomes necessary to fall back to a particular age of data files, the corresponding versions of software and equipment must also be available. This prerequisite includes data tables which may be entered as variables for processing such as pricing.

PERSONNEL

There should be *formal plans* and procedures for key personnel, including the assumption that the services of some people might be lost due to a disaster. Formal plans should indicate, for each critical activity, the persons qualified for its performance. Qualified persons should also be informed on the responsibilities and how they are performed in an emergency. The recovery plan should also include provisions for contacting key personnel both on and off duty.

If recovery of data might require extensive keypunching activities, the recovery plan should include assignment of priorities and sequences of activities which should be followed. There should also be estimates of manpower requirements for this special personnel area.

INPUT AND OUTPUT MATERIALS

A *checklist* should be prepared of all input and output documents and forms used, indicating all materials essential to continuation of EDP services, how much, and where it is stored. The payroll files and programs are of limited value if no paychecks are available.

In establishing requirements for protected storage of forms, it should be taken into account that some forms will have to be machine processed and handled at high speeds. This, together with the composition of special forms, will impact the temperature and humidity limits and, therefore, the specifications of adequate storage facilities.

RECOVERY DOCUMENTS

An item of particular interest associated with protection for documentation is the storage of the recovery plan itself. If the recovery plan is in a vault located within the EDP facility, it will not be usable during an emergency which made the vault inaccessible. Thus, the recovery plan itself should be maintained in such a way as to insure access under varying circumstances.

Example — This requirement came to light in the first disaster drill of the company cited earlier. All copies of the recovery plan were inside the IPF and were "destroyed" or not accessible during the initial state of the recovery process.

SPACE

One assumption to be made in the development of a recovery plan is that the space occupied by the computer operations center may become unusable. If this continues for an extended time, space must be available elsewhere. Typically, such arrangements would be on a contract basis. Plans should include arrangements for power, lighting, and other requirements in addition to adequate space.

Example — A company provided for emergency recovery space through a contract for use of a ballroom. Changes were made, including wiring, to be sure that the facilities were adequate for continuing computer operations. The recovery plan included designations for the location of keypunch machines, computer equipment, forms-handling equipment, and so on. The analysis which developed this phase of the recovery plan determined that it would not be economically desirable to provide normal environmental controls for full-scale computer operations under all conditions. An economic decision was made to provide fans which would dissipate sufficient heat to allow continuous operations in all but the severest hot-weather conditions.

INSURANCE

Insurance provides recovery of monies lost due to destruction or theft of assets. The premiums charged spread these costs across many insureds. However, it is always cheaper to remove the risk than to spread it plus sustain the costs of operating the insurance company. Therefore, insurance should be utilized only to cover risks that cannot be substantially eliminated or readily absorbed.

The risks that are introduced by the utilization of a computer for business data processing include:
- Damage to the computer equipment
- Cost of blank media
- Cost of acquiring the data stored upon the media
- Damages to outsiders
- Business effects of the loss of the computer functions

Standard forms of insurance coverage often exclude many of the hazards to which computer systems are particularly vulnerable.

Accordingly, the prudent businessman who is seeking to insure his risks must not only acquire such conventional forms as have been prior practice but must generally obtain additional policies or endorsements to cover the new, computer-associated risks.

"Named-perils" policies cover only the damage or the losses caused by specifically itemized perils such as fire, sprinkler leakage, etc. However, computers are vulnerable to many additional hazards.

Example — If the air conditioning system broke down on a hot summer day and if the indoors temperature rose to over 140°, the computer could be severely damaged. However, this would generally not be covered under a "named-perils" policy.

Broader coverage may be obtained by "all-risk" policies. These cover all hazards except certain ones which are specifically excluded.

Example — The change of temperature damage noted above is a common exclusion for coverage even in "all-risk" policies.

Appropriate additional coverage may be obtained by acquiring special data processing policies, "difference-in-conditions" (DIC) policies, or other special endorsements.

The application of proper insurance coverage in a data processing environment is a specialized and highly technical subject. The purchaser of such coverage should be careful to specifically check the policy for applicability to electronic media and devices. Insurance coverage should consider the broad business consequences of hazards in all areas of a business. The difference in applying coverage to data processing, however, lies in the unusual sensitivity that data processing equipment may have to certain hazards as opposed to the sensitivity of other business assets.

Security of the IPF premises and contents is usually a significant concern because of the concentration of assets within an IPF and their vulnerability. While prevention is most desirable, complete prevention is not obtainable. Accordingly, the total security plan must provide for reliable detection and correction capabilities.

This concludes the material on IPF controls. A summary of the relationships of IPF controls to causes of exposure is presented in Figure 18-1.

RELATIONSHIPS OF IPF CONTROLS TO CAUSES OF EXPOSURE

CAUSES OF IPF EXPOSURES

PREVENTION CONTROLS	HUMAN ERRORS				HARDWARE/ SOFTWARE FAILURES			COMPUTER ABUSE							CATASTROPHE			
	DATA ENTRY	CONSOLE ENTRY	WRONG FILE OR PROGRAM	FILE DAMAGED	INTERRUPT OPERATION	LOSS OF DATA	LOGIC ERROR	THEFT	EMBEZZLEMENT	FRAUD	ESPIONAGE	INVASION OF PRIVACY	MALICIOUSNESS	MISCHIEVOUSNESS	FIRE	WATER	WIND	CIVIL DISORDER
Definition of duties	1	1	1	1				1	1	2	1	2						
Segregation of duties	2	2	2	2				2	2	2	2	2	2	2				
Reliable personnel	2	2	1	1									1	2				
Competent personnel	2	2				1		1	2						1	1		
Job rotation																		
Housekeeping			1	1											1			
Equipment maintenance					2	1	3											
Air conditioning			2		1	1	1											
Scheduling								1			2	2	2	2				3
Limited physical access									2	2	2	2	2	2				
Restricted knowledge			2	1		1		1	2	2	2	2	1	1	2	2		2
File custodian				1				2	2	2	2	2	2	2	2	2		
Physical security			2								1	1	1	1				
External labels		1	2			1										1		
Internal labels		2	2			1							1	1				
Protect rings		2	2															1
Disk enable				2														
Containerized operations	2	2	2	2	2			1	2	2	1	2	1	1	1	1		
Training																		
Authorization					2	2	3						2	1	2	3	3	2
Manufacturer design															1	2		1
Physical structure								1										
Physical location																		

RELIANCE ON CONTROLS

3 — Reliably controls applicable cause

2 — Controls cause but should be accompanied by additional controls

1 — Useful but not especially effective

Blank — No significant contribution

Figure 18-1 (page 1 of 2)

RELATIONSHIPS OF IPF CONTROLS TO CAUSES OF EXPOSURE

CAUSES OF IPF EXPOSURE

	HUMAN ERRORS				HARDWARE/SOFT-WARE FAILURES			COMPUTER ABUSE							CATASTROPHE			
	DATA ENTRY	CONSOLE ENTRY	WRONG FILE OR PROGRAM	FILE DAMAGED	INTERRUPT OPERATION	LOSS OF DATA	LOGIC ERROR	THEFT	EMBEZZLEMENT	FRAUD	ESPIONAGE	INVASION OF PRIVACY	MALICIOUSNESS	MISCHIEVOUSNESS	FIRE	WATER	WIND	CIVIL DISORDER
DETECTION CONTROLS																		
Supervision	2	2	2	2				2	2	2	1	1	2	2				
Budgets	2	2	1					2						1				
Management reporting	2	2	2	2	1	2	1		1	1	1	1	1	1				
Operator logs			2	2		1	1											
Console logs (job journal)	1	2	2	1	2	1	2	1	2	1	2	2	2	2				
Library logs		2				1		1	1	1	1	1	1	1				
Control logs	2	2	3	2		2	1	1	1	1	1	1	1	1				
Keystroke verification	2																	
Hardware checks	1			2		2	2											
Operating system checks	1	2	2	2		2												
Scan output	1	1	1			1		1										
Fire detectors															3			
Application controls	3	2	3	2	2	3	2	2	2	2		2	2	2	2	2	2	2
CORRECTION CONTROLS																		
Recovery plan			2	2	2	2	2								2	2	2	2
File histories	2	1	1	1	1	1	1	1		2			2	2				
Error statistics		3	3	3				1		2			2	2				
Fire extinguishers															2			
On-premises backup	2	3	3	3		3		2	2	2	1	1	2	2	3	3	3	3
Off-premises backup	1							2					2	1	2	2	2	3
Discharge personnel								2			1	2	1	1				2
Insurance								2				2	2	2	2	2	2	2
Uninterruptable power					2													

RELIANCE ON CONTROLS

3 — Reliably controls applicable cause
2 — Controls cause but should be accompanied by additional controls
1 — Useful but not especially effective
Blank — No significant contribution

Figure 18-1 (page 2 of 2)

355

19
Audit of the IPF

In practice, the IPF examination is often performed before the examination of applications or the system development process. During the initial stages of the audit review, the auditor obtains summary level information about the IPF and its activities and uses this information to set the tentative scope of the overall review of the data processing function. He is then able to determine the extent of the work that will be required in the IPF phase as well as the tentative extent of application and system development work that will be required.

The objective of the IPF audit is the verification of effective implementation of the controls discussed in the preceding chapters of this section. The audit of the IPF requires a greater awareness of the EDP environment than the audit of applications. At the same time, this greater awareness need not be too extensive. One does not need to be a chicken in order to recognize an egg. The auditor working in this area should have acquired, possibly through experience in the use of general purpose audit software, a working appreciation for this more technical environment and an understanding that technical assistance may be required in certain areas of this part of the EDP audit. Such an awareness and background are basic to a realistic evaluation of operating controls.

STEPS IN THE IPF AUDIT

Figure 19-1 presents the steps required to perform the review and evaluation of IPF controls. In the process, the tentative extent of work to be performed in the application audit and system development audit areas is refined, based on the results of the IPF review. The steps may be summarized as follows:

Basic Information Gathering

■ Obtain and review summary-level information about the data processing department, its people, organization, hardware, software, applications, etc.

Detailed Information Gathering

■ To complete the understanding, interview various personnel to determine policies, practices, etc., preparing in the process such supplemental audit documentation as is required.

Evaluate Control Strengths and Weaknesses

■ Having completed the understanding of practices, policies, etc., determine which controls are essential to the overall audit objectives as well as to the tentative objectives of the application and systems development process audits.

Design Audit Procedures

■ Determine the technical proficiency required to perform the test work, select the verification techniques applicable to each area, and prepare instructions for performing the compliance tests.

Test

■ Perform the necessary compliance testing by using documentary evidence, corroborating interviews, and personal observations.

Evaluate Findings

■ Evaluate the findings of the compliance testing, relate those results to the applications being processed, and report.

Basic Information Gathering

The following summary-level information should be obtained prior to starting any audit fieldwork. This information should be readily available from the IPF personnel, from other working papers prepared during the use of generalized audit software, from audit permanent files, etc.

■ Organization charts for both the company and the EDP organization with brief information about the titles of personnel in various positions, the numbers of personnel in various groups; e.g., "4 programmers."

■ Information on the IPF's computer hardware and peripheral devices, including the CPU (make, model, size, etc., and whether rented, owned or leased); the number and type of tape and disc drives; and the number and types of other peripheral devices: terminals, console typewriter, printers, card readers and punches, key-verification equipment, etc.

DIAGRAM OF STEPS IN IPF AUDIT

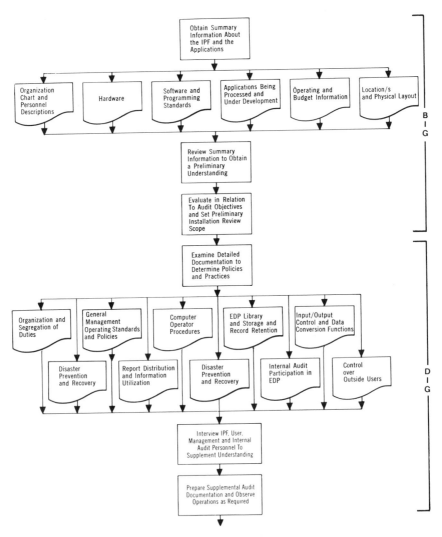

Figure 19-1 (Part 1 of 2)

DIAGRAM OF STEPS IN IPF AUDIT

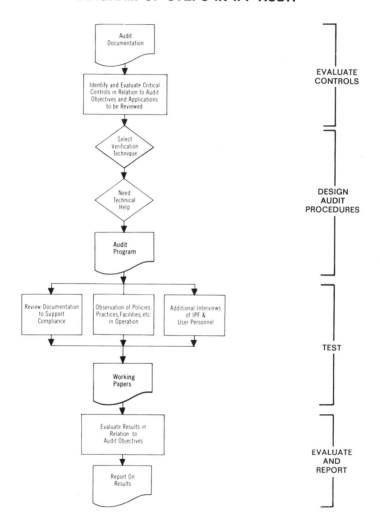

Figure 19-1 (Part 2 of 2)

359

- Information on the IPF's software: the operating system and whether it is manufacturer-supplied, written by the internal staff, etc., the version of the operating system, the primary program languages in use in the IPF, and whether generalized audit software or data management packages are used.
- A list of applications, both those presently being processed and those under development, with information describing the type of application, how long it takes to process, the dollar value of transactions and master file balances involved, and the processing frequency.
- Operating and budget information broken down by such categories as equipment, personnel, supplies, and the amount of computer time used per month for regular applications, testing, outside users, maintenance, etc. This information should also indicate if time is being used at outside service bureaus. In addition, the auditor should obtain copies of reports on equipment scheduling, equipment utilization, and programming backlog.
- A brief sketch or other description of the physical layout of the computer room.

The summary-level information should be reviewed to obtain a preliminary understanding about the size and complexity of the IPF. Evaluation of this information in conjunction with his other knowledge about the company will enable the auditor to make a preliminary judgment on the extent of review procedures that will be required in the data processing area.

The extent of the remaining review may range from nothing at all, because data processing has little impact on audit objectives, to a complete review of the entire IPF. Since the significance of the IPF is based on the audit significance of the applications it processes, the presence of even one application having audit significance may require some IPF control verification.

The application audit work may be conducted independently of the IPF examination if more than one person is available. The application work cannot, however, be finalized until the IPF work is completed. This will be discussed later.

Detailed Information Gathering

The auditor next obtains standards documentation (procedures manuals, job descriptions, etc.) about the IPF and reviews it to obtain a preliminary understanding of the policies and practices. Some of the relevant subjects which will be discussed in later sections of this chapter are:
- Organization and segregation of duties
- General management's operating standards and policies
- Computer operator procedures
- The EDP library and storage facilities and record retention

- The input/output control and data conversion functions
- Physical security
- Disaster prevention and recovery
- Report distribution and information utilization
- The use of the IPF by outside third parties

In certain areas, the auditor will interview IPF, user, and/or management personnel to supplement and to complete his understanding. Although a review of informational documentation is the primary technique used to obtain an understanding, some interviewing will always be required.

During the course of the interviews and as a result of the documentation reviews, the auditor will prepare varying amounts of supplemental audit documentation for his working papers covering comments in interviews and filling the gaps where documentation is limited.

Identify and Evaluate Critical Controls in Relation to Audit Objectives and Applications to Be Reviewed

Having finalized the understanding of the policies, etc., the critical controls must be identified, evaluated, and selected for testing in relation to audit objectives and the scope of application audit work. If control defects are identified in the organizational structures or resources, the degree of exposure identified will have a bearing on the selection of further application audit tests. The variable effects of such exposures will relate to the quality of the implementation of virtually all of the controls within the IPF.

As described previously in chapter four, "Control Concepts and EDP," and as applied in chapter ten, "Auditing EDP Applications," a simple but powerful technique for evaluating controls in the IPF is the Control Evaluation Table. A typical table for an IPF is illustrated in Figure 19-2.

The lower portion of the table shows the relationship between common business exposures and common causes of exposures in an IPF. These relationships are preprinted on the table in Figure 19-2 but should be tailored to the specific company circumstances when it is applied.

The upper portion of the table shows the relationships between the IPF causes of exposure and the controls that may be applied in an IPF. Again, the typical relationships that are preprinted on the table must be tailored for each specific facility where it is applied.

The relationships on the table are measured on a scale of one to three. Three indicates a very strong relationship — a cause will almost certainly lead to the related exposure, or a control will be very effective against a cause.

Two indicates a moderate relationship — a cause will probably lead to the related exposure, or a control will be effective against the majority of the occurrences of a specific cause.

One indicates a weak relationship — a cause might lead to the related exposure, or a control may influence some of the occurrences of a specific cause.

Relationships that are extremely remote are left blank on the table.

IPF CONTROL EVALUATION TABLE

RELIANCE ON CONTROLS
3 — Reliably controls applicable cause
2 — Controls cause but should be accompanied by additional controls
1 — Useful but not especially effective
Blank — No significant contribution

EXPOSURES
Erroneous record keeping
Unacceptable accounting
Business interruption
Erroneous management decisions
Fraud
Statutory sanctions
Excessive costs
Loss or destruction of assets
Competitive disadvantage

IMPACT OF CAUSES
3 — Very likely to occur
2 — Likely to occur
1 — May occur
Blank — Generally little effect

CAUSES OF IPF EXPOSURES

PREVENTION CONTROLS	HUMAN ERRORS — Data Entry	Console Entry	Wrong File or Program	File Damaged	HARDWARE/SOFTWARE FAILURES — Interrupt Operation	Loss of Data	Logic Error	COMPUTER ABUSE — Theft	Embezzlement	Fraud	Espionage	Invasion of Privacy	Maliciousness	Mischievousness	CATASTROPHE — Fire	Water	Wind	Civil Disorder
Definition of duties	1	1	1					1	1		1	2						
Segregation of duties	2	2	2					2	2	2	2	2	2	2				
Reliable personnel	2	2	1	1					1	1		2	1	2	1			3
Competent personnel																1		
Job rotation					2	1		1										
Housekeeping		1	1	1	1											1		2
Equipment maintenance																		
Air conditioning			2															
Scheduling							3	1	2	2	2	2	2	2	2	2		3
Limited physical access				2	2	2	1	1	2	2	2	2	1	1	1			
Restricted knowledge		2	1					1	2	2	1	1	1	1				
File custodian		2	1			1		2	1	1	1	1	1	1	1			1
Physical security															1	2		2
External labels	1	2											1	1				
Internal labels	2	2			1				1									
Protect rings	2	2																
Disk enable	2	2						2	2	2	2	2	2	1				1
Containerized operations	2		2				3											
Training	2	2	2	2	2	2										3	3	2
Authorization					1		1	1	2	2	1	1	2	1	1	2	2	1
Manufacturer design	2	1		3	2	1						3	3			3		3
Physical structure	1			2	2				3	2	2	2	2		3	3	2	
Physical location	2	2		2	2	2	2	1	3	2	2		2	1	2	2	2	2

Figure 19-2 (page 1 of 2)

IPF CONTROL EVALUATION TABLE

CAUSES OF IPF EXPOSURES

DETECTION CONTROLS	HUMAN ERRORS				HARDWARE/SOFT- WARE FAILURES			COMPUTER ABUSE							CATASTROPHE			
	Data Entry	Console Entry	Wrong File or Program	File Damaged	Interrupt Operation	Loss of Data	Logic Error	Theft	Embezzlement	Fraud	Espionage	Invasion of Privacy	Maliciousness	Mischievousness	Fire	Water	Wind	Civil Disorder
Supervision	2	2		2				2	2	2	1	1	2	2				
Budgets	2	2	1					2	1	1	1	1		1				
Management reporting	2	2	2	2	1									1				
Operator logs				2		2	1											
Console logs (job journal)	1	2	2	2	2	1	2	1	2	1	2	2	2	2				
Library logs	2	2	2	2		1		1	1	1	1		1	1				
Control logs	2	2	3															
Keystroke verification	2						2											
Hardware checks	1	2	2	2		2												
Operating system checks	1	1	1	2		1												
Scan output	1							1										2
Fire detectors															3			
Application controls	3	2	3	2		3	2	2	2	2			2	2		2	2	2
CORRECTION CONTROLS																		
Recovery plan				2	1	2	1	1					2		2	2	2	2
File histories			1	1	1	1	1	1					2		2	2		
Error statistics	2	1						1	2	2	2		2	2	2			
Fire extinguishers											2				3			
On-premises backup	2	3	3	3	2	3	2	2	2	2	1		2	2	3	3	3	3
Off-premises backup								2	2	2		1	2	2	2	2	2	2
Discharge personnel	1							2	2				2	1				
Insurance					2										3	3	3	.
Uninterruptable power	2				1	2	2	1		3	3	3	3		3	3	2	3
IMPACT OF CAUSES																		
3 — Very likely to occur	2	1	1	2	3	2	1	1	3	3	2		2	1	3	3	2	3
2 — Likely to occur	1		1	1	2	2	1	1	3		1		3	1	3	3	3	3
1 — May occur	1							2										
Blank — Generally little effect	2	2	2	2	2	2	2	2	3	2	1		3	1	3	3	2	3
	2	2	2	2	2	2		2	3		2		2		2	2	2	2

RELIANCE ON CONTROLS

3 — Reliably controls applicable cause
2 — Controls cause but should be accompanied by additional controls
1 — Useful but not especially effective
Blank — No significant contribution

IMPACT OF CAUSES

3 — Very likely to occur
2 — Likely to occur
1 — May occur
Blank — Generally little effect

EXPOSURES

Erroneous record keeping
Unacceptable accounting
Business interruption
Erroneous management decisions
Fraud
Statutory sanctions
Excessive costs
Loss or destruction of assets
Competitive disadvantage

Figure 19-2 (page 2 of 2)

When applying the table, the auditor may first tailor the relationships between causes and exposures.

Example — Invasion of privacy could never cause a statutory sanction if the IPF maintained no credit, payroll, nor other records pertaining to individuals.

Next, the controls and causes would be tailored for the controls and relationships that exist in the specific situation.

Example — If information gathering reveals that no fire detectors exist, they obviously must be deleted as a control over fire, etc.

With the completion of the tailoring to fit the specific situation, the table is ready for identification of those controls to be tested.

Usually, the auditor should start with the detective controls. If one strong (three) control for a single cause supposedly exists, it may usually be relied upon to detect that cause.

If no strong control exists, the auditor may be able to rely upon two or more moderate strength (two) controls. A single level-two control will not normally be adequate. Weak (level-one) controls will rarely provide enough control, even when several exist, to justify an auditor's reliance.

After picking the detective controls upon which he plans to rely (and test), the auditor must then turn to corrective controls. The analytic process for these is the same as for detective.

Preventive controls are also important, but evidence that they function effectively may often be inferred from the exceptions reported by detective controls. Relatively few of the preventive controls are even moderately strong; but if the auditor elects to rely upon those that are, the evaluation and selection technique remains the same as for detective and corrective controls.

If the auditor is unable to identify adequate controls for a particular cause of exposure, he must then conclude that a weakness exists to that cause; and his audit procedures should try to test for the exposures that might have resulted.

Design Audit Procedures

Having determined what controls need to be verified and weaknesses investigated, the auditor must determine the technical proficiency required to perform the tests. He may then select the verification techniques to be used. Certain of the more complex and technical areas (hardware and software) may require that the auditor seek help from a qualified independent consultant or EDP audit specialist. The auditor himself is the only one to make this judgment, as he will have all the facts about the potential control problems in the IPF and his own technical proficiency.

Unlike the application audit, where the auditor may utilize a variety of tools and techniques, there are only three basic verification techniques applicable to the IPF audit. They are:

- Review documentation supporting compliance
- Interview personnel
- Observe activities and operations

REVIEW DOCUMENTATION SUPPORTING COMPLIANCE

In verifying that controls exist and are working, the primary verification technique for many areas is a review of documentation supporting compliance with prescribed policies, controls, etc. This documentation includes supervisory signatures or initials on console logs evidencing review, daily work schedules, library logs on files in and out, etc. Applicable documentation is covered in the discussions following on each computer center operations area.

INTERVIEW PERSONNEL

Interviewing as a verification technique is primarily applicable in administrative efficiency areas and where there should be user and IPF liaison. This would not normally be observable or documented. Interviewing may also be required where compliance with policies, etc., is not adequately documented.

OBSERVE ACTIVITIES AND OPERATIONS

Controls in certain areas can be verified only through observing that they do in fact take place or exist. The auditor should schedule several short periods of time: one or two hours at a time on an unannounced basis to observe activities and operations. He will, for instance, observe that departments are physically segregated, that machine-readable media contain external labels, that the library is not open to unrestricted access, that file protect rings are removed and that supervisors are periodically in the computer room. Observation is particularly important for the organizational controls because there will frequently be no audit trail to support adherence to documented standards. Activities subject to verification through observation are also covered in the following discussions.

Perform Audit Procedures

Using the techniques noted above, the auditor will now test for compliance with the controls that are significant to the required reliability.

Evaluate Test Results in Relation to Audit Objectives and Applications Being Processed

The results of the compliance tests and the existence and adequacy of controls must be evaluated not only with respect to the audit objectives set for the IPF but in relation to audit objectives established for application examinations. In the event controls are not adequate, the audit scope must be adjusted accordingly to evaluate the effects of the weaknesses.

The evaluation process itself is basically the same as the evaluation performed after information gathering. The only difference is that the auditor now knows whether the controls really exist and how effectively they are implemented.

REPORT ON FINDINGS

Finally, the auditor should comment on weaknesses noted in a letter of recommendations.

The majority of the remainder of this chapter is devoted to a discussion of the individual areas of audit concern within the IPF. Figure 19-3 summarizes these areas of concern and the documentation, interviews, and observation verification techniques to be utilized in each area.

ORGANIZATION AND SEGREGATION OF DUTIES

An examination of EDP operations begins with developing a familiarity with the corporate and IPF organization structures, actual manpower situations, work loads, functions of departmental personnel, and, particularly, the segregation of duties. Significant organizational weaknesses will usually lead to associated weaknesses in other areas. Few compensating controls can offset organizational weaknesses effectively.

In order to understand the EDP organization, the auditor should review documentation which includes:

- Corporate and departmental organization charts
- Manpower and overtime reports
- Job descriptions

To the extent that organization charts, manpower and overtime reports, and job descriptions are either missing or outdated, the auditor should request that at least brief and current descriptions be prepared. In extreme circumstances, he may have to interview management personnel to develop his own brief documentation on organization and job descriptions.

This phase of the examination should provide the auditor with an overview of the structure and resources of the organization and the utilization of those resources. A primary concern in this area lies in the segregation of duties as it affects both working efficiency and potential conflicts of responsibility.

The auditor should determine that there is proper segregation of duties in areas and between functions.

366

AREAS OF CONCERN AND TECHNIQUES IN AUDITS OF EDP OPERATIONS

AREA OF CONCERN	DOCUMENTATION	INTERVIEWS	OBSERVATIONS
Organization and Segregation of Duties	Corporate and department organization charts. Manpower and overtime reports. Job descriptions.	Interview senior management personnel and prepare own organization charts and other documentation.	Verify lines of reporting, job descriptions, and separation of responsibilities.
General Management, Operating Standards and Policies	Processing logs. Daily operations schedules. Reports on completed jobs. Summaries of above.	If documentation inadequate, interview EDP operations management to identify any compensating controls. Develop awareness of capacities and costs as a basis for evaluation of utilization of resources.	Note availability of managers in computer center. Note degree to which management can observe operations.
Computer Operator Procedure	Operator logs. Error reports.	Not appropriate.	Series of brief, unannounced visits spread over all shifts. Observe neatness and orderliness of installation and such procedures as file handling, cleaning tape heads, accepting inputs, etc.
EDP Library and Storage and Record Retention	Library log of file, program, etc. in use Records of data files Records of disks and tapes Record retention policy statement	Interview management about IRS Ruling 71-20 agreements	Observe how files and programs are handled Observe accessibility of library, during all shifts.
Input/Output Control and Data Conversion	Analytic flow chart depicting control group activities. Console and operator logs. Conversion instructions Error reports	Interview users to determine if controls are being applied. Interview users to determine satisfaction level with equipment reliability and error resolution	Observe control group functions. Verify correction of errors in course of other duties.
Report Distribution and Information Utilization	Report schedules.	Interview users on adequacy of distribution.	Not appropriate.
Equipment and Software Reliability and Utilization	Records for utilization, cleaning, and recertification to tapes and discs. Preventative maintenance controls and logs.	Interview users to determine satisfaction level with equipment reliability.	Observe presence and use of temperature and humidity control devices.
Physical Security Disaster Prevention and Recovery	Plans of action. Certificates for devices. Contingency plans. Arrangements for backup facilities. Documented test procedures which have been performed on backup facilities. Fidelity insurance. Insurance for equipment damage. Insurance for reconstruction costs. Business interruption insurance. Duplicate application documentation.	Interview fire prevention personnel. Appraise quality of preventive measures and exposure. Interview management to identify and describe undocumented recovery facilities, plans, or arrangements.	Observe segregation of computer facility, access controls, protective equipment, and library controls over files. Visit night shift. Examine file labels. Observe off-premises backup files and facilities. verify usability.
Control over Outside Users	Copies of Agreements. Billing procedures. Operating reports.	Interview EDP manager to determine if there are other outside users.	During routine observations, note third party job handling procedures, if appropriate.

Figure 19-3

367

He should also determine that all job positions (librarian, computer operators, the input/output control group, and keypunch operators) are adequately described so there is no question on functional duties. Furthermore, he should see that all positions are properly staffed, eliminating the potential for overlap of responsibilities due to lack of personnel.

If conflicts of responsibility exist, the auditor should be alert to the possibilities the conflicts create. When such conditions are identified, the auditor must reconsider his application audit scope for any applications which may be affected.

Finally, once documentation is acquired or created, observations by the auditor will provide verification of lines of authority, job descriptions, and separation of responsibilities. Observation is important in the organizational area because *there will be no audit trail to support adherence to documented standards.* Therefore, verification is limited to the auditor's own opportunities to observe the organization in action.

GENERAL MANAGEMENT AND OPERATING STANDARDS

While reviewing organization, the auditor should become familliar with the quality of management standards as documented by internally created reports.

When adequate management reports are not available, the auditor should interview computer operations management personnel and determine what, if any, compensating controls exist. The auditor should also obtain a general awareness of the IPF's capacities and operating costs as background for later judgments regarding audit scope, substantive tests, and control recommendations.

In the observation phase of the verification of general management, the auditor should note:

- The presence of *only* the authorized personnel and files necessary for operations
- The typical availability level of management personnel in the computer center
- The degree to which activities in the computer area may be observed by supervisory personnel from within their offices
- The hardware in and the physical layout of the IPF.

The auditor normally will not be so technically proficient as to be able to evaluate the amount of hardware the IPF should have for the types of applications being processed. He may, however, be able to get an indication of excessive or insufficient hardware through relating the amount of hardware to other areas reviewed: the jobs processed and processing times by application reports. This indication may lead to a call for technical assistance. As to layout, the auditor is certainly qualified to evaluate the "housekeeping" aspects of an IPF.

The auditor routinely examines IPF documents for management reporting on operations and observes supervisory activities during which he will also encounter many opportunities to note potential improvements.

The auditor should review schedules for evidence of management participation before and after the fact. Interviewing management and/or observing supervisory activities may also be necessary. The observations of supervisory activities may also indicate situations of concern to the auditor which are of an operational efficiency nature.

COMPUTER OPERATOR PROCEDURES

Most operator-applied controls are verified mainly by observation. This activity should be relatively brief and unannounced — usually a matter of a few hours spread over different shifts in order to cover as many individual operators as possible. Prime opportunities for observations may coincide with audit procedures involving the use of test data or general purpose audit software. Such activities require the use of computers by the auditor, offering an opportunity for concurrent observation of the activities of computer operators.

To be certain that operating results are adequately reviewed, these activities should be observed and evidence of scheduling and review documented so they may be examined by the auditor during the review of operations.

The auditor should also pay particular attention to such elements as security and access, operator access to program documentation, or general purpose utilities that allow changing files through the console, housekeeping within the IPF, the cleaning of peripheral devices, the orderliness with which files are handled, and verification that inputs are authorized.

Both the existence of instructions and actual practices should be observed.

The auditor should note whether file protect rings are used and removed immediately to protect files from inadvertent erasure. If this is not done, the auditor should concern himself particularly with recovery procedures, which may be needed to reconstruct inadvertently erased files.

The orderliness of an IPF is both easily observed and important. In particular, the auditor should observe the handling of flammable waste materials and the handling of files within the IPF. The possibility that sloppy handling may lead to incomplete processing of files or the processing of incorrect files always exists and should always be examined.

The auditor should further observe the adequacy of external file (disc and tape) labeling procedures. Inadequate labels often may lead to inadvertent file destruction. On the other hand, extensive external information (beyond a simple identification) may not be necessary if the available controls involving internal labels are effectively enforced. The auditor should consider the use of utility or other programs to print internal file labels to verify that all magnetic media files have adequate labels.

Finally, the auditor should observe procedures for accepting inputs to the computer. In this area, his concern lies in the operator's enforcement of authorization procedures before input can be processed; e.g., one type of observation would be the examination of punched-card-input decks for the presence of verification notches indicating control within the data conversion section.

As he observes operator processing, the auditor may be able to reach some evaluation of professional competence of personnel. Within an EDP environment, such competence is as critical in the efficiency of operations as it is to successful implementation of controls.

The auditor who has used general purpose audit software frequently acquires a working knowledge of computer operations in the process. He will usually be aware of many techniques which substantially affect the efficiency of EDP operations centers. Of course, unless the auditor has extensive technical training, he will not be fully qualified to evaluate all the activities for which an operator may be held responsible. The level of technical requirements placed upon many computer operators is not beyond the evaluation capabilities of many auditors, even without technical backgrounds. However, as the size and complexity of IPF's increase and as more sophisticated multiprogramming operating systems come into use, these technical requirements will also increase. Unless he has received additional technical training, the auditor, in such circumstances, may do well to seek technical help from an EDP expert.

THE EDP LIBRARY, STORAGE AND RECORD RETENTION

During the observation of the IPF, the auditor should also observe how files, programs, and other sensitive media are handled within the library itself as well as into and out of the library and storage areas. He should determine first that the library and storage area (for sensitive media) are under the control of a person independent of computer operations and that the person is in fact maintaining proper physical control over the library. The control should extend through all operating shifts.

Examination of the library log for propriety of sign-outs by only authorized personnel should also be performed. Security of the

370

library; i.e., separation from computer operations (susceptibility to accidental damage or destruction) and access may also be reviewed at this time.

While reviewing library and storage procedures, the auditor should determine what the file-retention policy is for both printed output and machine-readable media. The audit tests may be extended to evaluation of the retention policy and tests of compliance. The adequacy of the retention policy should be based upon the users' requirements for operating continuity as reflected in a recovery plan. Statutory requirements may also be relevant. In the event the IRS has performed a Ruling 71-20 review, the auditor should obtain and review a copy of the resulting retention agreement signed by the IRS and the company.

INPUT/OUTPUT FUNCTION: A TWO-LEVEL REVIEW

The function of an input/output control group is reviewed at two levels by the auditor. During the IPF review, he establishes what the *general policies and practices* are in respect to the input/output control function; i.e., the accountability for data from receipt through data conversion, processing, error correction, and reentry and through final distribution of output to users. He also performs compliance tests to verify adherence to proper controls. Then, during application reviews, he will go into further detail on the input/output control function and how it, or its equivalent, *performs with respect to specific applications.*

The existence, or lack, of an adequate input/output control function is a primary control concern of the auditor. Its function of being responsible for the accountability of data is of paramount importance. The existence of this function is in itself a preventive control. In the event the function or its controls are found to be inadequate, the scope of application review work in respect to the accountability for data must be expanded.

A large part of the audit work to be done in determining policies, practices, and the adequacy of controls in the input/output control area is the same at the IPF level as it is at the application level. Only the emphasis changes; i.e., general policies and practices versus performance on specific applications. For this reason, the discussions of this in chapter 7 on "Application Controls" applies equally here and, for the most part, is not repeated below.

The auditor should obtain whatever documentation is available such as balancing logs, control sheets, edit reports, etc. He should also observe that controls exist regarding:

- Proper resolution of errors
- Identification of the causes of errors
- Receipt and distribution of input and output

Error Control

Application verification procedures, as discussed earlier, deal extensively with the identification and disposition of errors and exceptions. In addition, audits of IPF's should examine specifically the documentation and distribution of errors or exception conditions reported by the control group.

In the processing of some applications, error situations will be reported to the operator through the computer console most of which deal with functions of equipment or vendor software. Failure to resolve errors reported to computer operating personnel may be fully as serious as failure to resolve errors associated with the logical portions of an EDP application.

The principal documentation to support the *actual resolution* of errors and exceptions within the EDP operations center will be console and operator logs. Initials, as well as any other documentation, on the face of the reports should indicate that corrections and resolution of errors *were completed and reviewed by proper supervisory personnel.* In many instances, errors of this type will be resolved through computer reruns of the jobs in which errors were reported. Such reruns may be performed immediately if the errors are of a transitory nature. Otherwise, when extensive follow-up procedures are necessary, reruns can be handled at a later time.

Console and operator logs should indicate clearly whether the IPF allowed continuation of processing in the face of error conditions or whether reprocessing was performed. Indeed, the implementation of error-correction controls should be so stringent that interviews are not appropriate for audits at the EDP operations level. Only documentation is satisfactory.

Observation of error-correction procedures should not be attempted on a deliberate basis within the IPF because of the random nature of occurrence. Conceivably, an auditor could observe an operation for days and never encounter an error condition. However, in the course of observations for other elements of this audit activity, the auditor should observe the handling of any error situations encountered.

DATA CONVERSION FUNCTION

As is the case with the input/output control function, the data conversion function is normally reviewed at both the IPF level to determine general policies and practices and at the application level to determine its functioning with respect to the specific application being reviewed. The latter was previously covered in chapter 7.

At the IPF level, the auditor should determine that all data conversion procedures are in writing and current. The conversion procedures should require that all major fields of information be verified by some verifying operation like the use of redundant keystroke verification, check digits, batch controls, or other techniques. From a management and supervision standpoint, he should ascertain whether management or some other independent person reviews data-conversion error reports in order to identify potential problems and to evaluate conversion performance.

REPORT DISTRIBUTION

The auditor should observe the housekeeping and security of the output distribution activity. Particular emphasis should be directed toward the handling of sensitive outputs such as checks. The handling of blank-check stock at the beginning or end of runs is a common problem.

The primary audit procedures which are feasible involve verification of results through confirmation with recipients or comparison of files. Verification of anticipation controls used by recipients of important outputs may also be performed when applicable. Where information is distributed on-line, testing may be performed by using the integrated test facility technique.

HARDWARE AND SOFTWARE RELIABILITY AND UTILIZATION

The auditor should be concerned about:

- Equipment reliability
- Equipment and software utilization

Equipment Reliability

Concerns about equipment reliability lie in two areas:

- Computing machinery
- Media on which files are stored

Operating personnel and users should be interviewed in the course of every audit of EDP operations to help determine equipment reliability. This should be done regardless of the extent of the documentation covering equipment or file-media maintenance. To further determine if hardware and software are operating properly, the auditor may also examine downtime reports, machine-error logs, and maintenance reports.

Additionally, the auditor should observe whether appropriate temperature and humidity-control devices are in operation within the facility. Failure to maintain the proper climate may be determined from review of logs generated by temperature and humidity equipment and from a review of operating statistics to determine the extent of reruns, equipment downtime, or job reruns.

Equipment and Software Utilization

Equipment and software utilization is primarily a technical area requiring specialized, technical review expertise. In most cases, the auditor should not attempt to delve into this area unless other problems indicate it is needed. Generally, this will require technical assistance. In certain areas, the auditor's capabilities are generally adequate to raise questions about, if not to review, utilization. A discussion of the controls in this area is provided in chapter 23 on Operational Auditing.

PHYSICAL SECURITY AND DISASTER PREVENTION AND RECOVERY

The auditor should review this area at both the IPF level and the application level. The application-level review serves to further verify the adequacy or inadequacy of IPF practices in this area.

The auditor should examine the procedures which would go into effect in the event of a theft or a catastrophe such as fire, flood, explosion, and so on. However, he should also recognize that the simple existence of such documents does not provide much assurance that proper actions will be taken if crises develop.

The auditor should also examine vaults or other storage facilities for on-premises retention of files and program documentation to determine that they are secure from unauthorized access and are certified for their protective capacities.

Most verification of disaster prevention controls can be accomplished through direct observation by the auditor (supplementing this, of course, should be interviews with people directly concerned for specific disasters such as fire prevention personnel). The auditor should note whether the IPF is physically segregated from other activities of the company and the degree of ease with which an individual with destructive intent could gain access to the computer center.

Observation of the facilities will also show whether automatic or manual fire extinguishing equipment was installed, what agents are used, and whether protection of the computer center area appears reasonable.

Most of the remaining observation in the security and disaster area deal with the IPF library. The auditor should observe whether files and programs are released only by properly appointed librarians and only to authorized persons at the times these materials are needed. Lack of such controls affect the likelihood that improper processing or erasure of tapes or discs may take place. At the same time, the auditor should observe entries in the library log book and compare the accuracy of the entries with his observations.

Protective enclosures and storage equipment of the library should be examined, particularly if the IPF does not have certification documentation covering this equipment. The auditor should also visit the night shift within the IPF and observe the extent to which library controls are exercised continuously. Also, if any other storage areas are used within the IPF, particularly for important or sensitive files or documents, the protection provided for these areas should also be noted and evaluated.

Finally, the auditor should examine the file media in use or being held within the operations center to note whether external labels provide clear identification and retention dating and whether file protection rings were removed.

The actual existence of important IPF security and recovery controls must be verified in recognition of the fact that such items may be essential to the survival of the organization. Documentation may not be adequate, however; and alternative verifications techniques may have to be employed.

If insurance documentation is not available and if management claims that coverage has been secured, the auditor should seek written confirmations.

If adequate recovery-plan documentation does not exist, interviews of appropriate personnel should be conducted. Where no contingency plans have been documented, management might, in fact, have considered such requirements and reached some sort of arrangements. However, communication to the IPF staff cannot be relied upon when there is no documentation. If backup facility arrangements are not documented, but in fact arranged, the auditor might ascertain whether IPF personnel periodically visit such facilities to verify their availability. Above all, the auditor should determine that the backup facilities are suitable and that compatible capability will be available.

Moreover, observation of disaster and accident recovery capabilities may need to include physical inspection of backup master and transaction files at off-premises locations to verify that they, as well as supervisor or operating system programs, are current, available, and reconstructable. This test may be particularly important, depending on the circumstances. Adverse findings should be considered in the auditor's evaluation of any control situations heavily dependent on off-premises backup capabilities.

Since most disaster-protection procedures are clerical in nature, some lapses may be expected; however, substantial weaknesses may indicate serious exposure. If these are noted, the auditor should apply particular thoroughness in his review of the IPF's disaster recovery capabilities.

Regardless of the degree of disaster-prevention controls which exist, the ultimate capability for disaster recovery still remains extremely important in the prevention of organizational amnesia. In every case, there is always a likelihood that a crisis will be in an area for which no preparations were made or which will be beyond their capabilities. This is a simple fact of life. Therefore, while satisfying himself that the IPF is prepared for the worst, the auditor should still put little reliance on such measures. He should, instead, recognize that disaster-recovery capabilities are necessary, no matter how improbable a crisis may seem.

In addition, the auditor should recognize that disaster-recovery measures are appropriate for less-than-catastrophic interruptions of data processing services. The same procedures and measures, for instance, may be brought into play when files are accidentally erased or damaged.

CONTROL OVER OUTSIDE USERS

Many organizations with computers have some excess capacity which they may attempt to sell to help cover equipment rental costs. If the IPF under examination does this, the auditor should examine controls over billing procedures and security over the facility, programs, files, hardware, etc., while outside users are present.

The IPF operations log and the meter on each central processing unit provide the principal controls for identification of third-party utilization. Controls exercised to bill such time are similar to those commonly found in service and manufacturing job shops. Basically, a lack of billing controls may raise IPF costs if machine-rental agreements include charges for processor utilization. Even if there are no machine-rental penalties, there is exposure to loss of revenues which may be material, depending on the volume of such activity.

In any event, the auditor should obtain copies of any formal agreements involving the sale of computer time or services to outside parties and verify the appropriate documented accounting controls. An examination of rental and utilization statistics for the IPF may assist in identifying gross amounts of time used by third parties which were not accounted for. However, such procedures are not likely to be highly effective and should not be solely relied upon.

Moreover, in the course of interviews with the data processing manager, the auditor should determine whether third parties other than those for whom formal documentation exists occasionally use the computer. If any such informal agreements exist, the auditor should record their general terms and the levels of utilization involved for subsequent comparison with billings. Finally, during observation of general operations activities, he should note whether any third parties use the equipment. If so and if such use is material, he should observe procedures for recording use.

Since auditing concerns itself largely with the identification, evaluation, and testing of controls, an information processing facility emerges as a logical focal point for audit concern and activity. The basic skills, judgments, and instincts of an auditor provide important background and guidance. In highly technical areas, the auditor may sometimes call upon persons with specialized knowledge of computer equipment and software; however, the auditor's responsibility to satisfy himself as to the processing techniques and controls affecting audit objectives remains unchanged. In addition, there are important new, potential horizons in the application of audit skills to the efficiency and the control of procedures.

Section V
ADVANCED TOPICS

20

Advanced Application Systems

The subjects presented in this section are a further development of subjects already presented briefly in sections II, III, and IV. They concentrate on specific concerns that include combinations of elements of computer applications, system development, and information processing facilities.

The organization of each chapter follows the same pattern used in the preceding sections:

- Activities within the function
- Causes of exposure
- Controls
- Auditing

WHAT ARE "ADVANCED" SYSTEMS

Previous discussions of application controls in this book were primarily limited to batch-processing computer systems. Many auditors, however, are concerned with so-called "advanced" systems but the definition of "advanced" varies according to the individual's technical expertise. Two characteristics of computer applications commonly qualify to be considered advanced: those with on-line transmissions and those that involve a data base.

Application systems utilizing on-line transmissions may be common, sophisticated, or unique-level applications (see chapter 6 to review definitions of levels of application systems). On-line transmissions are becoming more frequent as applications become more complex and span multiple locations. Data bases are found generally in sophisticated and unique-level systems. Again, they are more frequent with unique systems than with sophisticated. Accordingly, some auditors may never encounter applications that incorporate on-line transmissions or a data base. Nonetheless, all auditors should be familiar with the characteristics and concerns of such applications so that they can recognize one should it be encountered.

ON-LINE SYSTEMS

Applications involving on-line transmissions fall into these major categories:

- Remote
    Batch transactions
    Job entry (RJE)
- Real-time systems
    Inquiry
    Update
    Programming
- Switching

Remote Batch Transactions

Remote batch systems generally are similar to conventional batch systems except that the batches of transactions are transmitted electronically. Such transmissions occur only at prearranged times with the computer equipment being dedicated to that batch during the period of transmission. Transmissions of this type are found most often in small and common-level systems (see Figure 20-1).

The new causes of exposure that arise with remote batch applications are the complete or partial loss of transactions during transmission. Noise in the transmission circuits (typically, telephone lines) may also alter the input data and make it inaccurate. Otherwise, the same causes of exposure exist in remote batch transaction systems as in conventional batch systems.

Remote Job Entry

Remote job-entry systems (RJE) resemble remote batch but are not limited to application processing. The remote terminal may function essentially the same as the on-site card reader, printer, and console used by the computer operator. The remote user may submit application programs, call operating system utilities, submit application transactions, and direct his programs and transactions to affect any available file. Like remote batch, the remote location may only send transmissions at prearranged times. Except for the limitations provided by the prearranged times and the concurrent availability of files, a remote job-entry system effectively creates an "open shop."

In addition to the same transmission problems that may occur with remote batch, an RJE system also generates most of the exposures associated with unlimited access and computer abuse that may be found *within* any information processing facility.

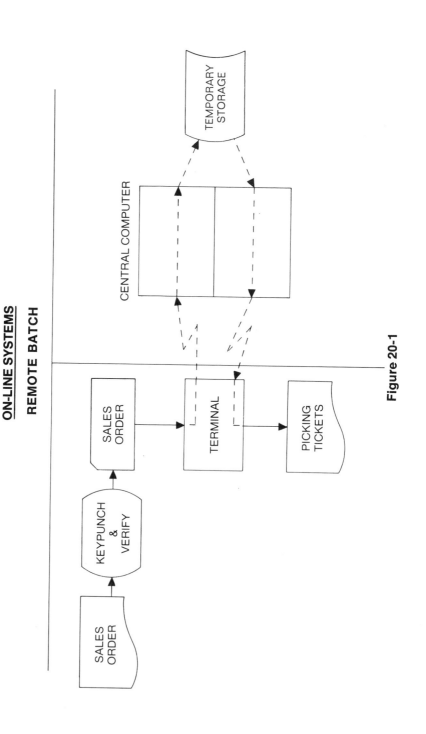

ON-LINE SYSTEMS

REMOTE BATCH

CENTRAL COMPUTER

TEMPORARY STORAGE

SALES ORDER

KEYPUNCH & VERIFY

SALES ORDER

TERMINAL

PICKING TICKETS

Figure 20-1

Real-Time Inquiry Systems

Real-time inquiry systems allow an immediate response (2 to 15 seconds) to inquiries for information from a terminal. Such systems are particularly common for bank tellers verifying account balances and retail establishments requiring credit authorization. The terminal user cannot input or alter master file information. The only type of transaction allowed is a request for information. In some situations, a log of requests may be maintained. In others, a memo file of the monetary amounts which have been processed may be recorded. However, unless the actual master records are updated at the same time, the system would still be classified as "inquiry only" (see Figure 20-2).

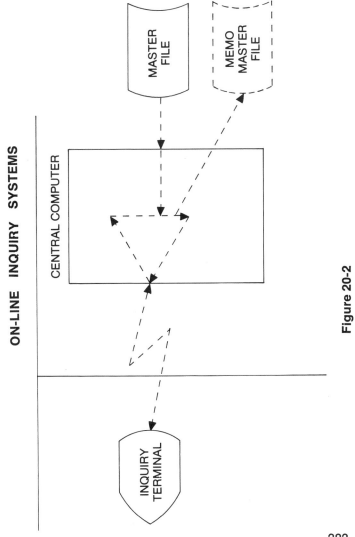

Figure 20-2

383

The causes of exposure that are changed by using real-time inquiry systems are:

- Invasion of privacy
- Information not current
- Information plausible but erroneous

Personal account status and credit information are limited to specified inquiries under various "privacy" statutes. Unlimited access which permits invasions of privacy could lead to statutory sanctions.

The immediate responsiveness of real-time systems often creates an illusion of timeliness that is not true. Many inquiry-only systems are updated daily by batch processing. Transactions which occurred subsequent to the submission of the batch inputs will not be reflected on the files. If substantial delays occur in transmitting the batch inputs, this may omit days of transaction effects. At best, the files will not reflect transactions that have occurred during the current day.

Transmission distortions of information may also occur in realline inquiry systems like any other electronic transmission; but, normally, the effects of this will be so immediately obvious that the inquiry will be resubmitted immediately.

Real-Time Update Systems

The next step upward in the sophistication of real-time systems are those which allow the master files to be altered through terminal originated update, file maintenance, or error correction input transactions. Such systems generally allow different types of transactions to be input by different levels of authorization (see Figure 20-3).

Under such systems, the transactions and processes which will be accepted are controlled by the application level of software. Realtime updating systems present difficulties in accessing or performing processes in any manner not accepted by the application logic.

Accordingly, the causes of exposure that are increased by using real-time update systems are unlimited access, hardware and software failures, unsupportable results, and human data-entry errors.

The unlimited access problem is similar to that of real-time inquiry systems except that unauthorized transactions can have far more substantial consequences than invasion of privacy. Rather than merely obtaining information, the real-time updating system will allow changes to the file by update, file maintenance, or error correction transactions, depending upon what the application programs accept. These transactions may be performed by anyone who has access to an appropriate remote input terminal. Such situations also exist in manual systems, if transactions may be submitted by such a multitude of sources that effective control over these sources must wait until they are collected at one point.

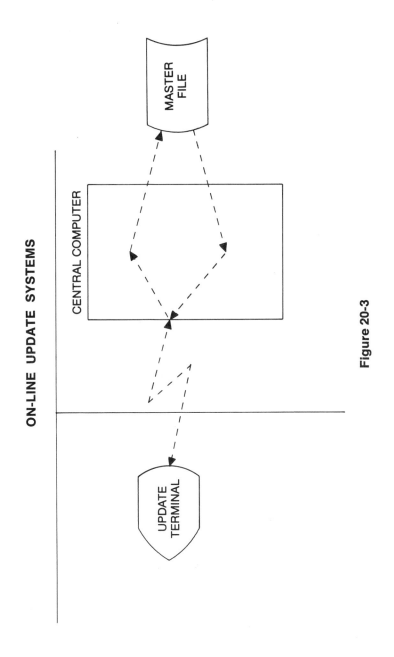

ON-LINE UPDATE SYSTEMS

MASTER FILE

CENTRAL COMPUTER

UPDATE TERMINAL

Figure 20-3

Example — Charges for services within a large hospital may be submitted by any member of the staff, which could number in the thousands.

Another cause of exposure arises if hardware or software elements of the computer system should fail during application processing. The person initiating transactions at the time of the failure may be uncertain of whether the current transaction was completely processed. Accordingly, such transactions may be lost or duplicated. Next, the direct submission of transactions on an electronic device may provide no opportunity for recording the initiated transaction on a hard-copy document. Furthermore, the files may be changed without any separate record of the transaction which caused the change or even a record of the fact that a change had occurred. The total absence of a transaction trail may prevent necessary corrective actions and make corroboration of the results impossible.

Finally, human data-entry errors may be submitted on the terminals for the same reasons that they occur with keypunch machines. That is, the data may be inaccurate, elements may be omitted, digits reversed, etc. If a large variety of users are allowed access to the terminals, the error rate may be somewhat higher than that which is customary for trained keypunch operators.

Real-Time Programming Systems

The final major classification of real-time systems is that which allows the remote submission of application programs or the calling of resident utilities. Such programs may be compiled and executed by the central computer and the resulting applications systems used to process all types of real-time transactions. Such programs may be directed to access any file stored on the equipment and change it in any manner whatsoever. Programs may also be devised to supersede or change the actual operating system which directs all other functions of the computer system (see Figure 20-4).

Real-time programming systems are generally incorporated by means of "time-sharing." A number of commercial and private services are available to a multitude of users. All that is required of the user is an appropriate terminal device and sufficient knowledge to gain access to the system.

Real-time programming systems provide the same capabilities as remote job entry except that they are available constantly without special arrangements. Again, the existence of such systems effectively turns the information processing facility into an open shop.

The use of real-time programming (time-sharing) systems gives rise to all of the causes of exposure one finds in an information processing facility except such physical causes of exposure as fire, water, wind, or civil disorder. Any of the human errors, hardware and software errors, or computer abuse may occur from a remote terminal device. Via remote electronic transmissions, any individual may effectively accomplish any computer processing that he could accomplish by standing within the installation and running the equipment personally.

Naturally, these systems also provide the causes of exposure found in real-time update systems:

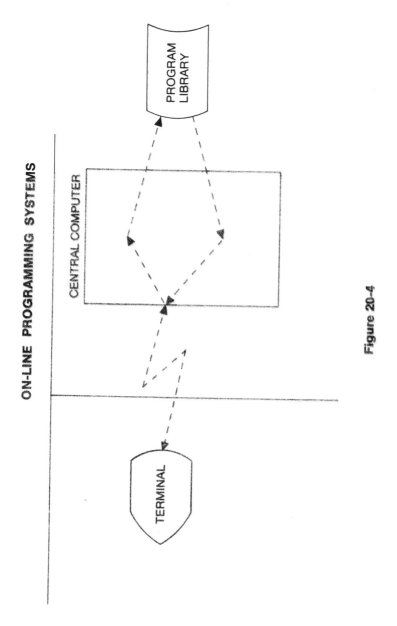

Figure 20-4

- Hardware/software failure
- Unsupportable results
- Human data-entry errors

These causes of exposure are just about identical with real-time updating systems.

Finally, application programs resident within the system may be destroyed through accidental or deliberate actions from a remote terminal.

Switching Systems

Advanced networks of on-line information processing facilities may be interconnected through a central switching facility. A switching facility is an information processing facility that provides a switching application by either dedicating the entire system or a portion of it. Such switching systems have existed for many years primarily in the telephone system. For maximum efficiency, computers that are specially designed for this function may be employed. However, general purpose computers may also be utilized effectively.

In addition to the familiar telephone system, switching systems and switching facilities have become familiar in recent years through the nationwide airline reservation systems. Currently, electronic funds transfer of banking, or consumer credit transactions are being done on a nationwide scale. This necessitates switching systems.

The primary function of a switching system is quite simple. It monitors a multitude of terminal or computer locations and receives the messages they transmit. Based upon data contained within the messages, the system transmits that information to its destination across appropriate transmission lines.

The causes of exposure that arise with such systems all relate to the reliability of transmissions. Transmission data may be lost or sent to the wrong destination. These are essentially the same things that can go wrong with the transmission of data in any application system. The differences between other application systems and switching systems are the volume, distances, and hardware.

DATA BASE SYSTEMS

A "data base system," as generally defined in computer terminology, is a system wherein large numbers of distinct data files are stored continuously on direct-access devices, all of which are accessible under a common "software controller." This software controller is known as a "data base management system," which may be provided by a computer manufacturer or an independent software vendor. Such systems customarily provide for cross-referencing so that, by simply knowing a common identification key, an application program may access any relevant record, no matter on which file it resides (see Figure 20-5).

DATA-BASE SYSTEMS

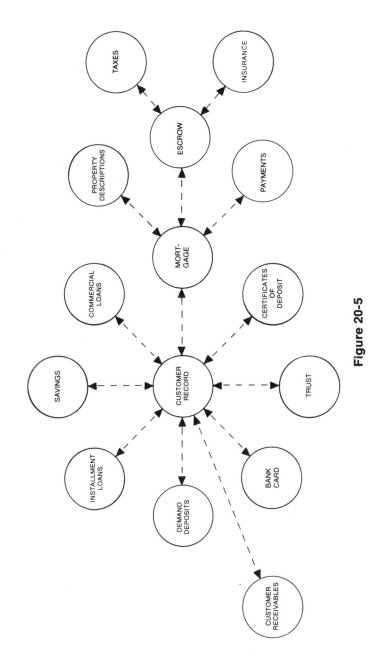

Figure 20-5

The file structures employed must be organized specifically to permit such access. This can be extremely complex. The two general methods that are employed are "networks" and "hierarchical" files. Although the type of file architecture may affect operating efficiency and accessibility of specific data segments, the architecture is not generally relevant to users nor auditors. If further information is needed regarding concepts of file architecture or the architectures used by specific data base management products, such information may be obtained from the data base product vendors or from recommended readings listed at the back of this book.

The new causes of exposure that arise under data base management systems include:

- Unlimited access
- Destruction of files
- Software failure
- Slow response

The increased concerns regarding unlimited access to file contents arise due to increased concentration of information assets. Without data base systems, an application program can only access information in specific files provided to it. The data base system effectively eliminates all "library controls" over files and allows unrestrained access to any file at any time.

The massive volumes of records actually associated with data base systems also complicate the development of adequate backup files for recovery purposes. A device failure or an application program may cause the destruction of machine-readable information just as readily as it could without the data base. Because the medium on which the data base is maintained does not readily permit a grandfather-father-son backup procedure, the volume of storage makes special backup operations much more costly. The situation could be likened to the effort required to copy every file in the entire library of a major information processing facility.

By utilizing data base management systems, the organization becomes dependent upon another layer of software in addition to the operating system. This software is extremely complex and may fail due to inherent discrepancies or new types of violations devised by users and programmers.

The introduction of a data base management system between the operating system and the application program also introduces another layer of computer "overhead," which consumes some of the processing capacity of the equipment. This can affect the productive capacity of the equipment. Relatively speaking, related records required by a specific application may reside in widely separate physical locations on the files. This will also reduce the processing speed due to the additional instructions required to locate the related records, extra movements of disc heads, and the storage requirements of the cross-referencing information. Therefore, the wholesale consolidation of business files may carry a substantial cost due to the reduction of processing speeds and the special devices and software required.

The causes of exposure in advanced systems are summarized in Figure 20-6.

NEW PREVENTIVE CONTROLS

All of the application control techniques that we have discussed previously are generally applicable to any of the advanced systems. However, in addition to these controls, we find several new controls:

ADVANCED SYSTEMS CAUSES OF EXPOSURE

Type of System	Causes of Exposure
Remote Batch	Loss of data
	Distortion of data
Remote Job Entry	Loss of data
	Distortion of data
	Unlimited access
	Computer abuse
Switching Systems	Loss of data
	Distortion of data
	Delay of data
	Misrouting of data
Real-Time Inquiry	Invasion of privacy
	Information not current
	Distortion of data
Real-Time Update	Unlimited access
	Hardware/software failure
	Unsupportable results
	Human data-entry errors
Real-Time Programming	Unlimited access
	Hardware/software failure
	Unsupportable results
	Human data-entry errors
	Computer abuse
	Destruction of programs
Data Bases	Unlimited access
	Destruction of files
	Software failure
	Slow response

Figure 20-6

Passwords

The principal control which is used to control the cause of exposure known as "unlimited access" is some form of a code normally termed a *"password."* Nothing effectively prevents passwords from being used in less sophisticated systems, but such systems seldom have the accessibility problems that require their use. Passwords may take on a multitude of forms. However, they may all be classified according to the following characteristics:

- Who you are
- Something you know
- Where you are
- Something you have

Passwords that ask "who you are" are the type that ask your name, job title, employee number, etc. Those that involve "something you know" may ask for some special cipher or for some peculiar information known only to you such as your mother-in-law's date of birth. Passwords that inquire "where you are" are those which can recognize the location of the device which you are using. Passwords that ask for "something you have" will usually call for the insertion of some identification card into a reader.

All of these methods can be evaded. You can always lie about your name. Secret ciphers don't always stay secret. Knowing only a location does not really identify the individual. And, finally, identification cards can fall into the hands of others.

Generally speaking, password controls are the most effective if you use some *combination* of the above approaches. Particularly, the combination should always include an identification of "who you are," not in general terms of job titles but what specific individual. This should be accompanied by either "something you know" or "something you have." The second item of information should be checked by the computer system against the individual's identification to verify that the person has identified himself truthfully. The passwords or cards should be unique to each individual and be changed periodically as a corrective control due to the possibility of their becoming known to unauthorized personnel. Finally, information on "where you are" may allow a final edit or corrective capability.

Password controls may be used at any level. They may be used to limit initial access to the system or to keep that individual from submitting unauthorized transactions. These controls may be extended to defining which files, records, or specific fields the individual may access with the transactions at his disposal.

Such password access controls should be found with real-time inquiry, update, or programming systems as well as data bases.

Physical Terminal Security

The terminal devices which are capable of accessing the on-line systems should be physically protected from unlimited access. Some terminals provide for a *lock and key* similar to that of an automobile ignition. The terminals may also be kept in rooms where *physical access is restricted.*

Authorizations

By their nature, on-line systems typically permit a large variety of users to access them. Mere limitation of access will usually still permit a large number of individuals access. To be effective, such access controls must be accompanied by an extensive set of *formalized authorization criteria.*

Individuals should be authorized to submit only those transactions that are compatible with their job functions and system training. Certain individuals may be allowed only inquiry capabilities, whereas others may be allowed to submit updating inputs and still others, error correction inputs. Where more than one application is online, users should be permitted to access only those applications and related files that are consistent with their job functions (see Figure 20-7).

Example — Given an on-line production control system, individual workers should only be allowed to input transactions reporting and updating the files for their own time on projects. The production foreman may be allowed to submit error correction inputs for this type of transaction. Clerks in the Personnel Department should be the only ones allowed to access the labor rates used to price the labor time inputs.

Protecting the physical security of an IPF can prove expensive. Likewise, huge amounts can be spent to control unauthorized electronic access. Regardless of the investment in security, an individual with sufficient resources, knowledge, and determination can always penetrate any preventive control. Therefore, top management *must* decide on what degree of risk they are willing to run and how much they are willing to spend for security.

Since no on-line application exists that can completely defy any penetration, a compensating control should always be provided to detect such penetrations. Application or system-level software should record access attempts, particularly those with invalid passwords. They should be recorded on a medium that is not accessible should the penetration be successful. Since unauthorized access cannot be completely prevented, the most important thing is to know when such an access had occurred.

NEW DETECTIVE CONTROLS

Line Protocol

Since most on-line transmissions are via conventional or special high-capacity telephone lines, certain common conventions must be

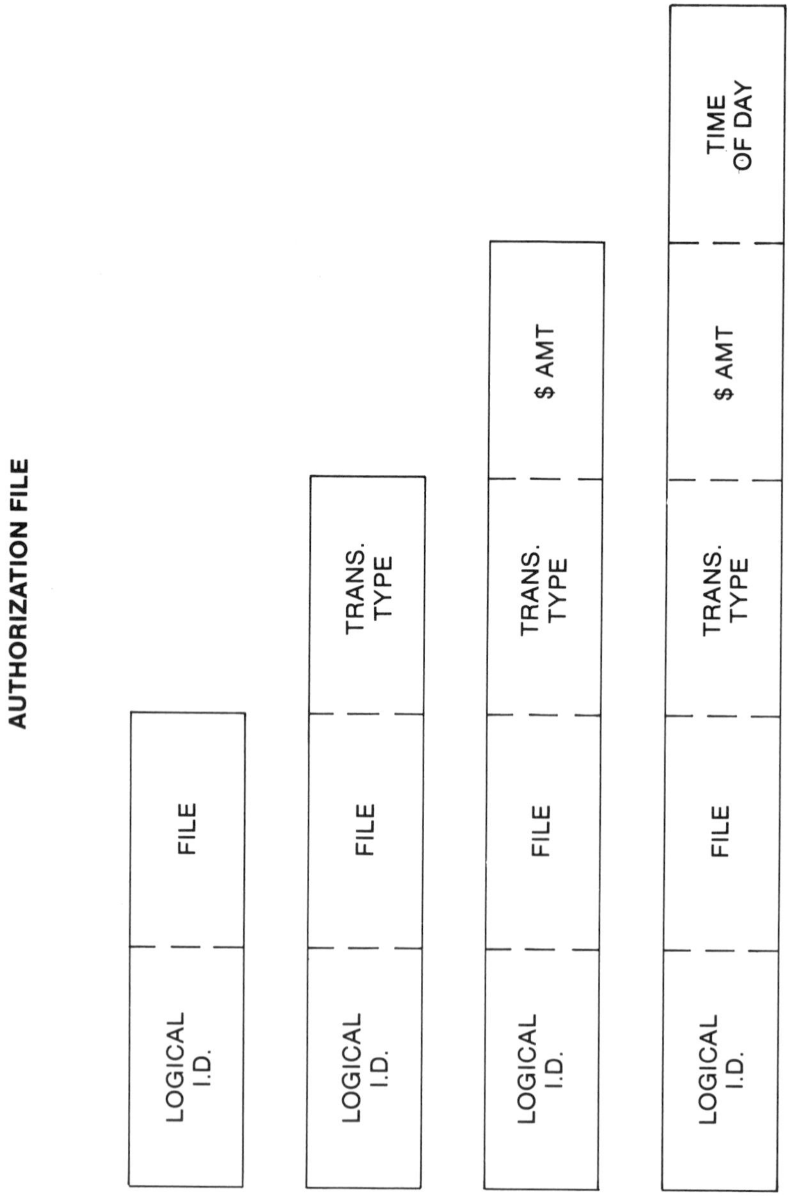

Figure 20-7

employed to handle the variety of transmissions from a multitude of user organizations. These *protocol conventions* are generally devised by the equipment manufacturers in cooperation with the telephone companies.

Transmissions will usually contain both administrative and transaction information. Much of the administrative information constitutes transaction controls. Some of these controls may include the following:

- A message header containing the terminal identification
- A sequence control number for the transmission or data item
- A message number
- Identification of the sending location
- Date and time
- An action code
- An end-of-message indicator

Up-Front Edits

Another control capability that becomes feasible with real-time systems is the direct use of *application edits* over the data being submitted by the individual actually initiating the transaction. While the nature of the edits does not change from the various forms discussed in chapter 7, the availability of real-time equipment does allow the movement of these edits from a processing step performed within the isolation of the information processing facility to a direct communication with the actual transaction initiator. This greatly simplifies the effort involved in error resolution and eliminates many of the distortions caused by unresolved and unprocessed input exceptions.

Access Logs

An *access log* is a transaction listing of attempted and successful accesses to the application system from terminals. It should consist of the administrative data describing terminal location, date and time, action codes, etc. The log of access data must then be analyzed, preferably by computer, to produce a periodic report showing the activity by location and data file as well as rejected attempts.

Authorized-User File

This detective control was discussed in conjunction with the preventive controls of passwords and authorizations.

Read Back

On-line systems allow a responsive *acknowledgement* to input data so that the initiating party can immediately verify the accuracy and completeness of the data he had submitted. This is normally a very valuable control in that he will usually detect distortions of data, many human data-entry errors, and many types of hardware or software failure. Preferably, the response should not be transmitted back until all related processing is complete. Immediate acknowledgement before processing actually takes place still permits exposure to undetected defects or failures immediately after the acknowledgement.

Redundancy Checks

Redundancy checks may be applied by the communications control units (a hardware component) upon data characters either "vertically" or "longitudinally." This control is quite similar to the "parity check" normally applied to data characters within the on-site computer equipment.

This control may be very effective in detecting distortions of data during transmission. However, if it is not provided by the hardware manufacturer, it may be rather difficult to implement in house.

Line Control Hardware

One of the hardware components generally found in an on-line transmission system is a *"line control unit."* This may be a separate hardware component; or, alternatively, the function may be performed by software resident within the main computer. The function of this component is to implement line protocol procedures, produce the access logs, perform the redundancy checks, and implement various optional electronic security edits.

Again, because this hardware or software function is customarily provided by a commercial manufacturer or vendor, each organization is somewhat dependent upon the specific features offered by the available vendors. Where such features are offered optionally, they should be employed. When important features are not available from the vendors, they may also be difficult to implement internally.

NEW CORRECTIVE CONTROLS

Rotation of Access

The preventive controls over access may tend to deteriorate with time. Passwords may become known, individuals may terminate employment with the organization while maintaining access capabilities, etc. To offset this deterioration, access controls should be periodically changed. The frequency of this change will depend upon the sensitivity of the applications and files.

Locks and keys should be changed periodically. Cipher passwords and identification cards should be changed frequently. Of course, the authorized-user file should be kept current.

Transaction Log

Primarily because of the difficulties which usually accompany recovery of data base files that were damaged or destroyed, an extensive and complete *log of transactions* should be maintained. This should include not only the application transactions but also the administrative and operator messages that accompanied the transmissions in processing (see Figure 20-8).

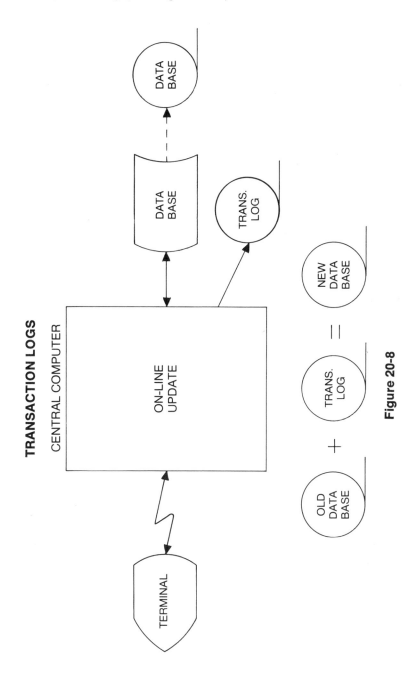

TRANSACTION LOGS

Figure 20-8

397

Some data base management systems provide this feature automatically, whereas in others it is either optional or must be developed by the using organization.

Whatever the effort required, the maintenance of a log of this type is essential. It is the primary source for recovery capabilities and is usually necessary for the implementation of many detection controls.

On-Line Instruction

This control is an advanced form of training in which the authorized-user file maintains a record not only of the transactions and activities individuals are authorized to perform but also as to whether they have been formally trained to perform these authorized functions on the application system. If an authorized user desires to perform some activity for which he has not yet received training, such *training* might be provided *on-line* in a conversational mode.

Recovery Journal

A *recovery journal* is similar to a transaction log except that it usually covers a relatively short span of time. It is specifically intended for swift recovery from minor hardware or software failures. It will be composed of administrative and transaction messages and will often be recorded on a high-speed, direct-access medium. With some of the more advanced data management systems, it may be accessed automatically by the recovery features of the system software.

Graceful Degradation

This term describes a number of individual controls that are desirable within on-line and data base systems. It means that, when a hardware or software operating failure occurs, the result is only to degrade performance and not completely disrupt it. The controls involve informing active terminal locations that a problem had occurred and providing direction as to how they may correct for any erroneous or incomplete processing that resulted. Automatic recovery, using a recovery journal, may be a feature of *graceful degradation.* Other control features may provide for automatic shutdown of the offending components and automatic transfer of functions to components that have continued to operate properly.

COSTS OF ADVANCED CONTROLS

The costs of controls in advanced systems are apt to take on substantially greater dimensions than was customary in batch systems. Terminals may need to be "intelligent" or have special identification attachments. Additional devices may be needed on the central computer to provide transaction trails and recovery capabilities. The application software may need to include special vendor options that carry a fee. Many of the advanced system controls carry substantial costs in addition to those required for "uncontrolled" operation of the system.

AUDIT TECHNICAL EXPERTISE

Because of the variety of additional causes of exposure and control techniques, the auditor of advanced systems must acquire a greater level of technical expertise than was necessary with batch systems if he is to effectively audit such systems. This is true, even if the auditor has the background of a professional data processor.

The environment of advanced systems is changing so rapidly that constant refresher courses will be necessary. This refresher training should be considered as "EDP technical training," not "advanced audit" training. As such, appropriate training may be acquired from a variety of commercial and vendor sources that are intended primarily for the technical development of EDP personnel. The audit methodology which was presented previously in this text is equally applicable to technically advanced systems.

Particularly, valuable use may be made of the control-evaluation-table approach. A control evaluation table for advanced systems in general is provided in Figure 20-9.

CHANGES IN AUDIT TECHNIQUES

Just as the existence of advanced systems brings about only a few new control techniques, all of which *could* be applied to batch systems, their existence also has a limited effect on the types of audit techniques which may be employed. All the techniques that were discussed in chapter 9 have some degree of applicability in advanced systems. To provide a recapitulation, a summary of techniques from chapter 9 is presented in Figure 20-10.

Integrated Test Facility

The integrated test facility (ITF) is a popular technique for the verification of on-line systems. It is somewhat easier to implement, at least for small volumes of test transactions, than with a batch processing system. This is because the auditor can submit his transactions directly through on-line terminals with little advance arrangement. Because of the immediate response normally provided, he can also revise his test data as he proceeds in reaction to computer responses that arouse his interest or concern. ITF's are also easier for an auditor to obtain in a real-time environment because systems development personnel often develop these capabilities for their own testing requirements.

ADVANCED SYSTEMS CONTROL EVALUATION TABLE

CAUSES OF EXPOSURE

Control	REMOTE BATCH Loss of Data	REMOTE BATCH Distortion of Data	REMOTE JOB ENTRY Loss of Data	REMOTE JOB ENTRY Distortion of Data	REMOTE JOB ENTRY Unlimited Access	REMOTE JOB ENTRY Computer Abuse	SWITCHING Loss of Data	SWITCHING Distortion of Data	SWITCHING Delay of Data	SWITCHING Misrouting of Data	R-T INQUIRY Invasion of Privacy	R-T INQUIRY Info Not Current	R-T INQUIRY Distortion of Data	R-T UPDATE Unlimited Access	R-T UPDATE Hardware/Software Failure	R-T UPDATE Unsupportable Results	R-T UPDATE Human Data Entry Errors	R-T PROG Unlimited Access	R-T PROG Hardware/Software Failure	R-T PROG Unsupportable Results	R-T PROG Human Data Entry Errors	R-T PROG Computer Abuse	R-T PROG Destruction of Programs	R-T PROG Unlimited Access	DATA BASES Destruction of Files	DATA BASES Software Failure	DATA BASES Slow Response
PREVENTION CONTROLS																											
Electronic security			2		2	2					2			2				2				2	2	2	2	2	
Passwords:																											
Cyphers	2	2	2	2	2	2	2	2			2			2				2				2	2	2	2		
I.D. Cards	2	2	2	2	2	2	2	2			2			2				2				2	2	2			
Device identification			1		1	1					1	2		1				1				1	1	1			
Physical scanners					3						3			3				3			3	2	2	3			
Physical terminal security			2	2	2	2	2	2			2			2				2			2	2	2	2			
Authorizations			2	2	2	2	2	2			2			2				2			2	2	2	2			
DETECTION CONTROLS																											
Line protocol	2	2	2	2			2	2		2			2		1		3		1		3	2		2	2	2	1
Up-front edits		2		2	2	2	2	2		2		2		2	2		1	2	2	3	2	2	2	2			1
Access logs			2	2	2	2	2	2		2			2	2				2					2	2	2		
Authorized user file			2	1	2	1																					
Read-back	3	3	3	3			2	2		2		2	2		2	2	2		2	2			3				
Redundancy checks (vertical or longitudinal)	2	2	2	2			2	2		2										3	1	2					
Line control hardware	2	2	2	2			2	2		2		2	2				2				2	2	2	2			
CORRECTIVE CONTROLS																											
Rotation of access controls			2		2	2	2	2		2		2	2		2			2			2	2	2	2	2	2	
Transaction log			2		2	2	2	2				2			2			2			2			2	2	2	
On-line instruction										2		1			2				2	3	1	3	2	1	3	3	1
Recovery journal	1	1									1				2	2	1		2	2	2	1	1	1	3	3	2
Graceful degradation				3					2						2				2								2
IMPACT OF CAUSES																											
	3	3	3	3		3	3	3		2	2	2	1	2	2		3	2	2	2	3	2	2	1	3	2	1
	1	2	1	2	2	1	1		2	1	2	2	2	1	2	1	1	1	2	3	2	2	3	1	2	2	2
	2	2	2	2	2	1	2	2		1	2	1	2	2	2	2	1	2	1	1	1	3	1	2	3	1	2
	1	1	1	1	1	1	1	1		1	1	1	2	1	1	1	2	1	1	1	2	2	1	1	1	1	1

PREVENTION CONTROLS
- Electronic security
- Passwords:
- Cyphers
- I.D. Cards
- Device identification
- Physical scanners
- Physical terminal security
- Authorizations

DETECTION CONTROLS
- Line protocol
- Up-front edits
- Access logs
- Authorized user file
- Read-back
- Redundancy checks (vertical or longitudinal)
- Line control hardware

CORRECTIVE CONTROLS
- Rotation of access controls
- Transaction log
- On-line instruction
- Recovery journal
- Graceful degradation

IMPACT OF CAUSES
3 — Very likely to occur
2 — Likely to occur
1 — May occur
Blank — Generally little effect

RELIANCE ON CONTROLS
3 — Reliably controls applicable cause
2 — Controls cause but should be accompanied by additional controls
1 — Useful but not especially effective
Blank — No significant contribution

EXPOSURES
- Erroneous record keeping
- Unacceptable accounting
- Business interruption
- Erroneous management decisions
- Fraud
- Statutory sanction
- Excessive costs
- Loss or destruction of assets
- Competitive disadvantage

Figure 20-9

SUMMARY OF APPLICATION AUDIT PURPOSES, TECHNIQUES, AND TOOLS

PURPOSE	TECHNIQUE	TOOLS
Gather information describing controls	Review program listing	
	Review logic flowchart	Flowcharting software
Verify processing	Audit around	
	Test data	Test data generator Audit software
	Integrated test facility	
	Parallel simulation	Tailored program Audit software
	S C A R F	
	Snapshot	
Verify results	Confirmation	Audit software Tailored program
	Comparison with file or physical	Audit software Tailored program
	Edit & reasonableness tests	Audit software Tailored program

Figure 20-10

The testing of real-time systems via the ITF technique may make it more difficult to submit high volumes of transactions. Since systems may be designed to respond only to human inputs from remote terminals, the auditor may not be able to submit large volumes of test transactions or make use of test data generators, which produce only machine-readable transactions.

In chapter 9, we noted several disadvantages of the ITF system or disadvantages which it shared with the test deck technique. Briefly, these disadvantages are as follows:

- The effects of the transactions must be removed from the company's records.
- A high cost is involved if program modifications are necessary to remove the effects.
- The technique provides some risk of permanently damaging the files.
- A thorough variety of exceptions may be difficult to identify.
- The volume of test data submitted may be limited.

Overall, the ITF technique retains the same serious disadvantages in real-time application that it has in conventional batch applications. It continues to present the same problems in developing unbiased transaction situations, in producing adequate volumes of inputs, and in independently producing the predicted results.

Parallel Simulation

The effective use of the parallel simulation audit technique with many advanced systems depends upon the existence of backup master files and a transaction log. Since both of these controls are usually considered to be absolutely essential for any real-time system, these requirements do not usually limit the effective use of parallel simulation in practical situations (see Figure 20-11).

No existing general purpose audit software language allows the submission and processing of inputs via an on-line device. Of course, if such a capability is required, various conventional programming languages may be used.

Actual submission of transactions in a real-time environment, however, is not really essential to the successful completion of parallel simulation, since the auditor is attempting to only simulate the *results* of transactions actually submitted. Therefore, he is free to develop his parallel system using any medium he desires. Therefore, working with transactions on a transaction log file is a highly desirable approach. The auditor can easily test this file, separately or in conjunction with machine-readable copies of related master files, using general purpose audit software.

Similarly, few general purpose audit software languages allow direct access to records stored under the control of many of the data

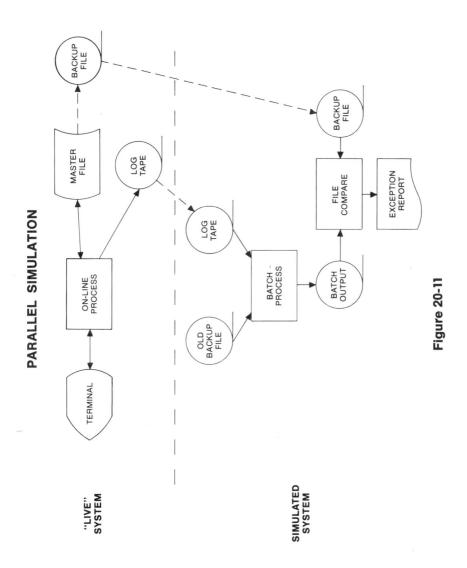

PARALLEL SIMULATION

"LIVE" SYSTEM

SIMULATED SYSTEM

BACKUP FILE

MASTER FILE

LOG TAPE

ON-LINE PROCESS

TERMINAL

BACKUP FILE

LOG TAPE

OLD BACKUP FILE

BATCH - PROCESS

BATCH OUTPUT

FILE COMPARE

EXCEPTION REPORT

Figure 20-11

base management systems whether in an on-line or off-line mode. In those cases where audit software can't directly access the data base records, three alternatives generally exist that will permit the auditor to use general purpose audit software.

First, some of the data base management systems have features which automatically write all or selected records onto magnetic tape for backup purposes in a format that can be read by most of the general purpose audit software systems. Second, the information processing facility personnel might have already prepared a "utility" (or can easily write one) to accomplish the same result because they frequently have need to extract special files from the data base.

Finally, some of the general purpose audit software systems, including STRATA, provide for user exit routines that can be written in an appropriate data base access language and processed in conjunction with the audit software system.

Therefore, the advanced system environment presents no particular problems to the successful use of the parallel simulation technique assisted by general purpose audit software.

The primary new concern in auditing some advanced systems is not what new audit techniques must be used but, rather, what new or increased causes of exposure arise. The relationships of controls, causes of exposure, and exposure are summarized in a Control Evaluation Table in Figure 20-9. A realistic appreciation of new causes of exposure and controls may require the auditor to obtain additional technical expertise. However, fundamental auditing concepts and approaches *do not change.*

21
Minicomputers

TYPES OF MINICOMPUTERS

The area of greatest recent innovation and technological change relating to computers is that of minicomputers. The price and performance revolution in this industry is evident in the vast consumer market for pocket calculators, which may be considered the smallest member of the minicomputer family.

Minicomputer is a general term describing machines that are smaller and cheaper than conventional, general-purpose computers. However, the term is used quite broadly and actually includes five major, distinct classifications.

- "True" minicomputers
- Microcomputers
- Programmable calculators
- Accounting computers
- Small business systems

"True" Minicomputers

Minicomputers are generally classified as having from 4,000 to 128,000 characters of main storage. A few models exist that are even larger. Accordingly, the term "mini" does not mean that they are necessarily smaller than general-purpose computers. The only thing that is generally smaller is the price, which may be as low as $1,000. The difference between a mini- and general-purpose computer of comparable core capacity is mainly in the variety and capacity of peripherals, application software, and vendor service.

In appearance, a minicomputer may physically resemble a component in a hi-fi system. Although powerful peripheral devices are available, the typical mini has relatively limited input/output capabilities. The combination of a miniprocessor with high-capacity I/O devices will often classify it as a "small business system." Examples of "true" minicomputers include:

- PDP-11
- PDP-8
- Nova 1200
- Hewlett-Packard 2000's

Microcomputers

These machines are smaller and slower than minicomputers. They may have from between 256 to 32,000 characters of main storage and operate at less than half the speed of minicomputers. The software, peripherals, and vendor service that are available are more limited than with minis.

A complete microprocessor "chip" may be no larger than a letter of type on this page. Because of this small size, the processor and memory modules are generally provided by the vendors on small cards. Although they generally disappear as an internal component of some "intelligent" device, the microprocessor may remain apparent as the processor for a calculator or even an accounting computer. Examples include:

- Itel 4000 Series
- Itel 8000 Series
- National IMP

Calculators

One of the most popular devices incorporating microprocessors is calculators. They vary from units displaying six digits and performing the basic arithmetic operations to desk models with 12 or more digits which can be programmed. The main distinction between a calculator and some smaller computers is the numeric and operations keyboard of the calculators. The keyboard allows the replacement of programming language commands with function keys. This greatly simplifies learning and use. Examples include:

- Wang 2000 Central Calculator
- Hewlett-Packard 9800 Series Desk-Top Calculator
- Hewlett-Packard HP-65 Pocket Calculator

Accounting Computers

A mini- or microprocessor may also be incorporated in a desk-sized unit specifically designed for bookkeeping applications. This typical "works-in-a-desk" device can process unit-record files by using some type of magnetic card under the constant direction of an operator who must select from certain programmed alternative decisions. While such machines are programmable, they are usually delivered with vendor-provided software specifically designed for selected general business applications. Examples include:

- Basic Four
- Nixdorf 820/110
- Litton ABS 1281
- Burroughs L-7000
- NCR-399

Small Business Systems

At the next higher level, a minicomputer may be incorporated into a small computer configuration that includes magnetic discs, an operating system for multiprogramming, high-level programming languages, and even multiple-user terminals. Such machines resemble the larger, general-purpose computers except that the storage capacity and speed will be limited. Examples include:

- IBM System 3
- IBM System/32
- Burroughs B-1700
- Honeywell 50/58

MINIPERIPHERALS

The proportionate cost of a mini- or microprocessor may well be less than 10% of a complete mini- or microcomputer. The total cost becomes even greater when input/output devices are added.

The most universal, and most limited, peripheral is the teletype (TTY). The next step up involves paper tape reader-punches and higher-speed character printers. If line printers, high-speed tape drives or mass storage devices are desired, their cost may eclipse the cost of the processor.

While all of the devices above are familiar to the large general-purpose computer environment, we also find a new line of peripherals in the mini market. These are magnetic tape cassettes and "floppy" discs.

The magnetic tape cassettes appear identical to the common audio-recording tape cassettes used in homes and cars. While obviously much more limited in capacity than the familiar 2,400-foot, one-half inch tape, cassettes still provide ease of storage and reuse.

"Floppy" discs somewhat resemble the sample phonograph recordings that are sometimes distributed in promotional mailings. They measure roughly eight inches in diameter and are flexible. Like their larger, high-speed cousins, they accept direct-access file structures.

These various peripherals can be accepted by most minicomputers and many microcomputers for either engineering or business applications.

APPLICATIONS

The applications for these devices vary quite widely and are expanding constantly. The mini- and microprocessors, by themselves, can be incorporated into many other machines. These include:

- Traffic controllers
- Elevator controllers
- Measuring systems
- Medical equipment
- Machine process controllers
- Communications peripherals for general-purpose computers
- Key entry data transcription devices
- Point-of-sale terminals
- Cash registers
- Watches

Minicomputers, micros, and calculators are often employed to solve scientific calculations. They may allow FORTRAN or BASIC on larger models, assembly languages on smaller models, and pre-programmed function keys on calculators.

Accounting computers and small business computers may be widely applied to common business applications such as payrolls, accounts receivable, general ledgers, etc.

ENVIRONMENT

The most common distinguishing characteristic of independent minicomputers is that they function under the direct control of the users. The centralized information processing facility is eliminated, and the machines return to the hands of the people who actually have the problems. The communications interfaces with programmers and operations are substantially eliminated.

Of course, an IBM System/3 may be operated in a central information processing facility, just like its larger cousins. In this case its designation as a "minicomputer" is irrelevant; and the exposures, causes, and controls over this system are substantially identical to that of a larger machine operating in a similar environment.

In the remainder of this chapter, we will address ourselves only to minicomputers that are operated directly by users of a business information system. The scope of this text does not include process control or scientific systems. Our primary concern is business information systems and, specifically, the concerns that accompany returning the machines to the users.

ADVANTAGES AND DISADVANTAGES

The decentralization of computer processing when minicomputers are employed improves the contact and involvement of the users. They are no longer tempted to abdicate their responsibility for the application systems. Also, they regain an intensive comprehension of the operating problems of the application. This must be considered beneficial.

While the users may actually operate the minicomputer systems, they seldom understand the internal functions. Programming of minicomputers is no easier than for larger machines. The technical services function that we found in the centralized information processing facility must still be provided — but is seldom available within the user's department. This remoteness of technical services can considerably complicate troubleshooting and application changes.

In many cases, the technical services function will be provided by the vendor. He may market his computer with associated application software for common business functions (payroll, general ledger, etc.) or for specific industries (construction companies, hospitals, etc.). The purchaser of such "turn-key" systems should expect, however, that some degree of tailoring to these programs will be necessary before he will be satisfied. The vendors are generally willing to make such alterations on a fee basis.

The primary risk of the new user acquiring such a system is that the vendor may not adequately understand his industry, company, or application. Furthermore, the costs of vendor support *may be* significant. The limited availability of technical support is certainly the greatest disadvantage to the utilization of minicomputers by businessmen.

Just as the rise of centralized IPF's promoted a concentration of information assets, these assets are rediversified when processing is done by individual users. While this may reduce the consequences of an individual accident or catastrophe, it may also limit the development of applications requiring an integrated data base.

Minicomputers do not need to be operated as separate, standalone units. Many models provide the capability to interconnect the minicomputer with other minicomputers or with a large central IPF. Such configurations are known as "distributive systems." Such systems provide a combination of available benefits by having a minicomputer under the control of the user, accompanied by the central power and technical support of a major information processing facility. Such configurations may allow the local user to perform his own processing on premises with specific data being transmitted to a central facility for consolidation.

MINICOMPUTER CAUSES OF EXPOSURES

As should be evident from the descriptions above, the unavailability of technical expertise is the primary cause of increased exposure. At the same time, the causes of exposures that normally exist in applications using centralized information processing facilities are somewhat reduced, particularly in the likelihood of processing wrong files or programs. The overall magnitude of virtually every exposure may also decrease.

The systems development causes of exposure are generally incréased due to the lack of available technical expertise. However, the extensive involvement of the user may compensate to some degree.

All of the IPF causes of exposure exist for minicomputers as well as for centralized facilities. However, the magnitude of the exposures is substantially less.

CONTROLS OVER MINICOMPUTER APPLICATIONS

The same controls are available for both minicomputer applications and larger systems. However, the importance and feasibility of many controls do change.

Training of user personnel becomes even more important than before. Depending upon the availability of technical support, this training may have to include programming skills and equipment maintenance. Indeed, the cost of training may be surprisingly large in relation to the cost of operating the total system.

The *application controls* provided by *vendor* software may be given to the user rather than specified by him. The user cannot demand many individually tailored application systems and controls if he is to receive the cost benefits of generalized application packages. Accordingly, the available controls may be excessive, appropriate, or deficient, depending upon the effort and understanding exhibited by the vendor. However, for the most part, because processing is under the immediate supervision of user personnel, there is less need to depend upon programmed application controls than with a remote, centralized facility.

MINICOMPUTER FACILITY CONTROLS

Because of the lesser values for equipment and files, fewer IPF controls will be economically justified. Few users will provide special fire detection or extinguishing equipment, and general security will be less.

One IPF control that must not deteriorate, however, is *backup*. The magnetic media utilized by minicomputers are fully as vulnerable as those used by larger machines. While the size of a reconstruction effort may be less, accidental erasures are still quite probable — with annoying, if not lengthy, interruptions.

AUDITING MINICOMPUTER APPLICATIONS

Application auditing of minicomputer systems is similar to that of larger systems. The auditor, as in other environments, must appre-

410

ciate the relative capabilities and constraints that accompany mini-computer systems. The auditor will find a greater likelihood that he can effectively audit around the computer because the record and transaction volumes will be moderate and the printed transaction trails will often be substantial.

On the other hand, if around-the-computer techniques are not effective, the auditor may find it very difficult to implement computer-assisted techniques. General purpose audit software for the IBM System/3 has only recently become available, and such software is generally not available for any other system. In lieu of this, tailored audit programs in RPG and COBOL may be necessary.

Minicomputers may be incorporated into business information systems in the form of accounting computers, small business systems, or "true" minis. Their effect is to return processing to the user; however, in doing so, they provide technical challenges that the user may not be qualified to resolve. While none of the application, IPF, systems development controls, or audit techniques change in nature, there may be substantial changes in costs, consequences, availability, and effectiveness. The most important consideration is to train the user to deal with the technical problems that accompany the many advantages.

22
Computer Abuse

ACTIVITIES WITHIN THE FUNCTION

The term "computer abuse" was defined by Donn Parker of Stanford Research Institute in a definitive study on the subject.[1] The definition that he provides is quite broad. It is: "All types of acts distinctly associated with computers and data communications in which victims involuntarily suffer or could have suffered losses, injuries or damage, or in which perpetrators received or could have received gain."

The roles that the computer plays in this definition are:

- Object
- Tool
- Symbol
- Environment

CAUSES OF EXPOSURE

As the *object,* computer services may be used without authorization; the contents of computer files or the computer may be stolen; or the computer may be vandalized by malicious or mischievous acts.

Example — The computer center of Sir George William's University in Montreal was destroyed by student vandals in 1969.

As a *tool* for abusive acts, a computer may be used to design or actually implement the act.

Example — The fraud at Equity Funding was largely consummated without the use of computers. However, the perpetrators

[1]Parker, Nycum, and Ora, *Computer Abuse,* Stanford Research Institute, Menlo Park, California, 1973.

412

found the computer useful in producing detailed support for one segment of the fraud: the fictitious insurance policy records.

The computer may be used as a *symbol* in an abusive act while actually not being involved in any other significant aspect.

Example — Some dating services have advertised the use of a computer to perform scientific partner matching when no computer is actually involved.

Finally, we find types of abusive acts which have existed previously but now also exist within the computerized *environment*. These include embezzlement, fraud, invasion of privacy, malicious alteration of records, and damages that are sustained by users and outsiders who are affected by defects in computerized activities which they are unable to correct.

In this chapter, we will analyze the various controls and auditing techniques which may be applied to the prevention, detection, or correction of abusive acts involving computers.

Since this book is directed to the business manager and auditor, we will address only those controls that are appropriate for internal use. Questions regarding controls that may be exercised externally to the business are not relevant to the purpose of this book.

PREVENTION CONTROLS

For an individual within a business to perpetrate an abusive act, he or she must have access to one or more of the following:

- A computer
- Data files
- Computer programs
- System knowledge
- A means of converting the above to personal gain

An effective control approach is to limit access to the above resources to the minimum number of individuals required to employ these resources for constructive business objectives. This approach embodies using a variety of preventive controls so as to include:

- Personnel screening
- Definition of duties
- Segregation of duties
- Dual access
- Physical-access security
- Electronic-access security

Another approach is to motivate individuals to abstain from computer abuse. Some of the preventive controls that may apply include:

- Professional ethics
- Licensing

- System design controls (see Section III)
- Fear of detection

Of the preventive controls, the most effective are those which prevent access. Such controls, however, do nothing to prevent acts of computer abuse by those individuals with authorization for access.

Strong motivation and substantial resources may enable the perpetrator to succeed in an act of computer abuse in spite of all reasonable preventive controls. Any security system can be breached. Proper control then becomes a matter of balancing the cost of controls with the risk. Various control approaches may emphasize prevention, detection, or corrective (e.g., insurance).

DETECTION CONTROLS

Some degree of *control* over computer abuse is exercised from sources *external* to the business. Particularly, external victims of computer abuse can be expected to file complaints with company officials when they become aware of damages.

The detection controls within *application* systems should be the most effective detection *controls* over acts of computer abuse affecting those application systems. Controls serving these functions will include many of the edits, control totals, balancing, etc., discussed in Section II.

Within on-line systems, controls should also provide *detection* of invalid attempts to *electronically access* the system. These should be reported and analyzed to determine the cause, source, and appropriate corrective action.

Detectors of physical presence will function to control acts of computer abuse involving actual presence in the computer facility.

Theft of certain types of information may also be detected through the use of *bait records,* whose use will alert management.

Theft of services may be detected by conducting a physical inventory of all files within the IPF and examining those with no apparent legitimate purpose.

Finally, use of effective *auditing* procedures, together with reasonable level of other controls, may disclose certain acts of computer abuse.

CORRECTION CONTROLS

In some cases, an act of computer abuse has no continuing effects on the business; and its correction is accomplished by simply halting the acts. This should be accomplished by *discharging* the responsible personnel and taking appropriate *legal actions. Outsiders* who are victimized by computer abuse may also exercise various types of *external* corrective actions. Such actions may be to the detriment of the business, because common law generally holds the employer responsible for any damages to outsiders arising from actions of his employees.

In addition to preventive actions to halt abuse, remedial actions may also be necessary. Corrective application controls will be the primary means to accomplish this. Accordingly, management should develop *contingency plans* to enable a rapid response to acts of computer abuse and minimize the resulting effects. Such contingency plans will frequently involve the availability of *backup and recovery* capabilities for files and equipment. Finally, *fidelity insurance* may reimburse losses.

A table depicting typical relationships between the exposures, causes, and controls is shown in Figure 22-1.

The new controls to be discussed in the area of computer abuse are:

- Professional ethics
- Licensing
- Fear of detection
- Bait records
- External controls
- Legal actions

Professional ethics are being promulgated by the Society of Certified Data Processors as well as other computer organizations. However, electronic data processing, as a distinct profession, is still in its infancy. *Licensing* of data processors involves statutory recognition which does not yet exist in any jurisdiction.

Fear of detection appears to be a highly powerful negative motivator with regard to many types of computer abuse. However, certain types of computer abuse are motivated by the opposite attitude: The perpetrators want to be detected so that their "ingenuity" will be recognized. However, such persons generally don't commit acts of computer abuse which result in serious damages. Accordingly, no business should avoid stimulating such fear of detection simply because it may bring the opposite result in some situations. In either event, fear of detection may have a significant impact on the magnitude of exposures.

Theft or misuse of name and address or other files may be readily detected by including *bait records* in the file. This concept is like the "bait money" commonly kept by bank tellers. If stolen, the "bait" is readily identified and traceable. Bait records are usually name-and-address records addressed to organization executives or security officials. Operating personnel are not aware of their existance or nature. If the name-and-address file is copied for unauthorized sale as an address list, the unauthorized material will be sent to the bait addresses. Some characteristic of the name will reveal the source to the knowledgeable recipient.

Similar "dummy" records or operations may be inserted in other types of files and programs to permit authentication of their source.

The potential effects of *external controls* and *legal actions* are difficult to estimate and virtually impossible for an auditor to verify. The effectiveness of controls exercised by individuals outside of the organization depends upon the degree of care and attention exercised by those individuals. This will vary widely from person to person. Although the auditor should be aware that this control exists and that it may be helpful, his inability to verify it should preclude any substantial reliance on this control.

Legal actions available to business management and outsiders vary widely according to the location. Some states have statutes that effectively include many acts of computer abuse within the criminal code. However, in many other locations, the statutes are still stated in terms that exclude the computer environment. Accordingly, the availability of effective legal actions will vary widely.

AUDIT TECHNIQUES

Many conventional auditing techniques are highly effective in verification of the controls needed to prevent, detect, or correct computer abuse. The following controls and related verification techniques were discussed in previous chapters. For purposes of cross-referencing, these controls and the location of previous discussions are listed below:

Control	Discussion Reference
■ Personnel screening	Application, systems development, and information processing facility (IPF)
■ Definition of duties	Same as above
■ Segregation of duties	Applications and IPF
■ Dual access	Applications
■ Systems design controls	Systems development
■ Physical-access security	IPF
■ Electronic-access security	Advanced systems
■ Application controls	Applications
■ Physical detection	IPF
■ Auditing	Applications, systems development, and IPF
■ Contingency plans	IPF
■ Backup and recovery	IPF
■ Discharge personnel	IPF and systems development
■ Fidelity insurance	IPF

APPLICATION AUDITING FOR COMPUTER ABUSE

The acts of computer abuse which represent the greatest potential exposures are embezzlement and fraud. Fraud involves misappropriation of assets through deceit. Embezzlement is theft or fraudulent misappropriation by a person authorized access. Such acts may occur on a sustained basis and may be difficult to detect. An ingenious programmer does not need to have physical access to the computer or files in order to commit theft or misappropriation.

The common practice of limiting access of programmers to the computer and data files is a useful control but, by itself, provides only a modest obstacle to a determined programmer. Barring unusually strong segregation of program coding and work assignments, many programmers have sufficient access to programs and knowledge of system functions so that, if unsupervised, they can modify programs to obtain access to the actual assets. This can often be done through collusion with an outsider, even when internal segregation of duties is very strong.

The manner in which application fraud and embezzlement may be implemented includes the following major categories:

- Unauthorized transactions
- Direct alteration of existing transactions or master files
- Internally programmed transactions
- Bypass of programmed controls

The first two types of situations, *initiation of "valid" but unauthorized* transactions and *altering* of transactions and master records, are problems that have existed long before the use of computers. Computers have, however, concentrated or centralized the location of such transactions and records and have transferred the transaction trail from media that can be read by people to that which can only be read by machines. This creates some new problems, but it does not create entirely new areas of concern.

The second two sources, the *internally programmed transaction* and the *programmed bypass of controls,* are new areas of concern arising from the computer environment. Before computers, processing was performed by people whose duties could be segregated to avoid unauthorized processing without detection or conspiracy. Now that processing is performed by computers and the previous segregation of duties has been substantially eliminated, much of the processing is under the control of the people who design the computer programs or who have access to them. They don't need direct access to the transactions or the master files nor the cooperation of the people running the computer. All they need is access to the programs. Since programmed controls may be selectively avoided, prevention and detection of this situation provides a significant new challenge.

While *application programmers* have opportunities to commit fraud or embezzlement within the individual applications to which they have or gain access, the opportunities available to *systems programmers* extend to all applications and files. Application controls, programs, and files are also more readily subjected to direct testing by users, systems development personnel, and auditors. However, these programs operate under the control of system software. Since system programmers have both knowledge of and access to such software, they can obtain unrestricted access to anything else they wish.

Strong *supervision* must be the primary control over systems programmers. Unfortunately, there may be no one else in the organization with the technical proficiency necessary to make even close supervision effective.

Alternative compensating controls (which may be objectionable) could include periodic *background investigations* or private *surveillance.* Another alternative is simply to rely on trust (which is no control) and carry substantial employee *fidelity insurance.*

The techniques available for audit detection of programmed embezzlement and fraud include the following:

Results

- Direct confirmations with outsiders
- Elaborate tests of reasonableness and results
- Comparison with files maintained *independently*

Processing

- Parallel simulation

The other techniques for verification of processing that we discussed — around the computer, test data, integrated test facility, SCARF, and tagging — may be effective in detecting many innocent errors; but they are either easily evaded or are, inherently, unlikely to detect programmed fraud or embezzlement.

Since auditing around the computer depends upon transaction trails produced by that computer, a programmer could readily disguise that transaction trail. Test data and transactions submitted to integrated test facilities may detect programmed fraud or embezzlement acting upon many of the records in the files, but they would probably miss anything involving a few selected records. The removal of assets through fraud or embezzlement will often be implemented through a single account to which the perpetrators have obtained access. There is little likelihood of a test deck or integrated test facility addressing this one account and detecting the fraud.

Test data and ITF's can also be evaded by causing them to be processed against a "clean" program. The effort required to obtain assurance that the program being tested is the same as the program in use may be impractical.

SCARF and tagging may detect fraudulently submitted or altered input transactions. They are very unlikely to detect programmed frauds or evasions since the SCARF or tagging program routines will usually be accessible to anyone in a position to alter application or system programming. They are also oriented toward input causes of exposure and not usually directed at internally initiated transactions.

Various types of verification of results techniques are effective in detecting many types of fraud and embezzlement. However, they, too, may be evaded with ease under certain circumstances.

Example — A common target for embezzlement of bank deposits are dormant accounts. Confirmation of such accounts is frequently ineffective for reasons relating to the dormancy — and the address available for confirmation might have been altered.

The only application auditing technique that seems to be highly reliable for detection of programmed fraud or embezzlement is parallel simulation. If this technique is implemented, using the complete set of master records and a comprehensive selection of transactions, the parallel simulation can detect unauthorized effects on any individual account. If the simulation is conducted, using an *independent* operating system, the technique should also detect those embezzlements and frauds that are implemented through the operating system.

Dependable detection of programmed fraud or embezzlement depends upon some additional conditions. However, these conditions are under the control of the auditor, not the embezzler.

Auditing for detection of computer abuse can involve extreme effort. Here, as in auditing for any other types of exposures, some realistic recognition of cost and benefits should be observed. In many industries, the cost to audit for many types of computer abuse simply exceeds the cost of probable consequences. In other industries, such as banking, material exposures may arise through computer abuse and should be a serious concern.

23
Operational Auditing

Operational auditing differs from other forms of compliance auditing only in its objectives. The *exposures* to which operational auditing is directed are primarily those which deal with *excessive costs, deficient revenues, competitive disadvantage,* and *erroneous management decisions.* Operational auditing emphasizes any or all of the exposures that do not directly affect the fairness of financial reporting.

Several different types of auditing fall under the general heading of "auditing." They really blend into each other somewhat as illustrated in Figure 23-1. Definitions may be obtained from the following sources:

- **Substantive auditing** — *Statement of Auditing Standards #1,* American Institute of Certified Public Accountants
- **Compliance auditing** — *Statement of Auditing Standards #1,* American Institute of Certified Public Accountants
- **Operational auditing** — *An Evaluation of Selected Current Internal Auditing Terms,* The Institute of Internal Auditors
- **Management auditing** — *An Evaluation of Selected Current Internal Auditing Terms,* The Institute of Internal Auditors

The *methodology* for operational audits is no different from that of audits of financial policies, procedures, and compliance. Since only the *objectives differ,* the auditor conducting an operational audit will concentrate on identifying and verifying those controls which tend to reduce the exposures listed above. Many of these controls are the same controls that effect exposures of a financial reporting nature.

The only reason for identifying an operational audit as a separate audit is because it emphasizes those areas of concern that are not normally covered in depth by a certified public accountant in

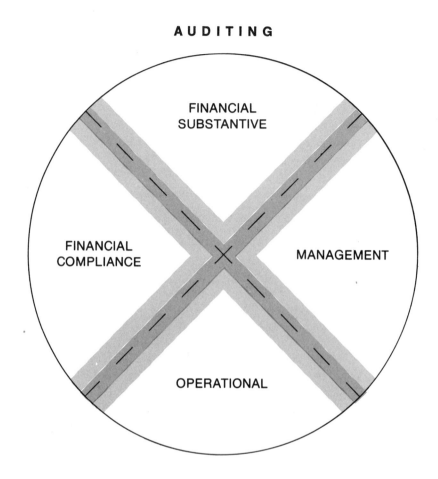

Figure 23-1

rendering an opinion on financial statements. Operational audits may be provided, however, by either the audit or the management advisory services arm of a CPA firm upon request.

From a viewpoint of an internal auditor, there should really be no bias toward either an operational audit or a financial audit. The internal auditor should provide equal emphasis to all types and causes of exposures. His comprehensive examination should naturally include appropriate operational concerns. To the extent that external auditors perform tests verifying financial controls, the internal auditor may elect to exclude the same procedures from his own testing because they would be redundant.

Even though operational aspects are not a primary concern of the external auditor, the certified public accountant should nonetheless take note of operational exposures which become apparent during the normal course of his examination of the financial statements. Though he may not be engaged for such purposes, many valuable comments and recommendations may be provided with little or no additional effort by simply recognizing the operational consequences of strengths or weaknesses in controls that are tested during the normal course of a financial audit.

CHALLENGING POLICIES AS WELL AS COMPLIANCE

Operational auditing should go beyond the evaluation and tests of compliance with controls, which is the primary topic of this book. The high-level policies prescribed to achieve organizational goals should also be challenged as to effectiveness. Even in a "for-profit" organization, profits are generally not the only goal. Obviously, profits are specifically omitted from the goals of nonprofit organizations and governments. Nonetheless, such organizations are still concerned with efficiency as well as the primary goals of their existence.

As related to EDP activities, the primary areas where policies should exist and be challenged are:

- Long- and short-range planning of applications, equipment, communications, and software. These policies should assure that user needs are properly planned and provided for by the data processing organization.
- Methods and standards for developing and maintaining systems. These policies should assure that changes are made in a predictable and effective manner.
- Effectiveness and efficiency of operations. These policies should insure that the processing of data is reliable, accurate, and economical.

There is no point in criticizing or praising compliance with controls that are really not appropriate to the organization's goals. The effective auditor must maintain a broad perspective, even while concentrating on detailed controls, and evaluate the entire function under examination not merely for compliance but also for effectiveness.

EFFECT OF EDP ON OPERATIONAL AUDITING

Even though the auditor may recognize that operational exposures are significant concerns in his examination, his practical capacity to evaluate these exposures may be limited by the technical nature of some of the causes and controls. The majority of auditors may be expected to be experienced only in financial auditing. This by itself is sufficiently demanding. He cannot normally be expected to also maintain the degree of technical proficiency that is expected of the full-time technical EDP staffs.

Many questions relating to computer operating efficiency are specially technical because their *solutions* may permit an immense variety of potential alternatives. The evaluation of these alternatives may require the services of a person who has an intimate knowledge of computer hardware and system software. However, the business observation that unsatisfactory conditions exist which are not being effectively acted upon does *not* require such a level of technical EDP knowledge.

AUDIT VERSUS DO

To be effective, the auditor does not need to have the same magnitude of technical proficiency as is required to actually develop studies of cost versus benefits or to implement operating changes. Rather, his job is to determine that the staffs of user and technical departments exercise appropriate controls with reasonable proficiency.

Even when an auditor of computerized systems has a background as a professional EDP technician, he can seldom maintain his proficiency at the same level as persons involved full time in the technological aspects of computer processing because of other demands on his time. The auditor must, to some degree, be a generalist. Even though he may start with a technical background, his concerns must encompass all aspects of business that concern management. Since the technical aspects of computer control and efficiency are only one segment of these broad concerns, the general auditor cannot possibly maintain, in the long run, a high degree of technical EDP proficiency.

For these reasons, we will distinguish between business logic and technical controls during the following discussion.

OPERATIONAL CONSIDERATIONS IN APPLICATIONS

Business Logic Aspects

The most important contribution an auditor can make in evaluating productivity of a computerized application is to challenge the value of the information being produced. This value may be viewed as a function of the timeliness and appropriateness of the output information provided to various users and to top management.

Many application systems have been developed without adequate participation by users. As a result, systems development and

424

EDP personnel often exhibit a lamentable lack of comprehension of user activities. They may produce great volumes of useless information while going to great efforts to make that production efficient. At the same time, users may simply accept the useless information without comment and without concern for its cost. The net result may be excessive costs, available information not utilized in business decisions, and decisions that are inferior to those of competitors.

The auditor with a more comprehensive business view of the user's objectives and the entire application process, may help reduce costs by simply identifying application reports that are of little or no use. He may also note situations where exception reports could well serve in lieu of full-detail reports or where reports could be produced on a "request-only" rather than on a regular basis. Finally, he may recognize unexploited opportunities for effective use of available data.

DETAILED INFORMATION GATHERING

The steps involved in the detailed information-gathering phase of an application controls examination provide particular opportunities for the evaluation of efficiency. Analysis of controls and activities subject to controls using an application control matrix provides an effective opportunity for identification of redundant controls and activities.

By focusing on the "activities subject to control" across the top of the matrix, rather than the controls along the side, an application system can be quickly stripped down to its "productive" activities.

By removing the controls, the auditor can consider the contribution of each remaining activity. This review often highlights the existence of unnecessary or redundant activities as well as unneeded controls.

Example — Through analysis of an application control matrix, auditors identified "paper shuffling" that essentially duplicated computerized activities. Elimination of this duplication saved $45,000 per year.

This same analysis may also reveal manual procedures which could be better performed by the computer or, conversely, automated procedures that would really be cheaper if done manually.

Example — Internal trailer labels may incorporate control totals of the record in a particular file. These totals, in turn, can be processed by application programs to perform automatic run-to-run balancing with negligible operating cost.

Technical Efficiency Aspects

There are two primary areas of *application efficiency* which deal primarily with technical questions. These are:

425

- Use of more appropriate *equipment*
- Use of a more appropriate *programming language*

Both may involve significant *costs to change.*

EQUIPMENT

Utilization of certain types of peripheral equipment may have a direct bearing on the efficiency which can be realized in the processing of specific applications.

Example — If an application uses a master file stored on magnetic tape which is updated frequently with only a small percentage of master records being changed, it may be desirable to change that file to direct-access devices which will make possible more efficient file processing for such applications.

Most considerations regarding equipment efficiency fall under the classification of the IPF, because many applications will generally be affected similarly.

PROGRAMMING LANGUAGES

The programming language used in an application has a direct bearing on the efficiency of processing and in the efficiency of program preparation as well as program maintainability. While these decisions are made during the systems development process — and it may be quite expensive to change language once the application is implemented — desirable changes may still be a relevant subject for an operational audit.

The basic choice in the programming of business applications lies between the choice of *assembly* and various *compiler* languages. The selection made relates largely to the trade-offs between the more efficient computer processing possible with assembly-level languages and the greater productivity for program coding inherent in the use of the higher-level compilers.

Example — If a typical payroll application were written in assembly-level coding, processing on the computer may be made quite efficient. However, since payrolls are subject to frequent modification due to changes initiated by government or labor organizations, the efficiencies in maintenance provided by higher-level languages may be more important than the efficient use of the machinery.

Opportunities for efficiency improvement should also be suspected when a time-consuming application is programmed in a language that is obsolete. These programming languages were developed for earlier models of computers. Their continued use generally adds some cost, since such languages require either special vendor software for simulation of the old machine or special hardware features which emulate older generations of computers. Users of out-dated programming languages pay two separate penalties: vendor charges for the simulation software or emulation equipment and loss of processing efficiency usually afforded by use of current programming languages.

Efficiency questions may be raised concerning the selection of a language appropriate to a particular application. For example, the FORTRAN language is efficient in both programming and processing of applications involving higher-level mathematics. However, the handling of business files in FORTRAN may be awkward. On the other hand, COBOL handles business files quite effectively but is not as effective in the processing of sophisticated mathematical equations. While any informed auditor may question language selection, effective evaluation will require significant technical knowledge.

COSTS OF CHANGING

The principal obstacle in the evaluation and implementation of recommendations with regard to application efficiency lies in the determination of the benefits and the magnitude of costs necessary to implement changes. Significant improvements in application processing costs often require proportionately significant programming and testing costs. Many systems development organizations have backlogs amounting to years of work. To justify the alteration of a particular application, the savings must be particularly dramatic or the required changes unusually simple. The preferable time for recommendations regarding application processing efficiency is at the time of their development. After their implementation, it is frequently too late.

OPERATIONAL CONSIDERATIONS IN SYSTEMS DEVELOPMENT

Application Efficiency

As noted above, the preferable time for consideration of appropriate peripheral devices, programming languages, etc., is at the time they are originally being selected. This is during the user and technical specifications phases of the development process.

The user and technical specifications phases should be preceded by extensive information gathering as to the existing and forecasted application requirements. Some of the relevant information would include:

- Master file volume
- Volume of various transaction types
- Proportion of master records affected during a processing cycle
- Growth rates of the above
- Importance of response times

- Application impact on IPF capacity
- Content of reports
- Content of master records

We should emphasize that it may not be the auditor's responsibilty to second-guess the efficiency considerations made by individuals having greater technical proficiency than he. *The auditor's principal concern should be that efficiency considerations are not ignored due to seemingly more urgent pressures to meet development budgets or delivery schedules.*

Systems Development Productivity

Compliance with standards for systems development projects has as much impact on the efficiency of the application development effort as on the quality and reliability of its product. Therefore, an operational audit of the systems development function is substantially completed when the auditor determines that project management standards exist and are in fact being used. Chapter 12 discusses the project controls which should be exercised over systems development to assure this efficiency. Beyond this, the auditor's main contribution to the efficiency goals of the organization may lie in his investigation of the use of programming productivity aids.

Programming Productivity

Just as the computer is used to improve the productivity of business applications, it may also be applied to the process of systems development. While the computer is of little direct use in the development of concepts for new applications, it can be of great use in the more routine phases involving program coding, documentation, and testing. The following types of software products can be used to permit the computer to increase program productivity:
- Source-language generators
- Decision-table generators
- Data-management systems
- Language optimizers
- Test-data generators
- Flowchart generators

SOURCE-LANGUAGE GENERATORS

Source-language generators are similar to some general purpose audit software systems. They permit the preparation of powerful source-language statements through shorthand notations or fill-in-the-blank specification sheets. COBOL is the language normally generated by such programming aids. The difference between these systems and general purpose audit software systems which also generate COBOL lies principally in the greater degree of technical knowledge required of the user of source-language generators.

428

DECISION-TABLE GENERATORS

Decision-table generators are closely related to source-language generators. These programming aids produce source-language statements from decision tables. Normally, such aids do not produce entire programs. Rather, they are limited to the program subroutines represented by the decision tables. Such generators can be extremely powerful in making possible an immediate conversion of decision tables — prepared as a part of the technical specifications phase of a systems project — directly into error-free source coding.

DATA-MANAGEMENT SYSTEMS

Data-management systems provide the next step upward from source-language generators. In addition to providing rapid preparation of program-generated instructions, they also provide file designs and file maintenance logic modules that often fulfill the major portion of an organization's file-management requirements. Such aids apply certain file-design constraints as a part of their construction. If these constraints are acceptable to the user, such software can provide substantial benefits in development effort.

LANGUAGE OPTIMIZERS

Language optimizers accept either source-level or object-level program instructions and alter them to maximize computer processing speed. They do this by systematically eliminating program instructions which are generally needed for a particular process but which are redundant in the particular situation or become superfluous when applied in a particular set of logic.

Example — Arithmetic operations normally require the computer to bring the relevant data from core storage to a register in the arithmetic unit and then return the results to a location in core storage. However, if several arithmetic operations are being performed on the same item of data, the transfers back and forth from core storage become unnecessary and may be deleted.

Some standard compilers include optimizers as optional features. Optimizers also exist as separate software products to supplement existing compilers.

TEST-DATA GENERATORS

The thoroughness of testing during the programming or system-test phases may be enhanced substantially by the use of automated techniques for the preparation of test data. Test-data generators accept parameter cards indicating the format and requirements of test data to be produced. Under the control of test-data generator software, the computer may be used to generate large volumes of test records and transactions.

FLOWCHART GENERATORS

Manual preparation of application flowchart documentation at the detailed-logic level is a very time-consuming task. Once developed, substantial additional effort may be required to revise the flowcharts due to various changes and corrections to the application programs.

Numerous commercial packages are available which will accept source-language statements and produce reasonably legible detailed-logic flowcharts on either a plotter or a standard printer. Flowcharting software often provides supplementary analytical reports regarding edits of the source statements, cross-reference listings of data-name usage, or flowchart compressions to highlight decision logic.

A variety of programming and documentation aids exist, and their widespread acceptance and marketability provide strong empirical evidence of their value. The auditor should be sure that the systems development activity at least considers the use of such software aids to increase productivity.

OPERATIONAL CONCERNS WITHIN EDP OPERATIONS

An information processing facility (IPF) — possibly more than any unit in a modern company — offers extensive opportunities for both improving efficiency and eliminating unnecessary costs. While many factors involving efficiency of EDP operations are highly technical in nature, the trained auditor's experience and judgment are still highly relevant in the evaluation of many fundamental management procedures within the IPF. Just as an auditor does not need to be a professional industrial engineer to evaluate many aspects of the efficiency of a manufacturing plant, neither does he need to be a computer science engineer to evaluate similar aspects of an IPF.

Business Aspects of IPF Efficiency

The general productivity of an IPF can be evaluated by using many of the general management concepts and tools familiar to all businessmen. Some of the subjects that should be reviewed include:

- Organization and segregation of duties
- Supervision and management reporting
- Equipment and software reliability
- Equipment-utilization statistics
- Operator procedures

430

ORGANIZATION AND SEGREGATION OF DUTIES

In examining an IPF's organization chart and job descriptions, the auditor may note conditions which may affect efficiency as well as control. Such important management considerations as span of control, conflict of duties, and communication responsibilities may substantially affect the efficient utilization of a company's EDP resources. In general, specialized duties within an IPF should be assigned to individuals as much to promote quality and productivity through specialization as to avoid conflicts that relate to safeguarding of assets.

GENERAL MANAGEMENT AND SUPERVISION

The exercise of responsibility supervisory duties depends directly upon regular reporting of operating statistics. These statistics should include the time or cost of various applications, reruns, program testing, etc.

Probably the most important of the management reports within an IPF is the daily computer operations schedule. Other reports on processing results, while not as critical as the daily operations schedule, represent the only feasible way in which IPF management can evaluate its own operations realistically.

Both short- and long-range forward planning should be in evidence.

EQUIPMENT AND SOFTWARE RELIABILITY AND UTILIZATION

Reliability of equipment and files has considerably more impact on efficiency than on financial exposures. Unreliable equipment or files may lead to a loss of data or to the bypassing of other controls with processing shortcuts. The problems of reliability are more substantial in the area of productivity. Such operating problems as machine halts and systems downtime result in the loss of EDP services for the duration of the interruption. Frequently, they also involve further time losses for reprocessing of interrupted jobs.

Measurement of effective hardware and software utilization is a particularly difficult technical subject. Since there are extensive interrelationships between the various hardware devices, manufacturer-provided software, application file designs, and the various individual application software programs, effective evaluation requires intimate knowledge of all these elements.

Some of the techniques that are available to evaluate equipment utilization include:

- Simulation software
- Software monitors
- Hardware monitors

Software simulators seek to quantify the interrelationships between all of the various factors that have a significant impact on the amount of work throughput that a particular computer configuration can perform. Unfortunately, the "work" performed by a computer does not have a commonly accepted definition. Since the relationships affecting "work" are highly complex, the only feasible way to address this problem is by developing mathematical models which can be processed on computers. Such models, which can be tailored to various IPF's, are available commercially.

Software monitors are programs that operate on large model computers concurrently with the various application programs and supporting software. They interrogate various elements of the equipment to determine the types of things that are being processed. This information is then analyzed to present a representative view of the extent and nature of the utilization of the various components of the computer.

Hardware monitors operate similarly to software monitors except that they are independent of the computer configuration itself. They are minicomputers that can be interconnected with the "main" computer to measure and record the level and nature of utilization of the many components of the computer configuration.

Generally, the approach in all techniques of evaluation is to identify and remove whatever element in the combined system of hardware and software is presenting a bottleneck. The upgraded system is then reexamined for further bottlenecks.

Evaluation of computer utilization is much more of an art than a science. While such tools are used to acquire great volumes of operating information, and even perform some of the analysis, effective evaluation and action plans require a superior level of technical expertise.

Although some EDP audit specialists may acquire this level of expertise, it is considerably beyond the capacity of most auditors — and a great many EDP professionals. However, all auditors of computerized systems should be aware of the need and availability of such information. They should be concerned about the quality of cost control if the IPF management exhibits no knowledge of such techniques and is accustomed to making significant investment decisions without appropriate information.

OPERATOR PROCEDURES

In the course of his observations of computer-operator activities, the auditor may be able to note efficiency-related situations. Again, this will depend upon the technical proficiency of the auditor. The auditor who is accustomed to the operating environment through his own use of computer audit software, should normally be well qualified to detect significant operator inefficiencies.

The methods of performing operational audits follow the seven standard steps of the compliance methodology. The only thing that differs is in the first step: the determination of objectives. If those objectives are oriented primarily toward the exposures of excessive costs, deficient revenues, competitive disadvantage, or erroneous management decision, then the subsequent auditing procedures are customarily considered to be an operational audit.

Many operational auditing considerations that involve computers demand an exceptionally high degree of technical expertise. However, at the same time, there are also many areas of operational evaluation which involve basic business logic that is essentially similar to that used in many other functions. The external certified public accountant does not normally perform operational auditing as a principle objective of his engagement. Nonetheless, he should remain alert to the operational significance of the various controls and other situations that he may identify and evaluate during the course of his financially oriented examination.

While the internal auditor may wish to distinguish his activities from those of the external auditor by classifying them as "operational auditing," he should be equally concerned with all sources of exposures. If the extent of his examination of nonoperational aspects is limited, it should be limited only to the extent that such controls have already been verified by external auditors.

Section VI
AUDIT MANAGEMENT

24
Managing EDP Audits

This final chapter will explore the affect of EDP systems on the many aspects of managing audit personnel in a computer environment. The presence of computers *does* change the manner in which an audit manager must direct his staff. While the subjects of his concern do not differ, the specific decisions that he makes within each subject may often differ.

The existence of a system, policies, and procedures are made more formal with the involvement of computers. Whereas the manual system might just have been "the way we do things around here," a major element of the procedures in a computer system is the invisible, but tangible, set of program instructions to the machine. In addition, the nature of the detail procedures may be substantially different than that which is found suitable in the manual systems. Accordingly, the involvement of computers *does* change the manner in which audits are conducted.

The subjects of audit management concern covered in this chapter are:

- Recruiting
- Staffing
- Training
- Timing
- Budget and scheduling
- Supervising and reviewing
- Reporting
- Cost factors
- Service bureaus
- Audit standards
- Independence
- Scope

436

- Certified public accountants' scope
- Internal auditors' scope
- Reliance by CPA's on internal auditors
- Cycling of compliance audits
- Repeat examinations

RECRUITING

Every audit manager is constantly faced with an apparent dilemma: Should I recruit auditors or EDP technicians to perform my EDP audits? Based upon our experience and observations, it probably doesn't make much difference. Whether EDP audits are performed by auditors having a general business background or by former EDP technicians, the effective EDP auditor must really have a combination of both talents. Therefore, inexperienced personnel from either background will not be particularly effective immediately in EDP auditing without at least moderate skill in the other discipline.

Few experienced EDP auditors are yet available in the general job market. Neither do most university curricula provide a true major course of study in auditing, much less in EDP auditing. As a result, most organizations find that they must develop their EDP auditors internally.

In their initial efforts, most organizations select a limited number of individuals to become "EDP audit specialists." These will often be experienced EDP personnel or audit personnel having a particular aptitude for EDP systems. In the course of development of an effective EDP audit function, there is commonly a temptation to create what effectively constitutes a separate audit department. This may be a serious, long-term mistake.

EDP auditing today is only the auditing of tomorrow. What an organization first sees as an EDP audit specialist is what all of its audit staff should look like in a few years. Even now, many organizations have virtually no information systems that do not involve computers. This trend is accelerating so that more and more applications will incorporate computer processing within smaller and smaller organizations. The day will soon come when any application system worthy of concern by any auditor will involve a computer in some aspect. Accordingly, exclusion of the existing audit staff from EDP audit training and experience will inevitably lead to complete obsolescence of these individuals and eventually make them *useless as auditors.*

The objective of the initial EDP audit specialists should be to act as a training cadre for the entire audit organization. So-called "conventional" auditors should be trained and involved in audits of computerized applications at a very early stage. The initial EDP audit specialists may be further trained in more technical or advanced audit skills or may be groomed to progress to positions in audit management.

No real consensus exists on the attributes that should be sought in recruiting the EDP auditor as either a cadre or an advanced specialist. However, some of the factors include:

- Intelligence
- Business education
- Computer education
- General inquisitiveness
- Ability to perceive systems relationships
- Salesmanship
- Writing skills

While outstanding qualifications in all of these areas would probably qualify an individual to replace the president of the organization, they also demonstrate that the effective EDP auditor must be much more than an EDP technician who has been transferred to the Audit Department. Recruiting such an individual will not be easy, but it is very important and worthwhile.

STAFFING

The principal qualifications that an audit manager should concern himself with when selecting staff for an EDP audit are:

- Some actual experience with computers
- Capability of communicating with data processing personnel
- A willingness to try new techniques and to learn .

The particular area of the EDP audit to be performed by the staff dictates the degree of EDP expertise needed. For example:

- Audits of the systems development process require the greatest EDP systems expertise. Technical assistance is often required for this area.
- IPF audits require a moderate degree of EDP operations expertise plus experience with application reviews.
- Application audits require the least EDP expertise because application audits in the manual phases of the examination are what lesser experienced personnel are, in fact, accustomed to. However, some EDP exposure — computer fundamentals and general purpose audit software training — is required at a minimum. Required EDP and general purpose audit software expertise will also vary in direct proportion to the complexity of compliance test procedures to be performed and of the application system (see chapter 6).

Qualified personnel *must be used* in completing an EDP audit. Such individuals *must* attain the necessary bilingual ability in the languages of computers and finance. They may be trained and developed through commercial or in-house training programs and on-the-job training. Although a lack of experienced individuals may create substantial difficulties in initiating EDP audit activities, these difficulties can be overcome by proper planning and adequate supervision.

Thorough study of this book alone will not in itself produce a qualified EDP auditor. Formal EDP audit training and practical experience must also be acquired. Of course, the level of experience required to audit competently in a computerized environment will vary according to the sophistication of that environment.

In staffing the engagement, the audit manager must consider not only the skills required but also the number of auditors assigned to various tasks. In general, as the complexity and size of the EDP review increases, the *proportion* of sophisticated auditors decreases. However, it is preferable to have only one auditor involved in any one of the following phases of an examination:

- Analytic audit and evaluation
- Tests of reasonableness and edits
- Use of test data
- Use of parallel simulation

On the other hand, more than one person may be more readily employed in confirmations, comparison of files, tests of manual procedures, and auditing around the computer. This is because they are more mechanical in nature, more time-consuming, and at a lower level of logic. Furthermore, these techniques are less susceptible to having things drop through "communication cracks."

Realistically, more than one person may be assigned to any given procedure. In the case of techniques where only one staff member is recommended, effective action requires a particularly thorough understanding of the controls. Because of the level of comprehension required, involvement of several persons is usually quite inefficient. The other types of procedures require lesser levels of thorough comprehension. The steps involved may be broken down more readily into small tasks. Therefore, several individuals under the guidance of one senior auditor may feasibly be utilized.

In the performance of some audit procedures, the auditor may desire technical assistance. The most common example of such assistance is the preparation of programmed selection routines for confirmations, selections for manual support, or edit and reasonableness test routines. Such technical support is frequently desirable but must be used with care to insure audit objectives and procedures are understood and complied with. When internal technical personnel program confirmation-selection routines, for example, the only thing the auditor can rely on is that the programmer will select only those records he thinks should be selected. This does not necessarily mean that the programmer will bypass any records intentionally. It does mean, however, that he may make decisions to omit the selection of certain records that he feels are inappropriate in the circumstances. The auditor's interpretation of what is inappropriate may well differ.

TRAINING

The rapid technological evolution of computer hardware, software, and management concepts requires regular training of even experienced auditors, just as it does for data processors and management. A number of organizations operate large-scale businesses offering education in EDP technology and auditing. An audit manager will generally find himself on the mailing lists of such organizations by merely subscribing to a few technical and EDP auditing periodicals. While they are not allowed to advertise nor solicit, most major CPA firms will also provide materials developed for in-house training to clients and others. The American Institute of Certified Public Accountants (AICPA) or The Institute of Internal Auditors should be contacted for more specific information regarding vendors of education services.

The AICPA now recommends, and many state license bureaus now require, that all practicing CPA's attend professional development education courses at a minimum rate of generally 40 hours per year. The field of EDP auditing is progressing so fast that 40 hours per year may not be enough in this discipline alone either for CPA's or internal auditors. The question may often become not one of preference but rather one of necessity for continuation of professional quality service.

TIMING

Timing considerations, when using the computer, differ significantly from those of a manual audit. The use of techniques such as flowcharting, test data, ITF or parallel simulation, and tools such as general purpose audit software change timing considerations. The principal reason for this is the availability, or lack of availability, of the computer and related data files under the existing data-file-retention practice. Since all data files are not retained and some may be destroyed only a few days after being created, the auditor must arrange well in advance for the retention of files to be used. In many cases where the auditor wants to use the computer, he must wait for some time to gain access to the equipment. Once he does, he may find that he has bugs or logic errors within his own tests. While the actual time used by an auditor in performing the necessary corrections may not exceed the time under manual techniques, the elapsed time will frequently be much greater because the auditor must again arrange for the use of the computer.

The auditor performing his first EDP audit will also require additional time because of his lack of experience. Even an auditor who is well trained in manual audit techniques will experience a steep learning curve when first using computer-assisted techniques. Full speed will normally be achieved after experience with two or three audits.

Another factor that tends to extend timing is the increased need for careful planning. In manual applications, the auditor can alleviate poor planning by making corrections or changes on the spot. When using a computer, such changes may not be as easy. While careful preplanning may appear to increase the time required for a first audit, it will save time in the long run.

BUDGETING AND SCHEDULING

Once the auditor has established the detail extent of the review and has selected the approach (or approaches) for his testing plan, he should establish a budget for each task and a schedule for the performance of the tests.

The time used to estimate budgets for the various audit procedures is highly dependent upon the complexity of the activities under audit and the experience of the auditor. In addition to the factors that can affect the time required in an audit examination not involving computers, consideration must be given to those which involve computers directly. These include technical sophistication of computer utilization, quality and quantity of assistance from technical personnel, and quality of documentation. Because of such variables, the appropriate time budgets for EDP audits are very difficult to generalize. They can only be determined by review of historical budget data on reviews and/or by an experienced auditor who has substantial information about the particular situation. This does not mean, however, that an auditor on a first-time review is justified in omitting the establishment of budgets because he feels uncertain. Even if they are subsequently found to be unrealistic, budgets will assist in the determination of future budgets, assist in the development of more accurate estimating capabilities, and stimulate a concern with costs through an awareness of a forthcoming accountability for costs in comparison with budget.

Although the scheduling of audit tasks is dependent upon the accuracy of the time budgets, effective scheduling is also essential to good audit management.

While the time involvement for a particular phase may not be extensive, the schedule should provide for a substantially longer elapsed time for its completion. Interruptions and delays in the audit of computerized financial information are caused by the limited availability of computer hardware and personnel. An auditor in a manual environment could perform audit procedures that involved only a limited proportion of the personnel or records at any time. The concentration of processing personnel and information assets that are typified in a computer environment substantially change the situation. In many cases, the auditor must personally employ the computer to gain access to files and records. Since the computer is expensive and its available time is limited, the auditor may encounter difficulties in obtaining such access. Accordingly, the auditor should plan to perform more than one examination phase during the same period of time. By alternating between tasks, he will utilize his time more effectively when he encounters delays in the performance of any specific task.

SUPERVISION AND REVIEW

During the evaluation of computer auditing, the auditor is frequently working in an unfamiliar environment and dealing with a level of technical complexity which far exceeds that of manual procedures. As a result, effective supervision of the EDP auditor is even more critical than for the auditor functioning in a manual-processing environment. This condition should not discourage technical-area probing. It should, however, be considered in determining the level of review to which audit findings are subjected.

All findings should be subjected to two types of review:

- **A functional-level review** should be made by those having both EDP audit and management-level audit experience. They will be able to apply their general business and auditing knowledge to computer situations.

- **A technical review** should cover any aspects of the examination that exceed the technical qualifications of the regular audit supervisory personnel mentioned above. The needed technical expertise may be available from computer audit specialists or from computer consultants.

The process of evaluating internal controls is the most difficult audit step to review. The reviewer often may only have a choice between accepting the judgment of the auditor or reexamining all the control documentation and comparing his separate decision. The former may not be very satisfying, and the latter may be excessively time-consuming. However, a third alternative exists.

If the auditor making the control evaluation utilizes a control evaluation table (as illustrated in chapters 4, 10, 14, 19, 20, and 22), he can provide clear documentation of the evaluation process. Thus, while a proper evaluation may be feasible without using a control evaluation table, its use substantially enhances an effective and efficient review. This will further enhance the general quality of such evaluations.

The entire concept of business information systems presumes that a common denominator exists for the measurement of the activities of a business: the dollar. In evaluating and following upon audit discrepancies and control weaknesses, the auditor must always remember to quantify his findings.

REPORTING

The final step in the conduct of an EDP audit engagement is, obviously, the reporting of results. Most of the considerations to be made in reporting apply equally to CPA's and internal auditors. Certain considerations that apply particularly to CPA's are specifically noted.

The highest level of reporting is the outside auditor's opinion on the fairness of the presentation of the financial statements in conformity with generally accepted accounting principles. In this report, the independent CPA must state that he complied with generally accepted auditing standards. These auditing standards require that all internal controls upon which the auditor relies be suitably studied, evaluated, and compliance tested. Therefore, to the extent of such reliance on internal EDP controls, the independent CPA commits himself to the quality of such controls. Furthermore, as a matter of policy, the CPA normally provides top management with a letter of comment and recommendations on various opportunities for control and efficiency improvements noted during the examination.

The function of the auditor is to provide an opinion on the reliability of the systems under examination, not to provide a tabulation of potential controls that were omitted. Where significant control omissions are noted, their impact must be determined. Therefore, the auditor's examination is not necessarily concluded when he completes his planned procedures. He must determine the exposure that results from omission or ineffective implementation of any controls. This exposure may first be estimated by using pessimistic error rates and transaction values. Then, if the exposure is significant, the actual error that was experienced must be measured.

Although the CPA's attest function is purportedly limited to rendering an opinion on financial statements prepared by management, he is normally expected to suggest adjustments if he finds areas of disagreement. Therefore, the auditor's testing procedures for the measurement of actual errors should be directed toward producing an audit adjustment of a determinable amount.

Even when the auditor can determine that the exposure or actual error is not significant and does not require an adjustment, his comments to management should indicate the amounts involved. This information will provide management with a basis for evaluating the relative significance of the auditor's recommendations.

When making recommendations concerning computer control and efficiency, the auditor must be particularly careful in his presentation. The following is a recommended outline:

- A general description of the control weakness or efficiency-improvement opportunity found
- One or more examples that support the finding
- An explanation of why the control improvement or efficiency change is desirable in the circumstance
- A recommendation on the action that should be taken

The style and terminology used in preparing these comments should be tailored to the specific audience. Where several levels of management are being addressed, the auditor should adjust his level of detail, use of technical jargon, and explanations of the need for change. The closer the recipient of the recommendations is to the specific problem area, the greater the detail the auditor should provide. Therefore, in addressing a Board of Directors, the auditor should be broad in his descriptions of the problem areas and should avoid the use of technical terminology. In addressing a data processing manager, however, the auditor may be quite specific and may feel free to use technical terms to the extent they are appropriate.

In general, each letter of recommendations should be addressed to the next higher level of management above the level to which the comments apply. Therefore, a letter to a Board of Directors may include comments covering all aspects of the organization. On the other hand, a letter on operations of a computer center should be directed to the immediate superior of the center's manager. Because the control and efficiency of a computerized application may affect a large number of departments and organizational entities, comments regarding application systems must often be directed to a fairly high level of management.

Before any tentative comments are released to their intended recipients, they should be reviewed carefully with all parties whose activities they purportedly describe. This review should consist of an actual review of a tentative draft of the letter of recommendations, not merely an exit interview upon the completion of on-site procedures. Although this is a good policy in any report of audit findings, it is particularly important when computers are involved. The auditor may readily misunderstand some technical aspect of control, or he may receive his information from someone who is not fully informed. Furthermore, the auditor may find difficulty in evaluating the cost feasibility of some of his tentative recommendations.

The main qualities offered by the auditor are his independence and credibility. Accordingly, he should review his tentative findings carefully with all parties concerned and release only those findings he can fully support in accordance with professional standards.

444

COST FACTORS OF EDP AUDITS

Two major cost factors distinct from those in manual systems are found in the examination of computerized financial information systems. The first is staff time. This was discussed previously. Because of the greater sophistication and the relative experience of the staff, many audit EDP procedures will involve greater expenditures of time than the auditor is accustomed to expending in manual environments.

The second cost factor relates to the utilization of computers. If practical, the auditor should utilize the same computer equipment which processes the applications he is examining. Little or no additional cost (unless the IPF is a service center) will result to the organization if this is feasible. In many cases, lease or depreciation charges are completely fixed; and the auditor's utilization has no marginal effect. The auditor is also well advised to use the regular IPF for reasons other than cost. The IPF may be relied upon to have the necessary equipment and capacities to suit the processes and file sizes that the auditor will encounter. Utilization of a different computer configuration may often cause unforeseen difficulties due to technical peculiarities of the equipment of which the auditor was not aware.

Obviously, the utilization of an outside computer facility will affect audit costs. However, the use of an outside computer facility can be justified whenever adequate audit procedures cannot be performed without the use of a computer or when the productivity of the auditor can be increased by a factor that offsets equipment costs.

If the utilization of computer hardware in the audit is simply a matter of convenience or efficiency, the auditor can justify its use to the extent that he increases his productivity.

SERVICE BUREAUS

The utilization of a computer service bureau means that a computer is involved in a business application system but that the involvement is external to the business organization. To the extent that an audit objective may be to verify the quality of the business application, the use of the service bureau can be no more ignored than it could if the equipment belonged to the organization.

Accordingly, an application audit in which a computer service bureau performs a portion of the processing must reach outside of the organization's legal entity and include the processing performed by the service bureau. This can generate a number of practical complications.

One service bureau may serve a multitude of user organizations in the same industry or in different ones. Frequent interruptions by a multitude of auditors from the various user organizations may interfere with operations. Even where an audit examination would not significantly interfere with operations, the management of the service bureau may resist an examination for valid or spurious reasons. This may lead to a dilemma between continuing the utilization of the service bureau and gaining substantial assurance that the application system functions properly. The need to ascertain that application systems function properly should prevail when such decisions must be made.

In many cases, the printed transaction trail and file details that are provided to service bureau users are sufficiently comprehensive that the application may be effectively examined by manually auditing around the computer. This means that the auditor may conduct his application audit with little or no interruption of the service bureau operations or contact with their personnel. While many such situations probably exist, the auditor must be careful to consider the implications of the information processing facility (IPF) controls over his application. This class of controls can be examined only by actually evaluating and testing the procedures within the service bureau.

Where a number of users are served by a single service bureau, these users may select a third-party auditor to conduct an examination of internal controls. Certified public accountants perform such examinations under standards prescribed by the American Institute of Certified Public Accountants and published in the audit guide *Audits of Service-Center-Produced Records.*

An opinion on internal control which is provided by an independent third-party auditor is not equivalent to a warranty that an application system will function properly for every user. The various controls exercised by a service bureau must still be supplemented by application controls exercised within the user organization. Remember that an application encompasses all aspects of a business function from the initiation of a transaction until historical reports are discarded. The operations of a service bureau only provide one segment in an entire system.

The user organizations who engage the third-party auditor should make clear those exposures, causes of exposures, and controls that they desire to have examined. A committee of the users should meet with the third-party auditor and directly participate in the development of the specific audit objectives. The resulting opinion on internal control will describe the *essential* controls that are represented to be present within a service bureau and an opinion as to whether they were effectively implemented during a stated period of time.

STANDARDS FOR EDP COMPLIANCE AUDITS

The general standards for the conduct of a compliance audit of EDP systems are the same as for the conduct of any other compliance audit. Professional standards for certified public accountants are prescribed by statements of auditing standards issued by the American Institute of Certified Public Accountants. These standards are mandatory for the conduct of an examination by CPA's in accordance with generally accepted auditing standards.

Internal auditors are not *required* to observe the standards prescribed for CPA's. However, most professional internal auditors are familiar with the public accounting standards and consider their content in the conduct of internal audits. Guidelines and recommendations are provided to internal auditors by The Institute of Internal Auditors within IIA's publications and periodicals.

Some of the most significant standards that may be recommended for both external and internal auditors are as follows:

- All controls which may significantly affect audit objectives must be reviewed to develop information concerning the nature and extent of such controls.
- Information which is gathered with regard to the nature and extent of controls must be evaluated in light of the audit objectives.
- All controls which are significant to the audit objectives must be tested to verify that they functioned effectively throughout the period under examination.
- All of the auditing procedures performed with regard to the above must be performed by an individual competent to perform the necessary auditing procedures.
- All of the controls and auditing procedures must be documented so as to provide evidence of professional standards.

INDEPENDENCE

Certified public accountants are required to be totally independent of any organization to which they provide attest services. This independence prohibits any financial interest in the organization, significant or abnormal financial obligation, close blood relationship to stockholders or executives as well as employment. In addition to avoiding those situations which would cause a CPA not to appear independent to the public, he must maintain an attitude of professionalism and objectivity. This same attitude should be maintained by internal auditors. However, they are obviously not prohibited from employment nor from financial involvements or blood relationships. Accordingly, while the internal auditor should be independent of the entities that he examines *within* his organization,

447

he can never be independent of his employer in the sense required of CPA's.

Independence of internal auditors can be maximized by having them report directly to an audit committee of outside directors. Even in this situation, routine activities, as well as compensation, will normally be influenced, if not actually controlled, by the chief executive officer or some senior vice president. While this relationship may limit the internal auditors' independence with regard to evaluating decisions or activities by top management, an audit committee will at least provide a ready vehicle for communicating any significant evidence of malfeasance on the part of such executives. Under no circumstances should the internal auditor report to operating-level management.

CPA AUDIT SCOPE

Internal auditors, users, and data processors should understand the scope of the CPA's responsibilities as well as the CPA's do. Without this understanding, duplicate efforts or serious omissions may occur in the total effort to limit exposures.

Compliance Versus Substantive Auditing

Compliance auditing alone does not constitute an audit under generally accepted auditing standards for CPA's. The purpose of compliance auditing within these standards is to determine the degree by which substantive auditing may be limited, if at all.

Substantive auditing is the verification of the specific balance sheet and operating-statement values and relationships. This may be accomplished through detailed examination of those balances, the transactions which generate them, and analytic review of the interrelationships. Substantive auditing occurs primarily as of the fiscal year-end of the financial statements, although substantive support of transactions may also occur throughout interim periods. Although the results of compliance auditing may predict a high degree of accuracy for related financial statement values, substantive procedures may still not be totally eliminated from an examination of a material financial statement item.

The relationship of compliance and substantive auditing to the formation of an accountant's opinion is illustrated in Figure 24-1. The prediction of financial statement accuracy may be stated in terms of statistical reliability and precision (confidence level and confidence interval). The extent of substantive testing must raise that reliability or narrow the precision to the level required to provide an opinion. The extent of these substantive tests may also be specified in statistical terms of reliability and precision.

448

RELATIONSHIP OF COMPLIANCE AND SUBSTANTIVE AUDITING

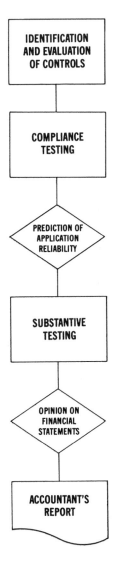

Figure 24-1

Levels of Certainty

The combined results of the reliability and precision obtained individually from compliance and substantive testing may be calculated by using "Bayesian statistics." Since the mathematical calculations involved in this approach involve discrete alternatives, we can classify these cases as follows:

- Materially understated
- Significantly but not materially understated
- Fairly stated
- Significantly but not materially overstated
- Materially overstated

After first defining "significant" and "material" values, the auditor may draw upon the results of his compliance auditing to *subjectively* assign a probability to each of the five alternatives above. If the ultimate reliability needed to express an opinion is then specified, calculations may be made to estimate the level of sampling reliability necessary for substantive tests to achieve the prescribed goal.

> *Example — Based upon compliance tests and evaluation of internal controls over the accounts receivable application, the auditor predicts that the year-end receivables book balance will be as follows:*
> - *Materially understated — 3%*
> - *Significantly but not materially understated — 4%*
> - *Fairly stated — 70%*
> - *Significantly but not materially overstated — 20%*
> - *Materially overstated — 3%*
>
> *Using Bayesian statistics, he can then calculate that he will reach 95% overall reliability that the balance is fairly stated by confirming a sample of receivables that, by itself, provides 80% reliability of being fairly stated.*

Substantive auditing of computerized application systems is beyond the scope of the current edition of this text. Generally, however, it closely resembles the techniques described in *"verification of results"* in chapter 9.

Business Viewpoint

In addition to performing the scope of examination necessary to fulfill the minimum requirements for generally accepted auditing standards, most CPA's make at least some additional effort to look at the general health of the organization and recommend improvements to management. *Understanding the organization under examination is just as essential to the determination that financial statements are meaningful as are universally accepted auditing procedures* such as confirmation of receivables and observation of inventories. The professional accountant would indeed be remiss if he failed to report meaningful findings gathered in the course of his business review and auditing procedures, even though they had no immediate or direct bearing upon the literal fairness of the financial statements.

By expending a nominal additional effort, the CPA may also extend his procedures into operational auditing concerns. The financial benefits that may be rendered by even a modest effort in this direction will often justify not only the cost of such an effort but possibly even the cost of the entire examination. Accordingly, most CPA's consider this an integral part of their normal client services. Consequently, CPA's "letters of recommendations" normally include some operational comments.

In addition to the basic attest function, CPA's frequently provide additional financial, tax, or management advisory services. The scope of such engagements is extremely flexible, according to the needs of the client and the in-house resources, and often involves computer activities or controls.

Application Scope

CPA's normally limit the scope of a financial examination to those application systems which have a direct impact upon the financial statements. Accordingly, they will rarely perform any examination procedures on the quality or compliance with control in nonfinancial applications. Even where computerized application systems have direct financial statement consequences, the compliance procedures performed by CPA's will usually be limited to those controls whose implementation could materially affect those financial statements. Other controls may be extremely significant to the limitation of other exposures but not be necessary to the performance of the CPA's attest function. Alternatively, the CPA may even elect not to rely upon controls that could have a material effect on financial results if he can otherwise perform substantive tests of those same results more feasibly or efficiently. The decision by a CPA to rely upon internal control is often one of audit economics. He is ethically obliged to his client to perform his examination at the lowest feasible cost. Substantive tests of certain applications may be cheaper than compliance tests.

IPF Scope

The compliance procedures performed by a CPA within the information processing facility (IPF) will be primarily influenced by the following three factors:

- The relative significance of the applications being processed
- The extent of compensating application controls
- The exposure provided by the IPF to the termination of the business

In some organizations, the significance of all of these factors may be so low that the CPA need not rely upon nor examine the IPF controls. This situation is probably rare. Most medium-size organizations would be ruined if the information assets within their IPF were destroyed. Some organizations are so small that manual processing could be readily reinstituted. Other very large organizations may have such a small proportion of their information assets located at any particular computer center that the destruction of a single IPF would not be disastrous. However, most organizations receiving financial audits from CPA's would be classified somewhere between very small or very large.

Generalizations about the usual significance to a CPA of other IPF controls is difficult because so many variables exist. However, the examination within an IPF by CPA's will certainly be more narrow in scope than that which should be performed by an internal auditor.

Systems Development Scope

CPA's should be actively involved in compliance audits of the *systems development* function to avoid serious problems with application controls in audits of future years. Controls over *maintenance* of application systems in operation during the year under examination will also be a part of this function.

The relationship between a CPA and his client is usually a long-term one. Accordingly, the CPA cannot afford to be concerned only with the year presently under examination but must also look forward to future years and strive to prevent serious breakdowns in application controls which could affect the financial health of his client or the effort required to perform an audit. Since the systems development process contains important controls that can prevent breakdowns in the controls of future applications systems, systems development controls should be a concern of every CPA in the course of a normal financial statement-attest relationship.

Reliance upon compliance with programmed controls within the year under examination is also dependent upon the effectiveness of controls over access and modifications to the programs which include these controls. Therefore, some verification of program maintenance controls would be necessary for every CPA who desires to test compliance with programmed application controls by directly reviewing and testing the application programs which contain them.

Other Scope Concerns

The normal attest activities of a CPA will seldom include additional procedures specifically intended to evaluate operational exposures or exposures to computer abuse. These areas of exposure are not generally considered as a part of the CPA's responsibility.

The CPA may participate in evaluating the *application controls* within systems under development even when they have not been implemented during the year presently under examination. As noted above, the CPA-client relationship is generally long term; and the

452

CPA may elect to evaluate application controls before they are implemented for reasons of efficiency or to assure that serious control weaknesses do not occur during subsequent fiscal years when the application controls must be relied upon. Serious control weaknesses in highly complex systems have been known to defy swift corrections and thereby prevent an unqualified opinion on the fairness of financial statements. Both CPA's and their clients view this possibility with extreme distaste and may elect to evaluate application controls prior to the implementation of the application system so that such situations will not arise. When qualified internal audit personnel are available, this function is more commonly performed by the internal auditors.

INTERNAL AUDIT SCOPE

Compliance Versus Substantive Auditing

The usual scope of examinations by internal auditors concentrates on compliance audits and puts little emphasis on substantive procedures, but they are concerned with a much broader variety of exposures than the fairness of financial statements. Although internal auditors may utilize techniques that verify the results of processing, such procedures are seldom employed for purposes of substantiating financial reports.

As noted previously, the mission of the modern internal auditor team is to act as a reconnaissance force for top management. The magnitude and complexity of many modern organizations prevents detailed supervisory involvement by top management in daily operating activities. In lieu of relying upon operating management to appraise their own effectiveness, top management will employ internal auditors to make such evaluations and to report to them. Accordingly, the scope of examination of internal auditors may be compared to that of CPA's as illustrated in Figure 24-2.

Quality Assurance Versus Internal Audit

To an outsider, the internal audit function may be viewed as a high-level element of the total internal control of an organization. However, the internal auditors must not be involved in the implementation of daily operating controls; or they will lose their independence in evaluating such systems. Specified individuals within an operating department may be assigned functions and titles that indicate they are auditors. Although their activities may closely resemble those of an internal auditor or a CPA, such persons should not be considered internal auditors as defined within the context of this book. Rather, they perform a *quality-assurance* function and represent an intermediate level of internal control *between* that of *operating controls and internal auditing.*

COMPARISON OF SCOPE FOR CPA'S AND INTERNAL AUDITORS

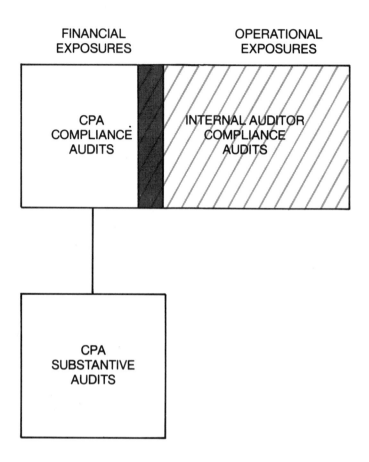

Figure 24-2

Example — Within the insurance industry, persons designated "claims auditors" are commonly employed to examine the activities of claims adjustors. They may evaluate the quality and implementation of control over payment of insurance claims. However, they report to the senior officer in charge of claims operations. They do not examine other functions of the insurance company and cannot be considered independent of the Claims Department. Accordingly, while the quality-assurance function they perform may be extremely valuable, they should not be considered as being the same as internal auditors.

Levels of Certainty

The scope of the examination within each area will be more detailed than that of the CPA in that the internal auditor will be concerned with a much tighter precision (confidence interval) than the CPA would normally consider to be material. However, the internal auditor should maintain some concern with the significance of exposures so that the direct costs of his efforts are at least offset by the benefits he provides.

Example — An internal auditor would be foolish to expend 100 hours of his time, if valued at $10 per hour, on auditing a petty-cash application that accumulates only $1,000 per year. Even if everything were wrong (which is extremely unlikely) the company would still receive no direct net benefit from his efforts.

At the same time, the internal auditor may not require the same reliability (confidence level) as the CPA. He will rarely be required to support adjusting entries, and he is unlikely to face legal liability if he fails to detect a material discrepancy, although he may lose his job.

Scope in Specific Functions

Internal auditors will perform compliance audits of EDP applications, information processing facilities, the systems development function, and application controls within systems under development. Their examinations will normally be concerned with operational and computer-abuse exposures as well as financial exposures. Their examination of financial exposures may be limited to the extent that similar procedures are already performed by CPA's.

In addition to his broader concern with exposures and with values not considered material by a CPA, the internal auditor will generally be involved in the evaluation of application controls of systems under development. While this service may be provided by a CPA, it is seldom considered a routine part of the attest function. The internal auditor is much more appropriate to evaluate development of application controls due to his lower direct cost to the organization and his greater availability for long-term projects. His experience with a broader variety of exposures also makes him preferable. Therefore, while CPA's may occasionally be called upon to evaluate development of application controls, it is generally the exclusive responsibility of internal auditors.

RELIANCE BY CPA's ON INTERNAL AUDITORS

Inasmuch as the internal auditor is himself an important internal control of his organization, his audit scope, competence, and objectivity should be considered by a CPA in determining his scope. Furthermore, the CPA may specifically request and rely upon certain procedures performed by the internal auditor. A healthy attitude of cooperation and mutual respect will usually produce a better total audit and also reduce total costs.

The reliance by CPA's upon internal auditors is guided by the AICPA's Statement of Auditing Standards #9 (SAS 9). This statement specifies certain tests of the internal auditor's work that should be made by the CPA in order to support reliance. These may include the following:

- Evaluate competence:
  - hiring practices
  - training
  - supervision
  - certification (Certified Internal Auditor or Certified Bank Auditor)
- Evaluate objectivity:
  - level of reporting audit results
  - level of administrative reporting
  - quality of recommendations
- Evaluate internal audit procedures:
  - adequate scope of testing
  - adequate audit programs
  - adequate working papers
  - appropriate conclusions
- Test internal audit procedures:
  - reexamine the same transactions or balances
  - examine similar transactions or balances
  - compare results

However, there is a limit to the reliance that the CPA is permitted. He must personally make any decisions in the following areas:

- Evaluation of internal control
- Sufficiency of tests
- Materiality
- Other financial reporting matters

456

CYCLING OF COMPLIANCE AUDITS

The effort required to adequately review, evaluate, and verify controls in sophisticated and unique application systems frequently requires more time than is available to either CPA's or internal auditors in any single year. Accordingly, most audit organizations customarily cycle their examinations of the different application systems within the organization over a period of three to five years.

This traditional cycling was fine for most manual systems, but it may no longer be appropriate for computerized applications. Some evidence exists that the typical computer application has a lifetime of only four years. While numerous exceptions to this rule may certainly be found, the efficacy of four or five years' cycling time is questionable.

CPA's are obligated by generally accepted auditing standards to review and to test all controls upon which they rely in each year that they express an opinion. To the extent that a single application system serves multiple locations, the testing may be performed at different locations in different years. However, compliance tests of controls which are being relied upon must at least be performed at some locations every year. Cycling of tests of different applications in different years by CPA's is strictly prohibited.

Example — For a centralized payroll function in a multilocation organization, plant-level controls may be tested at different plants in different years. Not all plants need to be tested in the same year. However, the controls in some plants and the controls at the central facility must be tested every year an opinion is provided.

Information gathering, documentation, and evaluation of controls must also be performed every year a CPA provides an opinion; but the level of effort required each year does not need to be the same. If a thorough job of documentation and evaluation is performed in the first year, this evaluation only needs to be evaluated for subsequent changes in the application system. The effort required to maintain a current evaluation of controls should not be significant. Furthermore, any deletion of controls upon which the CPA relies should be quickly detected through his compliance tests. Therefore, in terms of the evaluation effort required, the CPA may appear to cycle the control evaluation phase of his compliance auditing over the life of the system. It is probably inadvisable to exceed four years between in-depth control evaluations even when the existing application has not been replaced. In this time, the cumulative effects of minor control changes will often be sufficient to call for a completely new control evaluation.

REPEAT EXAMINATIONS

Eventually, the Audit Department should reach that milestone in its maturity when it repeats an audit of a computer application, IPF, or systems development function that it has examined previously. This will be a considerable benefit. Not only are working papers available from the previous audit, but there is also a period of experience available where the auditor can compare his predications concerning control with the actual events. Hindsight may be of great benefit in reevaluating controls and in estimating the likelihood of various exposures.

If the system has not changed significantly since the prior examination, the effort required to gather information, document the controls, and evaluate them should be considerably less than the first time. Even if an application system were completely replaced, the new system would often incorporate the best features from the old while taking advantage of new technology as well as experience. Relatively few new application systems are revolutionary; their ancestry is usually quite apparent.

The overall approach to audit management should be similar to the management and control of a systems development project as described in Section III. Both should be broken into separate, defined phases with specific end products. The phases should be broken into tasks or activities with time budgets assigned to each. Progress may then be measured by deviations in delivery of end products from target dates and in comparison of actual to budgeted time. The audit manager must be a proficient auditor so as to provide guidance and quality. In addition, he must be a skilled project manager.

GLOSSARY

Access Time
The time required for a computer to locate data and move them into the central processing unit.

Address
The code used to designate a specific piece of data within computer storage.

Aging
Identification of unprocessed or retained items in files according to their date, usually the transaction date. The aging classifies items according to various ranges of dates.

Alphanumeric
The character sets composed of letters, digits, and special characters ($, #, ", etc.).

Amount Control Total
Totals of homogeneous amounts for a group of transactions or records, usually dollars or quantities.

Analog Computer
A device which performs computational functions by using a nondiscrete representation such as variations in voltage.

Anticipation
The expectation of a given transaction or event at a particular time.

Approval
The acceptance of a transaction for processing after it is initiated.

Assembler
A computer program that accepts instructions in a symbolic code and produces machine language instructions. Generally, one machine instruction is produced for each symbolic instruction.

Audit Trail
See "transaction trail."

Authorization
Limits the initiation of a transaction or performance of a process to selected individuals.

Automated Error Correction
Automatic error correction of transactions or records which violate a detective control.

Backup
Files, equipment, and procedures that are available if the originals are destroyed or out of service.

Balancing
A test for equality between the values of two equivalent sets of items or one set of items and a control total. Any difference indicates an error.

Batch Balancing
A comparison of the items or documents actually processed against a predetermined control total.

Batch Processing
An application system where transactions to be processed are collected into groups and concentrated for processing into a brief span of time.

Batch Serial Numbers (Batch Sequence)
Batches of transaction documents are numbered consecutively and accounted.

Batch Totals (Batch Control)
Any type of control total or count applied to a specific number of transaction documents or to the transaction documents that arrive within a specific period of time.

GLOSSARY

Binary
A number system with a base (radix) of two. The decimal number 39 would be represented as 100111.

Binary-Coded Decimal (BCD)
A method of representing the decimal digits by a four-digit binary code. For example, the decimal number 39 would be represented as 0011 1001 in BCD but would be 100111 in pure binary.

Bit
An on- or off-state in storage representing a binary digit of 0 or 1.

Block
A set of data transferred as a unit between components of a computer system. A block may include one or more records.

Blocking Factor
The number of records incorporated into a single block.

Branch
A computer-language instruction that may cause the computer to next process an instruction other than that which is immediately following.

Buffer
Storage used to compensate for differences in the rates of transfer of data or in the timing of transmission of data from one device to another.

Bug
An inadvertent mistake in the logic of a computer program or in the wiring of a circuit.

Byte
A set of eight adjacent bits that can be used to represent one alphanumeric character or two decimal digits.

Calculation
The performance of various mathematical operations yielding a numeric result.

Cancellation
Identifies transaction documents in order to prevent their further or repeated use after they have performed their function.

Card Punch
A device which records data on a paper card in the form of a pattern of rectangular or round holes.

Card Reader
A device which recognizes data on punched cards and may transmit them to a different device.

Cathode-Ray Tube
A device similar to a television screen upon which data can be displayed.

Central Processing Unit
The portion of a computer system that contains the circuits controlling the interpretation and execution of instructions. Abbreviation, CPU.

Check Bit
A binary check digit.

Check Digit
A digit which is a function of the other digits within a word or number used for testing an accurate transcription.

Check Point
A point in time during processing when a record is made of the status of all the contents of the computer registers and main storage so as to minimize restart efforts should a failure subsequently occur.

460

Clearing Account
An amount which results from the processing of independent items of equivalent value. Net control value should equal zero.

COBOL
Acronym for Common Business-Oriented Language. A high-level computer-source compiler language developed for common business functions. Every COBOL-source program has four segments: identification, environment, data, procedures. The procedures statements resemble English.

Coding
(1) Successive instructions which direct the computer to perform a particular process. Also, the act of preparing code.
(2) The recording of values or characters having meanings which are not readily apparent.

Common Carrier
In data processing, a company which rents or leases transmission lines for communication purposes such as Western Union or AT&T.

Comparison
The examination of data by using logical or conditional tests to determine or to identify similarities or differences.

Competence of Personnel
Persons assigned to processing or supervisory roles within information systems have the technical knowledge necessary to perform their functions.

Compile
Machine language instructions generated from a high-level program language so that more than one object program instruction is produced for each source program statement.

Compiler
A computer program that compiles object language instructions from source language statements.

Completeness Check
A test that data entries are made in fields which cannot be processed in a blank state.

Console
A component of the computer used for communication and control by the operator or maintenance engineers. Usually, contains a typewriter keyboard and either a cathode-ray tube or a typewriter printer.

Control Clerk
An individual performing clerical duties associated with control over data processing operations.

Control Program
See "operating system."

Control Register (Batch Control Log)
A log or register indicating the disposition and control values of batches or transactions.

Counter
A component of a computer used to store numbers which may be increased or decreased to affect the process of counting.

C P U
Abbreviation for a central processing unit.

Data Base
An integrated file containing multiple record types or segments that may be accessed in a nonsequential manner.

GLOSSARY

Data Storage
Storage of transactions or records so that they may be retrieved upon request.

Dating
The recording of calendar dates for purposes of later comparison or expiration testing.

Debug
To identify and to eliminate faults in computer program logic or equipment.

Decision Table
A table listing all the conditions that may exist and the corresponding actions to be performed. It permits complex logic to be expressed in a concise format and may be used in lieu of flowcharts.

Deck
A collection of punched cards.

Default Option
The automatic utilization of a predefined value in situations where input transactions have certain values left blank.

Definition of Responsibilities
Descriptions of tasks for each job function within an information processing system. These indicate clear beginning and termination points for each job function. They also cover the relationship of job functions to each other.

Desk Checking
The manual process in which representative data are traced through program logic to determine that the logical processing is as intended.

Diagnostic Routine
A computer program designed to test and diagnose defects in computer machinery or violations of source program conventions.

Digital Computer
A device that may be used to manipulate data expressed as discrete values. Contrast with analog computer.

Discrepancy Reports
A listing of items which have violated some detective control and require further investigation.

Document Control Total
A count of the number of individual documents.

Documentation
Written records for the purpose of providing communication.

Drum Card
Automatic spacing and format shifting of data fields on a keypunch machine.

Dual Access/Dual Control
Two independent, simultaneous actions or conditions are required before processing is permitted.

Dump
A printed record of the contents of computer storage usually produced for diagnostic purposes.

EBCDIC
Abbreviation for extended binary-coded decimal interchange code. An 8-bit code used to represent up to 256 distinct characters and numerals.

Echo Check
A test of the accuracy of data transfer by retransmitting the data received to their source and comparing them to the original.

462

Edit
A general control term that includes format check, completeness check, check digits, reasonableness tests, limit check, validity check, etc. Generally implies implementation via a computer program.

Emulator
A hardware device that enables a computer to execute object language programs written for a different computer design.

Endorsement
The marking of a form or document so as to direct or to restrict its further use in processing.

Equipment Check
A control built in by the computer manufacturer to verify the accuracy of data transmitted, processed, or stored by units or devices comprising a computer.

Error-Source Statistics
Accumulation of information on the type of error and origin. This is used to determine the nature of remedial efforts needed to reduce the number of errors.

Exception Input
Internally initiated processing in a predefined manner unless specific input transactions are received that specify processing with different values or in a different manner.

Expiration
A limit check based on a comparison of current date with the date recorded on a transaction, record, or file.

Field
An element of data within a record that constitutes an item of information. Example: name, account number, amount.

File
A set of related data records.

File Maintenance
Changing information in a file through addition, deletion, or replacement usually to information that will have a sustained impact on future processing.

File-Protect Ring
A plastic ring approximately four inches in diameter that, when inserted in a recess on the back of a standard magnetic tape reel, depresses a switch on the tape drive to allow the drive to write upon that particular reel. No ring — no write.

Fixed-Length Record
A record that is the same size in all occurrences. Contrasts with variable-length record.

Flowchart
A diagram that presents through symbols and connecting lines either the logical structure of a computer program or the sequence of processes in a system.

Format Check (Form)
Determination that data are entered in the proper mode — numeric or alphanumeric — within designated fields of information.

Forms Design
Forms are constructed to be self-explanatory, understandable, and concise and to gather all necessary information with a minimum of effort.

FORTRAN
FORmula TRANslating system. A high-level compiler-source language principally incorporating mathematical expressions.

Generate
To produce machine language instructions from a set of user specifications.

GLOSSARY

Generator
A computer program designed to produce other programs. Based upon input parameters, a generator may apply decision criteria and produce a program suitable to the parameters.

Hard Copy
Printed reports, listings, etc., produced by a computer on paper.

Hardware
The machinery constituting a computer or peripheral devices.

Hash Total
A meaningless total developed from the accumulated numerical amounts of non-monetary information.

High Order
The left-most digit within a number representing the highest order of magnitude in the number.

Housekeeping
Broadly pertaining to the general upkeep and maintenance activities within an information processing facility.

Initialize
The instructions that set various registers and addresses to zero or a specific starting value at the beginning or end of a processing routine.

Initiate
Any financial or other event which should be recorded.

Inquiry
A request to obtain information without altering it.

Interblock Gap
The space on a magnetic tape between the end of one block and the beginning of another. Each gap will be of a defined length according to the tape drive so as to permit the mechanism to stop, start, and regain appropriate speed for processing. Sometimes misleadingly referred to "interrecord gap."

Interface
The boundary between one major responsibility and another. Frequently utilized in conjunction with relationships between the Data Processing Department and a user department.

I/O
Abbreviation for input/output.

IOCS
Abbreviation for input/output control system. A standard set of routines to initiate and control the input and output activities of a computer system.

Key
Identifying characters within a record used to locate it or to control sorting.

Keystroke Verification
The redundant entry of data into keyboards so as to verify the accuracy of a prior entry. Differences between the data previously recorded and the data entered in verification will cause a mechanical signal.

Labeling
The external or internal identification of transaction batches or files according to source, application, date, or other identifying characteristics.

Library Routine
A standard set of program instructions maintained in on-line storage that may be called in and processed by other programs.

Limit Check (Range Check)
Tests of specified amount fields against stipulated high or low limits of acceptability. When both high and low values are used, the test may be called a "range check."

Line Control Count
A count of the individual line items on one or more documents.

Log
A record on paper or machine-readable media of all transactions, operating instructions, etc., sequenced in the order they occurred.

Logic Diagram
Synonymous with program flowchart.

Loop
A sequence of program instructions that can be reiterated for a designated number of times based upon a condition in the data.

Macroinstruction
An assembly-language instruction that generates several predetermined machine instructions.

Master File
A computer file containing information to be retained and reused for reference or in file maintenance. Contrast with transaction file.

Matching
Matching of items from the processing stream of an application with others developed independently so as to identify items unprocessed through either of the parallel systems.

Mechanization
Consistency of processing is provided by mechanical or electronic processing.

Merge
To combine two files into one.

Multiprocessing
The simultaneous operation of more than one set of processing circuitry within a single computer.

Multiprogramming
The processing of two or more application programs by interleaving the execution of individual instructions.

Object Language
Machine instructions produced from a compiler or assembler program that accepts source language.

Object Program
A computer program composed of object language instructions.

OCR
Abbreviation for optical character recognition. The mechanical facility to recognize graphic characters using devices sensitive to light.

Off-Line
Equipment, devices, or files not electronically connected to a computer.

On-Line
Equipment, devices, or files that are electronically connected to the computer for purposes of access.

Operating System
A complex set of computer programs normally provided by the machinery vendor to perform some or all of the following functions:
- Schedule, load, initiate, and supervise execution of programs.
- Allocate storage, peripheral units, and other facilities of the computer.

GLOSSARY

- Initiate and control input and output operations.
- Detect and correct certain classes of machine and data malfunctions.
- Provide a means for communications between the human operator and the computer hardware.
- Produce a log of system operations.
- Manage multiprogramming, multiprocessing, or time-sharing execution of programs.
- Manage utility programs and language translators.

Overflow Checks
A limit check based upon the capacity of a memory or file area to accept data.

Padding
The completion of a block of data with meaningless characters so as to make it the prescribed size.

Passwords
The authorization to allow access to data or to process by providing a signal or code known only to authorized individuals.

Patch
To correct or to modify a computer program by directly altering the object code.

Periodic Audit
A verification of a file or of a phase of processing intended to check for problems and encourage future compliance with control procedures.

Peripheral Equipment
The auxiliary storage units of a computer used for input and output of data. All components of a computer other than the central processing unit and core storage.

Precoded Forms
Fixed elements of information are entered on forms in advance and sometimes in a format which permits direct machine processing so as to prevent errors in entry of repetitive data.

Prenumbered Forms
Sequential numbers on individual forms printed in advance so as to allow subsequent detection of loss or misplacement.

Preventive Maintenance
Maintenance of hardware occurring on a prescribed schedule so as to prevent breakdowns.

Program Flowchart
A flowchart that diagrams the processing steps or logic of a computer program.

Programmed Check
An edit performed by a program.

Programmer
An individual who codes computer programs in a source language.

Programming Language
A source language used to define operations that can be translated by software into machine instructions.

Random Access
A manner of storing records in a file so that an individual record may be accessed without reading other records.

Read Back
Immediate return of input information to the sender for comparison and approval.

Real Time
A computer system that will respond within a matter of seconds to an inquiry or a command.

Reasonableness
Tests applied to various fields of data through comparison with other information available within the transaction or master records.

Reconciliation
An identification and analysis of differences between the values contained in two substantially identical files or between a detail file and a control total. Errors are identified according to the nature of the reconciling items rather than the existence of a difference between the balances.

Record Layout
A diagram showing the nature, location, size, and format of fields within a record.

Record Mark
A special character used by some computer systems to designate the beginning or end of a record.

Recording
The creation of a record of a transaction on some medium.

Redundant Processing
A repetition of processing and an accompanying comparison of individual results for equality.

Reference Documents
Documents that serve to store information for reference.

Reliability of Personnel
Personnel performing the processing may be relied upon to treat data in a consistent manner.

Report File
A machine-readable file containing records that may be directly printed to constitute a report.

Reporting
Summary or exception information printed and used for management decisions or accounting entries.

Rerun
To reprocess a computer program usually because of a defect or error in the previous processing.

Rotation of Duties
Jobs assigned to people are rotated periodically at irregularly scheduled times, if possible, for key processing functions.

Routine
A set of computer instructions that will cause the performance of a particular process. A computer program may consist of one or more routines.

RPG
Abbreviation for report program generator. A high-level source computer language designed particularly to facilitate the rapid preparation of reports.

Run
The execution of a single computer program.

Run Manual
A document describing one or more computer programs within an application system.

Run-to-Run Totals
The utilization of output control totals resulting from one process as input control totals over subsequent processing. The control totals are used as links in a chain to tie one process to another in a sequence of processes or one cycle to another over a period of time.

GLOSSARY

Secure Custody
Information assets are provided security similar to tangible assets such as cash, negotiable securities, etc.

Segregation of Duties
Responsibility for custody and accountability for handling and processing of data are separated.

Sequence Checking
A verification of the alphanumeric sequence of the "key" field in items to be processed.

Serial Access
Data stored in a manner where all preceding records must be accessed sequentially in order to locate a specific record. Contrast with random access.

Signed Field
A numeric data field containing a designation of an algebraic sign.

Simulator
A computer program which attempts to imitate the consequences that will be produced by variable conditions in a real-world environment.

Simultaneous Preparation
The one-time recording of a transaction for all further processing, using multiple copies, as appropriate, to prevent transcription errors.

Software
All levels of computer programs that control the operation of hardware.

Sort
To arrange items or records into a sequence.

Source Document
A document from which data are originally acquired.

Source Language
A computer language utilized by a programmer and submitted to a translation process in order to produce object instructions.

Special Character
A visible character other than a number or letter (e.g., $, #, /).

Standardization
Uniform, structured, and consistent procedures are developed for all processing.

Storage Protection
A provision by the software to protect against unauthorized reading or writing between portions of storage.

Subroutine
A routine that may be recurringly called upon by a different routine to perform a defined process.

Summarization
To combine detail items having the same "key" into a single item with the same "key" and accumulated value.

Summary Processing
A redundant process using a summarized amount. This is compared for equality with a control total from the processing of the detailed items.

Suspense Account
A control total for items awaiting further processing.

Suspense File
A file containing unprocessed or partially processed items awaiting further action.

System
A broad term to designate an arrangement of entities that form an organized whole. Generally, meaningless unless accompanied by a modifier such as: computer system, application system, operating system, etc.

System Flowchart
A flowchart illustrating the flow of documents and operations in an application.

Systems Analysis
The function of determining what and how changes should be made to a business activity.

Telecommunications
The electronic transmission of data over a long distance.

Throughput
Useful work performed by a computer system during a period of time.

Tickler File
A control file consisting of items sequenced by age for follow-up purposes. Such files are usually manual.

Time Sharing
A technique of computer operations that permits a large number of human users to access comprehensive computer services simultaneously.

Track
The ring-shaped surface of a disc or drum or the segment of a magnetic tape running parallel to its edge.

Trailer Label
A record providing a control total for comparison with accumulated counts or values of records processed.

Training
Personnel are provided explicit instructions and tested for their understanding before being assigned new duties.

Transaction Code
A field within a transaction record that designates the nature of the transaction.

Transaction File
A machine-readable file containing transient information that will cause changes to a master file during a file maintenance or updating process.

Transaction Trail
The availability of a manual or machine-readable means for tracing the status and contents of an individual transaction record backward or forward and between output, processing, and source.

Transcription
Copying recorded information from one medium to another.

Translator
A computer program that converts source language statements into object language instructions.

Transmit
The movement of data from one location to another.

Transmittal Document (Batch Control Ticket)
The medium for communicating control totals over movement of data, particularly from source to processing point or between processing points.

Turnaround Documents
A computer-produced document which is intended for resubmission into the system.

GLOSSARY

Updating
Changing information in a file through the addition or subtraction from a value in a field.

Upstream Resubmission
The resubmission of corrected error transactions so that they pass through all or more of the detective controls that are exercised over normal transactions (e.g., before input editing).

Utility Program
A standard routine that performs a process required frequently such as sorting, merging, data transcription, printing, etc.

Validity Check
The characters in a coded field are either matched to an acceptable set of values in a table or examined for a defined pattern of format, legitimate subcodes, or character values, using logic and arithmetic rather than tables.

Variable-Length Record
A machine-readable record that may contain a variable number of fields. Contrast with fixed-length record.

Verifier
A device used to check the accuracy of a data transcription operation.

Verify
The act of determining whether data are accurate.

Visual Verification
The visual scanning of documents for general reasonableness and propriety.

Volume
An individual storage medium such as a tape reel, disc pack, etc., composing a complete file.

Working Documents
Functional documents used to transfer assets or information.

RECOMMENDED READINGS

Adams, Donald L. "Audit Review of Program Code — I." *EDPACS*. Reston, Virginia: Automation Training Center (August 1975).

Adams, Donald L. "Library System Packages — Revisited." *EDPACS*. Reston, Virginia: Automation Training Center (February 1974).

Adams, Donald L. "Performance Measurement in EDP." *EDPACS*. Reston, Virginia: Automation Training Center (May 1974).

Adams, Donald L. "Recovery from a Data Center Fire." *EDPACS*. Reston, Virginia: Automation Training Center (April 1974).

Adams, Donald L. "A Survey of Library System Packages." *EDPACS*. Reston, Virginia: Automation Training Center (July 1973).

Adams, Donald L. "A Survey of Test Data Generators." *EDPACS*. Reston, Virginia: Automation Training Center (April 1973).

Adams, D. L., and Mullarkey, J. F. "A Survey of Audit Software." *Journal of Accountancy* (September 1972), pp. 39-66.

American Institute of Certified Public Accountants. *Audit Guide: Audits of Service-Center-Produced Records*. New York, New York: The American Institute of Certified Public Accountants, 1974.

American Institute of Certified Public Accountants. *Statements on Auditing Standards*. New York, New York: American Institute of Certified Public Accountants, 1973, 1974, 1975, and 1976.

American National Standards, Inc. *Flowchart Symbols and Their Usage in Information Processing*. American National Standards Institute, Inc., 1971.

Anderson, Lane K.; Hendershot, Raymond A.; and Schoonmaker, Robert C. "Self-Checking Digit Concepts." *Journal of Systems Management*. Cleveland, Ohio (September 1974), pp. 36-42.

Arens, Alvin, and Loebbecke, James K. *Auditing: An Integrated Approach*. Englewood Cliffs, New Jersey: Prentiss-Hall, Inc., 1976.

Arkins, Herbert. *Handbook of Sampling for Auditing and Accounting*. 2nd Edition. New York, New York: McGraw-Hill Book Co., 1974.

Automation Training Center. *Index. EDPACS*. Reston, Virginia; Automation Training Center (December 1975).

Baird, Lindsay L. "An Analytical Approach to Identifying Computer Vulnerability." *Security Management*. Washington, D. C.: American Society for Industrial Security (May 1974), pp. 6-11.

Bank Administration Institute. *Auditing Bank EDP Systems*. Chicago, Illinois: Bank Administration Institute, 1968.

Boutell, Wayne S. *Computer-Oriented Business Systems*. Englewood Cliffs, New Jersey: Prentiss-Hall, Inc., 1968.

Brown, Foster. "Auditing Control and System Design." *Journal of Systems Management*. Cleveland, Ohio (April 1975), pp. 24-31.

Cadmus, Bradford. *Operational Auditing Handbook*. New York, New York: The Institute of Internal Auditors, Inc., 1964.

Canadian Institute of Chartered Accountants. *Computer Audit Guidelines*. Toronto, Ontario, Canada: Canadian Institute of Chartered Accountants, 1975.

Canadian Institute of Chartered Accountants. *Computer Control Guidelines*. Toronto, Ontario, Canada: Canadian Institute of Chartered Accountants, 1971.

Canning, Richard G. "Computer Fraud and Embezzlement." *EDP Analyzer*. Vol. II, No. 9 (September 1973).

Carey, J. L., and Doherty, W. O. "The Concept of Independence — Review and Restatement." *Journal of Accountancy* (January 1966).

Carter, Ciel. *Guide to Reference Sources in the Computer Sciences*. New York, New York: McMillan Publishing Co., Inc., 1973.

Chan, Stephen. "SEC Rules on Independence." *CPA Journal* (October 1972), pp. 843-844.

Cochran, William G. *Sampling Techniques — Second Edition*. New York, New York: John Wyley & Sons, Inc., 1963.

RECOMMENDED READINGS

Crowley, Thomas H. *Understanding Computers*. New York, New York: McGraw-Hill Book Company, 1967.

Davis, Gordon B. *Auditing and EDP*. New York, New York: American Institute of Certified Public Accountants, 1968.

Ditri, Arnold E.; Shaw, John C.; and Atkins, William. *Managing the EDP Function*. New York, New York: McGraw-Hill Book Company, 1971.

Ditri, Arnold E., and Wood, Donald R. "The End of the Beginning." *TEMPO*. New York, New York: Touche Ross & Co., 1969.

Dorricott, Keith O. "Appraising Computer-Assisted Audit Techniques." *CA Magazine*. Toronto, Ontario, Canada: The Canadian Institute of Chartered Accountants (August 1975), pp. 24-29.

Farr, M. A. L.; Chadwick, B.; and Wong, K. K. *Security for Computer Systems*. Manchester, United Kingdom: The National Computing Centre, Limited (NCC publications), 1972.

Georgen, W. Donald. "Rating Internal Controls." *Financial Executive*. New York, New York (April 1975), pp. 42-50.

Gruenberger, Fred, and Babcock, David. *Computing with Minicomputers*. Los Angeles, California: Melville Publishing Company, 1973.

Hagelbarger, David, and Fergerman, Saul. *Instruction Manual for Cardiac*. Bell Telephone Laboratories, 1968.

Horwitz, Geoffrey B. "Standards for Program and System Testing." *EDPACS*. Reston, Virginia: Automation Training Center, Inc. (November 1975).

Hudes, Albert. "Behind the Scenes at Equity Funding." *TEMPO*. New York, New York: Touche Ross & Co. Vol. 19, No. 1, 1973, pp. 12-19.

The Institute of Internal Auditors. *Modern Concepts of Internal Auditing, Establishing the Internal Audit Function EDP-Job Descriptions*. Orlando, Florida: The Institute of Internal Auditors, 1974.

International Business Machines Corporation. *Auditability Information Catalogue GB 21-9883-0*. White Plains, New York: International Business Machines Corporation, 1975.

Jancura, Elise G., and Berger, Arnold H. *Computers: Auditing and Control*. Philadelphia, Pennsylvania: Auerbach Publishers, Inc., 1973.

Larsen, Kent S. *Privacy, A Public Concern: A Resource Document Based on the Proceedings of a Seminar on Privacy Sponsored by the Domestic Council Committee on the Right of Privacy and the Council of State Governments*. Washington, D.C., U. S.: Government Printing Office, August 1975.

Loebbecke, James K. "Internal Control Evaluation: How the Computer Can Help." *The Journal of Accountancy*. New York, New York: American Institute of Certified Public Accountants (August 1975), pp. 60-70.

Loebbecke, J. K., and Neter, J. "Statistical Sampling in Confirming Receivables." *Journal of Accountancy* (June 1973), pp. 44-50.

London, Keith R. *Documentation Standards*. New York, New York: Petrocelli Books, 1974.

Mair, William C. "New Techniques in Computer Program Verification." *TEMPO*. New York, New York: Touche Ross & Co. (Winter 1970-71).

Mair, William C. "Parallel Simulation — A Technique for Effective Verification of Computer Programs." EDPACS. Reston, Virginia: Automation Training Center, Inc. (April 1975).

Martin, James R. *Design of Real-Time Computer Systems*. Englewood Cliffs, New Jersey: Prentiss-Hall, Inc., 1967.

Martin, James R. *Security, Accuracy and Privacy in Computer System*. Englewood Cliffs, New Jersey: Prentiss-Hall, Inc., 1973.

Martin, James R. *Telecommunications and the Computer*. Englewood Cliffs, New Jersey: Prentiss-Hall, Inc., 1969.

Mason, J. O., and Connelly, W. E. "The Application and Reliability of the Self-Checking Digit Technique." *Management Advisor* (September/October 1971), pp. 27-34.

RECOMMENDED READINGS

Massey, L. Daniel. *Computer Basics for Management — Second Revised Edition.* Boston, Massachusetts: American Management Association's Extension Institute, 1973.

McPhee, W. S. "Operating System Integrity in OS/VS 2." *IBM Systems Journal.* Armonk, New York: International Business Machines Corporation, Vol. 13, No. 3, 1974, pp. 230-252.

Meigs, Walter B.; Larsen, E. John; and Meigs, Robert F. *Principles of Auditing.* Homewood, Illinois: Richard D. Irwin, Inc. 1973.

Morrill, Chester, Jr. *Computers and Data Processing Information Sources.* Management Information Guide 15, Detroit-Gale Research Company, 1969.

National Fire Protection Association International. *Halogenated Extinguishing Agent Systems Halon 1301, 1973 — NFPA No. 12A.* Boston, Massachusetts: National Fire Protection Association International, 1973.

National Fire Protection Association International. *Protection of Electronic Computer/Data Processing Equipment 1972 — NFPA No. 2 75.* Boston, Massachusetts: National Fire Protection Association International, 1972.

Neumann, Frederick L. "The Auditor's Analytical Review — Some Sources of Information." *Journal of Accountancy* (October 1974), pp. 88-92.

Parker, Nycum, and Oura. *Computer Abuse.* Washington, D.C.: National Technical Information Service, 1973.

Perry, William E. "Auditing Computer Operations." *EDPACS.* Reston, Virginia: Automation Training Center (October 1973).

Perry, William E. "Concurrent EDP Auditing and Early Warning Scheme." *EDPACS.* Reston, Virginia: Automation Training Center (January 1974).

Perry, William E. "Concurrent EDP Auditing and Implementation Approach." *EDPACS.* Reston, Virginia: Automation Training Center (February 1974).

Perry, William E. "Selecting an EDP System for Audit." *EDPACS.* Reston, Virginia: Automation Training Center (April 1974).

Perry, William E. "Snapshot — A Technique for Tagging and Tracing Transactions." *EDPACS.* Reston, Virginia: Automation Training Center (March 1974).

Perry, William E. "Try ITF; You'll Like ITF." *EDPACS.* Reston, Virginia: Automation Training Center (December 1973).

Perry, William E. "Using SMF as an Audit Tool — Accounting Information." *EDPACS.* Reston, Virginia: Automation Training Center (January 1975).

Perry, William E. "Using SMF as an Audit Tool — Performance." *EDPACS.* Reston, Virginia: Automation Training Center (December 1975).

Perry, William E. "Using SMF as an Audit Tool — Security." *EDPACS.* Reston, Virginia: Automation Training Center (January 1976).

Perry, William E., and Adams, Donald L. "SMF — An Untapped Audit Resource." *EDPACS.* Reston, Virginia: Automation Training Center (September 1974).

Porter, W. Thomas. *EDP Controls and Auditing.* Bellmont, California: Wadsworth Publishing Company, Inc., 1974.

Porter W. Thomas. "Evaluating Internal Controls in EDP Systems." *Journal of Accountancy* (August 1974), pp. 34-40.

Prentiss-Hall Editorial Staff. *Encyclopedic Dictionary of Systems and Procedures.* Englewood Cliffs, New Jersey: Prentiss-Hall, Inc., 1966.

Reid, G. F., and Demiak, J. A. "EDP Implementation with General Purpose Software." *Journal of Accountancy* (July 1971), pp. 35-46.

Rennie, Robert. "Flowcharts for Audit Purposes." *The Quarterly.* Touche Ross & Co., (March 1965), pp. 13-22.

Robertson, Jack C. *Auditing.* Dallas, Texas: Business Publications, Inc., 1976.

Sawyer, Lawrence B. *The Practice of Modern Internal Auditing, Appraising Operations for Management.* New York, New York: The Institute of Internal Auditors, Inc., 1973.

Science Research Associates, Inc. *Computing Systems Fundamentals.* Chicago, Illinois: Science Research Associates, Inc., 1969.

SEC Accounting Series Release No. 126, Independence of Accountants: Guidelines and Examples of Situations Involving the Independence of Accountants. Reprinted in *Journal of Accountancy* (September 1972), pp. 83-89.

RECOMMENDED READINGS

Shaw, John C., and Atkins, William. *Managing Computer System Projects.* New York, New York: McGraw-Hill Book Company, 1970.

Skinner, R. M., and Anderson, R. J. *Analytical Auditing.* Toronto, Ontario, Canada: Sir Isaac Pittman (Canada) Limited, 1966.

Sleeper, Richard C., Davis William P., III. "Data Processing Risk Insurance." *EDPACS.* Reston, Virginia: Automation Training Center (three parts: November 1973, December 1973, and January 1974).

Steffen, Roswell as told to Miller, Curt. "How I Embezzled $1.5 Million — And Nearly Got Away with It." *Bank Systems and Equipment.* New York, New York (June 1974), pp. 26-28.

Weber, Ron. "Auditing Computer Systems, Using Integrated Test Facility." *The Australian Accountant.* Melbourne, Australia, Accountant's Publishing Company, Limited (May 1975), pp. 232-235.

Weiss, Harold. "Audit Review of Program Code II." *EDPACS.* Reston, Virginia: Automation Training Center (August 1975).

Will, H. J. *Computer Based Auditing — Parts I & II.* Toronto, Ontario, Canada: Canadian Chartered Accountants (February/March 1972).

Wooldridge, Susan; Corder, Colin; and Johnson, Claude. *Security Standards for Data Processing.* New York, New York: John Wiley & Sons, Inc., 1973.

Yourdon, Edward. *Design of On-Line Computer Systems.* Englewood Cliffs, New Jersey: Prentiss-Hall, Inc., 1973.

INDEX

ABDICATION
  management: 257

ABUSE
  computer: 259, 312, 344, 381, 388, 412, 455
  control evaluation table: 416, *sleeve*

ACCEPTANCE
  test: 287

ACCESS
  334, 344, 345, 365, 374
  direct: 407
  dual: 413
  electronic: 414
  file: 121
  limited: 413
  log: 395, 396
  physical: 393,414, 417
  restricted: 319
  rotation of: 396
  supervised: 323
  unlimited: 74, 381, 384, 390, 392

ACCIDENTS .
  70, 343, 376, 409

ACCOUNTING
  computer: 406
  unacceptable: 11, 74, 209

ACTION(S)
  external: 414
  legal: 414, 416

ACTIVITY(IES)
  application: 58
  flowchart of application audit: 162
  information processing facility: 306
  relationship between controls and activities subject to control: 184
  schedule: 270
  subject to control: 54, 59, 62, 111, 182, 425
  system development: 208, 215
  which provide control: 54
  work definition, level: 267

ADMINISTRATION
  computer: 26
  personnel: 26

ADMINISTRATIVE REPORTS
  297

ADVISORY
  management services: 422, 451

AIR CONDITIONING
  335, 347

ALL RISK INSURANCE
  353

ALLOCATION
  resource: 31

AMNESIA
  organizational: 111, 375

ANALYSIS
  controls: 8
  quantitative: 24

ANALYSTS
  systems: 274, 318

ANALYTIC
  audit flowchart: 108, 109, 179, 236
  auditing: 439

ANSI
  format of tape header record: 87

APPLICATION
  activities: 58
  advanced computer program: 201
  advanced systems: 380
  audit software: 118
  audit techniques: 131
  audit tools: 106
  basic understanding: 164
  causes of exposures: 69, 183
  characteristics: 78
  classification of criteria: 77
  common level: 380
  controls: 41, 82, 371, 410, 444, 452
  control evaluation table: 183, 186, *sleeve*
  control matrix: 2, 111, 113, 182, 282, 425
  definition: 17
  definition of controls: 98
  detailed understanding: 167
  documentation: 167, 295, 297
  edits: 395
  EDP auditing: 161
  error rates: *xv*
  features to test: 193
  file description for data division: 173
  flowchart of audit activities: 162
  maintenance: 295
  manual: 169
  objective of audit: 161
  objectives of controls: 82
  programmer: 418
  relationship of controls to causes of exposure: 95
  review and evaluation: 252
  run book: 169
  sophisticated level: 380, 457
  standards: 47
  steps in audit: 161
  STRATA flowchart: 154
  summary of audit, purposes, techniques, and tools: 132, 197, 400
  unique level: 380, 457
  unmaintainable: 259

APPROVAL
  86, 175, 275, 280, 297, 299, 324
  management/user review and approval: 239, 274
  technical review and approval: 274

ARITHMETIC
  operations: 125

ART
  state of: 80, 258

ARTIFICIAL
  intelligence: *xvii*

ASSEMBLER
  333, 426

ASSEMBLY
  326

ASSETS
  information: *xii*, 409
  loss or destruction: 12, 74
  safeguarding: 431

ASSURANCE
  quality: 453

ATTRIBUTE SAMPLING
  128

AUDIT (ING)
  86, 414, 422
  analytic: 439
  analytic flowchart: 108, 179
  application purposes, techniques, and tools: 132, 197, 400
  application techniques: 131

475

INDEX

application tools: 106
applications of software: 118
areas of concern and techniques with
    EDP: 367, 436
around or through the computer: 5, 135
439
committee: 448
compliance: 4, 20, 43, 51, 52, 421, 447
448, 453, 455, 457
definition of tools: 55
designing procedures: 55, 195, 364, 365
diagram of steps in IPF: 358
documentation: 52, 179
EDP auditing: 17, 161
EDP objectives: 20
financial: 208, 422
flowchart of application activities: 162
general purpose software: 117, 139, 151,
360, 369, 402, 411, 440
generally accepted standards: 165, 443,
457
information processing facility: 356
internal function: 20
management: 421, 453
manual specialists: 5
operational: 208, 421, 451
participation in audit: 262, 275
participation in system development:
280
procedures: 297
program: 55, 200, 201, 456
quality control: 148
questionnaire(s): 106, 107, 165, 301
relationship of compliance and substan-
    tive auditing: 449
reports: 203
sample review file: 146
scope: 203
steps and objective in application audit:
161
steps in systems development process:
294
software functions: 121
substantive: 3, 20, 51, 421, 448, 453
system control and review file: 145, 146,
282, 419
systems development process: 292
techniques: 55, 300, 399, 415
testing: 55, 156
trail: 88, 368

AUDITABILITY
49

AUDITOR
bilingual: 5
comparison with CPA: 454
concerns and objectives: 18, 51
EDP: 17
internal: 17
role: 205

AUTHORIZATION
86, 319, 334, 384, 392, 396, 414
chain: 61, 67
file: 392

AUTHORIZED
transactions on a blanket basis: 70
user file: 395, 396, 398

BACKGROUND INVESTIGATION
419

BACKUP
71, 192, 239, 320, 390, 403, 410, 415
facility: 375
files: 375
off premises: 348, 375
premises: 350

BAIT
records: 414, 415

BALANCING
86, 414

BANKING
307

BASE(S)
data: 26, 80, 124, 333, 380, 388, 398, 4
management system: 388, 402

BATCH
control: 176, 256, 373
processing: 84, 380, 399
remote: 381, 382
system: 399

BAYESIAN STATISTICS
449

BILINGUAL
auditors: 5

BINARY
85, 124
coded decimal: 85

BITS
124
diagram of parity bits on 7-channel
    tape: 337

BLANKET AUTHORIZATION
70

BONDING
345

BONDS
savings: 323

BUDGETING
capital: 31, 214

BUDGETS
47, 297, 317, 330, 360, 441

BUREAU(S)
service: 5, 360, 445

BURSTING
311

BUSINESS
exposures: 185
interruption: 11, 74, 210
small system: 407

CALCULATE
calculate-stratify form and diagnostic:
155

CALCULATIONS
60

CALCULATOR
406

CAPACITY OF COMPUTER
328

CARBON DIOXIDE
347

CARD
identification: 392, 396
magnetic: 345
punch: 332
punched: 124, 307, 315, 370
reader: 332

CASSETTES
key to tape: 307
magnetic tape: 407

CATASTROPHE
312, 346, 374, 409

INDEX

INDEX

INDEX

INDEX

tape header: 86, 87, 172
trailer: 172
unit: 406

RECORD LAYOUT
171

RECORDER
335

RECORDS
bait: 414, 415
fixed length: 124
variable length: 124

RECOVERY
71, 175, 192, 347, 349, 361, 399, 415
IPF: 343
journal: 398
plan: 375
software: 351

RECRUITING
437

REDUNDANCY CHECK
396

REFERENCE DOCUMENTS
62, 67, 69

RELIABILITY
83, 318, 342, 348, 431, 455
equipment: 373

REMOTE BATCH
381, 382

REMOTE JOB ENTRY
381

REMOTE TERMINAL
333

REPEATING SEGMENTS
124

REPORT
62, 66, 69
administrative: 297
audit: 203
discrepancy: 250
distribution: 361, 373
error: 67
exception: 66, 168, 172
layout: 231, 232, 281
production: 168, 172
status: 271
system planning: 220
utilization: 325, 327

REPORTING
317, 324, 443
evaluating status: 271

RERUN
326, 372, 431

RESOLUTION
error: 73, 190

RESOURCE ALLOCATION 31
RESTART
241

RESTRICTED ACCESS 319

RESTRICTION OF KNOWLEDGE
319

RESUBMISSION
upstream: 88

RESULTS
evaluate: 202, 365
testing: 134, 195
unsupportable: 73, 384
verification: 196, 450

RETENTION
file: 239, 320, 371, 440
record: 176, 360

REVENUE
deficient: 421
ruling 71-20: 88, 320, 371

REVIEW
84, 202, 239, 274, 297, 299, 304, 324, 44
application evaluation: 252
management and user: 304
postimplementation: 31, 219, 251, 26
275, 290, 299, 304
program flowchart: 133
program list: 131
status: 272
system audit file: 55, 145, 146, 282, 41
systems development process: 292

REVOLUTION
computer: *xvii*

RING
file protect: 321, 365, 369, 375

ROLE
auditor: 205
outputs: 65
processing: 67

ROTATION
access: 396
job: 319

RPG
117, 411

RULING
revenue, 71-20: 88, 320, 371

RUN
application and computer book: 169
RUN TO RUN
89

SAFEGUARDING OF ASSETS
431

SAMPLE AUDIT REVIEW FILE
146

SAMPLING
147
attribute: 128
combined attribute/variable: 128
judgmental: 148
random: 148
statistical: 149
variables: 128

SANCTIONS
legal: 210
statutory: 12, 74

SAVINGS BONDS
323

SCANNING
visual: 322, 323

SCHEDULE
324, 360, 431, 441
activity, work: 265, 270, 324
distribution: 324
short term: 270

SCOPE
448, 456
audit: 203
CPA with internal auditor: 454
IPF: 451

SCREENING
personnel: 413

486

INDEX